What people are saying...

Michael D. "Moon" Mullins with his usual flair has found a perfect way to bring life to the stories of America's Warriors. His lyrical way with words has opened a window into the past that is closing much too quickly. *Out of the Mist, Memories of War* touches the soul and brings the reader to a deep understanding of the sacrifices made by those ready to stand in the breach.

—D. H. Brown, Award-winning author of *Honor Defended*, Board member of Military Writers Society of America, Vietnam Veteran

Thanks for everything
Mike

Out of the ℳ*ist,*
MEMORIES OF WAR

Michael D. "Moon" Mullins

iUniverse, Inc.
Bloomington

Out of the Mist, Memories of War

Copyright © 2011 Michael D. "Moon" Mullins

All rights reserved. No part of this book may be used or reproduced by any means, graphic, electronic, or mechanical, including photocopying, recording, taping or by any information storage retrieval system without the written permission of the publisher except in the case of brief quotations embodied in critical articles and reviews.

iUniverse books may be ordered through booksellers or by contacting:

iUniverse
1663 Liberty Drive
Bloomington, IN 47403
www.iuniverse.com
1-800-Authors (1-800-288-4677)

Because of the dynamic nature of the Internet, any Web addresses or links contained in this book may have changed since publication and may no longer be valid. The views expressed in this work are solely those of the author and do not necessarily reflect the views of the publisher, and the publisher hereby disclaims any responsibility for them.

Any people depicted in stock imagery provided by Thinkstock are models, and such images are being used for illustrative purposes only.

Certain stock imagery © Thinkstock.

ISBN: 978-1-4620-5140-3 (sc)
ISBN: 978-1-4620-5139-7 (hc)
ISBN: 978-1-4620-5137-3 (e)

Library of Congress Control Number: 2011915504

Printed in the United States of America

iUniverse rev. date: 9/2/2011

The cover photography was shot at Brookside Cemetery in Windfall, IN. The crosses commemorate those men killed in action during World War II from the Windfall community.

CONTENTS

Preface/Acknowledgements   ix
    She Isn't Just Cloth   x

Introduction   xi

VETERANS' STORIES — WORLD WAR II

Sergeant Joe Thomas, World War II POW   2
Shoelaces   4
The Eye of Darkness   9
Old Claude   19
Saturday Night Surprise   26
A Walk in the Clouds   34
The Edge of Horror   58
BOHICA — For Real   68
A Woman's Life, Touched by War   78
Out of the Mist   83
Peace has its Price   107
A Pair of Queens   112
    POW/MIA   124

VETERANS' STORIES — VIETNAM

A Quiet Man Talks   128
    Blue Tag Unit   148
His Lucky Day   149
    Womp Womp Womp Womp   160
Flint   162
Moody Ripsaw   169
Sportster-Slim   178
    The 10th of May   185
Never on Sunday — Until Now   187
    My Pet   194
    An American Hero   196
Wilbur and Carol, a Love Story   200
    Topp Gunn   204

MIKE'S STORIES

The Moon in 'Nam	208
A Day in April	209
Southwest of Saigon	213
That was Close	215
Scared Awake	218
Just One More Step	220
Bone Chilling Times	222
On the River Bank	224
The Descent	226
The Groves	230
My Purple Heart	231
Just a Thought	233
The Rest of the Way Home	236
I Hadn't Looked at Him in a While	239
Vietnam Vets — the Embers of Anger	240
Serving America — It has been a family affair	246

VETERANS' STORIES — WAR ON TERROR

Leaving the Wire	262
Blinded	264
Infantry	265
Here You Stand	266
He is Home	268
Down in His Cups	271
Through My Eyes	273
The Torch	275
Loneliness	279
One Serves, One Stays	281
The Third Time	283

VETERANS' STORIES — DOOBIE CHATS

Doobie Chats   286

A PERSONAL PERSPECTIVE

The VA, a tough bus to catch	326
Today I Cried	329
Our VA	335
No Room in the Room, er, uh, System	342
Awakened Again	345
PTSD Compensation examination results	347
Saving Grace	351
Index	357

Preface/Acknowledgements

It is hard to write when you are crying.

The first line is all I was going to say at first. Nothing else is necessary. There are far too many people to thank in this book. There are far too many to thank now that it exists. A tiny dynamic little lady, an author from Kokomo, IN, challenged me to break away from my comfort zone — writing poetry — to write prose. I am not sure if I did that, but I wrote an anthology of short stories. I could not exclude a few poetic stories however. They burst into my head unbidden so they must not be ignored. She and I could not be further afield politically, but we both love the written word. Other names appear throughout the book. To each I say thanks.

My family listened to me speak of this project at every gathering. I am sure they are tired of it. They may as well get over that. It is not done — the hard part is ahead. And I have another in mind. Special thanks go to my wife, Phyllis. She allowed me to be a recluse at times. She accepted my perfunctory responses to her unwanted questions and my after-the-fact denials that I responded in any way. Being a writer's widow is akin to being a golf widow. Survivor's guilt transferred to some other kind of guilt and she wisely took advantage of that extended period of weakness.

Out of the Mist, Memories of War is not just a book to me. It is a life event. It is a living reminder of how blessed I am to be an American. The people I met while compiling stories for this book honored me. Those who know me realize that I was ready to publish a second book of poetry. Health issues altered my path, a little lady attacked my writer's courage, and divine intervention opened a different door enough to dare me to step through. It was a choice I had to make.

World War II, Korea, the Cold War, Vietnam, and the War on Terror are represented inside these covers. Military historians, families and friends of those who want to know more about the effects of war on both men and women at war — and at home — will find something touching when they read these stories. The stories are their stories. I am merely the storyteller.

She Isn't Just Cloth

Some wonder why we care so much about a flag.
She isn't just cloth. She is an army of souls.
The fabric of our flag, its every thread, is made with the American soldiers' spirit,
It is tattered dungarees, buckskin, BDUs, or fatigues, but always blood and bone.
It waves abroad and at home in spirit, in heart and soul, through the generations.
It is the heart of the warrior, reluctant or not, sacrificing for freedom.

Michael D. "Moon" Mullins, Vietnam Vet,
in respect of all our veterans

Introduction

As the daughter of a troubled combat veteran, I've spent a lifetime trying to understand the impact of war on the warrior. Some days, my father brightened a room like warm spring sunshine. Other days, chilly darkness covered him long before dusk. When I came home from school, would I find a fierce man glowing with pride or a broken boy crying in the corner? Inexplicable things made him angry — three-inch safety-pins worn on poodle skirts, the length of the paper boy's hair, Ozzie and Harriet, whether or not the neighbor across the street nodded when he drove past our house — me.

As a 19-year-old Marine, Daddy fought all 36 days on Iwo Jima — so we watched *The Sands of Iwo Jima* together many times. So many times that my mother refused to join us anymore. So many times that I knew most of the lines. Afterwards, we'd sit in our darkened living room, the test pattern buzzing on the television. Sometimes, silence drowned out the flickering buzz. Other nights, he'd tell me, one more time, how Smitty died because he had a belly-ache and didn't want to crap his pants in the fox hole where they all cowered, pinned down by mortar and machine gun fire. Once, I must have been about eight or nine, I declared that I wanted to be a Marine too — like him. He slapped me so hard that I fell backwards and hit the wall. "No daughter of mine is going to be a broad-assed Marine!" His eyes glittered with fury and I cringed, confused and heartbroken, expecting another blow. I loved and admired him — then and now. Understand? Not so much. How could I?

Mike Mullins is my age and also the child of a veteran. Like me, he grew up in a community where most of his neighbors participated, one way or another, in that enormous effort known as World War II. In fact, like me, many members of his family served in various wars over the years. Mike is a storyteller, a warm and generous man, a loving husband and proud father — and a Vietnam Vet. Like me, he admires and respects the "Greatest Generation" for all that they achieved. Like me, he wants to know their stories — because what happened to them in the 1940s changed how they lived their lives afterwards and that impacted who their sons and daughters became. Like me, Mike believes that to record a person's memories rescues him from being lost in the murky clouds of changing priorities. Like me, Mike doesn't write because he wants to, he writes because he must.

However, there is a vast difference between us. Mike has actually been in combat. It scratches his soul like an insistent cough tickles the back of a throat. Like Daddy, his memories are both delicate roses and infected boils. Like Daddy, he believes that war destroys the vulnerable, the unlucky, and the incredibly brave. Like Daddy, he thinks that others are heroes while his efforts never measure up. Like Daddy, his survival is an amazing gift — and evidence of his unworthiness. Like Daddy, his anger is inexplicable. How can we know the burdens he bears, the scars that cover both his flesh and his psyche? Like Daddy, he refers to war — that most confusing, frustrating, and horrifying of events — as black and white, and easier to understand than post-war life. Like Daddy, he can't stop talking about it.

This book is beautiful. Mike reveals himself, whether he means to or not, on every page. We see his eagerness to meet and talk with his aging heroes — and his sense of 'otherness' while around them. Through Mike's words, we see the complicated brotherhood of Vietnam Vets. His description of the way they reach out to each other, slap at each other, and comfort each other helps us appreciate their rich humanity. We see the rawness of Mike's relationship with his fellow Americans — he would die to protect us, but he doesn't understand us anymore than we do him. His anger shimmers across the chapters, but his affection warms and reassures us at the same time.

This piece helps us understand better. However, combat veterans have crossed some invisible barrier. We can welcome them back into our communities. We can love them, reward them, admire them — but coming home is complicated and nothing will ever be the same again. Mike Mullins' book is both a window and a mirror depending on which side of that barrier you stand.

Joyce Faulkner, President of Military Writers Society of America, award-winning author of *In the Shadow of Suribachi*, and editor of *Out of the Mist, Memories of War* by Michael D. "Moon" Mullins

SECTION I

Veterans' Stories — World War II

Sergeant Joe Thomas, World War II POW

I walked into American Legion Post #46 in Tipton, IN, one evening seeking permission for a book signing event. My book, *Vietnam in Verse, poetry for beer drinkers*, had been released a few weeks earlier and I wanted to do a signing in my home county. It was a quiet evening with few people seated at the bar. My eyes adjusted to the dimly-lit room and I scanned the faces, hoping to see someone who could answer my question. Getting permission to sell books in Legion homes has not been a good experience for me, even though I am a 30-year member. Each time I think about that I wonder why. I think they should welcome me. They should be fertile soil for what I do, especially since I donate so much of the proceeds to things supporting veterans. Organizational support is non-existent, but in many ways that is understandable. Too many of us write for any group to select whom it supports unless you are fortunate enough to be politically connected. I am blessed, however. What I learn from the people who I meet in the various veterans' settings is incredible, although most of that has been gleaned at other places than in Legion or VFW bars. This visit was about to prove a wonderful exception to previous experiences.

    I sat at the end of the bar until the bartender had a chance to speak to me, at which point I asked for an officer. Fortunately, the commander was there and we chatted a while, setting a date for my book signing. The Ladies Auxiliary leader, a woman with whom I've worked for years, arrived before I left and offered me a warm welcome. The atmosphere changed around me. An older member came in behind her and took a stool at the end of the bar. A beer magically appeared in front of him and people greeted him in a way that spoke of a status reserved for someone very special. My friend Virginia introduced me to Joe Thomas, World War II veteran and former Prisoner of War. I shook his hand, got a hug, and another beer appeared. I realized I was in the presence of the *royalty* of our world.

    Another older member joined us and fueled the conversation. The second gentleman was a Korean War era veteran who had served in the Air Force in stateside duty, but he urged Joe to share at least a little of his story with me. They chatted with each other and I became an interested spectator. I heard the end of his story that night and went home to write a tribute poem. Two weeks later, I returned to share it with him. Joe was pleased. If nobody ever saw it but him I had accomplished my goal. I presented him a gift from my heart. Within days, I heard from his family. A niece asked me for a copy.

She told me that I had said things in a way that meant more to the family than I could imagine. Words like that are scarce and give me purpose I never expected when I began my journey into the writing world.

Two weeks later, I returned to Post #46 looking for Joe. I was told he would be there soon — he walks the few blocks from his home every day, weather permitting. The walk is Joe's exercise and the Legion a large part of his social life. His stool is empty usually. If not, it will be. I took a seat nearby and waited, soft drink in hand. The smell of the grill forced me to order a cheeseburger and fries. That Legion Post knows how to do a good old greasy burger the way fast food joints do not understand. I was half way through the dripping burger when Joe Thomas sat down next to me. There was his beer — the magic still worked.

"Joe, I want to hear more of your story," I said.

I heard it that night. I wrote another poem. He loved it too. So did his family. It is not enough. I must tell the story in another way as well.

I looked into Joe's old face that night and saw tears. I closed my eyes to intensify his words.

"Damn these memories…they just come. For 65 years I've tried to turn 'em off," he said.

"What Joe?" My tone was subdued. "What memories will not leave you alone? Are they memories of lost soldiers?" I asked in an awed and reverent way.

By the time I met with Joe Thomas the second time, he was another of my heroes. He is a World War II Prisoner of War who survived; who was rescued; a man who was there to tell me his story and did so willingly. He was 83-years old, about to celebrate his next birthday. I waited as he calmed his demeanor, waited to hear another chapter in his story.

Shoelaces

"Shoelaces," he said, "Shoelaces."

"What about shoelaces?" I was taken aback.

He looked at me and said, "I was 18 at Anzio. We took the beachhead and I had been a cook. It all changed when we hit that beach."

I could see it in my mind. I saw him, 18 and green, in bloody water, wading ashore through the litter of torn bodies. Those floating bodies, bobbing in the waves on the shore, changed his role in that war from cook to infantry. As he explained to me, "his war started for real." Private First Class Joe Thomas began fighting his way to Rome. He was a Thunderbird of the 45th Infantry, part of the Army's 179th Infantry Division. The grand scheme was to catch the Krauts in a trap. Instead they were caught and Joe was a prisoner. In Joe's words, "I went ashore a PFC and death promoted me." In the landing he not only changed jobs, he got a battlefield promotion, through attrition, to Sergeant.

Memories come crashing out like the Colorado River in flood stage when they are released! They cascade and rumble out of control no matter how many times they have been unleashed. When a person opens the door to the locked chambers of the mind, the demons and the angels fly out regardless of the times you have visited that room. Joe has told his story before, at least to some veterans and a few fortunate historians. He belongs to a Prisoner of War Association as well. Each time there are little things that come back. Each time tears are as fresh as the images which rage behind eyes that see inwardly more clearly than out. Events are jumbled and happen out of sequence. I discovered in my own reminiscing about Vietnam that the calendar is inconsequential when talking with friends and veterans. Some incidents had more of an impact than others and leap off the floor of the memory chamber more often than others. You must grab a broom and sweep the dust off more obscure ones to give the whole picture any semblance of order. If you are to write about them you must step back and piece the puzzle together. Telling it is no different. Joe and I bobbed about like logs swept by the whirling Colorado roaring through canyons on the way to its end. The first time I talked to him, I heard the end of his story. The second time I heard the beginning. Now I want to tell them together, in some sort of flow, like a river of consciousness after the rainy season has passed.

Historians write that the landing at Anzio was such a complete surprise that the Germans were caught totally unprepared. The Allies were met with token resistance only and casualties were light. The 45th Infantry of the 179th Infantry Division had orders to make heavy fortifications along the way, yet they made amazing headway as they proceeded inland during the first week of the invasion operation. Fighting was sporadic initially, but the Germans moved rapidly to intercept and all of that was about to change. So was Joe's life as a soldier.

Joe Thomas, WW2 POW, in his "seat" with my son, 1st Sgt. Michael S. Mullins at American Legion Post 46, Tipton, IN

The Germans reacted with reinforcements which included elite troops, heavy armor, air support and a railroad-mounted artillery piece that caused more casualties to the Allies than all their other ground and air forces. The Army units continued to battle inland but progress was slowed to a crawl and fighting grew vicious. The landing occurred in mid-January, 1944 — but by early February resistance had stiffened and every foot of earth was earned with blood. Ultimately, the attack lasted into late spring of that year and the toll on both sides was remarkably similar. The Germans counterattacked in mid-February and Joe's part in World War II went from the proverbial frying pan to the fire. As the fighting intensified so did casualties. The 45th was caught in the crosshairs. The unit began taking an alarming number of wounded. Joe had his cooking gear taken from his hands and a carbine thrust in them. Having had no infantry training before he arrived in Europe, his only formal combat training was — combat. As the days turned into weeks he grew more skilled and progressed from Private First Class to Buck Sergeant in short order. Promotions through attrition were not unusual in World War II and Joe Thomas went from cook to non-commissioned officer in a few short weeks. The plan was to fight their way to Rome and back. They were going to trap the Germans in a gigantic pincer movement that would allow them to disable a large portion of the enemy force in that part of Europe. While his outfit was moving one direction another was supposed to move toward the *Jerrys* from a different one, effectively snipping their supply and reserve force pipeline. He fought on fields littered with bodies, walking through the dead and wounded. His friends dropped in large numbers, but Joe kept his squad moving the way his Company leaders directed. While they thought they were making all the right moves, the enemy had in fact reversed the tables on them. The German lines had bulged but not broken. It collapsed around them, trapping them between two forces. Joe's military life was again about to change course.

When the inevitable happened and more senior NCOs realized it, they pulled Thomas aside and gave him some terse advice. If capture was imminent he was to cover his stripes as quickly as possible however he could, or better yet get rid of his blouse and put on one from a fallen comrade if he must. Non-coms were not treated well when captured. Until the moment that advice was breathed aloud Joe did not realize how dire things had become. It was not long after those terrifying words landed on his ears than the face of reality crested a nearby ridge. He grabbed the field jacket of a dead GI and pulled it on just before the remnants of his platoon were captured. Joe thought he had done it in time, but one sharp-eyed German soldier saw the flash of his stripes before his arms disappeared into the sleeves. He, another sergeant, and a corporal were herded like a goat from the sheep and loaded on a separate truck when wheeled vehicles arrived. He was allowed to keep the coat.

Joe Thomas had no idea where he was taken. The truck was covered and all he knew was the trip seemed unending. He and his fellow prisoners were filled with dread, imagining nothing but the worst ahead. They knew that information was the key to victory and the Germans would do anything to extract whatever seemed of value from their American prisoners. Our enemies have never, in any war, been restrained by the same values as we, when interrogating (forgive me for editorializing — but it is true). Joe alluded to the fact that they tried to prepare for what they *knew* was in their future. He never gave many sordid details about that part of his interment in our discussions. Some memories are better left in their coffins.

The first night, the Germans put Joe in a basement somewhere and posted a heavily-armed guard. They ripped off his stripes and took them to someone — an officer, he assumed. He was beaten, as a warm-up for things to come. The enemy presumed that any soldier of any rank had a modicum of knowledge beyond that of the ordinary grunt. His cloth stripes were replaced with bloody ones. The next day the basement was used as a distribution center and further sorting was done according to rank. The guards separated Joe Thomas from his friends for longer term imprisonment.

The compound where Joe spent many months was deep inside Germany. His daily routine included questioning, filth, cold, damp, questioning, nasty rations, and limited writing privileges. Thomas joined more "experienced" prisoners who told him to sleep with his shoes tied around his neck at night. If he did not, the guards would steal them and sell them on the black market. He used his laces to secure his shoes to his throat at night. The soldiers were ruthless, but they would not take the chance of cutting them free. Joe said, "The shoes were mine. I fought miles in them. Nobody was taking them — they were life to me. My leggings were gone right after the landing. My shoes were my last defense and I guess my safe place in a way. They were really all I had."

While a captive, Joe was allowed to write a letter home every other week. On the odd weeks he could send a card, no more. The card went to Evvie, the letters to Mom and Dad. He smiled sadly and said, "Evvie was the redheaded girl in the next town who I saw before I left to the war." She was his angel and he clung to his parents. Joe said that reaching out to home may have kept him sane. He knew that anything he could not say to her on the postcards, they would share with her for him.

Somehow he still had his shoes when the Russians attacked and rescued him and the other POWs in his camp. They were saved! Joe still had his soles and his soul. They spent the next several weeks — and he did not know how many — marching 700 miles out of Germany to Russia. Joe said the march was endless, living on partial rations, with few clothes, in a harsh climate. But he was free! He was leaving Hell! He had no idea what was ahead but he knew what he was leaving behind. In an unnamed village along the way, a cobbler saw his shoes' condition and asked permission to help. The Russian soldiers allowed him to stop long enough to have them re-soled by a compassionate European. Joe's shoes were and are a symbol of all that his captivity was and what his rescue became. His shoelaces were his ties to hope. Joe does not know how long he was in Russia, but he remembers being put on a train and somehow arriving in Egypt. He was there for months. Joe called the time there a POW detoxification period during which the Army counseled many former POWs before they returned home. He lost track of time entirely during this period. I am not sure if the war was officially over by the time Joe Thomas returned to America. I did not press him with questions. I saw his face. I could not. I know one thing with certainty. World War II was over for him.

Joe Thomas was in the United States of America at last! He was on home soil. He did not say whether he got there by bus or train, but the police met him and drove him to his parents' house. An officer welcomed Joe home as a hero. He drove the young warrior home with deference and dignity. There were no red lights and no sirens as I understood the story. In fact, they arrived to find all the lights on. Surprised, Joe wondered how his Dad knew he was going to be there that night. He thanked the officer and went inside to huge, quiet embraces. (I am sure there was the appropriate community welcome later) It was not long until Joe's dad said, "Joe, go call Evvie and get her over here." He did both. She never left him again — until God called her home.

I cannot say how many times Joe got tears in his eyes. I cannot say how many times I have while writing this and the poems that preceded it. Joe Thomas concluded our meeting with a wonderful story that evening.

A few years later, Joe was working for a Chevy dealer near the Indiana-Michigan border. At the time, he was driving an old Mercury — all he could afford. It frustrated the dealership's owner to have that Merc on his car lot. He pestered Joe every day to buy a Chevrolet. He pressured, he cajoled, he berated — but Joe resisted. Joe never talked about his war history beyond the fact that he was a veteran. There were many around so that part was not unusual in the late forties. Government efficiency being what it was, Joe's POW compensation was not straightened out yet. The paperwork delays were as bad then as they are now. Many legislative acts were brand new and being clarified. The owner finally became aware of Joe's history through shop talk, but he did not pry. As it happened, when his curiosity could no longer be contained, he called Joe in to talk. It was the day Joe received his first POW compensation check of $23.64. The check was in Joe's shirt pocket. He intended to go to the bank at lunch to cash it — he needed the money. When the boss saw the check, he asked Joe about it and the whole story came out. The businessman was humbled. Apparently thinking about the grief he had been giving the man sitting across from him, he asked Joe if he could see the check. Joe reluctantly let him look at it. The man asked Joe if he could keep it for the afternoon. Joe agreed, but insisted that he have it by three and be allowed to go to the bank at that time. The owner agreed. When Joe returned at the prearranged time, the owner said, "Joe, this is not a very big check for all you have been through, but I want it. Would you use it to buy a new Deluxe?"

Joe was staggered. He could not believe his ears or his good fortune. He also could not refuse. He got his first new car and his boss got his first official POW compensation check. Oh, and his brother bought his worn out, old Mercury.

The Eye of Darkness

There is little good to be said about being a nation at war. We are that, however. The War on Terror is as real as any war ever fought. The nation did learn one thing from Vietnam, albeit learned in the throes of pain. She is not forgetting to welcome her warriors home — or to celebrate them at the appropriate times. In that vein, many national corporations reach out on Veterans Day, especially those that feed the public. My family and I ate in such a place on Veterans Day, 2009, enjoying a day of respect as well as good food. Near the end of our meal, a World War II vet rolled around the half-wall to the booth adjacent to us, where he scooted into a seat. My social butterfly grandson introduced himself before the old man picked up his menu.

My number three grandchild knows no strangers. He has been around military people since infancy. Our neighbor asked if the boy could come around and sit with him a minute, which was approved, of course. The octogenarian and the four-year old soon engaged in a wonderful conversation, only a portion of which could be overheard. What I did hear was about the old man's reunion vest and hat, commemorating his World War II service. He wore a number of badges and ribbons which aroused a litany of questions. We extended our stay a bit, but leaving became necessary. Other veterans lined up for meals deserved the space. I walked around to get my grandson — and met Ralph Dodge, veteran of World War II, the man about whom I now write. Before we left, Ralph gave the boy a dollar.

Ralph and I met in the small house where he resides behind his youngest son's home. The World War II veteran is a tough man, but age and illness trapped him. He asked for help and his son found a place for him. He is nearby yet retains his independence. Dodge spends his days with two Chihuahuas and occasional visits by a home healthcare nurse. Veteran friends check on him as well. He keeps a library of mementos in a scrapbook, framed pictures, and history books documenting World War II. His small television streams the news and his aging computer is near when he wants to get a message to his sons living far from him. His world is at hand. Like many older vets he needs cue cards for some of his memories.

Ralph Dodge is the product of a mixed marriage. His mother was the daughter of a French missionary working with the Tuscarora Indians in Canada. She married Grey Wolf, a member of the tribe. Ralph, or Little Wolf as he was known as a boy, lived part of his childhood in the Yukon.

His parents immigrated to the United States when he was young, where they settled somewhere north of the Chicago area. Chicago is where Ralph joined the Army Air Corps.

Ralph went on the warpath at the age of 15. Somehow he got a copy of his birth certificate and doctored it so it verified his age as 18. Many young men of that era lied in order to serve the country in the war. I asked him why it enraged him that much. He responded that his uncle was killed during the Bataan Death March. He wanted nothing more than revenge. Accepting that the Draft Boards were that gullible is always difficult. Ralph explained that he worked hard growing up. He looked older and he was strong. He said "In those days if you could do a man's job, you did it." The Army had fallen in such disarray prior to the war that they overlooked many things to get the different branches up-to-speed. The Board did not review his documents—and took him at face value. Ralph went to Basic Training and Gunnery school.

Most people celebrate their 16th birthday with cake. Dodge's fireworks emanated from two German planes (Messerschmitt and Focke-wulf) that he shot down that day from his position as tail gunner on a B-17. He got a third before leaving Europe in 1942. Ralph explained that life expectancy as a tail gunner could be as little as 49 seconds. He flew eight missions, accumulating five hours, 12 minutes and change. When the higher-ups sought volunteers for a new program, he stepped forward. He felt he was on the wrong continent for one thing. Ralph joined the Army to fight the Japanese. He sensed something else too. His run of good luck had to be near done. The program involved new technology with top secret equipment — and an eventual assignment in the Pacific Theater of the war.

Ralph Dodge, P-61 Black Widow squadron night fighter

Ralph arrived in the Kissimmee, FL, area for a school, but did not stay there long. He moved to the airfield at Boca Rotan for several months of training. The Army provided housing in Miami and bused them daily. The buildings were as scattered as the technology they studied. The military did not want the people or the information housed close together — that made too easy a target. The environment proved excellent, but the studies were challenging. He saw his first version of the P-61 Black Widow there too. Dodge became part of a new radar program designed for use in aircraft. It required a larger plane, with space inside, and room to adapt its separate equipment and additional manpower. Ralph said, "In those days, it was a court martial offense to even say the word *radar* off post anyplace." They learned the equipment and how it worked in the plane.

The Germans realized that something important was being done at Boca Raton. The buildings were spread. Guards controlled access and egress with irrefutable limitations. Their submarines patrolled the coast in an attempt to learn what was housed there. They shelled the compound almost every night. Even a random strike would interrupt the project, if not in its entirety. For security purposes, the American public had little or no knowledge about the activity on the base, but the enemy treated the area as a high-priority target.

The trainees acquainted themselves with the airplane. The P-61s were large airplanes. Four 50-caliber machine guns and four 20-caliber cannon were mounted on those used in Ralph's school. His assigned squadron flew them too. They also had mounting brackets for two 1600-pound bombs or extra fuel cells for longer flights. The parabolic reflectors for the radar unit fit in the nose of the aircraft. The electronics were contained in the boom controls. The gunner and radar operator shared space at the rear of the main fuselage and had access to the dual sets of controls for the equipment housed there. The P-61 in all its variations was heavily armored and powerful. It was still in the performance-testing phase when Ralph Dodge trained in Florida. When he completed the radar training school his next assignment was with his air wing in New Guinea. He made it to the Pacific War in 1943 with the 421st Night Fighters.

When his group arrived in New Guinea they preceded the arrival of the P-61s by several weeks. The pilots flew missions in other planes while their crew continued training and working in ground-based jobs. When the new planes arrived the Army Air Corps established several squadron bases on islands throughout the Pacific. Ralph Dodge became part of something for which the Japanese had no answer — air warfare at night. Our new fighters had eyes in the dark. Theirs had none.

Ralph asked what I wanted to know when we began talking. I told him the same thing I told the other World War II vets. "Tell it the way you want.

I will ask some questions as we go, but it is your story." Ralph replied that, "I can't remember so much about the combat as I do the other stuff, the stuff in between. We flew to Leyte, Luzon, the Philippine Sea, to Okinawa, to a lot of places. We had missions every night seems like."

I spoke to him at our big reunion in the fall before we had our real interview. I asked him there if it scared him to fly at night. While he thought about those missions, it seemed like a good time to revisit that question. His answer was the same. Ralph said, "Flying in the dark was easy. We had an edge. Nobody could see us. Our planes were black, our engines were muffled, and we hit them and were gone, like we were never there. You infantry guys had it a lot worse. But we had some characters. Man, we had some real clowns. Pilots are nuts. You gotta remember. I was supposed to be 19 over there and we had pilots the same age and bombardiers on the big planes the same age. We were a bunch of kids fighting a war and showing off like kids do." Then Ralph told me a story.

Ralph remembers an incident with another pilot in his group. That guy flew like he was born with a stick in his hand. He loved to display his skill if he got the chance. There were nurses in and out of their quarters for different reasons during the war. One day a captain's dinghy dropped a nursing major and her aide by headquarters to take care of some paperwork. It was his squad's job to get her the rest of the way to her destination. Mr. Hotshot drew the straw for the right to fly the pair forward to the Luzon hospital. The P-61 held three crew members, but the pilot knew nobody minded being crowded for a trip like that. He rearranged so the major could sit with him in the main cockpit. The radar operator squeezed back in his portion of the rear turret to make room for the aide between his seat and the gunner's spot. It was tight, but the discomfort worked for the men involved. At the back of their area, a door was fitted on the bottom of the radar operator's space. Held by a simple latch, supported externally by wind pressure, the door offered easy last minute access without bothering the pilot. The crew carried mail to the other islands at times, or dispatches came to them at the last moment. The door proved convenient for last minute additions to their cargo. The door made a lasting impression on the radar man during the flight that day.

The pilot barely contained his joy. His moment to shine broke through everything the day that he won the chance to help those nurses. His stars converged. He made a smooth take off and drew away from the air strip, when the chance to show his skill broke through the clouds. Even a flight like this was not a simple joy run. When they flew they also had a military purpose. He received his orders to fly cover for a Navy vessel sailing the same direction. The pilot poured the power to his engines and banked into a steep climb to make altitude. The plane shot up with so many "Gs" that the door in the radar hole popped open. The radar operator went through the hole and out! He braced himself against the door at take off with the extra passenger without a thought for anything like that happening. Positioned with the gunner, she couldn't see him. By the time she felt the decreased pressure against her body, the door had slammed shut from the wind buffeting it, the door had latched itself again and there was no sign of him. Unable to operate the intercom she sat in his seat in stunned silence until they touched down at Luzon.

When they taxied to a stop, deplaned, and gathered to walk to the hanger she tried to explain what happened in cries and shouts, as the story was told later. The pilot, panic stricken, did not even know how to report it. The pilot slowed her down and asked her to tell her story again. She is alleged to have said, "All I know sir, is that one minute he was there and the next he was gone." The pilot could not say he was showing off. His only recourse was to report a freak equipment failure and file a "Missing in Action Report" for his radar operator. And he was—for the next seventy two hours he was missing in action.

Headquarters received a message from the Navy three days later that one of their ships had recovered a crew member from a P-61. Marines on board the ship that the plane escorted saw what they believed to be a bag of mail fall from the plane. At least they thought that at first. Then its…his…parachute deployed. The ship could not hale the aircraft because they ran a different radio frequency. The captain brought his ship about, dropped a rescue boat, and got the man aboard. It took three days to track down his squadron and get him to his airfield. Ralph laughed and said there were a whole bunch of lucky guys with that one. Nobody went to the stockade and nobody died. The story cleared a fog bank for him too.

Ralph loved the P-61 and praised its safety. The plane was powerful and tough. It could not be seen or heard at night. If silhouetted against the moon it became visible, but he felt like a ghost in the night sky the rest of the time. Before they began receiving numerous escort missions with the Navy or intercept missions seeking enemy aircraft, they flew secretive missions for the Marines. Some of the squadrons did on-the-record cover for Army units during island assaults. His unit did several off-the-record operations for Marines near New Guinea. They could not get approval for some reason, but Ralph said, "It was not like it is now. Our generals cared more about saving our men and winning the war than they do now. A few politicians run the wars now and don't care who gets killed. Our officers weren't politicians. They did what it took and kept the politicians out of it as much as they could. I think that is why we won our War and we haven't won one since."

During some assaults the Marines found bunkers which were impenetrable. The Army and Marines exchanged radios and established a code system so they could communicate. Ralph's group had a resourceful supply sergeant who found some old fuel cells which he confiscated and stored at their airfield. They learned how to make their own napalm. One and one made two. The make-do napalm bombs were very useful against the machine gun bunkers. The P-61s powered in low enough to drop the napalm, making the assaults much safer for the Marines. Fired-up Japanese cooperated with them better. I asked Ralph if they absorbed much damage on the unauthorized attacks. He replied, "Never. The machine guns shot through horizontal slots at ground level. They could not shoot up and down at their airplanes. The only time they took any fire was from shoulder fired weapons. Sometimes we got hit by light machine guns, but nobody got hurt." He went on to say that was why they never could understand the refusal from higher authority for their requests to support the operations. The simplicity and relative safety of the operation to the aircraft, the improved success for the Marines made it seem a simple decision to those on the ground.

By the summer of 1944, the squadrons engaged in daily ops of all kinds. Enemy aircraft were growing scarce as Allied Forces turned the air war in their favor, but the P-61s iced the cake. The advantage they added put the Japanese in a complete defensive posture. Ground radar and intelligence predicted flight paths or plans. The Army Air Corps flew patrols all over the China Sea, the Philippine Sea, and the Pacific. The various squadrons flew cover in Navy shipping lanes. American eyes in the darkness spotted the enemy when the enemy could not see them. Ralph said they could pull up from below, swing in behind a Japanese bomber searching for one of our airbases and blast it out of the sky before it knew anyone was there. The heavy cannon were in the pilot's control. Many of the Japanese planes had very little armor. The 20-mm rounds would pass back to front, even killing the pilot and co-pilot whether or not the plane exploded. Often the Black Widows got so close that a "kill" became virtually guaranteed.

Dodge explained that the weapons systems designed for the P-61 included a two-scope system if needed. The cannons utilized both A and B scopes. The A scope displayed range and azimuth. The B scope displayed elevation and azimuth. When the pilot had his target directly in front of him the scopes showed 0/0 and he was "dead on." The machine gunner saw the same view and radioed the pilot a confirmation. The gunner controlled a pair of 50-caliber machine guns behind and above the pilot. The gunner could pivot to operate the rear pair, or if the radar operator was not busy, he operated them. The flexibility aided in the aircraft's combat success. Some squadrons' aircraft were not equipped that way, but Ralph's group employed the dual yoke, twin 50-caliber model.

Ralph claimed that the most dangerous aspect of night flying was not flight, but landing. Unlit or dimly lit runways were a challenge. He had absolute faith in his pilot. Dodge said the man flew as though the plane were an extension of his own body. He could make it do anything. They landed strictly by the altimeter. Ralph called it an "absolute altimeter" that was calibrated zero to 500 feet. When the wheels touched the ground, they were at zero. He won money one time on his pilot. They gambled against another crew and about which pilot could land with the most airspeed and still stop short of the runway's end. He won some cash but about lost his lunch.

The missions came every night. Usually they operated with a two or three plane team. The P-61 groups covered a lot of ocean. They lived for night missions. Their bodies and minds were tuned to the work. Their eyes were trained for night use. If they ventured out during the day, they wore sunglasses. Their rooms were darkened. The light bulbs were limited to seven watts. Ralph claimed that on a clear night, flying at their normal elevation, he could see a cigarette lighter flare on the horizon miles away. The radar and the men became skilled at another thing which proved a pleasant surprise to the Navy. They found that they could spot enemy aircraft carriers from the night sky. They could see the elevator lights on the deck when it moved to lower or raise planes. If the P-61s carried bombs, the radar gave them precision bombing capability. If not, they had heavy cannon, although their wing configuration made it impossible to perform like a dive bomber. At the very least, they relayed excellent enemy position information to the Navy.

I asked if he felt more like a bat than a Black Widow. He said they did live like bats in many ways.

Ralph Dodge learned to love the South Pacific. He reenlisted near the end of World War II to finish the war there. I asked how many missions he flew. Unsure, he put the number between 500 and 600, including his time flying during the occupation of Japan. The P-61 did not get the reputation that many fighters did. It got into the fight too late. It was the final nail in the coffin for the air war. The pilot and the radar man shared kills, thus it was difficult to name aces. Since crews sometimes rotated based on the constant demand for missions, they never knew for sure who was flying with whom when an enemy went down. Black Widows were used as escorts for the Marine contingent taking the Japanese diplomats to the Navy. The Navy escorted them to sign the Peace Treaty.

Ralph reminisced a bit about New Guinea as he thought about the time he spent near Japan after the war. He said some people could not acclimate to the tropical climate. About a third of the men lost in New Guinea were actually killed by the environment. It became a joke about the snakes. A small viper bite killed within minutes. Ralph laughed as he told it, "You were better off to sit down and smoke a cigarette than if you ran for help. You lived five or six minutes longer." He mentioned two places where he lived specifically — Honshu and Bofu. There were air bases in Burma, China and many of the island chains. At one point his station was on one of Japan's outer islands. Ralph learned to fly while stationed in one of those places. Never certified, his flying was unofficial. As the Radar Operator he was a Second Lieutenant, but when the P-61s were relieved and the manpower reduced after the War rank began to dissolve as well. He did not say directly, but he alluded to the fact that his role changed in the months after the war. His remained on his pilot's crew. Pilots had to get a specific number of stick hours during certain periods and he accompanied his pilot on occasion. During one trip, his old boss asked him to cover the controls while he took a nap. They were flying an AT6, which had space for such things. Ralph had filled in before when the Major encountered personal foul weather the night before a flight. On this particular occasion they remained aloft until fuel became critical. Dodge, forced to return to base, performed something he had never done when he could not awaken the sleeping pilot—a landing. They bounced to a halt. That woke the pilot. Upon arrival at the tower the Major got a butt chewing. Nothing could be admitted, so when he was ordered to do two Saturdays of "touch and goes", Ralph slipped in too. The back-up pilot needed preparation for the future as well.

Property ownership was illegal for our military men. American servicemen like Ralph — bachelors — found working arrangements that proved beneficial. He provided funding and his house girl bought property for them. When he transferred, she travelled ahead. It was a good arrangement and his living conditions were wonderful. As more recruits, including the ever increasing female presence in the military, came to the Far East the pressure increased to cease certain behavior patterns. By 1948, MacArthur found it prudent to force personnel who had served there for an extended period of time to return to the States to reenlist. When that happened, there were no guarantees that the new assignment would be in the Pacific region. Ralph remained in the Army Air Corps until 1949 when he was discharged. The civilian world did not fit him well. He joined the Merchant Marines, where he became an engine man. Somewhere along the way, he joined the Naval Reserve as well. In his words, "I threw those papers in a drawer and forgot all about them. While I was in the Merchant Marines I started some correspondence courses. What else you gonna do when you are off-duty on a ship going somewhere slow?"

Korea broke out. Ralph Dodge received a notice that he was needed again. Many Merchant Marines did, but he did not do it in that capacity. He wore Navy blue. His old Army paperwork showed his rank as a Radar Operator. His Merchant Marine work, even if only for a few months, showed him working in an engine room. The new assignment made him a Petty Officer in the Engine Room aboard the Essex. Ralph said, "Of all things. There I was on a one-lane aircraft carrier listening to those Gawd-awful jets take off and land. I just stayed below decks for three years. I came out and told 'em what to do and checked on 'em once in a while. They knew what to do. A lot of them were Merchant Marines too." He went on the flight deck one time and hated it. It was too noisy. Ralph said they floated around out there off the coast for three years doing their jobs. He also said he could tell how war was changing.

Ralph had a friend who was prosecuted late in the *police action*. His buddy shot a mama-san in a rice paddy. A young officer heard about it, reported it as murder, and Army officials came after him. The man went through hell. Witnesses and finally their Korean scout testified that the woman was working for the North Koreans. She sat there in the paddy calling in coordinates to enemy artillery and was getting them slaughtered. The scout figured it out and got word to the closest infantry unit. Ralph's buddy happened to be the man with the best chance at ending the barrage. The man was found innocent, but the incident was a harbinger of things to come in warfare. Dodge believes that cases like that have become common since then.

When the conflict in Korea ended, Ralph went back to the Merchant Marines for a few years. He became a Chief Engineer in the ship's engine room. Longshoremen impacted how they operated in the fifties. Ralph said, "You couldn't say much to anyone anymore. If you did more than speak to them in the morning you were harassing them. I just gave 'em orders and went back to my room and studied my correspondence course even harder. I thought I may as well get some schooling." Dodge left the Merchant Marines in the fifties and returned to the Chicago area.

Ralph Dodge lived for adventure. He had grease and speed in his blood by the time he settled down to make a living. The years in the Army Air Corps and at sea pushed him toward working on mechanical devices. His business linked to auto racing, which evolved into his own stock car racing experience. He met a young lady not long after she graduated from high school. She was different than the other girls in her class and different than the other women he knew. Ralph said, "That girl could turn a wrench!" He hired her. It was not long before he discovered that she was not only a great work partner, but his true life partner. They worked on cars and started a family together. Over the next several years she pressured him to drive too. She was not to be denied. Ralph said she was as tough behind the wheel as with the tools. One weekend tragedy struck. His beloved wife died at the track, forced into the wall in a freak accident that took her life. Ralph found himself with eight sons to raise, the youngest of which was five years old. They had four single births and two sets of twins. He was angry at her for years, but he could not stay where they had shared their life together. He packed the family and headed west, rolling with the tumbleweeds into Arizona.

Many endeavors fell in Ralph's contrail in the west, but none were dull. The story he shared with me came from his old scrapbook. I saw certificates of appreciation from the National Rifle Association, from the National Olympic Committee, a variety of sheriff's associations, and other military and civil service organizations. He moved from job to job, but was always connected with serving the community and the country. His proudest achievement came when the Women's Rifle Team he coached went to the Olympics. They won the Gold Medal in Barcelona. Ralph was not the head coach, but he worked with two of the girls who made the team from the western region. His expertise in safety and marksmanship earned him the position with the National Rifle Association. An autographed photo of him standing with Charlton Heston is treasured as highly as anything in his album.

Ralph fast-forwarded through his life in the book. He said proudly, "I kept the family together, the boys did well in school, and most of 'em made it through college. Two went to the Naval Academy and two to the Air Force Academy. When they were grown, I hit the road."

Dodge's eight sons make him proud. Seven of the eight served the country. All seven retired from one of three branches of the military. Only the Army is not represented by them. The eighth chose to remain a civilian. The others obtained government work after they left their respective branches of service and most live abroad. They seem to have their father's wanderlust. Ralph moved about the country, never working in one place long again. In the nineties he was hit on a motorcycle by a drunk driver. It cost him his right leg. The accident turned him into a recluse for years, until he moved to Kokomo, IN, near his youngest son, where I met him.

The tumbleweed does not beat Ralph Dodge by much. He has miles of life behind him. Ralph wiped the dust from his books and his memories with me. He allowed me a glimpse through his eye in the darkness.

Old Claude

My father never spoke much about his experience in World War II. Dad was an ornery but quiet man in most cases. There were moments when he came close to raising his voice. Those were times when hell rained down from above, and I am not talking about an airborne assault. He was Airborne in WWII, a member of the 517th Parachute Regiment Combat Team. When he rained he rained with undeniable results.

Dad weighed about 145 pounds when he was in Europe, but that did not prevent him from being chosen to jump with a BAR (Browning Automatic Rifle). They were heavy weapons for an airborne assault. Gear took dad's body weight to around 200 pounds and that was a load for his five feet, nine inch frame.

Family lore, much of it provided by a career Army uncle, unofficially declared that dad made three jumps, but only one is documented in his permanent, but partially destroyed records. That is not unusual as soldiers moved often from unit to unit based on need on the battlefield. Paperwork did not always keep up with fact, therefore I can only say with certainty that dad jumped during the Anvil Operation, which was part of the Normandy Invasion.

Before dad died in 1980, I did get a few questions answered, but not the way I wanted. I simply could not get his lips unlocked when it came to that War. Even though I too was a veteran, he remained reticent. My uncle told me to ask dad about the scar above one of his kidneys. I did. Dad never answered. I did learn that he made a jump that landed him in a river where he got very serious frostbite. I may be the only person who remembers the story. There were some shared with my godfather, Nile Butner (also deceased) and the uncle I mentioned, that occurred in my earshot which landed and stuck in small pieces. Dad was taken to England because of his feet at some point, but he went back to the War later. The Army wanted to remove his feet but he refused. He struggled with foot problems the rest of his life. Dad's DD-214 showed his combat, his awards and a rating of 100% disability. He never drew a dime. When I asked him why, he said, "I am going to leave that money for guys who need it worse." I did not realize until many years later how that unselfish attitude affected me. It influenced me and I am fighting my way through that roadblock still today.

Places like Ardennes and the Black Forest always register with me. I remember dad talking about being attached to two different units which were in effect wiped out and then getting reassigned again. Officially Anvil is the only thing I can document. The rest are just fragments, perhaps figments of my youthful memory. Where do those tales originate? I have nobody to whom I can turn, yet the images, the memories haunt me. Deep inside I know they are real. In the 517's history it is noted that a number of their men were loaned to other units before they officially entered the War. Could dad have been part of that advance? Could he have been there when the group came finally, as a complete unit? Something tells me it is so. Something tells me that he was already a hardened veteran, strictly by chance, before others arrived. My mother often discredited my uncle's stories. My father did not. He simply sat in silence.

One thing my parents did was keep dad's pictures together and protected. As my sons matured, they enjoyed seeing them when they could, imagining what dad may have done along with me. He had photos of his buddies and a few taken in France. I cannot remember all the names he mentioned in hushed tones when I was a kid. As is the case with most vets, he spoke with wistfulness about those whom he believed survived. His eyes got a far-away look when he got to certain faces. I understood later what that meant. I also respected his reticence and did not pursue things further until years later. Then it was too late to fill in most of the blanks. However, a trip to the hills of north-central Virginia in 2007 helped open the coffin of memories buried with him.

My older son had served for 17 years by that time. Ten of those years were spent in the regular Army. At that point he and his wife decided to come home for educational and familial purposes. She too planned to be a career soldier. Part of their plan was to convert their time to the Indiana National Guard. Son went Airborne, following in the footsteps of his grandfather. Not mine. I was but a simple grunt. My daughter-in-law is Airborne as well, attaining the "exalted" position of Jump Master. My son converted to the Infantry before his second tour in the Middle East (she went too — on his second tour). He wanted his Combat Infantry Badge. He got it. I asked him to step out of the footsteps of his father and grandfather and forego earning his Purple Heart. I said all of that to say this — along the way he began researching military history in general and his grandfather's specifically. He located photos of my dad's unit on line and even a Jump Manifest. We discovered names with arrows pointing to various faces upon closer inspection of that document. My father, Bernard W. Mullins, had served with John C. Williams in Headquarters Co. of the 3rd Battalion, 517th Parachute Regiment. They had history. They are history.

My progeny located and contacted the son of the man whose name appeared on the manifest. He forwarded the information to me. I called and had the tremendous privilege of speaking with Old Claude, a.k.a. J.C. Williams. I learned that he not only remembered my father but remembered serving with him. One corner was lifted from the memory sarcophagus. I saw an opportunity to get a better peek at the ghosts of times past. I asked permission to visit him at the first opportunity. He agreed with pleasure. The chance came sooner than I expected. My son attended Pathfinder School a few months later. We discussed a trip with his wife and my son to attend his graduation, if he managed to do that. He did and we made plans, including a detour to see Claude.

July of 2007 found us traveling to a destination a few miles west of Blacksburg, Va. We took a laptop with all of dad's photographs loaded on it and drove from Fort Benning, GA. We were instructed to call Old Claude when we got to his part of the world. I drove and perspired with anticipation for many hours. Upon arrival and securing overnight quarters, I made a nervous, expectant call. Claude told us how to find him the next day. It was difficult to sleep that night.

I struggled to stay calm during breakfast and motel check-out. I drove through the lovely hills of the state where my father was raised. I hurried, but slowed to tick the miles off by tenths as we searched for our destination. We found a lovely older home on a hillside and followed the winding road to Claude's driveway while my mind raced. I tried to corral my thoughts. I wanted to speak as though I had some common sense when I arrived. The old man was looking for us and his excitement was obvious. My relief was immediate, but followed soon by surprise. We stopped in his drive and he walked right by me to my son's truck. As it turned out he spotted my son's airborne license plate. He greeted him first then greeted my wife and me. It was funny. Some ties pass through generations and bloodlines. It was a *Geronimo* moment for two, no three, people who jumped from perfectly good airplanes.

I stretched, more quietly than usual, and looked around. There was a lot of grass on that hillside and it was obvious it was all his. I could sense that. I saw a tough old man of eighty-six incredible years who still mowed his own grass. I realized once again why his generation, my father's, had earned the title of the Greatest Generation. As I stood there in my reverie, voices penetrated and I realized Old Claude was inviting us in for ice cream and pie. Southern hospitality never ages.

We met Mrs. Williams and broke bread with them, but it was better than bread. She had baked a homemade apple pie and scooped ice cream on it. I felt guilt for having those grand old folks serve me. Like all gracious people they would have been insulted had we refused the food. We talked about their family and he asked questions of my son regarding his service. I was pacing myself, chomping at the bit, hoping to find a gentle way to pry open Claude's memory bank. Finally he opened the conversation about his and my father's time in Europe together. I began by asking him if he had salvaged any pictures. He did not, but was thrilled to learn that we brought my father's with us. He had never been that close to a laptop, but he was not as interested in that phenomenon as he was in the treasure it contained. I hurried to the car to get it while he and the others chatted. All of us resisted third helpings of dessert. I for one did not want to fall asleep when I knew all my attention was needed during the time I was allotted.

We poured through the photos that my wife had scanned. As we came to people he recognized he slowly thought about the faces. He did not know all of them. They were some men who were close to dad after Old Claude was wounded. He laughed at a picture of a mule and whispered to me that he would tell me a little about that when the women were not near. There were several shots which included the mule and all were taken in and around a village somewhere in the mountains of France. As it turned out, those pictures were taken prior to the major offensive when he was severely wounded. He did not pinpoint it for me, so I have no specific date for it, but it was a more pleasant memory than the next one.

When we got to his Company photo, I heard him take a breath. He touched the screen as he connected the names with the faces deemed significant by the arrows. He mentioned a couple to whom he had spoken years later. Two faces brought tears to his eyes as his fingers hovered there for long moments. After many deep breaths, he asked for some time to clear his head. We walked outside, Old Claude, my son and me.

Conversation lagged as Claude reflected quietly. He laughed and told us about the mule. It seems that when they went into a French village, that mule would stop randomly in front of a house. Invariably there were women inside who were *friendly* to American soldiers. He said the mule meant more to his platoon than almost anything else. His laugh and twinkling eyes conveyed more than his words. It was time to return to the house. He quietly led the way. When we arrived we saw that my wife, my daughter-in-law and young grandson had enjoyed Mrs. Williams as much as we had Claude. I never asked what they talked about while we were outside. I was too immersed in my own purpose and the recollections that Claude was sharing.

Old Claude continued with the faces that caused the interruption. They were dead. He and those men had been hit by an artillery shell at the same time. He awoke a day later when bodies were pulled off him. Those two lifeless soldiers had shielded him from the view of Germans searching for survivors. When American soldiers reclaimed the position, Claude was discovered in the crater clinging to life, with both arms almost severed from his body. He credited his dead buddies with saving his life. For the next two years, he moved from hospital to hospital, undergoing nine surgeries to save his limbs. He came home and worked more than 40 years at a local factory, raising his family and remembering. That is why he lost track of dad. His war ended that day while dad's dragged on until December 24th, 1944 when he too was wounded and left the battlefield. Claude's breathing labored, his words slowed, and his eyes misted. He said he had looked at all the photos he could stand. It was time for coffee.

I asked Old Claude if he could tell me a little something about dad. He could and he did. They jumped into Italy together and fought through the Alps side by side. Their Platoon Leader was killed when they reached the foothills. They could not turn back. As a group, they decided one thing. There would be no prisoners taken as they fought through the mountains. They did not have the means to care for them, or the manpower to deal with them. The cost of the War had been steep to that point. Besides, they wanted to even the score for the Platoon Leader. They fought on without one. They knew what they had to do and where they were going. I was struck by the pain in his face as he labored to tell his story. His words evoked images in my mind. There were Germans waiting as they struggled uphill with weapons thrust ahead of them. Those soldiers sweated profusely as the air grew thin, their breath coming in gasps, their fear swelling in their throats, fingers tight on the triggers of their weapons. Eyes straining, they knew they had to find a pass through the mountains. There was nothing behind them to give them relief and nothing ahead but possible death.

My newest hero, John C. Williams, told me that they fought and fought — finding Germans behind every rock formation. The casualties were high. They fought and fought — and fought. They killed. There was no negotiating table. Both sides had to use the same approach. There was no quarter asked and none given. They were killed too. They climbed. They fought some more. When they battled their way down, they realized the resistance was lessening. Old Claude implied there were no victors, only survivors. When they arrived in the valley on the French side of the mountains, replacements were waiting, along with a new Platoon Leader. After being fed and permitted to get some rest, the new Old Man told them he was asking no questions about what had transpired in the mountains. Then he reminded them they were back in the United States Army and all rules applied once again. It was then that Claude informed me he simply could no longer speak about that period in his life. He had been carried through those mountains by soldiers who refused to leave him behind. The memories were as painful as the wounds. He was tiring. He was in pain. We knew that it was time to take our leave. I was trembling inside, many questions answered but many yet roiling around in my heart and mind. Still, he had shared a golden treasure with me.

The interview was over. Another history book was read to me, but on a whole new level. We learned little more after that. Two years later I saw a handkerchief dad sent his youngest sister from Europe. We did more research, seeking more information about some of the faces not connected to Claude's story. There was an Oriental man who we discovered was Japanese and from CA. He was honored in that state in 2005. My attempt to contact him failed. I learned he was part of a Japanese Engineering Company that had served with dad in France. The Army would not allow them to fight in the Far East. Modern historians take the position, with some imagined moral high ground invented from having not lived in the moment, that America treated Japanese Americans badly during World War II.

Sadly they were treated badly. But these modern historians did not live then. They cannot understand the absolute fear that gripped the entire country after that sneak attack. Thousands of good people were herded like cattle to internment camps and kept there under surveillance for much of the war, if not all. The reviewers of that period were not at Pearl Harbor. Nobody knew for a long time the "who or why" about that treacherous attack. If they had lived then, if they had lost a loved one there, if they had heard the bombs, felt the ground shake, heard the screams of agony in the water as the sharks attacked and the flesh melted from the bones of burning men, then perhaps they may have had a more realistic perspective. Yet, all that notwithstanding, many of those people served in all kinds of war-time jobs and did so with heroism and honor. It took some time for Americans to sort their emotions and bring those citizens back to the fold. Some World War II veterans still have not. Others cry with horror at the memory at what both sides did to the other.

As we chatted about things other than the War, we learned more about this tough little man. He was diagnosed with cancer a pair of years before we met and doomed to death once again. He fooled the local medical community and lived. He had lessons to impart…to me. I called him a few months ago. His wife died in 2008, but his son lives with him now on that hillside. He has cancer again. Old Claude had received more than 30 different cancer treatments when we last spoke. He tired after a few minutes on the phone and wished me the best. I doubt I will ever hear his voice again. I will try again — however, I am reluctant to do so. I know I will shed some tears. As I write, he still lives, at least in my mind. I do not want to know officially that he too has passed.

That day, he walked with us to our vehicles and I had to ask one more question. "Claude," I queried, "Can you tell me how dad served?"

Old Claude looked at me and replied, "He did his job son. He did his job. We all did."

I left Mr. John C. Williams' home that evening with respect and reverence mixed with sadness at what we are losing in the country now. We are losing these soldiers, their stories, the understanding of the price paid for what we enjoy and inherited, and above all, the chance to learn from them. I waited too long to ask my father what he did and what it all meant. There is no assurance he would have answered, but the lingering doubt will always be a sore spot in my consciousness. I drove away in deep thought but somehow with a little better understanding even though my questions remained unanswered in many ways.

When I got home I left the story unwritten for months. It intimidated me. I did not want to think about it. It seemed that writing it was somehow akin to writing a final chapter in a book that I did not want to finish. Months later it beckoned me and here I am writing. I have Father's DD-214 in front of me, hoping that it will tell me something he did not, or fill in a blank that Claude did not. What do I see? Even this is generic. I wish I could see deeper into the shadows of this war. I am searching.

From my father's DD-214:

"Place of Separation — Hosp Center Cp Carson Colo — 13 July 45"

"Battles and Campaigns — Rome-Arno Southern France Rhineland Ardennes"

"Decorations and Citations — Eame Ribbon Combat Inf Badge 4 Bronze Sv Stars Purple Heart Good Conduct Medal"

"Wounds Received in Action — Belgium 26 Dec 44"

"Date of Departure — 17 May 44; Dest-Italy; Date of Arr-31 May 44"

"Date of Departure — 07 Mar 45; Dest-USA; Date of Arr-19 Mar 45"

"Reason and authority for Separation — Cert. of Disability Discharge"

There are still many "whys" and "whats" in my mind. As a kid I would look at his Bronze Stars and not realize there was a difference between a campaign medal and an award for valor. As far as I was concerned he was a hero. I know the difference now. I wrote that Dad was wounded on the 24th of Dec. That is the date Uncle Hansford used in his notes and the one I remember. Uncle said that Dad told him that was when he was hurt, but that he did not get medical help until later. Perhaps that is why there is difference on his paperwork. I have no idea.

All of this changes his status in my mind not at all. He was my hero.

By the way, I did call Old Claude again. He died in late 2009. I cried.

517th /combat record:

150 days of combat in Italy, France, Belguim, and Germany
Casualty Rate 81.9% or 1576 troops; 247 KIA

Saturday Night Surprise

John Graham and I arrived before the main crowd tromped into the mid-19th century building where our group meets every month. Greeted with, "You guys are in for a treat tonight," we wondered what the agenda held. Soon, veterans from the Gulf War and Vietnam began to squeeze through the old door. From the veranda, we heard our host Dave call to make some room, "They are here." In came two grizzled men in their eighties. Two World War II vets were our guests of honor for the evening.

He brought them to the center of the long, narrow living room where we waited with as much dignity as his excitement would allow. They were introduced to us by their personal chauffeur for the evening, Doctor Frantzer. "Men, these men are Seaman Second Class James Smith and Private Earnest Elliott, veterans of World War II. James survived the sinking of the USS Indianapolis and Earnest survived the invasion of Okinawa and several other islands in the South Pacific." Surprise is a word that fits some occasions. Not this one.

Dave called me over to make a special introduction to the two men. He told James Smith that we must spend a little time together tonight, at least. He realized how difficult it would be, but there should be some time for us. Men crowded around to shake their hands already, so I knew the moment I'd carved out would be difficult to find. Earnest deserved his own place in the sun as well. Talking at length with either seemed impossible. Our meeting on the last Saturday of January, 2010, loomed large in my memory book now.

These monthly gatherings are always memorable. Stories, laughter, and some sadness rule. Wherever veterans meet, that is true. We shared a meal, looked at the trophy room, where many new things were displayed on the shelves since my last visit. I saw an opportunity to spend some time with James Smith. Dave gestured for me at that time, too, having saved the chair when it became vacant. I wasted no time, squeezing by and into it as though I were playing a childhood game of musical chairs. We were reintroduced, with the additional explanation to Mr. Smith that I write stories about veterans.

I contained myself, but barely. A survivor of the Indianapolis — I could not believe I sat with such a man. Never had I considered having this opportunity. James Smith is a hardy, laughing, and warm man. We shook hands and he asked me if I was a veteran too. He thought so, but he wanted a little more information, which he received. I learned very soon that he has been involved with ten books and films about the sinking of the Indianapolis, so questions about it are nothing new. James carried a book, which was new, and a scrapbook. The latter he shared with four of us while we sat there talking. Throughout the evening he signed copies of the book as we chatted. Some of the men who came that night were aware he was attending and prepared.

James Smith, Survivor of the sinking of the USS Indianapolis.

The USS Indianapolis took part in the Battle of Okinawa. The sea battle and invasion, as huge as the Battle of the Bulge, extracted a heavy toll on the cruiser. Smith remembers the attacks she endured. The ship was hit by a kamikaze and one heavy bomb penetrated the deck. The ship's captain, Captain McVey, went to the deck and helped the hands there push the enemy plane off the ship. The bomb passed all the way through the ship and exited the hull. James remembers the total chaos, the fires, the crew manning guns and returning fire. During the battle witnesses confirmed a myth was *not* myth but fact. He heard that torpedo attacks by aircraft had been known to be made with kamikazes strapped to the torpedoes guiding them to their targets. Survivors extracted from the sea from other sinking vessels swore to the accuracy of the story. The battle left the Indianapolis so damaged it had to leave the battle and steam for a stateside port to undergo major repairs. She sailed at slow speed, listing, all the way to San Francisco. After repairs, the USS Indianapolis sailed back to the Pacific, back to the war — and into its sad history.

Jimmy, as he was known at the time, went ashore illegally while in Pearl Harbor to celebrate his 21st birthday. The USS Indianapolis had stopped to refuel after being dry-docked in San Francisco. They were sailing back to the war under orders. The crew received instructions to stay aboard. In fact, their identification cards were confiscated. James Smith had retained duplicates for just such a situation. He knew the ship's refueling allowed enough time for him to slip away and he was not about to miss his chance. Jimmy went to see his girlfriend at Pearl, where he partied too long and too hard. He paid a high price for it. Sea Dog Smith got busted. James Smith found himself in the ship's brig when it sailed on its secret mission to deliver parts for the atomic bomb. This was a solo run and top secret — all of which came out much later. Smith's punishment paperwork, including the 100-dollar fine, was locked in the ship's storage. He literally subsisted on bread and water while under lock and key for the entire five days. While he remained in the brig, the ship sailed to Tinian to deliver the payload it carried. After off-loading there, the Indianapolis put to sea again, sailing for Guam where it prepared for the attack on Japan. Orders sent it in secret to Leyte — alone. The second night out, Smith was released from the brig in the afternoon.

On the night of July 30, 1945, two torpedoes hit the USS Indianapolis while James Smith rested in his rack. A Japanese submarine could not believe its good fortune. It had found an American heavy cruiser on the open sea, unescorted by sea or air, in the dark of night. James showed me pictures in his scrapbook where the projectiles hit the ship, or the best descriptions offered by surviving eye witnesses. Both hit mid-ship, but in front of half-way. The second of the two appeared to be closer to the boilers. The first impact woke James at 12:05 AM — and rolled him from his rack. The second hit immediately after. James grabbed his life jacket, ran out of his room and forward. He discovered the way already blocked by fire, oil, and debris. The ship listed seaward minutes after the explosions. James turned around and walked aft, almost straight into the water. The ship sank in 12 minutes. He said the fantail went first and the bow pointed skyward. I asked him how he managed to get away, how he kept from being sucked down by the ship or the prop. He said, "I hauled ass."

Mr. Smith watched as men slid down the hull of the ship into the water, only to be sucked under as she sank. The bow jutted sixty to seventy feet in the air until the Indianapolis was swallowed by the sea. Other men dove. There were a few rubber rafts freed, but the large life boats were still secured to the ship — and with them, the supplies. They were also trapped on the side sinking into the sea. The water making equipment never got repaired in San Francisco. Damaged by bombs on the prior mission, the Navy never gave them time to get everything fixed before they sailed again. They had no potable water when they sank.

The crew's training instincts told them to gather in small groups for a number of reasons. The primary one seems to be the stronger one supporting the weaker, not just in the physical sense — but the emotional too. Eleven hundred men sailed on that ship. Seven hundred and ninety-seven went in the Philippine Sea that night in total darkness, according to James Smith. It was pitch black, waves swelling to 15 feet. A known risk to survival, aside from wounds and exposure, was the shark infestation problem which haunted pilots and sailors alike. Grouped together, they could watch for rescue, and attack — and support one another in many ways.

Some men grabbed debris. The life jackets they wore were designed to work for 48 hours. Before that time elapsed, shark attacks began. James assured me that sharks *do not* always bump their prey before they strike. Men stricken with delusions simply swam away from their groups. The groups could not always see others due to the swells. Some men attempted to drink the sea water. It killed them and they died in great pain. As men succumbed to the elements, those still living took their life jackets. Removing them from the dead meant that survivors could stay afloat longer. Floating longer meant living longer. Night passed into day, into night again, into day.

James told me about his good fortune. His group was led by Lieutenant Commander Hayes, the ship's doctor. They maintained discipline — and stayed together better than others. Hayes kept them focused, convinced them to work together. Their odds for survival were not good, but death would have to come for them. They were not going to it.

James Smith indicated one of the ironies was that the oil which covered them eventually helped them. Those coated in oil were protected from overexposure to the sun. He was one of those. I asked few questions as he told his story. However, curiosity made me ask why they did not get strafed by enemy aircraft, or even the sub that sank them. Smith responded that the enemy could not see them because of the rough seas. The enemy sub must not have called for air cover. Their captain knew the torpedoed ship went down. Surface vessels and aircraft may have assumed that they escaped in the cover of darkness. He did not know for sure. One thing he did know — nothing showed on the horizon and nobody could communicate.

James Smith had bobbed in the water four days and was into the fifth, when the first sign of a miracle appeared in the sky. A PBY flew overhead, saw them by some stroke of luck, and circled back to them. The pilot, disregarding orders as it became known later, landed the cumbersome sea plane nearby. Seaman Second Class Smith was among the first to be saved in an accidental rescue. Pilot Marks put the plane down and loaded so many men that he damaged his plane. Unable to get airborne, he radioed his position, and demanded assistance. The rescue led to the revelation of an historical miscue on the part of the Navy. Three-hundred-twenty men were fished from the water over the next few days. The full drama played itself out over the course of years in investigations and attempted cover-ups, but will live forever in history books. Three-hundred-sixteen men lived.

The USS Indianapolis went down about 500 miles from Guam, where the survivors were taken for treatment. Food ranked high on James Smith's list of needs. He survived nine days without a meal including his brig time. Hospitalized sailors and officers, the captain among them, remained there for several months. The Navy found itself mired in the muck of embarrassment and poor explanations. The top brass did everything it could to throw the entire mess on the shoulders of the captain of the ship. Jimmy Smith discovered a lot about what transpired while on Guam and still more years later.

The Navy sent the heavy cruiser on a solo mission without telling anyone its course. The captain requested escort which was denied. The people on radio duty ignored his distress calls and they went unreported. The first Navy position taken blamed Captain McVey for the ship's sinking, with the official position that he failed to put the ship on a zigzag course. No rescue effort was initiated because nobody knew they were missing. The Navy brass had kept the mission quiet. Upper echelon communications were a complete failure. The Navy cover-up failed due to the level of protest from eye witnesses and those involved in the rescue. The entire incident demonstrated an astonishing level of incompetence. In one final attempt to brand the captain forever, after the war, the Navy brought the Japanese submarine captain to testify against him regarding the ship's maneuvers. The Japanese captain said even if he zigzagged, it would have made no difference. The ship was a sitting duck out there on the horizon at night, all alone. The skipper of the USS Indianapolis was exonerated. The Navy was not.

James Smith served in the Navy from 1943 until 1946, when he was discharged. After his ordeal at sea, he was dry-docked. He worked ashore in San Diego for the rest of his tour of duty. We passed most of our time talking about the sinking of the Indianapolis, but he sailed with her on other missions. For example, he was there for the invasion of Okinawa. It would be grand to know more about that, but what he blessed me with is so unique that I remain overwhelmed with its inclusion in this book. With this short story you will find a photocopy of a chart James managed to keep from his Navy years. It is an original piece of history he allowed me to photograph. It is the sailing order for the largest battle formation in the history of our Navy, at least until then. I cannot imagine one bigger since. It is the sailing order for the invasion of Okinawa. There are 40 ships with primary name designations and nicknames noted on the plat. The formation noted the distance between vessels. It shows 100-miles wide by 100-miles deep. The beige parchment in James' possession is treasure. He has protected it faithfully for years. Smiling and laughing, he also showed me the pictures in his album of reunions and ceremonies, news articles with interviews. In each he wears the USS Indianapolis cap and jacket he wore the night I met him. It is now his uniform.

James Smith is funny, full of life and mischief. The last story he shared, laughing all the while, included another problem with his Navy uniform. He turned to a large photo of himself in his "whites" with his hat cocked jauntily to the side. Jimmy said, "See how I got that thing shoved off to the side like that? Ain't supposed to wear it like that, but the girls liked it that way. It looked better. And I liked the girls likin' it." He had a pass and was having a good time in San Diego when he got picked up by the Shore Patrol. His hat was cocked to one side, in the "girl position." He refused to square it on his head as ordered. Being out of uniform was added to his charges. Jim just cackled at the memory. The mind ages sometimes, but if you manage to hang on to it, the memories don't.

James followed the trials and inquiries for years as a survivor, wondering how he wound up where he did on July 30, 1945. The tragedy of that night shaped his entire life. It is part of every day. He weeps about it and he is celebrated because of it. He never stops living it. There are reunions, although fewer and fewer of them remain (51 now). America often finds a way to salute him and remember what happened that night. There is a monument dedicated to those who did not survive and books written to tell the story of those who did.

◆ ◆ ◆

Good fortune allowed me the opportunity to share time with another man who shaped our country. One more spoke with me that night. Unable to sit with him as long, I managed to chat with Earnest Elliott before they both left. Earnest held the floor in another room.

Earnest talked infantry with other men while I talked Navy with James. He served with the Bloody 32nd Infantry Regiment, also known as the Red Arrow by some and the Spearhead by others. They went to the South Pacific and fought on several islands. Earnest called himself an island hopper. It is incredible that he survived as many as he mentioned. New Guinea, the Philippines, and Okinawa — the 32nd is known for their attacks on several. Earnest said, "When we went in some place we never backed up. We took a place and we kept it." The outfit also fought on Leyte, Peleliu, and helped secure a place called Kwajalein. I am not sure how many of these he made.

While checking spelling on Wikipedia — a good, quick reference for that — I also learned that the 32nd is known for fighting for sixty of the bloodiest days in island history at one stretch and walking 16,910 miles. That is more than any regiment in history up to that point. After only three days' rest, the unit went to Korea to receive the surrender of the Japanese Army south of the 38th parallel. Earnest Elliott indicated he served in the South Pacific theater of World War II for a "few years."

James and Earnest…two more amazing men who gave a generation the title, "Greatest."

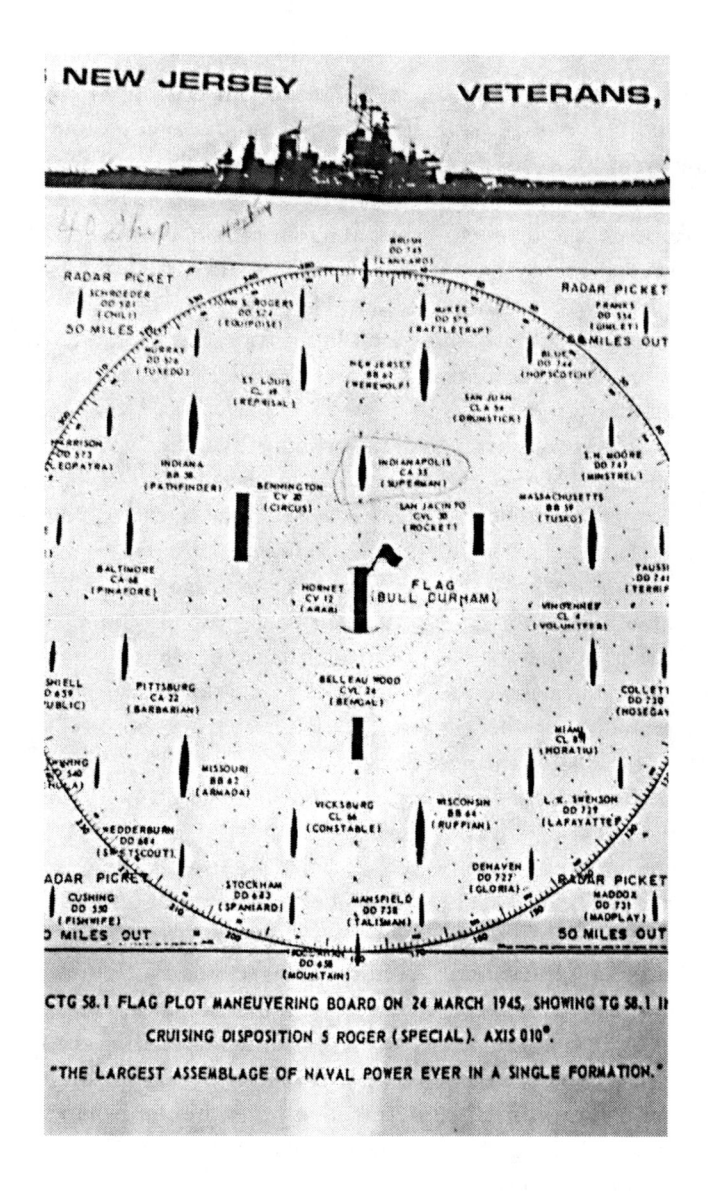

CTG 58.1 FLAG PLOT MANEUVERING BOARD ON 24 MARCH 1945, SHOWING TG 58.1 IN CRUISING DISPOSITION 5 ROGER (SPECIAL). AXIS 010°.

"THE LARGEST ASSEMBLAGE OF NAVAL POWER EVER IN A SINGLE FORMATION."

A Walk in the Clouds

My favorite bluegrass band, *The Grascals*, was playing at a wonderful campground venue in Indiana. The Bean Blossom camp ground is known for many events, but Bill Monroe's music festival is the largest family event held there each summer. My brother Jim and I went. Our brother-in-law, Danny Roberts, is a member of the band, but the unbiased fact is the group is great. Jim and I rarely have the opportunity to do something together. We have very different lives and schedules. He pretends to be a golfer — and I gave that up when I threw a nine-iron into a water hazard several years ago. We agreed to a different kind of trap on this day. Jim picked me up and we drove to southern Indiana.

The music festival was a trip of more than 100 miles. We actually talked. It was productive. I learned something. His best friend during high school was also his best man when he married. Jim's friend's father was a "Marsman" in World War II and helped secure the Burma Road. I have known Jim Modisett as many years as my brother, although not as well. He is a local farmer and business man known for his stories and ribald sense of humor. I've seldom been around him when he did not make me laugh. He is a big man with a booming voice and a commanding presence. I did not realize he was a World War II veteran. My brother suggested I ask him to talk about it — something he seldom did. I called the next day.

I arrived at the Modisett home at the appointed time, looking at the wonderful old house with the same admiration I had as a teen. It has always been a mansion to me. More than 50-years old, the property is graced by stately trees. Many years had passed since I had been there. Jim's dogs acted as a doorbell, so he was waiting for me.

He led me to his television room where he spends a major portion of his day, watching the various news channels — from hard news to market reports. Jim and his older son Greg, keep abreast of commodity trading and feed cattle for resale. They don't farm much now. Jim and his wife Diane have two sons, the younger of which is Jeff, a successful attorney and former Indiana State Attorney General. Greg lives nearby and manages the family business. Jeff resides in California. Jim pointed me to a chair.

I have way too much fun with some of my interviews. This one was no exception. We reminisced. Jim's voice boomed with questions about what I had been doing, where my brother was, and how I got started writing.

He pointed a big finger at a stack of books on his coffee table and said, "I got those out to show you. I don't have to say much. You can sit there and read."

"If I wanted to do that I would have gone to the library, Jim. I want to hear about you and your experience, not somebody else's take on it," I answered. "You aren't getting off that easy."

He laughed. "You are right. The books don't always tell it. I haven't tried to remember much of it in a long time. Sometimes I talk to some of my old buddies, but there ain't many of us left now. I have a hard time grabbin' hold of names and dates. It all runs together." I soon learned that was his favorite way of saying he was digging into his treasure chest of memories.

Jim has one thick volume which is his pride and joy. It was *Marsmen in Burma* by John Randolph, written in 1946. His copy was a gift several years ago. Jim is mentioned in it several times. He is pictured in it more than once. I was sitting with a man whose action was documented in period-correct text, not simply a story about to be written by my hand. Jim Modisett was a member of the Mars Task Force, a Marsman — a member of the advance group of allied soldiers which helped secure Burma. He walked over 300 vicious miles, driving mules and fighting, to reclaim the Burma Road *after* an arduous trip to reach the place where the journey was to begin.

Modisett introduced the subject by telling me he left India at Ledo, walked the Ledo road all the way to Myitkyina, Burma, the jumping off point for his adventure on the Burma Road. He called it a 300-mile walk in jungle and mountains with a bunch of mules. Then he said, after it was over, he had to walk out with them — over 600 miles. Jim, like every soldier I ever met, added the caveat that "the Army never did make any damned sense." If I had not begun asking questions that may have been his complete story, but I knew his exit included a small item referred to as the *Hump* — the Himalayan Mountains.

Jim Modisett was drafted in 1943 and trained at Fort Sill, Oklahoma, for six months. His advanced training occurred at Fort Carson, Colorado. Jim did not spend any time remembering the troop ship experience. Anytime I have been told about that it has been unpleasant. His next stop of importance was Bombay, Calcutta where he became a member of the Mars Task Force. That was when he and the other soldiers learned what they were about to do, or die trying. They were the 5332nd US Army Brigade, a Long Range Penetration Force for Burma. Jim was in the 613th Field Artillery Bn. (Pack), 475th Infantry Regiment (Special). The Task Force is included in its entirety on the US Army Special Forces Honor Roll web site. More intense and specialized training began while in India as they prepared to jump off for the mission to secure the Burma Road, and thereby Burma.

Jim Modisett

The trip across India was harsh. They left their quarters with a surfeit of material. The officers and non-commissioned officers told the soldiers to take what they wanted, including comfort items. Jim indicated they packed all kinds of ridiculous stuff, which came as a shock to me. We agreed that some inexperienced leader had false ideas about what they could take on mules and in carts. He was confident that none of Merrill's men were included in the planning. When they left, many of the men carried packs that weighed as much as 90 pounds.

Their water passage was made on what Jim described as "scud" boats. The soldiers split the next six days transferring from boxcars to cattle cars. It was hot, nasty, and dusty. They boarded planes along the way and flew seated on the floor of old cargo/supply transports to complete the journey to Myitkyina, Burma. There they began the hard journey into Burma. They tackled Mother Nature, the partially-built road, and the Japanese.

Camp Landis was an established outpost about ten miles north of Myitkyina. It was a virtual tent city. The soldiers had not yet been responsible for carrying the huge loads they had packed. More training prepared them for the coming battle. Now that they were about to actually engage the enemy, this was their real education. Each unit trained separately. The effort was more coordinated at this point. Infantry, artillery, field medical staff, and the Quartermaster units arrived at varying times, as well as other key support people. The mules were not all there yet. Once again, Jim referred to the old book and showed me pictures of the orderly chaos of a self-sufficient Army outpost far afield. The remnants of Merrill's Marauders were there before the inexperienced soldiers of what was to officially become the 5332nd Brigade (Provisional).

The Marauders had taken the Japanese airfield at Myitkyina a few months earlier in a vicious battle. Hundreds of Japanese were killed in the weeks it took to secure that airfield. The base was necessary to take that part of China and all of Burma. That group had been disbanded except for those who were to become part of the provisional force planning to take complete control of Burma. The 475th was the designated unit for the occupation of Myitkyina and had participated in the final effort to push Japanese resistance out of the city. The infantry unit was tough and included the remaining soldiers from Merrill's Marauders. They were seasoned and did not know the meaning of retreat. With part of the 124th used to re-man as new comers arrived, they were a formidable force. By the time the rest of the Task Force arrived, there was little mop-up work to complete. It would grow to accommodate a complete brigade, but the foundation was there.

◆ ◆ ◆

A rag-tag combination of battle-worn special operations troops fought the battle that won the airfield. The rest of the US force consisted of cooks, medical staff, truck drivers, combat engineers working on the Ledo Road, and anyone who could still walk and wield a weapon. From that victory Camp Landis was born, on the banks of the Irrawaddy River. The "borrowed" troops returned to their work when the "greenhorns" for the 475th arrived. The new American base was secured for the rest of the provisionary force's arrival, including Jim Modisett. Seasoned, battle-hardened soldiers introduced the battle-virgins to the facts of life. Training took on a whole new reality. Parade Grounds teach you how to march. Battle teaches you how to fight. Merrill's Marauders were a non-traditional fighting unit. Among them were a very unusual group of soldiers who Jim called the Kachinas (people native to the territory where the Marauders operated in the China campaign, as I understand it). There was a Chinese unit attached to the Brigade but it was not to engage. It was held in reserve, which actually suited the Allied Forces involved in the operation coming from all points, not just the Mars Task Force.

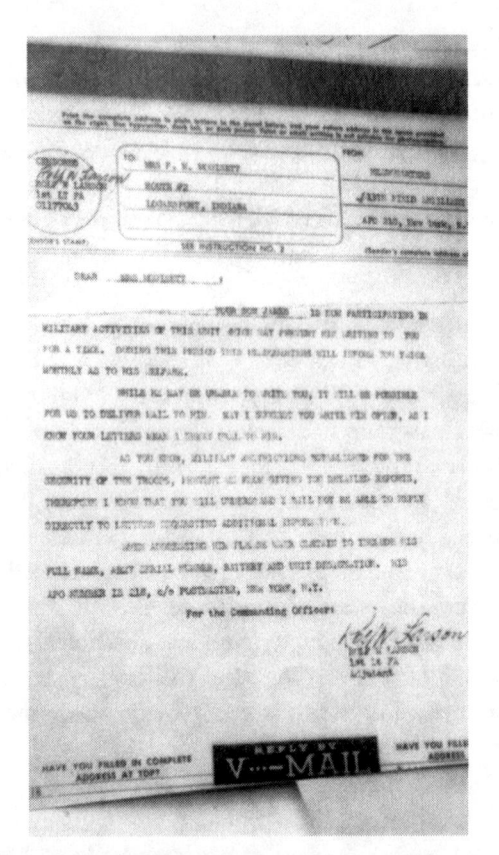

Telegraph sent to Jim's parents stating that he would not be contacting them for the duration of an operation, but that mail would reach him.

When they left Bombay, Calcutta, they disembarked with all of the unnecessary materials. Their officers had no clue what marching and fighting meant either. While they prepared for their strike into Burma, the truth unfolded. The mules could only carry so much, as could they. The villagers reaped the benefit. Modisett indicated they loved it. The excess material became either an outright gift to the locals or was traded for something that would be useful on the trail. The soldiers sorted through their treasures and retained only that which would be of use in the days and weeks ahead. The Marauders had not had a decent supply chain for months. It's not difficult to imagine the derision they heaped upon the new troops. Jim was a big kid. At 6'2", 225 pounds, he could *heft a load*. Jim and others had brought radios, extra clothes, and he even included a camp stool. He kept a small mirror in his marching pack and discarded everything else, including his most prized item — his new tennis shoes. He said it was a good thing. It was hot and the temptation to strip away clothes was strong. The rivers they crossed were all mountain-fed water, the coldest he ever experienced. He and the others were immersed frequently for one reason or another. The bridges they built were bamboo and usually constructed in ten minutes over the smaller streams. Jim noted that the Irrawaddy was not far from them at any time during the entire battle for control on the Burma Road.

I had to find spellings for many of the rivers and locales Jim Modisett remembered. In so doing, I also read more formal recitations about the Task Force and its incredible accomplishment. Soldiers are the boots on the ground. Our perspective is often quite different than that of the historians, or even that of the officers who later recount the story of an action. The tales told over a dusky campfire or along the trail during a march have the taste and smell of muddy reality. It is there that the splatter of blood or the stench of gunpowder and sweat gives a perspective which scholars ordinarily cannot share. Each soldier sees through his own eyes, hears with his own ears, and interprets with his own experience. Jim shared his impression of the history leading up to the moment he became part of it. That is the story being told here, not the story told by someone thousands of miles away at a different time. What he expressed are the words and feelings of the *moment*, of his impressions *then*, *there*, and of those with whom he shared the *then* and *there*.

Jim Modisett's tale of his Marsman days turned into a history lesson for me. He was *grabbin'* memories of the things that he heard at Landis from the Marauders who made it out of the mountains and lived to fight the rest of the way through Burma. Think of it. They fought in China and then in Burma! All of these people retroactively earned what today is the Special Forces patch in our United States Army! I got just as excited listening to Jim. But I have to get back to the *boots on the ground* history lesson.

Jim believed that the whole China operation was a "dirty, dirty deal." He admired Vinegar Joe Stillwell, who was hired by Chiang Kai-shek and Madame to chase the Japanese out of China — however it was done. Supposedly he had full authority to do whatever it took and complete control. The master plan was an operation that would set the table for a more formal, open attack by Allied Forces to come in from another position and sweep the country clean. Modisett said that Madame Chiang Kai-shek was a leach and whore — a gold digger who worked behind the scenes, scheming constantly to get more money from the American government. She was very good at it.

Stillwell was to attack from the Chinese side and push outward. He had a nucleus of non-traditional soldiers who he had trained, remnants from the island-hopping in the South Pacific. Jim said that in many ways those soldiers were misled into believing it was going to be good duty. Some were mercenaries and others survivors of the worst battles on the islands. Many had been on Guadalcanal. They were promised copious supplies and support with soldiers in reserve if they were met with hard resistance. Stillwell had Chinese forces in his command as well as Brits and the Chinese guerillas known as Kachinas.

Stillwell had Frank Merrill take over the American troops, the famous Merrill's Marauders. Their training was so harsh it became legendary. The political battles were probably worse. Stillwell was prey to the ever-changing political climate and became a pawn in the battle between Chiang Kai-shek and the American government as more and more money was leveraged from US coffers. Leadership changes were more unpredictable than the mountain weather. Stillwell undertook building one of the longest supply roads ever constructed, all the while engaging an enemy. The Chinese Army deserted him. The Brits would not stand and fight. The Americans had a morale problem, feeling they had been left holding the proverbial bag. Madame Chiang Kai-shek was leading the attack on Stillwell, but her husband knew he was the key to the bank. In the meantime Merrill, ill health and all (he had heart problems), by remote and unfailing harshness, drove his men through the mountains to victory. His officers followed his directives implicitly. It was as though he were there directing the operation himself. There were 2000 casualties, many to malaria and injuries sustained in the mountains. They had no supplies, often no water, and no support. One account Jim showed me said that the only thing that ever made a Marauder run was dysentery. The Japanese did less harm to the Marauders than the terrain and the environment, yet the fighting was vicious. Jim Modisett is convinced that Stillwell was ill-treated by the American government, used and abused by the Chinese. The entire Army's effort was not as appreciated by anyone as it should have been. Jim went to The World War II Memorial in DC in 2009, where he reunited with other Marsmen. He spoke with a former 124th Calvary/Infantryman. They laughed together, remembering what could have saved the Marauders at one point. Jim's fellow veteran said, "They could have stopped a lot of that with some Pepto." They also saluted the fact that the Marauders had beaten a mechanized force on foot...an incredible feat...not to mention fighting over 7-8,000-foot mountain ranges.

Jim recalls how pleased he was when told that he would be handling mules to move his 75-mm Howitzer down the Burma Road. He was a strapping farm boy and that was just fine with him. All the mules had not arrived at Camp Landis yet, but the information shared with him indicated they would have six mules per gun. They would mirror mountain operations in Europe during World War I and in World War II. The mules were a key component in the penetration plan. The gun was broken down and divided among three of the mules with the ammo distributed among the others. The artillery crew manned the animals under the supervision of a skinner from the Quartermaster unit. Quartermaster units were assigned to each Infantry regiment and their support components. The Brigade had a shorter than usual training time, but a year from its birth, it was ready for battle. The 475th Infantry sent advance units toward Myitkyina in mid-November. Final marching orders for the rest of the Brigade were delivered in mid-December, 1944, during the Christmas monsoon season.

Marsman Modisett remembers well the morning they assembled in front of their tents to hear their final battle pep talk. Their commander, a young Colonel who patterned himself after George S. Patton, mounted a beautiful roan horse on the road before them, as though he was on parade that morning. He was an officer new to the battlefield, a 30-year-old man from Boston, young and polished. The colonel was there as a Marsman in Burma, with dreams of victory ahead—of glory Jim imagined. He spoke to be remembered that morning. He was proud of the picture he made atop that glorious steed there in the rain. The part of his speech that still rings in Jim's ears today are the words, "We are all coming back, or none…" as he rode to the head of the column to begin the march down the Burma Road. Jim commented that he never saw him again until they were almost at the front. By that time, he was humbled — muddy and on foot like the rest of his command — and he never spoke to anyone.

The last elements of the 5332nd Brigade (Mars Task Force) splashed into the mud the morning of December 17, 1944. The Brigade began its march into history. The big farm boy Jim Modisett found himself carrying the load of a mule in the beginning. His gun section had to carry parts of their artillery pieces. Initially there were too few mules, therefore those that were available labored under the heaviest loads and the men carried the lighter parts. Progress from the very onset was a struggle as the monsoons were some of the worst in recent memory. Raw soldiers and experienced alike labored to make distance on the rough terrain south toward Myitkyina, even though that part of the trip was a cakewalk compared to what they found on the other side of the distant mountains. Jim's luck was consistent. His stature kept him in the forefront when a job required brute strength. While at Landis he was picked to chop wood for the chow hall. When they began walking the Ledo/Stillwell Road toward the Burma Road intersection, he was chosen to replace a mule. He had the heavier parts of the artillery that the missing mule would have carried. In the early days they did not even have wheels. They dragged the heavier equipment. Soldiers and animals waded in mud up the hills and down toward that crossroads town where they would rejoin the rest of their force. It had been assisting with the airbase security. From there the march down the Burma Road would begin in earnest.

There were two Artillery battalions — the 612th and the 613th. Jim was in the latter. They were composed of four sections each. The former was attached to the 475th while the 613th supported the 124th Cavalry turned Infantry (it had been a storied Texas National Guard unit in World War I and peace time). When the 124th arrived in India, several of its original Texans had been siphoned off and absorbed by the 475th. The 475th Infantry had been fighting since the summer months in support of the shredded Merrill's Marauders. Jim's 613th had joined a former Texas Cavalry unit that was neither cavalry any longer nor purely Texan. It was still filled with that Texas cockiness though, according to him. The 475th once again embarked on the attack ahead of them. It took several days for 6,000 men to get in motion. Once they passed the rivers, the 475th would flank in one direction and the 124th would maneuver in another. The plan was to pinch the Japanese toward another main force and squeeze them into the Chinese forces — and then into the sea. They crossed the Irrawaddy River just east of the town and the terrain worsened immediately. Turning east, they had to help the combat engineers construct a bridge over the next river they had to cross. It was the fast-flowing Shweli River.

Jim explained that the process was pretty miraculous. The locals taught them a how to use bamboo materials, including the pliable inner parts, which were flexible and very strong when woven. They used it to secure the strong, rigid outer pieces. They extended the spans so that they became quite long over the great rivers they crossed — yet they were only six-feet wide. The columns were single-file while crossing the bridges. Modisett laughed when he told me they were strong but awfully saggy.

The Japanese were being pushed ahead of the column. The 475th ferried the first soldiers and others crossed on pontoon construction, but it was slow. As the column proceeded, improvements had to be made in order to move at a faster pace or they would have spread too thin. Modisett commented that had the Japs remained on the far hills while they worked on the bridge, they were extremely vulnerable. It could have turned the tide of what was to happen later. But they didn't attack.

Modisett was surprised how quickly they built the bridge and made the crossing. Once on the eastern side of the river, the trail began to climb into higher elevation. In the heavy rains, it was constantly one step forward and two back. Even the mules could not make much headway. Often their loads shifted and the men had to drag them up the hills. The burdens moved as the ropes securing them stretched in the torrential rains. The pack animals were precious. The teamsters from the Quartermaster units had convinced them that they must be tended to before they took care of themselves. It was common knowledge, but no doubt was left before they ever hit the road. If a mule slipped off the trail, they secured it instantly and muscled it back on the road.

As the lower hills loomed, they saw greater elevations just behind them. Within days, they were in mountains that were much more impressive. There were pockets of resistance all along the way. The units fought the enemy every night. At first, Jim made no mention of battle. He spoke only of the challenges of the travel and what they endured to make the climb into the heights. I had to pry any mention of fighting from him. He did tell me that somehow, before they began the ascent into the mountains, or perhaps even before they crossed the Shweli, the rest of the mules arrived as did the last of the Quartermaster soldiers. The mules brought supplies and lightened the burden of the soldiers shouldering extra loads. *I must insert a thought here: most combat soldiers, me included, do not keep a daily journal. Jim and I discussed this link between us during our talk. Days run into days, weeks into weeks, and months into months. They are all the same. One loses the sequence of events. It is impossible later to create order from disorder, to write a calendar from chaos. It is not important. Survival is. You mount up, you step out, you fight, you eat, you rest, and you get up again. You follow orders. You pray to be there at the end.*

The demand for supplies was incredible. Army Air Corps flights were dropping supplies with parachutes. Oats for the mules were as important as ammo for the weapons. They were wrapped in burlap. I interrupted Jim to ask if they burst when they hit ground. He replied that I was the first person to ever ask him that, and yes they did. The Army once again failed to look at the obvious. The first air drops splattered feed all over the place. He and the other guys had to scoop it up by the handful while Infantry guarded their flanks. Finally somebody in supply figured out that the feed should to be double-bagged. After that, if the inner bag burst the oats were still inside the outer bag. They could be grabbed and carried away. Nobody liked being exposed in the openings where they had to drop supplies. Often the chutes drifted. There was no way to avoid that. As they got into the mountains re-supply got more and more difficult.

Modisett's strength was a point of pride, but also a thorn in his side, I think. Somewhere during that trek in the mountains, he became proficient in the use of a weapon he never anticipated using. He mentioned it in passing, almost as though it was an afterthought. It is important. It points to the role he played when they were not in a position to utilize their artillery pieces. Jim became a BAR (Browning Automatic Rifle) man. A heavy weapon such as that is usually reserved for regular infantry, or a heavy weapons platoon. He was expected to handle his mule and a heavy automatic rifle, all the while climbing those mountains. As I wrap my mind around that image, I find myself in awe. I sat with a man who almost skipped telling me anything about his fighting moments, yet I know there were snipers, times when they were stopped dead-still—fighting to move forward. He managed a mule with arty pieces on it while being expected to lay down heavy suppressing fire with an automatic weapon. And all that was in the mountains during monsoon season. Jim stated that the ridges and hills they tackled in the winter weren't really mountains compared to what they encountered in the spring. That was when they topped out at 6 or 7,000 feet. He considered those mountains. In hindsight, the 3-5,000-foot elevations were foothills by comparison.

They fought their way through the first mountain range and started down the slope when Jim was "volunteered" for another select duty. After encamping on a ridge one night, his platoon sergeant called him to his position and told Jim he had special duty for him. Jim and a few of his buddies were picked to be an advance party. Sarge led them off the ridge. They dug-in well down the hill near a clearing just before total darkness. It would be morning before their questions were answered. Silent alertness and tension replaced dreams on the mountainside that night.

The sun broke the sky and began a new adventure for a select few from the 613th on the hillside. The sergeant pointed at the field after the men ate a quick, cold breakfast of C-rations. They saw rice paddies surrounded by small dikes to their front. He told them to move out and take a position near one of the dikes close to them — and take their entrenching tools. They began their move and the bullets began to fly all around them. Jim mentioned that fact casually. He said "bullets were everywhere." That was it for detail. "The next thing I knew, we were knocking the dikes down." They moved from one square to the next until they had a large area cleared and open, free of obstacles. Jim's sergeant explained to them that they had just built an airfield in the clearing. Once again, Modisett turned to the old book. He found a dog-eared page, turned to it — and there was a picture of him and a few other guys standing near a short-strip Army supply plane, the first to land in that part of the Burma Road fight. Jim laughed and said, "That ol' boy landed okay. He bounced a few times, but he got her in okay. He got shot in the hand on the way though. The pilot said he was turning to get in position and a bullet passed through the cabin and hit him in the hand. He was curious if he would get a Purple Heart. I never saw him again. We built other fields at other places, but he never came back." I asked Jim how they communicated with the pilots to get them on location and he showed me the radio that was in the picture. All they had was the crank field radio. It was kept on higher ground until they made contact. It was only good for short distances in the mountains. Jim Modisett indicated that quite often they could not even communicate with the units behind them. I inferred from the comment that he was almost always in the advance party with his BAR and went back to his 75mm cannon at night for his arty missions.

Jim had to take a short break and get another of his favorite soft drinks.

While he opened it, a newsflash appeared on the television regarding an incident in the War on Terror in Afghanistan. It troubled him. He said it bothers him that we teach our children to go to war. Jim said that he never spoke of it because he was always worried about the message he sent. There were things he wanted to say, but he was afraid he would say the wrong things. Jim believes that politicians always have it wrong and don't send the right message either. I had a moment suddenly with an old soldier who wanted to get it off his chest. Jim Modisett was talking about what he could not say to his sons in the way he wanted, yet I know by their characters that he gave the message to them. I asked him if he was talking about the difference between having "a willingness to fight for what matters and what is important and having a desire to fight?" He looked at me and boomed, "By God! That is it. Being willing, but not wanting to fight just for the hell of it." I expressed something then that I have come to believe. It has developed as I talk with these incredible old soldiers.

I told Jim that many of his era miss what I think is the important part of the lesson. They are reticent and say nothing for the very reason Jim expressed to me, but unlike him some didn't share the message by deed either. For me, the message is you have to fight for what you believe in, you have to stand firm at some point and not be so tolerant that you have no standards at all. That is not tolerance — that is foolishness and cowardice. You have to know why you are fighting, you have to have commitment, and you have to get up when you are knocked down. Jim's generation did that. The proof is there in observation. Rationing, war bonds, parades, welcomes home, unity, steadfastness in the face of deprivation…all things that are intrinsic to the Greatest Generation. But they did not necessarily make them part of their legacy. They did not explain them, they merely lived them. We, as a society today, waiver. We cannot grasp the enormity of that kind of commitment to anything. Jim said that he was afraid he could not find the right words and would leave the wrong message. I replied, "Saying nothing is often the worst message of all." I had often wondered why World War II veterans never talked. Perhaps this was in the minds of many of them…this and that they wanted to protect us from the images in their minds… of the horror.

The small contingent of Kachinas traveling with them acted as scouts. They traveled in small teams ahead as well as on the flanks of the main column. Extraction of information was a talent they possessed far beyond the Americans' skill set. The locals seemed unable to resist their requests for information. I questioned Jim repeatedly about the fighting he experienced along the route. He informed me that they had fire missions every night. Small pockets of resistance were a daily nuisance. Each village was a challenge, although he did not name them specifically. They did halt at several and treat their animals and regroup. A veterinarian unit accompanied them as well as a field medical team. The Mars Task Force was a self-sufficient.

They were short of supplies at times, but successfully improvised when necessary. Jim told the story of a friendship he made with a muleskinner from Texas who was part of the Quartermaster Corps because of a water shortage they experienced once. His buddy was a taciturn Mexican named Poncho, who got along with nobody. He rarely talked, but he liked Jim. It may have been Jim's farm background, but whatever it was Pancho and Jim did fairly well. The muleskinner was a master with the mules. He kept them in great shape. When Jim talked to him, the answers were always guttural mumbles. In Jim's words, "Pancho was a rough son-of-a-gun." Pancho changed the mules' shoes and let them know if the animals needed serious attention. Jim ran out of water on the trail. He saw Poncho taking a big swallow from his canteen and decided to see if the mean hostler would share a snort with him. The grumpy Mexican mumbled something and handed Jim his canteen. Modisett unscrewed the cap, tipped it up, and took a huge gulp. He choked, gagged, and almost died as the liquid fire hit his parched throat. It was not water or anything resembling it. Jim discovered in that moment that Poncho lived on whatever form of alcoholic drink he could get. In that part of the world it was Saki, and his canteen was pure, unadulterated Saki, probably of the homemade variety. Jim never asked Poncho for another drink.

The chase continued. The Japanese retreated through the hills. The 124th followed. The 613th had fire missions night after night. Jim indicated that they were outgunned by the Japs' larger armament. They developed a strategy of working in close and firing their own lightweight cannons like mortars. The Japanese 105s and 155s were firing into their rear positions while they were actually inside their range. They were pointing those 75-mms almost straight in the air, lobbing rounds inside the trajectory paths of enemy fire. It was very effective. They were successful in taking out the positions. The Japanese Army incurred casualties and retreated through the mountains, staying just ahead of the pursuing Marsmen. Thirst… mud…rocks…mountain trails wound round and round…shoot…get shot at…inflict casualties…have casualties, but thankfully Jim said they were not as bad as the injuries. Up and down they climbed. They slid off the beaten path. They pulled mules out of ditches, the mules pulled them up the steepest inclines — and they swam streams and floated their cannons across on make-shift rafts. The days dragged one into the next, as did the weeks. They turned into months as spring broke. The Marsmen were nearing the Japanese.

The Kachinas sensed, or extracted the information in their inimitable way, that they were walking into an ambush. They were infallible scouts and like the Apaches in the 19th century, the officers who understood guerilla warfare heeded their advice. The Kachinas indicated they should turn off the main road and follow them through the mountains along an alternate route that they had learned about from the people indigenous to the area. It was alleged to be a good trail that would circle and take them behind the Japanese. Jim said that there was no hesitation. They went.

The main road where they marched disappeared. It soon narrowed to a path and wound upward to the sky, rising into higher mountains toward a pass. It was grassy but well-worn. The mules and men again helped one another. Jim said there was no way horses could have gone where they went. Behind them on the main road, they had been experiencing heavier and heavier shelling and mortar fire. The Japanese had to wonder what had become of them. They hoped that the enemy believed that they had fallen back to dig in and regroup. Jim turned several pages in his book and found more pictures to show me. I looked where he pointed and my jaw dropped in astonishment. "It is a virtual Grand Canyon!" I blurted. I was stunned looking at the photos of the sheer cliffs and the ribbon of a trail they traversed. Jim told me that the scouts said they were around 8,000 feet in the mountains when they bypassed the enemy on that detour. The photos depicted soldiers, mules, and equipment winding for what seemed like miles in a coil around a deep ravine. When they began the descent, they were in fact positioning themselves for an attack by the Japanese — if they had not caught on to the maneuver and changed positions. Their fate had been altered due to the information gathered by the scouts.

Jim Modisett lost his best friend before they took to the hills to avoid more casualties from the heavy shelling. He and John Trimble of Texas had been part of an advance party again. They were below a ridge, dug-in as outposts. Jim and his team were on one side of the road while John and his were on the other. They were in individual, temporary positions. That evening, the Japanese walked in-coming rounds down the mountain more successfully than usual. Much of the time, they over-shot their positions. Not on this night. One round hit John's foxhole and killed him instantly. Jim found a parachute when he learned John's fate the next morning. He and the others carried John further down the mountain to a lovely spot and laid him to rest. Jim made a marker for him with his own hands. Jim showed me a quote in one of his smaller books. I will paraphrase it. It was written by a Marauder who said it about the dead left behind in their march through China and down the Ledo Road. "Let the chips fall where they may…only know the name of the man ahead whose mule's tail you hold…on the walk." I thought about it. That is essentially all that is relevant in the battle to survive, that and to get to the other side. And as the man said in that book, the title of which I never saw, "live to tell the story."

Before they cleared the mountains, the chaplain traveling with the

124th held a church service to commemorate all that had happened. He had ministered to individuals, but apparently he had a desire to convene a more formal gathering before they engaged what could be a major enemy force. They were in a lovely site that he deemed the ideal place to give thanks and ask for intervention. Jim said it was the right thing to do under that mountain ridge on that morning. Modisett related this part of the story with an unusual solemnity and without further detail — but it was there in his mind as a brief silence ensued before we walked down that mountain together any farther.

The balance of Jim's reminiscing was a reverie about events along the Burma Road. He fought every day. The smartest thing he participated in was a major artillery barrage against a fortified Japanese position when they had the enemy pinned down at one point. Neither could his unit advance. Jim said that much of what they did was mop-up. For some reason, the enemy retreated the length of the road. They seemed unaware that at first they had the Marsmen outnumbered, but as the days wore on they became scattered. Their own disorientation was their undoing.

The next 32 days were constant battle as the Marsmen closed on the enemy. It was heavy combat. Modisett swam more streams. The Burma Road and the Irrawaddy River were never far apart and all streams flowed into it. Historically, towns and trade routes followed the great waterways of the world. It was not any different in Burma, an ancient country. Jim crossed the Equator twice. They burned temples and villages. The Japanese strongholds were rousted. Our soldiers thirsted, hungered, but fought-on Jim became expert at building temporary landing strips for balsa-wood airplanes. The soldiers could build a bridge in what seemed to him ten minutes. They marched and fought by rote. They were machines and time was meaningless.

The artillery barrage that impressed Jim so greatly was an idea the artillery officers had one night. Our forces were established on high ground with the Japanese below them. Our spotters could see them below. They wanted to make the Nips believe they had more guns than they did. They positioned their batteries together on the ridge, tied them together with telephone line and established a firing pattern that would replicate what they hoped sounded like an entire Division. There were 12 guns in each battalion. They were joined again as the points of the pincer were closing. They were pushing toward the Chinese boarder and Burma was almost secured. The Japanese artillery units fired on them, but the rounds were long, thus sailing beyond their position. The Marsmen returned effective fire and broke them down before the incoming could do damage.

The 75-mms were to be fired one after the other, a minute apart. Fire one, wait a minute, fire two, delay another minute, fire three, a minute gap, and so on down the line until they were done and start over at number one.

The rotation allowed the barrels to cool so they would not warp, yet there would be an unceasing barrage of cannon fire. It also allowed them time to change targets based on forward observer information. Jim said once they commenced firing, they did not stop until the sun broke in the eastern sky the next morning. They had no replacement parts, thus the timing plan fooled the enemy and saved the equipment. The idea worked like a charm. It did exactly what the officers hoped. The Chinese Army was moving in by daylight too. During the night the Chinese had seen direct hits on Japanese positions. They confirmed that the Japanese forces were in disarray. It appeared that they were convinced there was at least an American Division poised to descend on them. Advance parties from both Allied units observed the Japanese retreating into the forests. When they reappeared, they were camouflaged and prepared for full retreat, which they did as quickly as they could get their units mobilized. They did send some small teams to positions to delay the Americans descending the mountain long enough for the withdrawal. The scouts and advance parties had to locate and eliminate them before the Marsmen could successfully negotiate the road to the valley.

There were more mountains along the way, but Jim considered them hills compared to those they had just left. In one of them, he encountered an historical place that found a way into his memory. It was the hospital founded by an American doctor who did medical work in Burma prior to World War II and for years after. His name was Gordon S. Seagraves and he is a legend in Burma. He treated the hill tribes for decades. The natives helped our soldiers because of what he had done, despite their treatment by both the Chinese and Japanese. They treated our wounded under shelters made with old parachutes. They were richly rewarded by our passing through with gifts and the supplies our forces could spare. Seagraves was a surgeon and an expatriate who lived for his work there, the son of missionaries in Burma. He left with Stillwell before Jim arrived, only to return after Burma was once again secure. Our forces did not stay in the area long, but continued to fight and pursue the Japanese toward the border with China.

They halted a few days later near mountain village where a small Chinese unit had also established a camp. The two forces did not co-mingle, but they were not far apart. Jim did not even realize they were in the area. The Allied forces had been in a pitched battle with the Japanese, but resistance was lessening by the day. The soldiers needed to recover before they renewed pursuit. Jim had seen something which interested him as they passed through the village. He reconnoitered on his own successfully. By dark, the story of his adventure had made the rounds and he found himself being interviewed by his platoon sergeant. It was suggested that he correct the situation. If he did not, there could actually be a full-blown international incident. Jim went back to his sleeping position and shared his quandary with his squad. It was dark. Returning the "spoils of war" was going to be more difficult than had been commandeering it. One of his buddies was filled with curiosity and volunteered to accompany him. They discovered the area where the item had been acquired was under guard. It was an unexpected hindrance. Jim's buddy thought he could eliminate the obstacle. Silently, as all good "special forces operatives" can, Jim's friend used stealth and subdued the unsuspecting amateur watching the area. Jim returned the item and they slid into the darkness without starting a brand new war.

As they left, the night chill was descending. Temptation, success, and revelry were coursing through Jim's young veins. He saw a haystack and thought the night chill could be fended off better there than in a hillside foxhole. They slept in the straw and did so in great comfort. When they awoke, they discovered a pond immediately adjacent to the haystack. Jim's friend stood watch while he stripped and dove in for a quick bath, which was something of a treat. Unfortunately he was caught completely naked. The natives saw him and his buddy. They reported them to the Chinese officers who had actually camped in the village. While they were being reported, other Burmese people nearby were more sympathetic. They retrieved Jim's clothes, and then got the two Americans out of town.

Jim and his co-conspirator were not in Chinese chains, but they were not out of the proverbial woods either. They spent the day performing extra duty. Later in the day, Jim was summoned to the Old Man's area. It seemed that the Chinese Colonel desired the company of one big, blond haired American GI for supper. The request was being honored. Jim went, wondering every step of the way where he was going to spend the next night, and perhaps the next several. When he arrived at the Chinese encampment, Jim was ushered into the senior officer's quarters. After the appropriate amount of quiet pressure had been applied, the officer began to quiz him in broken English. Eventually he asked Jim to join him for supper. They shared food and a better quality Sake than Jim had gotten from Pancho. Later that evening, the Colonel told Jim he was dismissed, but gave him a handwritten note to take to his Platoon Commander. The next morning his lieutenant told him the note said, "The big GI funny scoundrel. Tell him stay safe."

They fought and drove all the way to China. The engineers were following them and repairing the road as it was deemed secure. They continued receiving supplies by air. How much would they use the road? Regardless, it belonged to the Burmese, not the Japanese. Along the way he collected a Samurai sword, still in its sheath. He also has some photos which he obtained somehow from another combat photographer who got drunk with them. I hope to see them some day. He went on to tell me that the Japanese swore to commit Hara-kiri rather than be captured. That was common. They did it too. Jim encountered a combat photographer who had actually taken a picture of an officer in the act. Jim saw it. When they secured the area well enough, they established another major base camp. They built an airport runway long enough to accommodate larger aircraft was built. Jim worked on that too. He assisted with landing one of the first L-5 supply planes in Burma. He and his squad built themselves a bamboo hut as well. The Marsmen were here long enough to get in trouble again as well. American soldiers fight well — and with youthful exuberance, they celebrate equally as well. Apparently they discovered a cow in the neighborhood and decided that a feast was appropriate. They ate it. Trouble arrived before the steaks were digested, I imagine. Jim used the word "abattoir," which I had to research. The cattle were used in the rice fields according to him. The complainant told his superiors they were not "abattoir" and that word is what Jim "grabbed" from his memory of the event. The dictionary indicates that it means butchery. My inference is that the cattle were *not* to be slaughtered. At any rate, good times there or no, they no more than got the hut completed than they had to move. It is probably just as well. They were good at war and may have found one to start if they had remained in one place much longer.

Memories continued to dart into Jim's mind as we chatted. The veterinarian services were there for the animals. The quartermasters handled the mules, trained muleskinners, but also trained the dog handlers in those days. Several military occupational specialties emerged from the Quartermaster Corps. The field hospitals were crude but kept the soldiers in the battle. Jim recalls having to use the dental service at one point. The chair was mechanical as was the drill. The dentist had to operate the machine — and that is what it was — with a foot crank. He was in the chair and the drill was turning in his tooth when the dentist was interrupted. He did not say why, but you could see in his face that the memory was vivid. Jim assured me that having a drill stop in mid-torque in your tooth "hurts like hell."

The Marsmen pushed all the way to the Chinese border. They did what they were sent to do. They were a long range penetration task force and they penetrated. Jim read something to me again. It is worth repeating. He read, "Let the chips fall where they may…only know the name of the man ahead whose mule's tale you hold…on the walk." That was essentially all that was relevant during the battle. He continued with, "to survive and get to the other side, to tell the story." He and his fellow soldiers had done that. They arrived and suddenly the war was over while they awaited instructions as to what was to be done next. The US dropped bombs on Japan. They had fought for months, stayed in some places for days at a time and actually trudged over and through incredible terrain for 32 days and they had secured Burma. Did anyone really think they could when they sent them?

The Allied Forces began their operations in China and Burma under the command of Vinegar Joe Stillwell. He had been in and out of control for years. The governments had forced changes repeatedly. Jim pointed out that five generals ran the operation at one time or another. In the end, a man who he disliked was brought in to wrap things up. He would be properly political. That man was British and he quickly claimed credit for everything even though the master plan was Stillwell's. The British had been led by Vice Admiral Lord Luis Mountbatten. He was named Commander of the Allied Forces in China. In Jim's words he was another "British prima-Donna." When the battle was done, he called everyone together to make his speech. Mountbatten was forever making speeches when the bullets were cooling on the ground and the guns were silent, or that was the story that Jim heard. The good Lord always made them from a cigar box that his aide-de-camp carried with him at all times. He also made sure he faced the sun so that his lovely face was in the light and at its "rosiest best." The Mars Task Force soldiers despised him. Jim said that he began the speech with, "We did this" and went on to that, and on and on and on, but he was not even there…Jim added that at least Monte was with his guys in Europe. Jim noted with some derision that Mountbatten was a respected man. His yacht was blown up off the coast of Ireland years later.

Soon after Mountbatten delivered his speech, the Army chose Jim to take the mules back to China. I stopped him in his story then. "Why didn't they just take them to the sea since it was not far," I asked. Jim laughed at me. "Did you forget? It was the Army. Does it do things the easy way, or the way that makes the most sense?" Jim then told me that the brass chose not to negotiate passage through that corner of China to Vietnam, or to a decent port. There really were no good deep water harbors where they were at the end of the fight for Burma. Their first choice had been Indo-China, but the negotiators were not combat soldiers. They were not included in the talks. As usual they were pushed aside by the administrative types when things were safe. Their voices were not heard. The people who made the decision that walking the mules back north on the Burma Road was the best choice had no idea about the conditions or the terrain. Jim reiterated that it was the Army way. I agreed… it is the Army way.

Jim Modisett was one of the chosen few again. He was one of a half a dozen regular soldiers who joined muleskinners and veterinarians to handle the mules. They were protected by a small number of Infantry soldiers. They were going to China the long way. It had been decided. Supplies were flown over the Hump, but the men of the Mars Task Force were going to take the mules across the Hump into China and make a good will gift of them to the Chinese people as a gesture from the American government. Jim was going to climb the Himalayan Mountains. He was about to take a walk in the clouds.

Jim and the other Marsmen soon found themselves on the road again. It took 21 days to traverse Burma this time. They crossed the same mountains, swam the same rivers, passed through the same villages, and fought through the same mosquito-infested jungle areas. It was full summer this time, however — and incredibly hot. They had packed the mules with as many supplies as they could, yet some drops still had to be made for them. The small contingent of men with the large contingent of animals did encounter one band of Japanese soldiers who were hidden when they went south the first time. They fought them off successfully. The Americans were fortunate that the animals were well trail-broken for the trip back. In three weeks, they were at the foot of one of the most formidable mountain ranges on earth.

They began the ascent toward the sky and it was not long before the rocky trail became ribbon thin. I asked Jim if he found himself wishing for Hannibal's Tibetan bulldozers, the elephants. He laughed and said, "We never thought about that." I had pictures in my mind as he told me the story in his simple terms. Jim was actually dismissive of the adventure. He again turned to the old book to show me pictures of mule-wide trials, rocky and broken, with animals and men (they were aerial shots and he must have been in one of them) actually hanging off one side and scraping the other as they wound-up the mountain. I have read that passes in that mountain range can be as high as 11 or 12,000 feet in elevation. Jim assured me that the air got thinner and thinner. It was cold. After having been in the jungle, they suffered when they reached the peaks but they kept moving. They had no interest in camping there and the animals were ready to move after very brief rest periods. I was awed by the photos. I told him that the trail was certainly not the highway to heaven, even if there were monks somewhere in the mountains. It was absolutely stunning to think about it — yet he spoke in calm tones, as though it was really not a big deal at all.

Jim was convinced about the value of mules in all terrains after working with them for months. During his time in Burma and across the Himalayas, he only remembered losing three animals. At one point crossing the Hump, one of the animals slipped over the edge. They were in an area that was not quite so sheer…fortunately…and the animal was wedged against boulders. They rigged a sling and recovered it. The mule was bruised and gimpy, but able to move. In the steeper parts, the men grabbed the mules' tails and let them pull them up. Even if it had not been steep, the thin air made the effort so amazingly hard that they needed the help. The Infantry soldiers had to use the same tactics as well.

Jim told me about one pass that was particularly treacherous. He called it "Aluminum Alley" and it was one he had heard about before he left. He saw with his own eyes that it was more than legend. Pilots feared it and he learned why. In the peaks, they literally walked among the clouds. They were filled with ice crystals. Planes flying the Hump often encountered horrible turbulence and crashed into the sides of the peaks. Others had instrument failure and still others' engines literally froze. Pilots were known to pass out due to oxygen starvation too. Jim saw the results for himself. More than one plane fuselage jutted out from the side of the mountains as he drove his mules through. He heard a story about some combat reporters who had survived a plane crash into one of the mountains. They were missing for three or four days, but survived somehow and were found. Another jumped from a plane and made his way back down the mountain to tell the story. The pilot went down with his plane trying to find a place to land safely. During the walk in the clouds, Jim saw planes flying *below* him.

They crested the mountains, too, and made it down safely. When they arrived at their destination in China, orders and officials were waiting for them. They established a camp and rested, but not for long. They were instructed to join the villagers and build a fence to contain the stock. Jim estimated they enclosed about 3,000 acres. The muleskinners, with the help of the Marsmen, were soon at work putting new shoes on every animal in the temporary pen. The officers made plans to distribute the gifts brought to China by herculean effort, but irony struck before the plan could be enacted. The mules began to die. The veterinarians could not determine what was wrong initially and things worsened by the day. The answer came to them at last. It was encephalitis. The mules had been exposed to mosquitoes and flies of all kinds during the walk back through the jungle as they crossed Burma. Apparently the cold air of the mountains had suppressed the symptoms, but when they settled in the valley it did not take long for the disease to take its toll. They lost almost the complete herd. They went to sleep and died. Jim's strength and size trapped him again. It bothered him this time too. He had a real affection for the animals he had worked with for so long. His lieutenant assigned him to the burial detail. He and a few of the other soldiers had to bury every one of those mules.

The pain, the effort, and the time had essentially been wasted. The walk in the clouds, the highway to heaven was paved with good intentions, but the attempt was beaten by nature. It is truly ironic. Mother Nature had done the most damage to Merrill's Marauders. She also wrought havoc on the most important machine, other than the American fighting man, utilized by the Mars Task Force…the mule.

The Marsmen dispersed after the Burma Road was complete and Burma was secure. China changed its relationship with the United States of America after World War II. Some soldiers stayed behind in China for a variety of reasons. We had limited military responsibilities there. Jim Modisett was among them. He liked it and his service commitment was not over yet. He volunteered to stay in Shanghai and did not return to the States until February of 1946. Jim was assigned a job in a warehouse on our post there.

Jim Modisett got decent duty at last. He was outfitting soldiers returning home. His days were spent providing new gear to soldiers as they rotated out of China. Jim had access to all sorts of supplies and he made the best of it. One day, he met a pilot who had lost his bomber jacket. It was a significant item that set him apart from the common soldier out on the town. It identified him as an officer, but more importantly told the "ladies" he was a pilot. He had been to the warehouse in hopes of finding one, but his first search left him wanting. Before he left, Jim heard his story. He managed to pilfer one from somewhere and made a friend. He did not know it, but it was like making a deposit at the local bank and letting it draw interest. A few weeks later, Jim was downtown taking care of some personal business. He happened to be in his Company's big truck in heavy traffic. His brakes failed and he rear-ended a local. The incident caused a near riot. It could have also caused him military punishment and his job at the warehouse. Fortunately that day, the Officer of the Day for the MPs was his pilot-bomber jacket-guy. He cleaned up the mess and told Jim they were even. I am not sure if Modisett is an Irish name or not, but he had that sort of luck, at least on one occasion.

There is one man who was lucky that Jim never caught up with him again after he came home from China. China is the jade capital of the world. Jim saved his money and purchased a beautiful piece for his mother. He managed to carry it with him several places until he met a man he thought was going to be in the right place to mail it home for him. He was a soldier from Macon, GA. Jim trusted him with a gift that he desperately wanted to get to his mother. When he arrived home, after getting his discharge at Camp Atterbury in Indiana, he discovered that it was never sent to her. Jim is still angry about that.

Jim Modisett was happy to finish the bulk of his military duty overseas. He would not have been happy in a parade ground setting. He has always been a character. He will always be. He still talks to a few of his other Marsmen, although there are not many left now. And that is something. Really something. They are among the elite.

Jim and I were winding down when he remembered an article one of his World War II buddies sent him a short time before we talked. It was about the mules. Jim handed it to me. As he did he said, "The mules were important in WWI and a Japanese Engineering outfit used them in Europe too. The Germans used to zero in on them because of their shiny coats. The Army figured out they had to be fed potassium manganese to dull their coats." I responded that I knew about the mules in the Alps. "My Dad's parachute regiment worked with the 442nd Engineers." Jim then showed me what his friend sent. It was an article about the mules and how they got to Burma. They had never paid a lot of attention to it, although somewhat curious about it at the time. Modisett said he learned more in the article than he had ever known before.

The mules were sent by sea and it was a horrible job for the guys who had to accompany them. They were loaded below decks and they actually got seasick. Mules cannot vomit. That leaves only one way out when they are sick. Jim asked if I could imagine how one of those boats smelled. I told him I did not want to think about it. He said the muleskinners that sailed with them on those boats deserved some kind of special medal or something. That took some kind of courage beyond understanding. The Quartermaster Corps was disbanded after Korea he thought, but the canine handlers came from there, as did supply, and some other things. In World War II, they were truck drivers and all kinds of things. In the article, he discovered that they kept the mules alive on boats and got them off the boats and on shore when they landed. He also had never heard one of them complain about their animals in a mean way either. The Japanese submarines tried to sink them because they realized they were coming. They succeeded in sinking one. A complete load went to the bottom. The Germans sank a boat named the "Jose Navarro" he thought as well, in 1943. It happened on Pearl Harbor Day. Another was sunk going around the Horn in the Suez Canal. Mules were so important in the war effort according to Jim that they became a high priority target for the Germans and the Japanese. The Army bought so many thousands in World Wars I and II that they went from selling for $80 a head to $250 — and that was a lot of money in those days. Jim was tickled about getting that article. After 60 plus years, he was getting some questions answered.

Jim's wife, Diane, arrived home about the time we were closing down for the afternoon. He told her what we had been doing. They married in the late 40s and had their honeymoon in Colorado. Diane told me that they stayed in the hotel across from a fancy place called the Broadmore, which was the nicest place in town at the time. When Jim was at Fort Carson that was where the officers and their wives roomed. It was ritzy and considered way too good for common folks. It was still that way when they were there together. Many, many years later they went back to celebrate something. Jim and she got rooms there. It thrilled them to do that. It was some kind of justice, a personally gratifying moment and celebration of success. They went into the gift store and browsed. There was an elderly lady working. Diane saw an old and very elegant ring in the case that caught her eye. Jim told her to look at it. They are farm folks and Jim looks and acts the part. The lady warned Diane that it was quite expensive. Diane told her that it was quite alright — she wanted to see that very one. Diane loved it and it fit perfectly. Jim asked her if she wanted it. She simply nodded. They bought it and left quietly — the perfect ending to their stay.

Jim and Diane reared two strong, intelligent sons who know how to get up when knocked down. They are successful. Jim has been successful. He worried about saying the wrong words. He worried about giving the wrong message about fighting. He did not. He left the right message. Jim and Diane have grandchildren who got the message as well. Their grandson served in the Navy. The message lives.

Jim got some answers about his mules after sixty years. I got an amazing story. I heard about his walk in the clouds.

The Edge of Horror

The stories in this book were hard to write. Some were harder than others. This is one of those. I had pillow talk all alone one morning about this one and it dawned on me why it was difficult to start. Merle Voris has been in my life a long time. My Life Clock is ever ticking toward four decades of him and his family being close to me and mine. How do I turn a page in my Life Book and not find something there about his family? How do I isolate on Merle only? Even the story he told me when we talked did not do that. I have a hard time separating him from his family. They are all intertwined in my life. I did not realize they empathized with my family when we first arrived here. We were new to this small farming town. They had come here from their home in Ohio and understood the difficulty of moving to a new community. Voris roots were deeply planted in the Johnstown, OH, area. They came here to be part of a major, local farming operation, lending expertise and strength to this small community several years before we came on the scene.

When we first moved to Windfall, IN, I was not close to his children, except his youngest. They were all older, even the youngest, but she was close enough that we became friends in band and choir, MYF (Methodist Youth Fellowship) and other school functions in which we were involved. We even tried a date once. We were friends and it did not work. Merle and his wife Esther were pillars of the community and in my church. I had just officially become a teenager, having grown beyond the 6'2" mark, and had all the accompanying awkwardness, when we met. I was intimidated by them. As the years passed I have come to love the whole clan, grown close to the descendants, seen what they do and did. They have a remarkable intelligence in their DNA and it shows repeatedly in the generations. They are staunch and wonderful friends. We have shared living and dying — marriages, births, and funerals. Now, having shrunk back toward the 6'2" mark, I asked him about his experience in World War II at last. It is time to share the story.

Merle prefaced his story with general comments about World War II. He was sitting in a room visiting with two fraternity brothers during his freshman year of college on December 7th listening to the President announce the attack on Pearl Harbor. They were sharing the shock just like Americans all over the country. One fraternity brother, Dallas Hange, went to War at the end of the year, the other sometime later. Dallas was a junior or senior. Merle was one of nine members on the State Future Farmers Agricultural Executive Committee and returned to farming, including Dallas and the other young man in the room. Six of the nine members fought in the War. Merle was one of three to survive. Neither of the two in the room that morning came home alive. Two of the six who did not come home were even in his church and youth group. They were the only sons in the family — and even the only children. Merle noted that "this is the thing that rips the heart out of surviving veterans when they remember that many families saw the end of their family line in that war. The War cost them more than anyone can ever imagine in personal history. The family was gone. There were not going to be any more of them!" He spoke of the high cost in human life, the sacrifice made, the pride of those who served, marching into the War knowing what was at risk, yet they went. He remembered when his son Dave took him to see the World War II Memorial in Washington DC in 2006 and how all these memories flooded his heart and mind. He thought of the hundreds of thousands of men and women who served and died. He spoke of them almost in a whisper.

Merle Voris was a farmer. He farmed quite a bit of ground and raised a lot of livestock. It was important to the country. Steelworkers, coal miners, and farmers often had high draft points assigned. They were critical to the war effort right where they were. Merle had a lot of points and mentioned that he had three times as many as required to keep his deferment when you added points for being married and having a child. By the time his number was getting close, he had decided he was not asking for a deferment. He was not a hero, but he had seen several of his buddies go to war and duty called. Merle went to Arkansas to the Infantry Replacement Training Center, where he became a Platoon Leader due to his college training and background. He was made a *sergeant* but got no stripes and no pay, just added responsibility. While there he naively volunteered for Officers Training School. The next step in his journey was Fort Benning, GA. He was headed for the Infantry at that point, but had weeks of schooling ahead of him. His wife and baby daughter went with him to that school. Neighbors and family tended the farm. Again he was Platoon Leader. It was there that he had his closest encounter with death in World War II — training exercises. One particular exercise was observed by serious brass and he was put in charge because he had met several challenges successfully. Merle noted that his successes were largely due to the fact that he had a real, live Tech Sergeant serving under him who had survived the battlefield. Merle turned to him, wisely, in times of doubt. They worked as a team. Together they did well and both made Second Lieutenant.

Merle Voris.

    Merle graduated with another Buckeye and invited him to ride home with his family for a short leave before they reported to their next duty station. They drove north in his 1936 Ford, taking turns at the wheel. It is a long drive today. I can imagine what it was like then. As they crossed the state line from Tennessee into Kentucky on Friday night, a car careened down a mountain road and struck them broadside. They slid off the road, tumbling onto the car's right side into the ditch. Merle climbed over the driver and out the window. He stood on the side of the car, pulled a very upset little girl out of the car, got her bleeding nose under control — and her cries of "displeasure"— while standing atop the car. While he was busy with that, the dazed driver got his senses and reached in the back to check on Esther. He was panic-stricken and began yelling, "My God, she's dead!" He reached out of the window with his hand covered with red mush and red liquid running down his forearm. The man was totally beside himself, yelling into the night. Merle was trying to get in position to see what was happening. Neither of them could hear Esther saying she was okay until Merle got his friend calmed. Merle and Esther had purchased some watermelons in Georgia to take home. One of them had burst in the accident. The driver had reached into that mess and believed he had a handful of Esther's brains when he withdrew his hand! She was bruised and banged, with other scrapes and abrasions, but her brains were where they were supposed to be. A car came along and picked them up, took them back to Tennessee to a small town doctor who had a clinic in his home. They woke him and he treated their wounds. The man then returned them to their car.

Back in those days, I assume they righted it and got it running again. The cars were made of *real steel* and very little plastic or other material. The missile that hit them was probably piloted by a drunk and had disappeared into the hills of Kentucky without so much as checking to see if anyone had lived. Thank God a Good Samaritan happened along. They completed the drive home in the 1936 tank (by today's standards), enjoyed the short leave and Merle returned to Fort Rucker, Alabama.

The War in Europe ended while Merle was in Arkansas. VE day passed. Two days before he graduated from OCS, victory was declared in the South Pacific (VJ Day) which ended the War with Japan. When he returned to Fort Rucker, he was assigned to the Seventh Cavalry as part of the Occupational Force and sent to Japan. If the war had not ended, he would have been part of the Invasion Force, but the President made a decision that saved many lives. All their training had been done with taking Japan's homeland in mind. He remembers the landscape of Tokyo and Yokohama as he flew into Japan. Merle said it was "flying over the edge of horror." Everywhere you looked were twisted, melted beams, burned dwellings, and rubble. You could see where the river beneath had boiled. There was a noticeable change in the timber of his voice as he described the scene to me, as though he was seeing it again in that moment. I believe he was. Some memories are very vivid when we dredge them from the muddy lakebeds of our minds. He was convinced that the destruction was worse than that of Hiroshima and Nagasaki. Later he met soldiers who had been in those places and they assured him that in fact it was.

Merle Voris and I spoke about the impact of the atomic bomb on the War. He, like several other World War II veterans with whom I have spoken, is convinced it saved millions of lives. They do not speak of simply American lives, but lives of the Japanese people. Members of the military, academia, and the American public have spent decades debating the wisdom and morality of using atomic bombs. The Japanese soldiers knew we were going to invade. They were a product of a culture which swore a blood oath to an emperor that was more important than their lives. The entire military force would fight until the last round and use it to commit suicide rather than lose. The entire populace had sworn to die before subjugating itself to a conquering invading force, including women and children. When we invaded we found confirming documentation indicating such a plan. Merle discussed it. He saw the bunkers near our planned invasion point. Our military knew we would lose Soldiers, Marines, and Sailors by the tens of thousands were we to invade. Our political leaders knew that we would have to pull forces from Europe to supplement those in the Pacific to complete the invasion. It would be a bloodbath like nothing in history. It already was, but predictions multiplied those costs tenfold in some scenarios. The "bomb" was drastic but humane compared to the options. It worked. It saved countless lives, even as horrendous a choice as it was. The firebombing of Tokyo and other cities did as well.

Mr. Voris not only saw the edge of horror when he arrived in Japan, he lived and worked in it. All of the occupation forces did. The Japanese people lived the horror. That was the price paid for attacking our country. They had plans for doing the same thing to this country, as Merle quickly discovered. His first assignment was Platoon Leader, but he was soon Company Commander. It was not long before he was in charge of Battalion S-3 (investigation and intelligence). The officers in the 7th Cav were rotating home at an amazing rate as they accumulated enough points to fulfill their service requirements and Merle's duties evolved rapidly. His new military occupation required being out "amongst 'em" as some special ops guys laughingly called it. The area of occupation was the east side of Boso Peninsula, where the invasion would have occurred had it happened (the plan's actual name was Operation Coronet). The Japanese had established a last line of defense about 40 miles from the emperor's palace and that was where Merle's investigations took place. The city nearest the Palace had mostly been left unscathed by the bombings yet the buildings nearest the AO were ash heaps. In Merle's words, "they were ashes with metal twisted by the intense heat so tangled that they were almost unrecognizable." He and his charges had to interrogate the citizenry about any war materials in the area, confiscate it, and record it for immediate disposal. Even the school children were part of the war effort as they were enjoined in it by using them to install tiny screws and like items in the smaller parts required to support the military. The war machine had factories scattered throughout the neighborhoods so it was impossible to attack them without collateral damage. One of his investigations led him to a warehouse that was full to the overflowing with currency which they had stored for use when they invaded the United States. It was US currency, or what they were going to use as US currency when they were in control of invaded territory. There were bunkers and incredible fortifications which had to be discovered and destroyed, located throughout the area. According to information I read after talking to Merle, there were oaths taken that one million "shields" in the form of men, women, and children, would die from the beachhead in this area and the Palace to protect the royal family. Part of his duty was to find the plans for the locations of supplies as well as the hidden fortifications required for the defense of Japan. He went into schools and buildings, questioned the populace, led searches, faced the unknown at each turn, and lived with stress he still did not speak of even during this interview. He did not have to — the haunted laugh revealed it.

Remember the old sit-com, "F Troop"? Merle Voris was part of F Troop, Seventh Cavalry of the First Infantry Division. That unit was no joke. They were the Honor Guard for General MacArthur when he took command of the Occupation Forces in Japan. Merle had a huge job at an important time in our country's history and in Japan's history. We began to pacify and restore a conquered nation. Merle helped me gain a much better understanding of what that meant. The discourse was difficult about the period when he rambled through the rubble of Tokyo and Yokohama. Bodies littered the streets. The charred remains were not just structural. We reverted to a story about his earlier experience when he was "green as grass." Merle was a wise man even then. One of his first challenges was a riot at a downtown bank. Division called him to fall troops out to quell the riot. He called on his First Sergeant to handle it since that man was a seasoned warrior. All the weapons had been locked in the armory. A small mob of Koreans had made a run on a bank demanding their money and when it was not forthcoming, the Army had to control the mob. Second Lieutenant Merle Voris and his First Sergeant led a successful crowd control operation that day.

Another job that challenged Voris was managing the guard operation at the Palace. He commanded the 26 soldiers who performed the dual task of controlling entry in that area. He had two teams. The first post had two soldiers who stopped GIs from entering beyond a certain point. The second post required two soldiers to control the Japanese, except at the times they were allowed to pray to the Emperor. The Americans never questioned the practice. It was a major part of the cultural complexion of the country and was not to be interrupted. One day Merle went to inspect the guards. He found a vacant post with helmet and gear, including a weapon and ammunition, stacked there, minus the soldier. He was angry as he walked to the other post. Pickles, the missing guard, was there chatting with his very good buddy. Merle put him on notice of pending discipline. As soon as it was practical he had them both replaced at their posts and reported to Headquarters to request a court martial. It was a serious offense. Leaving a post was bad enough, but leaving it with a weapon and ammunition in occupied enemy territory bordered on dangerous to the extreme. Merle's CO was an officer who had gotten a field commission. He did not want the paperwork or the complications of a trial during the occupation. They came up with alternative punishment. The men were forced to march with full field packs, and anything else they could burden them with, in front of their quarters all day for several days. One day, they were cleaning their gear and one of them discharged a weapon accidentally. I thought it was a bit like letting Barney Fife load his one bullet on "Andy of Mayberry" when I heard the story. True to the Army way, they were transferred to the artillery. Merle heard they only made it there two weeks before getting in trouble again. He maintained they were doing their best to get mustered out of the service. They did not care and wanted everyone to know it. Sounds like *Mash*, does it not? The funny thing he heard after that, before he lost track of them entirely, was the Army tradition ran true to course again. They were made MPs (Military Police). Did someone say Barney Fife?

Merle spent months being trained before he went to Japan. His time there was brief albeit eventful, leaving him a lifetime of memories. He was fortunate to meet some good interpreters, some of whom were Americans of Japanese descent. Merle was even welcomed in some Japanese homes where he found people who were gracious and understanding. He made a lifelong Army friend named Joe who resides in Asheville, NC. They still communicate. Merle was the old man of the group at age 22 while Joe was a mere 19-years old. There were two Joes with whom Merle had gotten close while stationed in Japan. The other was a Texan, Chaplain Joe. He was a large man given to a love of parades. He joined in adorned with twin pistols at every opportunity.

Merle has been a committed Christian his entire life. A couple of ironies struck him while we chatted. The Officers Club was above the Chapel. After a Saturday night of revelry, the clean-up resulted in water dripping between the cracks into the chapel below during services. Ashville Joe was often a Saturday night participant. Merle got him to attend a service finally and his life changed. The other irony that Merle recalled was when his job required him to teach a class — another Army requirement in peace time is making work — which was harsh for a former Sunday school teacher. He had to teach how to kill silently. Then he prayed that nobody ever had to use the skill. The most awkward duty he had was teaching the men about "personal preparation" before they socialized in town and then "inspect their personal hygiene" before they returned to their barracks.

Near the end of Merle's military commitment, orders came down for him to make a decision where to spend his last three months. The Army wanted to use his civilian expertise in a way that benefited another eastern country. China had turned away from its ally status. The countries it was to assist us in rehabilitating it deserted. In fact, became aggressive toward them. Merle got to choose between Korea and Okinawa. The claws were already displayed in the former thus he opted for the latter. He found himself bound for the island of Okinawa and the small chain of islands close to it. He was an agricultural expert. He was unusual for his time. Merle combined heritage and education. The Army wanted him to help the natives reclaim their farms during his remaining time. Okinawa had been bombed. The northern half was a disaster area but the southern half was still suitable for farming. He focused on that area. The US provided tractors and other equipment which Merle taught the farmers to utilize. He showed them some modern techniques of farming.

He also went to a smaller island where horses were supreme but nearly wiped out during the war. Merle negotiated with another farmer to get some stock to start again. He remembers how small their horses were due to constant in-breeding. The first one he took over on an LST was a one-year-old horse which he was able to carry in his arms, a fact that amazed him then and still. A memory that brightened his eyes was that of a young girl as she planted the first of the fruit trees he helped provide in an area where the Japanese had destroyed their orchards.

Three months passed quickly and Merle found himself aboard a captured German hospital ship bound for San Francisco. He and three other officers landed in the States together, shared a room in a hotel and a phone to call their families. They were home! The trip across the Pacific had gotten them close enough to share some expenses and a giant platter of shrimp. The drink of choice for the evening was milk! They did not founder, but they drank and ate their fill.

Merle called home and got word to Esther that it would not be much longer. His son had been born not long after he arrived in Japan. He had a daughter before he left and a son he had never seen. Merle did not know his son had been born for a month after his birth. Someone in the chain of command had said, "The War is over and the country is in debt. We cannot afford to fly the mail now, even though it is free." When I heard this I wondered if he and the other GIs reacted like I would have as planes landed each day full of "dignitaries" knowing that my mail was languishing somewhere on the open sea in a tired old freighter. (It is a scene a lot like that in Haiti when the dignitaries were filling the flight patterns awaiting a photo-op while relief supplies could not be landed stacked up behind them.)

Merle did call Esther from Japan once. AT&T had phone service from Japan to the US. It was not cheap. The call cost him about $30 and I asked if that was not all he made, even as an officer. He laughed and replied that he had saved his cigarette rations. He reminded me they could be bartered. Two cartons became enough cash to make the call. Merle made arrangements with his parents to have Esther at their home at a certain time and the call was completed. Her parents did not have a phone. We talked briefly about the differences now in technology and how soldiers can communicate via e-mail. It made me think about my turn. Even then a phone call was rare and it was a "mere" 42 years ago. We could exchange tapes. I tried to imagine the connection he had sixty-four years ago. Was he shouting with excitement or to be heard or both?

The Army discharged Merle at Camp McCoy, Wisconsin, and he flew into Columbus, Ohio from there. He saw his son there on the tarmac for the first time. Merle planned to use the remaining three years of his college scholarship to attend Ohio State. He had GI Bill as well. He and Esther found a three bedroom home in their home town which was 25 miles from the college. He was going to commute. They could have made it work, but the people who owned the home would not rent to people with children. Merle had rented his farm and sold his livestock to the farmer who rented the place. When his plans for school disintegrated, he decided to return to farming. He bought his stock back at twice the price even though it was two years older and much less productive. War-time inflation had done that for him.

The cost of the war was time away from his family, scenes he could never describe fully to those around him, and even derision from certain family members who said he was never really in the war. These people never went at all and had no clue what anything was like, either in combat or in the occupation battle, yet they had the gall to comment. It was good that Merle was the kind of man that he was and is.

I asked Merle if he was surprised by Pearl Harbor. He said that most of the people he knew were shocked when it actually happened, but that it was expected. Most people thought Hawaii was at risk and Japan would attack. Our involvement in Europe was a greater surprise to him. People in the Midwest were even concerned about the West Coast. Hawaii made that a real possibility. It put the Japanese within striking distance. America today has no idea how close some Japanese ties were with the Hawaiian Island population. Our West Coast population had families in Japan, as well. At the time, although sad, the reaction was understandable. We were attacked…a sneak attack on a Sunday morning. People were fearful.

Merle spoke of his duty in S-3 which required that his outfit be observant of any attempted communications between former combatants, any attempt to reorganize, and any attempt to arm. He mentioned a place called Chosi Peninsula where some soldiers remained in uniform. When American soldiers passed by they made no attempt to hide the hate and loathing in their faces. Many Americans have forgotten the Bataan Death March, the way our enemy not only killed but killed with glee, tortured with a desire to inflict maximum pain before death delivered mercy, and made no attempt at mercy for any civilian population in its path.

Life offers balance much of the time. We choose the things to which we cling for better or worse in many ways. I have given in to my demons. At other times, I fend them off successfully. Merle and I found that once again veterans of all wars share a common understanding about suppressed memories and survivor's guilt, or self-doubt about not having done enough. That seems to go with the territory. The two Joes are important parts of Merle's experience in Japan. He has some shining moments from his stint in the Army. America stood with her military. One event lives in his mind surrounded in a golden arch. He clings to it lovingly. Christmas came during Merle's training at the Infantry Replacement Center in Arkansas. The Army attempted to dissuade wives from joining husbands during the holidays since the facilities there were woefully inadequate. It did however grant a special dispensation to those with children. Arrangements were made through the USO for the few efficiency apartments in the area and Merle and Esther were supposed to have been successful in obtaining one of them. Esther traveled cross-country on a milk train to see him. I did not fully appreciate the gravity of that venture until Merle gave me a better explanation. A milk train in those days stopped at every cross road in the rural areas and picked up a large urn of milk, then dropped it at some major distribution point. It did it along its appointed route, turning the trip into an arduous adventure that wore on those who traveled alone, much less a woman traveling with a toddler. By the time Esther reached her destination she was about as frazzled as one of the cinders along the route. The weather was cold, rainy and altogether miserable. Merle met her at the rail station and they went to find their quarters. They had the address but were given the wrong streetcar number. After walking up and down the street a pair of times, they knocked on the door of the last house at the end of the lane. An elderly couple answered the door, informing them what had happened. They pointed across a muddy field at a house visible through the heavy mist.

"That is the house you want. If there is no room there tonight you come back here. We have room."

Merle said they walked through the rain, cold and miserable, shielding the baby, only to find nobody at home. It was getting late. In desperation they returned to the first house. Esther was out on her feet. The little girl needed be inside and fed. The people had kept an eye out for them and welcomed them into their home. The guest room was wonderful. They were childless but the lady's ninety-year-old mother lived with them in an apartment above the garage. The next morning they awoke to the smells of a breakfast, which made the day break with a smile regardless of the Arkansas weather. Merle noted that the lady could not read or write, but she cooked! After breakfast, they got ready to check on the apartment once again. The couple told them that room or not, they were coming back for Christmas dinner. They did. The Voris family dined with a wonderful American couple — and the couple enjoyed a child at their table for Christmas.

Merle Voris is my friend. His life, his family, and his influence are intermingled in my life. I think of him and I see the faces of his wife, his children and grandchildren, even the great-grandchildren I know. I have witnessed the intelligence, the work ethic, the purpose, the loyalty that is his legacy. I know his influence. Merle has been a leader in my church since 1962 when I moved here. He has been a Gideon, a business leader, a community leader, a true patriarch. He does not see it sometimes, but he is truly a World War II veteran. He paid a price.

BOHICA — For Real

I greeted Jim with, "Hello, you rotten old booger!" as he entered his brother's home on a warm June morning. Dick Davis laughed at my formal salutation. I was there to talk to Jim. He was a little late from his morning workout with his wife. Dick had me wait, knowing it would not be long before Jim arrived.

"You know me too!" said Jim, as we shook hands.

I have known James Davis for more than 30 years. Jim is not a neighbor, but his sister Sue is. I have gone to church with his brothers and most of his relatives for more than three decades. When he is in town, we laugh and joke — but it was only recently that anyone told me I should ask him about his military experience. Jim's brother John suggested I interview Jim while he was home during the summer of 2010. I was shocked when John told me that Jim had been drafted twice — late in World War II and again for Korea.

Jim Davis is in his eighties and is a big, tough man. He is a cancer survivor of 15 years. Jim will tell you he should not be here, but he has a huge heart and character. His wit is great and his laughter is right below the surface. His cane slows him and the ravages of his disease are obvious, but when you meet him you know you are in the presence of a fighter. I enjoyed getting current on personal things before getting to my interview's purpose. How did he get drafted twice?

Jim Davis was drafted late in World War II and went to Basic Training at Fort Bliss, TX, for eight weeks. Fort Lewis was his next stop for additional training and preparation for debarkation to his overseas assignment. He was bound for Japan. Jim was assigned to the 35th Infantry Division and boarded a Liberty Ship for a long, slow voyage across the Pacific Ocean. It was a small ship for such a trip and he remembers it well. The crew was Filipino, as our Navy was taxed and many civilian transports were contracted late in the War. Jim related that they sailed in stormy seas almost the entire way. They were buffeted by huge waves and the small ship was out of the water almost as much as in it. Everyone on board was seasick, including the crew. The head was an abomination. If you were not sick when you visited it, you were before you left.

While at sea, the Armistice was signed. When Jim left the State of Washington, he thought he was going to war. When he made land in Japan, his duties were incredibly different. Jim says he got the greatest education of his entire life in the next nine months. Jim Davis did not remain with his unit. He was given a Temporary Duty assignment (TDY) to a "debugging" crew and travelled to every major city in Japan. His job was spraying DDT on every living or dead being in the country. The population was being eaten alive by flies and lice from the death and destruction. Jim may be able to see and smell that memory still. Any former warrior can recollect an impression of that overwhelming nature — napalm in the morning, bombed villages, gunpowder from a prolonged firefight…they linger in your senses. He and the crew with which he travelled performed a huge health mission on the island. They were saving the living from being infected by the dead.

Jim Davis returned to America in late 1946 to complete his two-year military commitment. He was home from the War by April, 1947. Jim laughs as he recalls his Saturday night before Easter Sunday that year. A strapping, 21-year-old veteran who had seen a world he could not yet explain, Jim still lived in his mother's house. He had an incident after an almost all-night celebration of his return. Jim stumbled in as the sun began to peek through the dark, mostly sober by dawn's early light. He went to his bedroom and prepared for bed. His mother, Winnie Davis, a tiny little lady I was privileged to know, came to his room and said, "Jim Davis, you get dressed young man. You are going to Sunrise Service. You are in my house, you live by my rules. I don't care where you have been." He went.

Pursuit of life was Jim's next adventure. He succeeded in getting a job at Chrysler Corporation and worked steadily until a strike was called. He crashed into another of his family's rules at that point, but Jim never met a rule he was afraid to challenge. His father, Tom, was a railroad man and an old time preacher — a good man by any definition. He instructed Jim that he could not get a job on the railroad. He taught his children that they had to work and work hard. Each of them has followed that rule their entire lives. Jim quietly managed to get a job on the very railroad where Tom Davis worked — without his father's knowledge. Jim's story moved from that period to the time when he met his first wife, Ruth Ann (deceased), who he married while working at a canning factory in Greentown, IN.

Jim Davis was 24-years old, gainfully employed, a veteran of World War II, and married. It was 1950 and he got a notice to report to the Draft Board in Tipton, IN. He was in shock. That had not happened to anyone else he knew. He reported as required, but not alone. His father tagged along. Tom was not about to let his red-haired son go to this meeting without him. It was a safety issue. Jim told the lady at the office that there had to be some kind of mistake and was assured that there was not. She told Jim that the Board had declared him on "Inactive Reserve" since he had seen no combat. Jim Davis had never been informed of any such declaration, nor had his father. Neither of them had received a notification. By this time, Tom was close to losing his religion. He intervened as well. The two men were almost holding each other away when the lady looked Jim in the face and said, "Report as instructed Mr. Davis. It won't hurt you." What kind of words were those to use on a man? Report to a war — "it won't hurt you."

A shocked and angry Jim Davis drove to Indianapolis, IN, the next morning for his swearing in ceremony. It happened. Not only was he sworn in, he was outfitted and given seventy-two hours of leave. He was ordered to be aboard a train for St. Louis, MO, three days later. That was to be his first stop on his trip to the West Coast. The Army had decided that returning veterans needed no conditioning, no Basic Training, and no time. They were going straight to war. He had little time to get his personal affairs in order. Jim Davis was shipping out to Korea. Jim returned to his house mad and with a plan. When he got home things were folded and other things began to unfold. Later that evening, he heard from an old friend from World War II. A buddy named Rust, from western Illinois, contacted him. The same thing had happened to him. Rust decided to head toward a meeting point so they could travel together. Jim told Rust that he was not reporting on time. He was getting his wife situated before he went anywhere. He did not give a damn what Uncle Sam wanted, he was taking care of his family first. Rust said they would go down together. They established a rendezvous time and place and took care of their business.

Jim boarded the train in Indianapolis days later in full uniform, orders in hand. A grizzled old sergeant spied him, stopped him and demanded to see his orders. "You are AWOL soldier" said the lifer. Jim did not say a word. "I never saw you. Get on the damned train." Eight days later, Davis and Rust were in Saint Louis. They went to a bar there while waiting for the train to Kansas City, the next leg of the journey. Two police officers questioned them there, but again they were released. Too many people remembered World War II and understood what was ahead of these soldiers.

They were not as lucky in Denver, CO. Jim got off the train during a water stop to get a candy bar and paper. Two fresh-faced MPs saw him, checked his orders and put him against the wall. They were kids and Jim's temper got the best of him that time. He laughed when he told me his reaction to them. Jim Davis said, "You young sons-a-bitches, I been once. You don't know nuthin' from nuthin'. I'm reportin' and I'm gonna go fight. At least, let me go tell my buddy on the train what the hell you're doin'." Jim said they immediately went and pulled Rust off the train too, put them both in chains, and held the train until they got orders from their sergeant. They were loaded aboard the train under guard and traveled to California as prisoners.

They arrived under guard and were taken to the stockade in chains. Jailhouse scuttlebutt informed them that their unit had not sailed yet. It had been forming up for several days as new trainees reported for duty too. They had made it in time, albeit with less decorum. Jim told Rust they would not be held. He was confident they would be on board when the ship sailed for Korea. Jim was right. A few hours later a sergeant had them released and took them to the nearby Post medical facility. They were given all their shots in short order, their boarding orders, and taken to a place to bunk for the night. Jim related that they were still not with the rest of the unit, but that was a formality. He realized they were being watched, but their next stop was Korea.

The sergeant retrieved them the next morning for chow. They were taken to the debarkation point where they found a good spot to wait under an exhaust vent spewing warm air. They dozed until the rest of the soldiers arrived. It was not like his trip to Japan. He was one of 10,000 soldiers boarding a huge troop ship, a twin-stack Navy vessel, this time. Jim remembers the talk as they sailed under the Golden Gate Bridge. Several of the guys said they would never see home again. He said, "They didn't, but I never felt that way one time. I knew I was coming home just the way I left for some reason. I never doubted it. And God did it."

The voyage was one of training and learning about the fighting unit they had joined. He was in the First Cavalry this time. Their orders would be revealed later. They knew their purpose. Only the specifics were still a mystery.

The ship made a couple of ports along the way where soldiers de-shipped. He heard they were getting more training. The officers had been reviewing soldiers' records while at sea. By the time Korea was the destination Jim Davis was one of 2800 remaining on board. They were the soldiers who had allegedly seen action in World War II. Command had determined they needed no refresher courses. They were chosen to make the beachhead at Inchon. Jim never fired a weapon in war. It did not matter. His military records indicated he was Infantry and all of his training fit their needs — on paper.

At last they were in sight of the coast of Korea. They circled while the landing craft were lowered. The sergeants and line officers prepped the grunts to climb down the sixty feet of rope ladders dangling down the sides of the bobbing ship. They were told to do it well. Anyone who didn't was dead. They had no time and no way to retrieve floaters. Besides, anybody who missed would probably be crushed or drown due to the weight they carried. The non-coms were brutally frank. Jim said, "There was no time for bullshit. He added, "I was scared to death. Anyone who says he wasn't is a damned liar." Jim Davis carried approximately 160 pounds of gear by the time he went down the rope. His load increased tremendously when he stepped to the railing. When he got there the sergeant handed him a 30-caliber water-cooled machine gun and said, "Big Guy, you are a machine gunner now." He was issued a 45 and ammo for both weapons. Jim had never operated a machine gun before. Neither had he climbed a sixty foot long rope ladder.

Jim landed safely somehow in his LST and made the beach for the assault on Inchon. The early landing forces were helping organize later waves of soldiers by assigning them to units as they waded ashore. A sergeant saw him carrying his newly acquired weapon and waved him over to his location. He directed Jim where he was to go and asked him if he knew "how to use that thing." They were taking fire, but the area had been heavily bombarded before they landed. Jim told him he had no idea. The sergeant then said, "You're gonna learn how to detail it in eight minutes or you won't live to see another sunrise soldier." Jim listened and learned right there on beach, under fire. The First Cav broke through at Pusan, helped recapture Seoul, and began its march to the 38th Parallel.

Jim Davis's equipment included C-rations, some spare parts for his machine gun, anti-freeze for it, ammo, canteen, his web gear, four pairs of socks, the limited personal hygiene supplies he could carry (which did not last long), and normal battle gear. His weapon fired 250 rounds per minute and out-performed the air-cooled version easily. The latter had problems with barrel warp when hot. Jim had an assistant gunner with as many as six men carrying ammo when they were well supplied. From that day on, Jim did not go a day without a fight for almost two years. He had no shower for two months, went without washing his hands or feet for over three weeks and did not eat a warm meal for three months. Jim and his fellow soldiers never slept a night through during that whole time. Korea is as cold in the winter as his home state of Indiana and as miserably hot in the summer. His unit outran its supply lines several times. They marched and fought, slept a little, awoke, marched and fought — all the way to North Korea. He carried his spare socks in his blouse in cold weather so they would warm his feet when he changed. Jim said if a man took care of himself the best he could, he made out okay. "We had good clothes, and we sure tested them." The men were tested too.

One night his lieutenant woke him and told him to get on his gun. Lt. Boone was with Davis the entire time, except for recovery periods twice. Boone was out of the field for wounds two times, but he came back. He was a field officer and the two of them had a special respect and relationship. This particular night Boone, another big redhead, was running the company. The Captain had been killed a short time before. Boone said they were about to be attacked by a bunch of Chinese. Jim said he saw about 250 enemy soldiers cresting a ridge in the moonlight. He started firing and they just kept coming. His platoon fought and the Chinese all died, like wheat being mowed down by a scythe. Jim had made Sergeant First Class by this time. He was a good soldier and by action and attrition he was ranking non-com by this stage in the "police action." At different times he was Acting First Sergeant and other times he was Platoon Sergeant. At all times he retained his 30 caliber. It was his. They were always undermanned so it was not an issue for any of his officers. Jim was good with the weapon.

Veterans do not remember war sequentially. Jim is no exception. Thoughts of one outstanding event lead to another. Days and nights run together. When every day is stress and a battle to survive they blur into sameness. Memories stand out when there is something that makes them a different color in the mind than the bleakness of pain etched in the darkest recesses of the mind.

Boone is one of Jim Davis's passionate memories, as is his Company, and later Battalion, Executive Officer. The XO had been with him on the ship going to Korea and was with the unit during the entire two years of battle as well. He backed Davis in every time of need. Boone and Davis kept each other alive. The XO got them what they needed whenever he could. He also kept Davis out of trouble more than once. One story that Jim interjected was a trip for supplies when they were back in Seoul late in Jim's tour of duty. Jim got distracted by something and ran the Company Jeep into a rice paddy, damaging it badly. He came close to getting killed that time — closer than almost any time in combat. The XO covered for him and made the incident disappear. He saved his stripes. Jim never forgot.

Davis's unit worked with South Korean forces and the Greeks. Jim said the Greeks were a mean, hard drinking, fighting bunch of wild men. He did not drink when in the field, but there was no time they did not drink. The Europeans relished hand-to-hand, face-to-face combat. Jim was astonished at their love of looking in the eyes of their enemy when it came time to kill. He did not say, but he made me wonder if they were around when the Cav punched out of Pusan early in his tour or later when they began their break to the north. Jim remembers with vivid detail how it felt to reach the 38th Parallel, watching the retreat of the North Koreans into their own territory. He was standing within eight feet of MacArthur when the General spoke the famous words so often quoted. He heard Macarthur say; "I will have you home by Christmas boys, if the Chinese stay out of it." It was not long after that when the order was given to pull back.

Truman angered the troops by not allowing them to pursue the enemy into North Korea and history recorded what happened to MacArthur. The soldiers were already somewhat disheartened during the drive to the north. In an attempt to slow them, they had even been deprived of ammunition, which demoralized and threatened their lives. They thought it was a simple supply issue, but the soldiers began to wonder if it was political after the call for withdrawal came. The machine gunners received sufficient ammo, but the riflemen had been getting only eight rounds each — two clips. Jim Davis remains angry about that and MacArthur's removal yet today.

The First Cavalry began a long, slow fight back toward Seoul then. There were many hills taken and relinquished, many battles fought. There were waves of Chinese and North Koreans attacking and killed. There were many Americans killed and wounded. The battles ran into each other. He cannot remember the hills' numbers. They all had one. It did not matter what it was. He had close calls, but he fought on, unscathed. Jim was trailing a column around a hill, with his Company's Captain ahead of him, when a soldier from a sister company ran up behind him and pushed him off the trail into the ditch alongside. There was a sniper in a tree he had not seen, which the point man behind them noticed. A man he did not know until then took five rounds in his legs before Jim took the sniper out with his machine gun. Jim managed to track his Good Samaritan later and they became lifelong friends.

Along the road south they had new recruits. Some were good, others not so much. One of the latter brought out the Patton in Boone. One went over the hill when he was supposed to be on his watch and almost got soldiers killed. The Captain said let him go, let the North Koreans or someone kill him. Jim recalls he was a loudmouth from Detroit, but he does not remember his name. Boone had an idea he could not have gone far; it was too dangerous and there simply was no place to go. He asked Jim to go with him. They tracked the guy and found him not too far away. Boone told Davis, "I'm gonna make him a soldier or kill him myself. It is up to him." He walked up to him, pulled his 45 and shot between the man's legs. He said, "You can get up and be a soldier, run out there and let them kill you, or let me kill you right here, you coward. But you're not gonna lay in that hole. Your choice." Jim said the guy never said a word, got up, and walked back with them. He became one of the best soldiers in the outfit.

There were always hills. It seemed that some general somewhere wanted them to take the high ground. They had taken one overlooking a river. After securing it they knew that there would be river patrols operating there soon after. Jim walked around the rim of the hill to check for machine gun emplacements that would provide the best covering fire for patrols along the river banks as well as boat traffic near their position. He rounded a knoll and walked straight into a Chinese soldier. They scared each other half to death. The Chinese soldier spoke in better English than Jim. Neither raised a weapon. They looked at one another, smiled, turned around and walked away. Jim told Boone what happened when he returned to his platoon area. Two days later Boone returned from a meeting and told Davis the rest of the story. The enemy combatant wanted to surrender. Jim scared him so badly that he forgot what he was coming to do. He found another unit and turned himself in there and told the entire story there himself. He had been educated in CA prior to the war. He did not want to fight but was conscripted. The Chinese soldier surrendered, but more than that, he provided important intelligence which made a significant difference in a battle they fought a few days later. Jim got some serious ribbing from his buddies for missing an opportunity to capture an enemy soldier instead of just throwing him kisses and waving goodbye.

Lt. Boone and Jim Davis built memories together in ways only soldiers do. Jim remembers another battle when they were walking near a command Jeep when the enemy had them sighted in with mortar fire. The enemy was dropping rounds in with a typical bracketing fire approach. The in-coming was getting closer and closer when they were forced to finally dive into a ditch beside the road. They had gotten supplies somewhere, including some liquor for the platoon. As Boone dove he ordered Jim to "save the whiskey, I'm gonna need it tonight!" The in-coming mortar fire was from a sixty millimeter mortar. They decided to take it out and it turned into a serious fight. There was an enemy force dug in nearby, requiring several days to defeat. No battle was won without a high price. This was no different. The First Cavalry took enormous losses in Korea. This battle was north of Seoul. Jim said the first time he saw that city it reminded him of Chicago. When he finally returned there after two years of constant fighting, there "wasn't one brick sitting on top of another."

After almost two years of fighting, the First Cavalry was relieved by the 45th Infantry. Jim Davis was going home — again. This time he was on a large troop ship and he was the NCOIC (Non-Commissioned Officer-In-Charge) of enlisted men on board. Boone was with him as was his other friend, the Executive Officer. One afternoon while at sea, the XO asked Jim if he had not had an AWOL in his records at one time. Jim told him that he did. The XO informed him that all records were in the hold of the ship and in the XO's keeping. They descended the ladder into the hold, searched the storage area until they found the right files and — POOF — flames — a certain report went up in smoke somewhere in the middle of the Pacific Ocean. Jim witnessed firsthand that steam will open a sealed envelope.

It was 1952 and Jim Davis was back in the States again. The rest of the voyage was uneventful. As his instincts had predicted, he sailed under the Golden Gate Bridge in once piece. He was battle-worn, hardened in ways difficult to describe. He was a gunner, a Sergeant First Class, a combat veteran. When they landed and settled in, his XO found him again. The officer had promised him a steak and a drink at the Officers Club when they got home and he came to deliver on that promise. When they arrived the guards at the door blocked their way, telling Jim he was not allowed in the room. The XO, who was a Major by then, said, "By God, he goes where I go. You guys damned sure haven't been there. I am buying him a meal and a drink. If you don't let him in I will tear this damned place apart. You want a piece of it?" Jim was amazed. His old boss was serious. They admitted him. There were enough combat officers present that he was made welcome. They knew.

Only a long train ride home was left. Jim was once more the NCOIC. There was an officer on board and 207 other enlisted men. They had orders and money. They also had an itch to get home. They were home from a soon to be Forgotten War. Their first stop was in the Rocky Mountains somewhere. The soldiers had time to visit a small town bar. It got a bit rowdy. Jim had to hold the train, but he lost a few guys who were close enough to home that they found another way. It was a sign of things to come. He had no way of retrieving them. They steamed all the way to Minnesota. It was worse there. The numbers dwindled even more. Chicago. Lord. If it kept up they could ride a couple of buses. Lafayette. Now they could ride a bus. When they arrived at Atterbury, there were perhaps 23 men left on the train. The officer asked Jim what they were going to do. Jim said, "We report, turn in the paperwork we have left, process the hell out, and go home. Good luck sir."

Jim Davis got a ride to Indianapolis. He managed to arrive at the bus terminal just as a bus was boarding for a destination that included Elwood. "Hold that bus," yelled Davis. He arrived in Elwood and found out what a cab cost. Jim was supposed to call his wife, but things moved too quickly along the way. He decided to surprise her. It was eight dollars to ride to Windfall, IN. He surprised everyone. After everyone picked themselves off the floor his sister, Kat, gave him her car keys and told him to go home. Jim reminded her that he had no license. She told him to go. He went. He surprised Ruth Ann.

Davis was not quite done with his military duty. He had to report to Fort Leonard Wood in Missouri. He and his wife relocated for the balance of his tour, but he had thoughts of making the Army a career. Jim was considering an application for Warrant Officer's School. When he reported for duty good fortune was again at his side. The Commanding Officer was a combat leader who recognized what Jim had been through. They discussed his future. At the time there was no real opening for him and the CO told Jim to take some time reviewing options. Soon a school was started there that the Old Man wanted Jim to help operate. Jim joined forces with a young lieutenant who also happened to be a Hoosier and a former railroader. They were going to run a joint military training facility for engineering and metal-working. The clerk assigned to them was a local boy whose father ran a car dealership. It was a good gig for all. The kid's dad had a lake cottage in the Ozarks. As things evolved they all had sufficient down time to utilize it and the duty there was incredibly good. Jim was sold on the Army as a career. Ruth Ann was not.

Jim Davis is a veteran with an amazing story. He graced me when he shared it. Jim communicated with many of his old war buddies for years. Rust died shortly after they came home from Korea. Years later, his phone rang. It was a call from one of his Cav soldiers. The voice on the phone said, "Sarge, you don't remember me I know, but you made me a gunner, a corporal, and a soldier. I'm in Indiana and I want to stop and see you." Jim could not do it then. He was fighting his cancer. Many months later he tried to contact the man. Jim had fought off the Death Angel. His old comrade had not.

Drafted twice. BOHICA. Bend over, here it comes again. For real.

A Woman's Life, Touched by War

I unloaded my small trailer one afternoon and heard the sound of footsteps in the street at the end of my back driveway. I saw Marie McKinney walking her son's Pomeranian. She returned my wave of recognition and stopped to talk. I graduated with her son. Naturally the family news followed, including news of Jake her husband, whose health failed, requiring full time care. She began quizzing me about my book, *Vietnam in Verse*, at which point she dropped a bombshell on me. Marie had been married before Jake. Her first husband was killed in World War II. Once again I found myself standing mouth open and speechless. How could I keep learning things about people I knew well as a teenager and not know so many things? How?

Our talk that afternoon led to a series of chats which, bit by bit, revealed amazing facts about Marie's life. I determined her husband's story had to be included in *Out of the Mist, Memories of War* somehow. It took time, but I accumulated enough information to begin organizing notes and start writing. A lightning bolt struck me from the sky! This is not a story about him, or the other people in Marie McKinney's life. It is her story. World War II intruded in her life multiple times. War and the effects of war changed the direction of her life. This story is really a story about a woman's life touched by war.

Born in Queens, NY, Marie McKinney was a city girl. She grew to young adulthood in the east, while playing on the sandy beaches of the New Jersey shore where her grandmother lived. She recalls watching the Hindenburg fly over her grandmother's home on more than one occasion. When it began making flights, she remembers her grandmother's agitation at its sandbags striking her house as it made altitude on the flight to Europe. More than once a sandbag landed in her yard, but on one occasion a bag damaged the roof of her house. The evening the Hindenburg crashed, Marie remembers in detail. They watched the airbus descend as usual. Soon they heard sirens. She said they could not actually see flames in the sky, but they knew about the accident. Two of her uncles served on the volunteer fire department. The sirens called them into service. They called her grandmother to tell her what happened. Later that night, they returned from the disaster — shaken and covered with the filth of fighting the fire. Marie listened with fright as they described what they saw that evening, but the thing they both agreed reverberated in their ears shocked her then and stayed with her always. They said the screams of the trapped horses inside the great blimp were ghostlike, and almost human. It was haunting for them. Marie said she cannot tell the story without remembering those words.

Marie entered high school as World War II erupted. It was as much a part of her life as homework. Young men left school to go to war. The War became a daily topic of conversation. A teenager, she attempted to enjoy all the normal things any other teen of her generation enjoyed. They all did, but everything was experienced among the rubble created by the chaos of an all-consuming war. They went to the beach. Warning flags waved often, calling them from the water when oil slicks appeared on the waves. German submarines nuzzled our coastline as the enemy attempted to gather information about our shipping lanes and shipbuilding yards. Observation posts were built all along an area that her people were accustomed to using for pleasant relaxation. Nothing was the same.

Marie dated a senior during her first year of high school. He graduated and rushed off to join the Army, as did most of the young men of the Greatest Generation. He was killed on Leyte. One of her friends, a quiet young Jew she admired, left to become a member of the first "ranger" group she recalls. He jumped somewhere in France on D-Day. She heard he was killed when his parachute failed. She graduated in 1944 and the War raged on, while she read about it, saw the results all around, and watched young men come and go. She went to work; life went on, but not exclusive of that war.

Marie met George Simmons while he was home on leave. George came home to be with his mother during her last days of life. Notified that death was close, her cancer made his leave taking a necessity. George was Navy, having served since World War II began, or just before. He reenlisted prior to meeting Marie. They met, experienced a whirlwind romance and married in a matter of weeks. Marie, swept off her feet, learned a lot in a short time about her Navy adventurer. The horrible jaundice and the seeping lesions on his legs reminded him of the negative impact the tropic environment placed on his health. George Simmons suffered from both when he and Marie met. Neither disease mattered to him. He loved the Pacific. Returning weighed heavily on his mind, while she tugged at his heart.

George served as a submariner when he first went to sea, but he wanted surface duty. When the PT boats became active they appealed to his sense of adventure. He volunteered. George loved the speed and power of the lightweight boats. He told Marie how the crews removed armor despite the violation of Navy regulations against it. The boats were even quicker and more maneuverable with it gone. He and the others believed they were safer if they could avoid being hit. George explained that they attacked and withdrew before the bigger ships could get their guns on them. She got a firsthand account of naval warfare, at least from his perspective.

Before he came home, he sailed with Lieutenant John F. "Jack" Kennedy on PT-109. George told Marie that one of his most difficult missions at that time had been leaving people behind as they escorted the boat carrying General McArthur away from Corregidor. He realized the General's safety was imperative; leaving Army personnel, nurses, and civilians behind to fall into Japanese hands ripped his soul apart. He struggled with it at night. He wanted back in that fight. George could have gotten different duty, but he wanted to go back to the Pacific. Marie agreed and he went.

When Simmons returned to his precious PT boats his assignment to another boat came as no surprise to him. Soon he began normal duty patrolling the islands during the day and raiding convoys at night. One day they took fire from shore while near the island of Borneo. George's boat commander decided to eliminate the gun position. They attacked. The PT boat crews showed no reluctance about beaching their boats. They were light enough to put into the soft sands of most of the islands where they operated. The powerful engines dragged them off the beaches quite well when slammed in reverse. The crew attacked the Japanese machine gun crew, eliminating it, but made one mistake. They did not see the second gun emplacement. George Simmons was killed in the ensuing action. His crew destroyed the second Japanese emplacement, but left Simmons buried there on that deserted section of beach. With a patrol to complete, the tropic heat precluded taking a dead man on the deck of their boat.

As they returned from the night's work they floated close to the location of the previous day's fight. They looked ashore only to see a small group of natives digging George's body out of the sand. They knew headhunters lived on the island; George's friends were not going to let him be desecrated. They circled the boat and once again beached her, firing on the natives. His PT boat crew retrieved his remains and returned to their base.

George Simmons is buried in the cemetery at Pearl Harbor. Marie's older daughter took her there a few years ago to see the memorial and visit George's grave. He is buried a few places from Ernie Pyle's grave site. He is among friends in his beloved Pacific. Marie, married for nine months, with her husband a matter of weeks, found herself a widow by the age of 20.

Marie grieved, but like so many women touched by war, played the hand dealt to her. She became a telephone operator. George Simmons was killed on July 10, 1945. World War II ended on August 14th without him. The memory of a few weeks left its print on her consciousness.

The beaches returned to normal. Several months later, in 1946, Marie and a friend took a break from work to eat on the beach. They enjoyed the sound of the waves, the breeze from the ocean, and the time away from the buzzing switchboard. A tall, handsome, blonde man walked up to them and interrupted them without any hesitation. He introduced himself as Clark McKinney (Jake). Not to be driven away, they chatted a while before the lunch break ended. Somehow he and Marie made a date for later.

In the Army, Jake called a small farming town in Indiana, home. He attended a military training school for radio operators there in New Jersey — another military man. Marie could not do it. World War II was a fresh wound, but Japan was being occupied by our soldiers. She did not want another relationship with a military man. She did not meet Jake as promised.

Jake persisted. He was stationed at Fort Monmouth, New Jersey. At every opportunity he hitchhiked to her town to see her. He decided to go home for his car. Jake told her about his Mercury, but when he went home he decided to get something that would impress her. While home he sold it and bought a friend's Ford convertible. How could she resist a tall, good looking, blond man with a convertible? She could not.

She discovered that Jake could have been exempted from serving in the Army. His family farmed. He did not want to do that. McKinney lied about his age to get in; yes, he was younger than she believed. He wanted to go to war, but just missed it. Once more she was in love with a man compelled to serve his country. More than that, the city girl found herself away from her precious coastal living in a small country town, learning a whole new way of life. They had married in a fever and he went to Korea, where he served in an infantry unit as a sharpshooter on the DMZ at the 38th Parallel, after all the radio training. Tensions were building and Marie knew she faced the possibility of another husband at war. And this time she faced it with a child coming.

Marie calls her oldest child, the daughter who took her to Pearl Harbor, the last USO baby born in Tipton County, IN. The USO had a program which provided full prenatal care and support for the wives of US military serving overseas in combat zones. Korea was heating up when Jake McKinney served there. Washington, DC, could not determine how to handle the North Koreans or the Chinese. Problems with both screamed into the headlines before the ink was dry on the peace declaration with Japan. Jake received his discharge before hostilities erupted between North and South Korea. Marie lived through it, but did not have to suffer war's direct impact this time. Jake did meet another man from his home town when he left. Jim Luster arrived as Jake left, another story to be told in the future.

Jake passed away two weeks before Marie shared more about her experiences from World War II. That is not the only conflict that has touched her life. One evening, we sat together and she opened a letter that Jake kept. It was written by his father. Jack McKinney served during World War I. Jack, the fox hunter extraordinaire — I remember him too. The old man of the clan served as a cook for an infantry training unit in Texas and never had to leave there. Marie's two firefighting brothers left New Jersey to get in the war when she was a teen. They both joined the Sea-Bees. One worked in dry docks around the world and the other worked somewhere in the Pacific. Neither spoke much about it. She had a brother who served in the Army and one in the Navy. All maintained the usual reticence. Marie's older daughter served in the Air Force, as did my class mate, Marie's son. Both are Vietnam era, serving in various ways. Her grandson served in the current War on Terror.

Marie McKinney's life has been touched by war — some would say it has been slapped by it.

Out of the Mist

I learned about Harry Hall at my dentist's office. The staff there adores Harry. They know I love telling stories about veterans and support me as much as they can. I had an appointment soon after one of Harry's days *in the chair*. They gave me a quick synopsis of his World War II experience. I tried connecting with Mr. Hall a few times over the next few months, but his health interfered. He was reluctant for another reason as well. It took some time to pry him loose from that reason. I waited several months before contacting Harry again. He fought cancer and had a series of draining treatments. We spoke at length, but he decided to explain his prior reluctance to set a date with me. Harry planned to write his own story, from childhood through his military experience, and professional life. He shared his background as a product of the coal fields of West Virginia who went on to become a successful life insurance agent and retirement investment advisor. It was a wonderful exchange, even if not in person. He tired, but before he disconnected, he asked me to call him back in a few weeks. I agreed. I was much more concerned with his health than I was his story — or my book. I realized I had spoken to another special man. His recovery out ranked everything else in importance.

Time passed. I thought of Harry many times. I missed him by minutes at the dentist's office again. I asked about his health without intruding on him and learned he was improving. The timing was right for a call. It pleased him when I did. Before the conversation ended I asked how his writing was progressing. Harry indicated that his younger years, the years in the coal mines, were about complete. I asked that he allow me to write the story about his service in World War II. I was both proud and pleased when he agreed — and we set a time and a date. Anticipation filled me. The days dragged until the moment I parked in front of his home.

I sat face-to-face with Harry Hall at last. He is a tall, handsome man, half way through his eighty-seventh year at the time of our meeting. He is winning a war with cancer, but hearing aids are mandatory. Harry is a proud man, neatly dressed in casual clothes which made me shabby by comparison. Each time I meet one of these gracious, marvelous heroes from World War II, I pray I can be as strong and as together as they. The man before me that day was eloquent and organized. He began by outlining what we were about to do. He wore his years of being a professional like the white shirt and dark pants he donned for the day. He was efficient. Harry assured me he had written about his days as a coal miner, but he was concerned about telling me his story. He and I talked about his having been trapped underground, surviving an explosion, as well as a fire, while in his teens. During our phone conversation, he explained that those things made him seek surface work. He wanted something other than what his family members had traditionally done for as long as he could remember. I assured him that I knew he had taken care of that history quite well. My purpose was to write about his military experiences, but anything he felt would help create the background for that was fine. It was his story. He could tell it however he wanted.

Harry Hall & his wife Jerri

Harry insisted on establishing something before we got into the meat and taters of his story. He was compelled to establish his credibility. There was no avoiding it. His first words convinced me that at some point he had been doubted. I could not believe that and remain troubled by it. Anybody who ever met him, listened as he spoke of his experiences, and remained dubious, has a clinker where his heart is supposed to be. I listened in shocked silence as that idea railed in my mind. He told me he was a replacement for the 28' Division in Europe. Originally Harry planned to be in the Air Corps. He in fact was in the Air Corps long enough to receive ten hours of flight training. All of his military misadventures relate to his introduction to the Draft Board when called to report.

Mr. Harry Hall's concern about having to tell his story perfectly was repeated.

I assured him it was not an issue. No veteran I ever met remembers perfectly — things become jumbled for anyone who has experienced combat. I discovered that the concern was not necessarily about his telling it to me. It had been the case when he told it to a representative of Senator Richard Lugar's office. One of the most satisfying things he ever experienced was being part of the project Senator Lugar sponsored involving the historical preservation of veterans' experiences. It pleased Harry that Lugar's project confirmed his version of events when he was imprisoned by the Germans in World War II. He was vindicated. Harry's story became an officially documented part of the Congressional Record.

Harry said, "This is big to me. It may not be big to anyone else. I have often wondered if people believe me when I tell them. I couldn't prove anything. When the guy came up from the VA in Indianapolis for the project that Senator Lugar sponsored and questioned me, I told my two stories. He told me point blank that they had been corroborated before he had ever talked to me." Harry went on to say, "You will never know how happy that made me. The stories are very sentimental and it is important to me." It has to be a tremendous emotional relief. Harry has been validated before God and Country. His mind is at ease after more than sixty years.

I replied, "You know what? You know in your heart what happened to you. It doesn't matter what another soul on this earth thinks, sir. You were there. To me, what you tell me is the gospel. It does not matter what some stuffed white shirt believes in DC."

Harry interrupted me, "But it pleased me very much. Those two things that happened to me were very important that they be reported accurately." I realized that he wanted them recorded accurately for history by an objective source. Harry continued by telling me the VA man asked him what color coat the man in his story had on and he answered quickly — "A white trench coat." The VA rep said, "Yes, we already knew that." Harry then assured me that the detail for our initial conversation would come back out in the proper sequence of his story.

Harry Hall was born May 31, 1923, into a large coal miner's family. He did not know that coal miners were granted draft deferments until he reported after receiving his notice. He had quit the mines and began working for Du Pont, where he had been employed for a month. Harry did not like it there and decided that he had enough of it too. The Draft Board officials informed him that he was deferred due to his employment there as well. Harry replied that he did not want a deferral, but that he had an appointment in Pittsburgh to take the qualification examination for the Flying Cadet Program. The opportunity to fly airplanes thrilled him. Flying was his main goal in life. Harry informed the Draft Board members that his appointment was on a Wednesday in the near future. He was going to it too!

The Draft Board, located in Morgantown, West Virginia, Harry's hometown, became a major player in his life. He hadn't anticipated that. When Harry explained his plans, the members replied affirmatively and indicated it was good to know. Harry went on to tell them that if he failed the exam, he still wanted to go with the draft. On the Monday before his trip to Pittsburgh to take the examination, Harry received his official Notice to Report for Duty. The Board had beaten him to the punch by two days. He returned to the Draft Board and demanded to know what was happening. The Board representative responded that he could take the exam as he planned, but he would report as required. Harry wanted to dispute it, but could not. He was forced to accept it. Harry's flight test was canceled. His plan derailed, Harry instead landed in Fort Hayes, OH, where he fell ill before his initial orders were delivered. The sickness resulted in his transfer to a post in Alabama. There testing spun him toward mechanics school. Hall had no interest in auto mechanics, none at all. For some odd reason the only thing he got from the school was the firing order of a six-cylinder engine. He retains it yet today — one-five-three-six-two-four.

There is one other minor incident that Harry recalls. He had a wee bit of trouble with a Drill Instructor there. A particular DI did not like Harry and the feeling was reciprocal. Hall was the high school marching band's drum major. He knew how to march. The Drill Sergeant did something every day to harass Harry. He managed to get him out of step one day during marching drill. The maneuver forced Harry to do the *skip step* twice, resulting in a cinder in Harry's shoe. Harry attempted to march and kick the cinder out of his shoe simultaneously, which placed him in the DI's hands.

The Instructor hit Harry in the small of the back with the stick he carried at all times. Harry had added to the DI's enmity by also trying to convince the Army to make him the company clerk. Harry could type. He had no inclination to be a mechanic. Harry tried everything he could to land another job and you do not do that in the Army. At least you did not do it then. Things did not work that way. Harry had fueled the fire of discontent. The DI hit Harry and Harry "piled him up in a blackberry briar patch." The Drill Instructor apparently saw a "wanna-be" clerk without realizing he was tangling with an ol' coal country boy who learned how to fight at a tender age. Harry got hauled to battalion headquarters for an appearance before a Major there. The Major circled around Harry for what seemed forever at the time. The officer shouted in Harry's face, "You are lucky rookie!" repeatedly. Hall thought he was going berserk.

The Basic Training group graduated at last — and Harry survived it somehow. The ordeal was over for him. After the ceremony, the unit had a huge beer bash, with the beer furnished by the Army. He learned in the meantime why he had not gotten in real trouble over the Drill Instructor incident. It was why they called him "lucky." They were not going to have him in their command for the next stage of training. He had been selected for the Army Air Corps prior to graduation. They were upset that he was destined for other things. Harry left after graduation for an airfield in Mississippi to begin training there. But he could not leave without adding another notch to his "legacy" there.

Throughout Basic, Harry managed to hang on to his old guitar. A soldier in his unit borrowed it on occasion, but always returned it with one or more broken strings. The tension built between them, but Harry maintained his silence. He needed no more trouble. At the party, the string-breaker demanded that Harry go get his guitar and play some tunes for them. Harry declined. As the beer consumption increased, the soldier's requests became more belligerent. Harry finally told him that the thing only had four strings thanks to him. He then told the man that he was not even thoughtful enough to borrow something and return it in working order, so "What made him think I was going to do him a favor?"

The other soldier, not content to let things calm, confronted Harry again. This time two of his buddies stood with him. Harry looked at him, suggested he get the beer, and they talk about it. Harry returned with two pitchers, approached them and spread his arms wide. He proceeded to throw the contents into the guy's sidekicks' faces — and the faces of anyone close to them. It was on! The room split — half for them, half for Harry. The ensuing several minutes became chaotic. The officers and NCOs were hard-pressed to keep an all-out brawl from erupting. Harry found himself literally dragged to the Company Headquarters once more. He laughed at the memory, eyes twinkling, and said, "The Old Man was madder this time than the first time. He walked more circles around me than he did when I put the DI in the briar patch. But I already had my orders." Harry's satisfaction knew no bounds. He was back on track toward his personal goal.

Harry Hall shipped out the next day for the small airfield in Mississippi, where he processed into the United States Army Air Corps. His flight pattern seemed established. Next, he went to Stephens Point, Wisconsin, and became a flight student in the 97th College Training Attachment. The Army commandeered the state teachers college there and converted it into a facility for the initial phase of fighter pilot training. Harry said it was a "great, beautiful place, even if it was cold in the winter." He loved it there. The college offered a wonderful cafeteria and even a bar. His training included intensive classroom studies and flight time in a Taylor Cub. The Army pilot cadets were required to complete ten hours of flight time to qualify for the next phase. Everything went fine until the group as whole reached around the seven hour mark. A fellow pilot trainee died in a crash.

Rumors flew along with the students. They believed he froze at the controls for some reason, but the instructors were close-lipped. No official information was released. Enough of them had been in the air that a theory developed. To a man, they were given control of the craft under unusual circumstances. The novice pilots also received instructions not to discuss the situation on the ground. An order like that never kept a soldier from developing a theory. It was Harry's turn to man the controls. As he did so, determination showed in his attitude that he would not make the same mistake. Soon airborne, he sighted on the church steeple all the young pilots used as a marker for the airfield. It lay to the right of the main runway. It had become a favorite target of the young pilots when they were given control of the stick. They dove at it and took the butt chewing that followed. Harry smiled into the windscreen at the thought. It was his turn at last.

They circled at the edge of town when the motor began to sputter without warning. Harry quickly looked at the flight instructor awaiting instructions. There could be no delay. The instructor asked, "What are you going to do?" Harry replied, "What do you want me to do?" The response was, "You are going to land this plane some place."

Harry replied in a calm voice, "I guess I will find the best flat field near here and set it down." Looking him in the eyes, the Flight teacher stated, "Then you better get busy and pick out the field you want. You are losing altitude."

Harry scanned the fields for a likely place to land. He tried to keep the nose up on the light aircraft, determined to land safely. He fought the stick and struggled to glide without losing altitude as hard as he could. In the midst of his battle the instructor said, "Take us home to our field." Harry thought to himself, "There is no way. I don't have the altitude and there are trees on the way in. It is every bit of three miles." As they approached the runway, losing altitude slowly, but losing, Harry never gave up. Nearing the trees the instructor said, "Let me have it" just as the engine barked to life. They landed safely and nothing more was said. Weeks later he told a fighter pilot about the incident while at a base there. He said the engine failed. It must have gotten ice on the carburetor or something. The experienced pilot assured him it did not. He was being tested. The instructors want to know how student pilots react to adverse conditions. They test their panic levels. The teacher turned the engine off intentionally. They did it to everyone. The fighter pilot insisted that Harry passed an important phase of his flight instruction that day.

Harry Hall completed flight school with flying colors, both in the classroom and in the air. Ten hours of flying time was deemed enough to pass through to the next phase. He had a study partner who was a whiz at math while he had a knack for physics. They had each other's backs in class.

He was ecstatic and things were going just where he wanted. Orders came for Santa Ana, CA, for pre-flight school. He was thrilled — until a bucket of ice water was thrown in his face. Before departure orders arrived, bad news landed. All ground personnel who had been diverted to flight school were being reassigned to their former branch of the Army. That was the biggest blow he ever took while in the service, "probably even combat was not worse than that." Harry's dream of being Captain Harry Hall, wearing the wings, the whole nine yards, was gone. Nothing, however, could erase the good memories taken from the time at the airfield in Wisconsin.

Harry Hall experienced his first Christmas in the Army at Stephens Point, Wisconsin. If the soldiers lived more than seventy-five miles from base, they could not go home for the holidays. Harry and one of his buddies were trapped there. They planned a two-man party for Christmas. Harry told his pal that "they would buy a bunch of liquor and drink their butts off." Instead, they were surprised to get an invitation from a local family to celebrate with them. Several families hosted soldiers who were unable to go home. It was America at war, not just part of her. At the appointed time, a car came to pick them up and two beautiful blondes knocked on their door—a sister for each of them. When they arrived at the home, they were ushered inside and got another huge surprise. A large decorated tree was across from the door. To its right, there was a liquor cabinet stocked with "at least seventy-five bottles of booze. There was liqueur, cognac, brandy — you name it — they had everything but the kitchen sink." Before we sat down to eat, we were half tanked," Harry laughed. He continued to explain that their hosts were wonderful Polish people who treated them as though they were part of their family. Harry and his buddy had an amazing time. They became wonderful friends with these people. Until the time they left Wisconsin, they were companions — bowling, going to movies, and sharing Sunday dinners. Harry remembers their names as well as their street address. He went on to say that "Polish people are the salt of the earth and what the Nazis did to them was almost as bad as what they did to the Jews."

Harry learned little things from people met along the way. Those lessons were as important as his Army training. He shared the stories as sidebars, but they were part of the evolution of Harry as the soldier. He told me a significant tale that he referred to often in the months ahead. The seasoned pilot who he met in Florida shared some important wisdom. It became a calming influence for him when he felt sorry for himself. When they met, Harry vented all his woes about his lost dream of becoming a pilot. He fumed about the Draft Board in Morgantown. It went on and on. The pilot interrupted him, "Harry, you might have gone to pre-flight, gone to flight school, and then went on your first mission and got shot down. That would be the end of it." The veteran gave Harry a different perspective in one short conversation. He went on to say, "You are here aren't you? That is what you always have to remember." Harry stated it turned on a light for him — yet his desire to fly ate at him all through his military experience. But everything he did in training and in battle, he reminded himself that "I am here."

Adapted to Wisconsin weather, Harry found no major changes when he arrived at Camp McCoy. He began his ground pounder (infantry) training again. The day he arrived, everyone was on a 25-mile march, which gave him time to store his belongings. The next day he was assigned to a unit. Although slim, Harry was one of the taller soldiers and his height got him selected as a Browning Automatic Rifleman (BAR). Harry had no interest in the Infantry but the Army did not care. He was going to do it — and this time there was no going back.

Hall was, and is, adventurous. He trained hard, but he pushed the envelope too. While at McCoy, they got a weekend pass. He decided to inspect some of the local bars in the nearby town when he discovered an unattended supply Jeep. Harry decided he could be more efficient in his inspection tour if he had wheels. He borrowed the Jeep. Harry also got caught. While waiting for his court martial, an NCO making the rounds soliciting volunteers for immediate overseas duty stopped to talk to him. When asked for specific information, the NCO told Harry that the Army needed 500 volunteers for immediate European combat assignments. Harry told him that he could not do it since he was waiting his court martial. The NCO replied, "I can take care of that soldier. The Army isn't gonna mess with that. We need volunteers. I can make that go away right now." Harry asked, "Where do I sign?"

Harry arrived in Fort Meade, Maryland, where he processed for overseas duty. In short order, he hopped to New Jersey and, along with thousands of American soldiers, boarded the Mauretania. The former English cruise ship, pressed into action as a troop ship in World War I, sailed performing the same duty in World War II. She was manned by a British crew headed for England. The English do not like salt, according to Harry, and the food reflected their taste. He despised it. The crowded ship afforded them little to do. He passed his time gambling and established a craps game in the cafeteria. If he could not enjoy the meals, he could find something else positive there. Harry was hot, winning half the money on the ship at one point. However, as the crowds grew in the limited space, the crew grew angry with him. They demanded Harry give up the game or do something that decreased the size of the on-lookers. Being the kind and thoughtful gambler that he was back then, Harry changed the game to blackjack. Harry laughed, telling me that at one point "I had so many 2000 franc notes that I could have papered the walls of this room (indicating the room where we sat)." The Mauretania put in to port in England long enough to let some of the people disembark, and set sail again for France. Lady Luck changed for Harry before they crossed half of the 19-mile channel. By the time they landed, Harry was so broke he had to borrow money to buy a pack of cigarettes. Where they went ashore, it proved to be a reality check for Harry. The cost of war hit him right between his young, cocky eyes.

As they crossed, Harry learned they were putting in at Utah Beach. Everyone knew the story of what had happened there in June, 1944, and he did not understand why the Army chose that location. He found a map and saw that it was most logical. It was the shortest path across the English Channel. They made the beachhead, off-loaded, and wound their way inland. It was a somber bunch of young soldiers who, with little noise other than clanking canteens and other suspended gear, passed markers on hundreds of hastily-dug graves. Harry saw the reality of war as they marched by signs of the huge price paid for the real estate where they walked in relative safety. They marched inland to a holding area where they awaited transportation to their assigned units.

Harry Hall, Infantry soldier and BAR man, became a replacement for the 28th Division, the Bucket of Blood Division. He was then assigned to the 112th Infantry Regimental Combat Team. They boarded a train and traveled across France to join their units. Everywhere he looked, he saw the remnants of what happened before his arrival. The countryside through which his train passed revealed more reality to him and his fellow troops. They stopped in Le Mans, France. The troops had time to stretch their legs. Soldiers did what soldiers do — they behaved as though nothing bothered them. They tasted the local flavor — in a pub. Harry and a new companion discovered a bar where the cognac was palatable. They savored it until the moment the train whistle beckoned them to hurry. Harry told his drinking chum they had to go as they barged out the door. The train was beginning to roll. Harry laughed, his eyes twinkling again, as his mind conjured that old image once more of a train creeping for about five miles until all the GIs caught it as it left town. Harry said, "We ran like the wind." Their next stop would be…

Arriving at the replacement area for the 28th Division, Harry questioned the unit's nickname. The outfit fought in the thick of things always. The Bloody Bucket Division took a high percentage of casualties. He heard that it was not unusual for them to absorb around a third of their forces in casualties for every major engagement. And they were engaged on a regular basis. They were on the leading edge of the hedgerow hopping across Europe. His assignment to D Company, 112th Regiment, as a BAR man introduced Harry to combat without delay. They loaded on a truck and rolled toward their area of operation (AO).

Reaching a drop point, their small group of uninitiated infantrymen left the truck with general instructions about the direction of their unit. Harry and two others got separated in the dusky light. They wandered on their own in territory broken by fields and ridges. As dark approached they faced a decision. They topped a ridge with a choice to make — left or right. One soldier persisted in his desire to go to the left, the other was undecided. When asked his opinion, Harry said he made the best decision of his life there on that ridge. He convinced them to go nowhere. Harry preferred to remain where they were and bed down for the night until first light when they could see where they were going. They heard heavy artillery fire exchanged. They saw the detonations where the rounds impacted, the red fire in the sky. Harry said to the man pushing to move to the left, "You want to go left, but you don't know why. You just think you should." He told the other guy, "you're just gonna follow. I am staying right here." They agreed that it made sense. It would keep them from getting captured or killed by the enemy and they wouldn't get shot by their own people.

Harry awakened the next morning to see a dead cow 20 feet away. The others scrambled awake in the morning chill to the same sight. They slithered to the top of the ridge to get their bearings only to see several more carcasses scattered about. Sunrise proved the wisdom of staying where they were. To the left, they clearly saw a German encampment. American soldiers were not too far away on the right. Their unit was there and they were as well, in quick order. Going left in the dark would have ended the war for them. Stragglers must not have been that unusual. Harry did not mention any questioning when they joined the company. They were instructed to dig in as soon as they reached Delta Company. They began digging what was in reality a large dugout. It was eight-feet long, four-feet deep, and four wide. They covered it with logs and any kind of debris they could locate that provided protection from aerial attack. The veterans suggested the stronger it was, the better. It was their shelter. The very first night, it rained for the duration. Harry woke up in an inch of water. The company spent the day tearing weapons apart and drying, oiling, and reassembling them. Headquarters Company was nearby to make sure that the work progressed as it should. That night the patrols began.

While in this area, Harry went on patrols one after another it seemed. All the platoons did. Harry and his BAR volunteered for extra patrols. It was appreciated — the more fire power, the better.

Their area was seamed with ridges, making it prone to ambushes. He preferred the patrols to duty in camp. One time, he walked close to a big, older soldier from Alabama. The man had a large family. Harry believed that made him edgier. They heard stories about Germans in American uniforms who spoke English getting near Army patrols and suddenly opening fire. They were both nervous, but Alabama more so than Harry. The two men encountered such a situation. Alabama drew a bead and was about to squeeze off a shot. Harry knocked his arm down, saying, "Wait a minute, wait a minute!" The other soldier turned on him angrily, but enough time had elapsed so that they saw the on-coming troops were indeed Americans. Another unit had strayed into their field of operations, narrowly escaping a "friendly fire" situation. Harry looked at me and said with the remorse born of experience, "It happens in combat."

Their AO, the perfect place for that sort of mishap, needed a different strategy. Soon the officers in the 112th ordered the ground-pounders to establish a system of listening posts — and rely less on roving patrols. Their sergeant instructed them to string telephone line in various directions with small noise-makers attached. Digging a small foxhole followed. They would rotate duty manning the observation hole. Those in the listening post were equipped with a radio.

Harry said it was eerie. At night, he could actually hear the Germans chopping wood, opening something metallic, and speaking to one another. If winds were right, he heard doors opening and closing. When the noise makers rattled, there was always an immediate response from the automatic weapons at his rear. Our forces sprayed the entire field blindly, from one side to the other. Harry believed he was going to get killed by "friendly fire" every time it happened. The night turned red with tracers the fire was so intense. The Company Commander controlled what they reacted to and what they ignored. One night, Harry called the rear and reported they heard track noises. He reminded me that if you have ever heard them you never forget the sound. There is only one thing that sounds that way — a tank. Harry and his foxhole partner thought they heard more than one. After a delay, the response from headquarters indicated that they were just jumpy and imagining things. They were not. The probing forces for one of the Panzer Divisions approached. The 112th became engaged in its biggest battle in theater in the months that followed.

The 28th and the 112th fought their way across France, toward Germany. Harry indicated, "It must have been around Thanksgiving when they picked a few of us to send back for some hot chow — especially some hot soup." Harry and his BAR were included. The Sergeant positioned Harry at a crossroads in a small village. Placed in a bar's doorway, he instructed Harry to observe the road they had not traveled, to cover their rear. Never trusted alone before, Harry was alert but nervous. His information indicated the road was mined. Surely anyone coming from that direction would be blown up and that would be enough warning so that he would not be surprised! The BAR was mounted on its tri-pod, placed on "fast-fire," which was a 20-round burst before it had to be re-set. Very little time had passed when Harry heard somebody coming on the road laced with mines. He stood where he got a better view and received a shock. In the distance, a German soldier walked toward him, looking down at the road ahead. It was obvious the soldier realized where he was and avoided the mines. Harry thought, "There has to be an explosion soon now. He can't miss 'em all," but there was not. His squad leader did not give him any instructions about what to do in a situation like this. Kill or capture? The German came closer and closer. Harry had him in his sights, under his trigger, yet he did not shoot. Soon he heard the German saying, "Comrade, comrade, comrade." The Nazi, his enemy, walked right up to him with his hands elevated. Hall held him at bay while he did a quick search. He discovered a small pair of binoculars, not unlike opera glasses, and packed them away. They were practical. The captive's personal items included a candle which Harry described as something useful in the field if you were in stationary base camp. He left these items alone, as he did the man's expensive gold watch. Later he heard someone in HQ confiscated it. Harry held the German soldier at attention until his crew returned, at which time he was pleased to turn the captive over to another authority. They returned with the soup, enjoyed an almost warm meal and plodded back into the war.

Division leadership established a rest program, attempting to give a few soldiers a little time away from the war in small groups. They had fought non-stop for months crossing Europe. Having cleared France, they determined that the small town of Luxembourg was perfect for the plan. Each unit sent soldiers for a few days to bathe and relax. Harry Hall was among the 30 chosen around Christmas in 1944. It was the first time since he made the beach in August that he and his BAR were separated. Unarmed, he was in a safe area. He focused on being clean, sleeping in bed, and enjoying a wonderful old European town. At night during his stay there, they were bombarded by artillery fire. The in-coming rounds took them by surprise. Window glass covered them in bed. The floors, littered by shards of wood and glass, could not be crossed without footwear. Showering soldiers found themselves almost trapped. Harry grabbed whatever clothing he could and evacuated to the street, where others were gathering. Unprepared for attack, the armory was soon open and distributing new M-1s to the unarmed soldiers. The NCOs created a couple of squads and made quick preparations to defend the town.

The confusion and chaos of the attack turned into a modicum of order. Harry's squad received instructions to proceed to a nearby abandoned service station. They were to hold that intersection. Stopping the Germans there was imperative. By the time they got there, it was almost reduced to rubble. They had no anti-tank weapons and from the night's sounds, it was a tank assault. The enemy infantry, already on them, indicated they were in danger of being overrun. Harry said they had no more than entered the building than a Panzer was "right in their faces." They pulled out the back, where he waited a minute. The Germans "swarmed into the building." Before they fanned out he tossed in a grenade. Harry believes he "killed a bunch of 'em. Had to."

Running to the right rear of the building, Harry emerged in the glare of a pistol flare fired about 15 feet away from his position. It lit them all up, including the enemy group of five or six. He emptied his clip. With nothing left to do but die, he dove over a low wall behind him into a gully, not knowing it was a deep ravine. Luckily it was muddy, or when he "busted his head" at the bottom he would not be here today. There was no return fire. He ran into another guy from his team. They headed for the woods nearby. Arty fire was hitting the treetops above them. Harry indicated it is a sound you never forget. Tree limbs crashed all around, with shrapnel hissing into the night. "It did not matter whose it was, it was going to kill you if it hit you. It was awful." Deep in the woods, they ran into some more lost Americans. They were soldiers from A Company, 110th Regiment. They were searching for their main body, also hit by Panzers. That unit's officers called for the tank destroyers from his unit to assist as the line was vulnerable at that point. The two American units had intermingled in the confusion of the nighttime attack.

Harry and the other soldier from the 112th remained with the 110th overnight. The next day it became obvious that searching for the 112th would not work. They joined the 110th in an ambush established in a damaged, deserted church near another small town a few miles away from Luxembourg. The 112th, like the 110th, was charged with keeping the Germans from making progress west. They could hear the Panzers coming. Harry climbed to the upper part of the church where he could see further with his *borrowed* binoculars. He swears he saw no fewer than 50 Panzers crossing the fields. There may have been 100. It was an awesome — no, horrible sight for him. He saw one leaving the small town, heading toward them in the early morning light. There was one driving down the street of the town, too. He saw a sergeant jump in front of it, armed only with his rifle, gesturing wildly. The NCO put the weapon to his shoulder and opened fire until his weapon was empty. Then he stood there. Harry watched in shock as the tank crushed the man. Harry looked at me — "The man just lost it or something."

Harry watched the tanks advance toward their position. A tank destroyer hidden behind a barn not far from his church building took out the first one. While that transpired, another Panzer closed on his position. Harry was close to the tank destroyers' position when they began taking a tremendous amount of fire. The Germans had them spotted and they were going to eliminate them.

The Panzers could not fire their big guns while moving. Discretion being the better part of valor, it was time for Harry to change locations. He could hear other tanks getting closer. He began running. Harry remembers the sound and feel of his canteen slapping his hip. As he neared a fenced pasture, he broke an old training rule. Infantry training taught that grunts hit the deck and roll under a fence when on the fly. Harry vaulted that one for some reason. He does not know why to this day, but the angel on his shoulder was good to him in the war. Harry laughed, "When I lit on the far side running, enemy fire chewed up the dirt at my feet where I landed." The Germans had expected him to react according to his training manual. They all ran, stopped, gathered again, delayed the German advance, and did it again.

The battle along the road was incredible. It was ironic. The 28th was being chased the direction it wanted to go. The Germans could not flank the Division to drive it back. At one point, Harry talked to a young replacement who, filled with questions, asked him, "Should I cross to the other side of the road?" Harry replied, "Why? There is no reason to." The kid kept insisting he should for some unknown reason. Harry told him at last, "Kid, I can't tell you what to do." The youngster rose and made it about half way across the 30-foot distance and got "bumped off." The thought saddens Harry still. He says he is so glad he did not tell that young man to go — he does not have to live with that.

Harry had to get moving again. Once more, they gathered in a forest. He met another young man — a tall, nice guy who never wanted to make a decision about anything. The kid, from the 110th, seemed to follow Harry's lead in everything. Fighting their way into another village, they sought some kind of cover — a place to rest for a few minutes. Harry suggested they find a house with a basement. Successful, they discovered a small abandoned place and entered. Harry peered down the stairs trying to see what it offered in the way of cover. The sound of pursuit took decision-making time away from them. They ran down the stairs. Nothing there permitted them a hide-away. There was nothing to crawl under or squeeze behind. The enemy found them almost the moment they landed on the last step of the stairs. They were surrounded by Germans with bayonets mounted on their weapons. And those weapons were thrust into their midsections. Harry believed they were dead on the spot — that they were going to stick those knives right in their bellybuttons. They were yelling, "Achtung! Achtung!" The German soldiers took them to the street above.

The ranking officer there, a captain or major, Harry was not sure, began searching them. He found Harry's personal items and stood there smiling. The smile soon vanished. Harry had been warned that were he to be caught ever, it would be bad news if he had any German material in his possession.

When the officer discovered Harry's confiscated binoculars, he went mad. His face turned red and he smashed them into the street, then stomped the pieces. Another soldier standing beside him grabbed Harry and spun him around. The second German held a burp gun against Harry's stomach. Harry could feel the bullets going through his body. He was convinced that he was about to die right there in that small town's street. But something stopped them — maybe an officer who outranked them both. When Harry looked around, there was a huge tank. It may have been a tank destroyer or command tank. It had a gigantic Swastika on its front and a heavy shield.

They pushed Harry that direction and ordered him to climb on it. Soon underway, they were under attack in seconds it seemed. They were taking large caliber rounds and Harry was stuck outside exposed to American shells. Harry tried to shrink, but it did not work. He attempted to climb inside with the driver. He was beaten back. Harry is convinced that they were 20-mm rounds to this day. They were huge! They moved as fast as the machine would carry them, over terrain that reminded him of the country near his home in West Virginia.

Harry believes they moved about three miles, where they joined with other German units which had thousands of American prisoners. The day became the most depressing one of his life. From his position on the tank, he saw lines of POWs. He estimated about 20,000 of them and his heart sank. He noted at this point of the story that he has a book which states there were approximately 8,000 POWs taken during and after the Battle of the Bulge. He indicated that the Germans fielded 13 Infantry Divisions and nine Panzer Divisions to firm up the defenses blocking the assault on Germany. Harry saw that power and the POWs and "could not believe we could stand against these guys. He worried about it." At that moment, he believed we had lost the war. All he saw was doom.

His voice cracking, he continued to tell me the story of his captivity. Harry went to Northeast Germany to a prison camp named Stalag 9b, which housed French, Jewish and other prisoners. The Nazis added Americans to its vast population. The reception people gave him a little piece of bread and some water. They confiscated all his personal belongings. The whole time he was there, he never had enough to eat. It was a way of life. The Americans did their best to get along.

Harry encountered another prisoner who was a stabilizing influence. The man carried a small New Testament in his shirt pocket. It had bullet fragments in it. Harry saw them with his own eyes. The man, hit in combat by a round next to his heart, was saved when his Bible absorbed the bullet. He found his faith there in battle. The man used the Testament to help the other prisoners.

One morning, the Germans marched them all out of their building. It was winter and eight inches of snow covered the ground. Harry's left foot was severely frost-bitten. The German guards kept them at attention in formation all day. It was brutal — without food, drink, and warmth of any kind, even as poor as those things were. Someone had stolen a loaf of bread, killing a baker during the act. The guards were going to kill everyone in order to find that person. Somebody was going to provide the person or the information about who the person was. If that did not happen, they were all going to die there in the cold. The story was they got the thief. Harry said, "I don't know if he was turned in or if they found him, but they got him. Otherwise I would not be here."

"They were running things tough. They were picking out people with Jewish names and even people who just looked Jewish, but they didn't have enough for a special work detail. They wanted 30 more and promised more food if people volunteered for it. I did and it was the worst decision I ever made." They brought in a train to move them. They loaded them on cattle cars which were the nastiest things Harry had ever seen. The make-shift latrines were horrible. Harry reminded me that he was from coal country and had seen some pretty crude facilities in the mines. The crap-box was eight feet by two and never emptied while they were aboard. In fact, it had been used and filled before they were loaded. The urinals were tall, milk-can-like things that were already full too. They smelled so bad that they pushed straw around them so they could urinate in that. Every time they hit a rough spot in the tracks, the stuff splashed over the sides. They were four days in transit — without food. The most vivid thing in his mind is Christmas Day on his holiday train. He was hungry and thirsty. Harry Hall scraped the frost from the barbed wire and stuffed it in his mouth. It gave him the sensation of eating while providing some much needed moisture for his body.

During the train transfer, the POWs were trapped in their cars during an aerial dogfight. Somebody strafed them. They never knew if it was a Nazi plane or Allied. The man next to Harry was shot through the throat and killed. The prisoners broke from the train only to be fired on by the guards. After being herded back aboard, the guards locked them into the cars and sought cover alongside the railway. Hot lead continued to pierce the sides of the flimsy cattle cars, killing more prisoners until the planes left the area. They completed the journey with the corpses, arriving in Camp Berga — to discover broken promises were the least of their misery.

Harry Hall learned the story of Camp Berga very soon. The smells there told him even before the words slammed into his ears. A Jewish slave labor camp, the Germans drew no lines when it came to spreading the misery around. Manned by German SS-like troops it was a viciously-operated facility.

Harry said he did not think that the staff there was SS, but they were only a notch below. They were highly trained and disciplined. He picked the Jews out soon. They were dressed alike and housed together. He was still in his uniform and remains mystified to this day that it survived his ordeal. The work detail was digging 15 tunnels back into the mountain, each around eighty feet deep. Harry gleaned the information in bits and pieces. As far as he could determine, they were all going about the same depth. At first he thought they were constructing a bunker complex, but later heard the Germans planned to develop some exotic fuel system below ground. The mountain was made of very heavy slate and the shafts had no ventilation. Since there were mere Jews and other POWs working in it, safety precautions were unnecessary.

They began work at sun-up and kept at it, often with no food breaks, until sundown. The non-Jewish prisoners muscled the slate removal carts, two to a cart. His job was on a cart. Harry remained underground until the digging crew knocked down a couple giant pieces of slate. He and his partner loaded them — and they were *heavy* — on the cart, removed them from the tunnel and dumped them. Two prisoners filled a cart. Harry indicated his coffee table as a rough estimate of the length of a piece and approximately eight inches thick. Hard work beyond comprehension and little food turned them all into even worse specimens of humanity than they had been. Bread and water were the staples in their diet.

Harry, no matter how emaciated he became, retained his fire. One day he decided pushing his luck was worth whatever it cost him. It took a partner, however, and that day Walter had to agree. After hearing his plan, Walter agreed to torment the Nazis. There was a creek at the end of the downhill rail run to the slate dump. The cars were almost exact duplicates of those used in the mines in Harry's West Virginia. The carts tilted for slate dumping. The men used a large piece of lumber to both brake at the end of the run and dump the car. Harry thought he could use the same lumber to make the car flip into the stream. The Germans considered it a river. Harry needed Walter to feign falling when cued so he could run around the cart and jam the wood under it at the right moment. It had to look like an emergency stop — it had to appear as though Harry were rushing to his partner's aid. Timing was crucial.

Harry and Walter moved a load or two more as required. The day passed and the guards relaxed a bit. The moment came, Harry signaled Walter and it was game on for them. The next load would be the one. They exited the tunnel and rolled down the track as usual. The cart gained a little momentum. Near the bottom of the run Harry signaled Walter who stumbled and fell on signal. Harry's partner earned his Oscar that day. Harry jammed the lumber under the wheels of the cart at the point he hoped it would provide maximum air time. Harry said it flipped beautifully. Splash-crash! It landed in the river, about a third of the way out from the bank, on its top. The guards heard it and came on the fly. Harry could not understand the words, but he understood the gestures. They were so angry that regret edged near the surface of his face. Looking at Walter, he saw the same dread appearing in his eyes as well. Harry, shoved to where Walter climbed to his feet slowly, joined his partner in waiting for the Firing Squad.

The Americans realized that Germans had no compunction about killing POWs. One of their numbers had tried escaping. He was caught and shot. The Germans wrapped him in a white trench coat and laid him in a wagon to decompose, as a reminder to the rest as to the results of escape attempts. The prisoners had to walk by the wagon every day, twice a day. They worried in stone-faced silence.

They received another lesson then. They discovered how much the Nazis hated Jews. The guards went to the shafts, dragged some Jews out and down to the river. The Jews were thrown into the icy water and forced to right the cart, drag it ashore and push it back on the tracks. Harry and Walter stood by, heads hanging in guilt, watching an un-intended consequence.

Harry, strength waning, decided he would make an escape attempt. There would be no such foolishness like stealing bread. That did nothing but alert them. A nearby barn had a hole in its floor, which he was convinced led to the outside. His plan included another distraction involving a fake fall. This fall would get nobody in trouble — and he thought he knew someone willing to be his accomplice. Once confirmed, he would establish the timing. He realized another element was necessary. As they marched back to their building at the day's end, the leader of the column carried a lantern. It had to be extinguished. After another discussion with his accomplice, they adjusted the plan without difficulty.

When the timing was right, the conditions deemed correct, the plan kicked in on cue. Harry's buddy fell, the light went out and Harry scurried into the hole. He remained there, like a rat, overnight. When enough time elapsed the next morning, he chose to make his exit. Peeking out of the barn's door, he confirmed that work seemed to be progressing as usual. No searches were being conducted in his area. He stayed low and started across a field behind the barn. Harry had not gone 30 feet when he found himself surrounded by a bevy of farmers. They all had very sharp pitchfork tines pointed at his midsection. It was another of those "I am dead" moments. They held him until the Nazis came. Harry never went into detail about the punishment meted to him after the incident. He did mention during our talk that after so much abuse, death is not so undesirable.

Every day for months, Harry had to pass a low brick building when he marched to work in the morning. When he returned at night, it was along the same path. He smelled flesh as he did so. He knew what it was, but it was confirmed later. The Jews were gassed there. He knew the soldiers carted them from the caves when they had been worked until there was nothing left, when they were useless. Once when we spoke on the phone, he mentioned seeing them loaded on boxcars and hauled away. Stacked like cordwood, the Germans did not even check for life as they loaded them on the trains. If they were not dead, they soon would be. An oppressive air hovered over Camp Berga which anyone who was there and survived, remembers forever. It was a death camp, a slave labor camp. He lived it for months — and he survived — somehow.

April 1, 1945 arrived. The Germans had the Allied prisoners fall out and be counted. Harry remembers that morning well. There were 304 of them. They were told they were going to march somewhere, but he had no idea where they were going. He also had no idea how they could possibly do it. Many of the men could barely stand. The poor food, terrible conditions, and intense labor left them mere skeletons. For months, they had scraped roots from side ditches, unidentifiable roots, but something they could chew. The Germans rationed their water, provided a sliver of bread, and all the cattle-beets they wanted. The beets destroyed their intestines. Livestock struggled to digest those crude, bulbous monstrosities. They are about the fourth level of preference on the beet chart for animal feed. Every man there had more parasites in their digestive systems than anything normal to the human species. To the man, they had cramps almost constantly and diarrhea became normal. Marching? How?

There was one thing all the prisoners knew from observation. If a man turned pale gray, he had about three days to live. Many of the 304 included in the morning count looked like the clouds forming overhead. Shocked, Harry received his personal items from one of the guards. They kept them from the time of their capture until that moment. His blue folder was there. His family pictures were there. The old picture of the girl he dated was there. His two to three inch piece of mirror was there. If he looked at himself, he could get his "death notice." He chose not to look right away, but he could not resist for long. A very faint gray, he recognized what it meant. He also knew what lay ahead on the trail. In camp, the guards shot prisoners when they fell out on the job. If a man dropped from complete exhaustion, the guard held his pistol behind the most exposed ear and shot him. The other prisoners had to bury their own. Harry's man with the Testament had volunteered for the work detail too. He read the 23rd Psalm for every burial and he read it several times at Berga. Harry's instincts told him that he would get more than one chance on the march as well.

Weaker, Harry knew that were he to escape it had to be soon. Not knowing their destination, his logic told him it could be some place even worse than the one they left. The first day's march went as he predicted. He checked the mirror. Grayer. Tomorrow would be the day.

One thing in his favor was that the guards were different when the march took place. Before the time the German officers announced the march, there was a literal "changing of the guard." The highly trained cadres were pulled to the front, where apparently things were not going well for the Nazi Army. They were replaced by much kinder soldiers of the everyday type, more like our men. The replacements were the infirm, the wounded and recovering, the battle weary, the very young, and the very old. They would follow orders on the march, but with more reluctance and less pleasure.

Harry began marching after a meager breakfast of bread, water, and leafy things he yanked off some carrot tops near a fence row beside the road. It did not take long before the marchers began to lag and the lines stretched. He checked his mirror. The gray in his countenance was more marked. Why not now? He began to fall behind. Soon he had dropped behind by two miles or more and nobody seemed to notice. Harry just fell face down in the road and laid there. He really did not care what happened at that point. It was not long before he heard voices speaking in German. They approached him. Bullets piercing his hide would not have surprised him. They may not have disappointed him. Que sera. Harry stated, "I didn't know many German words. I should have, but I didn't. I knew bread and water. That was it." Hands grabbed him and rolled him over. He mumbled the words he knew. His eyes flickered open to see a big, stout German farm girl standing above him. Suddenly she shoved a raw egg in his mouth. He remembers thinking, "What do I do with this?" The uncooked food took care of itself. She dribbled water into his mouth next. They lifted and moved him to a nearby village he did not even remember walking through, where they hid him away upstairs in some sort of building. He thinks it was a barn. During the day the girl brought him morsels of food. He slept in the warmth of the straw there until the next morning.

Even a little recovery emboldened him. Harry climbed down the next morning with the intent of making a getaway. He emerged from the darkness to find himself once again surrounded by German soldiers. Soon Harry was back with the same group, in the same marching order, going to the same place, only a few miles further along.

They marched from April 1st until April 23rd, 1945. During the march Harry learned that the Germans had violated the Geneva Convention by keeping the American POWs at Camp Berga, not to mention how they treated them. They were virtually treated the same as the Jews except for the gas chamber. The Nazis were losing the War and they did not want to get caught with them there so they moved them in an attempt to cover it up. In looking up spellings on-line (Wikipedia) I discovered our government aided in the cover-up and never told the American public that it happened. At any rate, Harry and the other POWs marched. The further away they got, the more relaxed it seems they were. Harry never mentioned a goal. I wonder if they were marching until the American forces caught them. They were in a village days into the journey and the Germans found some peas. Harry believed he could remember how to make pea soup. He was elected to try.

Harry entered a barn to attempt his long unused cooking skills. He tried his best, but the recipe eluded him. Not wanting to waste all the peas, he was ready to concede he could not do it alone. He stepped to the door and he heard that old familiar sound of tank tracks rattling in the distance. It was a chilly, misty morning. He could not see, but he could hear. Afraid of getting caught in a cross fire, Harry ran back in the barn and climbed into the rafters. Hearing no firing after a few minutes he decided to jump down. "What if they are Americans?"

He dropped to the floor. It hurt. He turned an ankle. He told himself, "It is not that bad, I am getting outside!" He checked his mirror for some reason. He was gray. He realized," If they are here now it is too late. I am a dead man anyway." It was depressing.

Harry ran into the street and looked down the road, down the mountain toward the sounds. Harry said in muted tones, "I never considered myself a patriotic man before that moment. I can't describe the joy or the feeling I had then. I can't put the happiness into words. It was incredible. You had to be there.

I looked and there they were. There it was. There is nothing like seeing Old Glory fluttering on the front of a Jeep followed by hundreds of tanks, all coming out of the mist — to save you."

The liberators embraced Harry and the others on the spot. The celebration was immediate. The American soldiers brought champagne. Giving Harry his own bottle, they insisted he drink up. He was too weak to remove the cork. Somebody removed it for him and he tipped the bottle to let the liquid flow. The next thing he knew it was three days later and he was in a German hospital with a German doctor and nurse standing over him. She bathed him with kerosene to kill the lice. Americans talked in the background, discussing the cablegram they prepared to send his family at home. They determined he had no survival prospects. The notification to his next of kin had to be done. Harry, unable to speak and near death, could still hear their words. Harry looked at me then, and said, "Never assume that a person in that shape can't hear you. Since that day, I have never forgotten that. I was aware of everything going on around me. They weighed me, but they stepped away. I could not hear the numbers." Harry's voice grew weaker as we talked about that moment in the hospital. His emotions and the pain of the memory challenged his iron control just a bit. He lived to be transferred. He looked at me and said, "I fooled 'em."

In a hospital in Reims, France, Harry's weight, taken where he could hear it that time, had improved to almost 80 pounds. A team of doctors prescribed vitamins and shots in a desperate attempt to save his life. Harry indicated that he had 30 vitamins a day of every kind along with 50 shots a day. It was painful. They injected him in every corner of his body, every joint and any fleshy surface where they could find one. The most painful injection, liver extract, swelled the injection site at once. Harry laughed and said, "I am not sure I gained weight, but I sure swelled up all over." They struggled with his jaundice. His color was horrible. One day the doctor came to his room, punched him all over, with the best punch to the stomach and said, "Son, how would you like to go home to the States? It will be as a litter patient, but I think we can let you go now. Before we do though, I have a surprise for you." During one of their talks, the doc told Harry that he truly believed Harry probably did not weigh more than 70 pounds when they got him to that German hospital after his liberation. His survival was a miracle.

At 2 AM, the doctor came to Harry's room with some aides and a wheelchair. He told Harry that he had not gotten any pleasure from his stay in France and that "by Golly, he was going to at least see the City of Lights before he left." The doctor loaded Harry in his car and drove Harry to Paris, just the two of them. Doc had a bottle of cognac along with them, poured Harry a drink and took him on a tour of the town. Harry said he had two drinks and it was a "bad mistake," but the night was wonderful. Sick when he returned to his bed, doc got him to the air field the next day and he flew home to Fort Mitchell.

Once stateside, Harry went from Army hospital to Army hospital. Questioned repeatedly, it seemed as though the Army could not learn enough about his imprisonment or could not keep his records straight. Harry could not count the number of psychologists he talked to either. They did what they could to help, but he is not sure they knew what that was. It went on for months. Harry needed extensive treatment. At last the Army offered him a choice about where he wanted to be for an extended stay in one place. The facility in at Sulphur Springs, WV, was the best in the country. There was another near Butler, PA, which, although not as good, appealed to him. A girl he dated in high school lived in Butler. Harry thought she might help him recover as much as the Army doctors. He chose that one.

Harry had a tremendous number of physical problems aside from the psychological issues. His medical problems could never be cured entirely.

What happened to his digestive system and his stomach were unlikely to ever be better. The Army doctors were correct in that prognostication. They have never gotten better. They have been a lifetime set of issues, but the issues have not been limited to those. Almost all of Harry's medical problems are linked to his imprisonment in the Nazi POW camp.

The girl from high school, once a good Catholic girl who considered studying to be a nun, was open to Harry's invitation for a dinner and dancing date. After he settled in, he called on her and they went for a night on the town. She slammed straight whiskey shooters with the best of them. At the night's end, they went to her place. She laid out the ground rules, and they were liberal, but she told Harry they could play anytime almost — but. The "but" was defined with clarity. His friend had changed. She loved a married man with two kids. When he called, Harry waited. Harry laughed and said, "I wasn't the only one war changed."

Treatments continued. Harry slowly assimilated into the local society. His physical issues improved and contact with people helped him cope with his wartime tribulation. He met another girl. They dated a while, but she giggled all the time and it drove him bonkers. Her roommate, however, seemed calm and wonderful. When they arrived home after a date, the friend always had something baked and they had a better time then, than on the dates. Eventually — given that they seemed mutually attracted — they engineered more group events. Harry succeeded in slipping from one to the other. They celebrated their sixty-fifth anniversary on May tenth of 2011. Harry, shocked at her acceptance of him, thinks the loss of her first husband in World War II gave her a better understanding of life than the others he met after he came home. That understanding helped him heal and cope. I met her and she is a tiny angel.

Harry Hall's successful career as a sales agent and counselor allowed him to retire to Florida several years ago and play the game he loves — golf. The value of family led him to Indiana which gave me the opportunity to meet him. During all these years, the Veterans Administration System has neglected him in my opinion. Had it not been for Senator Richard Lugar's History Project, it would still be neglecting him. It is shameful.

Harry has very bad hearing. He is also very proud. The day of our interview he knew what he wanted to say. Questions are difficult. He told his story well and that sufficed. His comments about the levels of VA compensation over the years saddened me. I may be wrong, but it has been my understanding that any surviving POW is supposed to get lifelong support from our government. Harry did not. He was unaware that an organization even existed until a few years ago. Nobody in that organization volunteered any information to him until about eight years ago. Until Senator Lugar sent people to see him (and the man that interviewed him cried when he heard his story, as did I upon hearing and writing it) he never got the appropriate level of compensation. I think I have this right. I was really upset.

For 30 years, he drew 20 percent disability. It doubled to 40 percent when someone saw how low it was. When the man named Parent came to see him (I had the impression this was the man Senator Lugar got involved) it moved to 100 percent and he even got some back pay, but it is like ninety with ten for being unemployable. Harry never belonged to a POW group until just a few years ago. Nobody ever told him about it. If they had, he would have gotten some representation. Where were his VA Service Officers in the states where he lived? Where were his VA advocates in the facilities where he received treatment? When Harry left the Army, the United States of America did not acknowledge that we had people imprisoned at Stalag 9b or Camp Berga. The country did some time later. Why did our leaders not seek the survivors and reach out to them? The VA should be ashamed. Harry is an amazing man.

As far as I am concerned he should get a huge check tomorrow. All I offer is limitless respect.

By the way, he would make a great golf coach even now. And he says he will play again. I believe him.

Peace has its Price

The more involved I get with story collecting, the more it has become apparent that we may be guilty of devaluing what soldiers and sailors have done for us in times of peace. In fact, I am not sure there has ever been real peace. The Cold War had a kind of stress that is indescribable in many ways. The arms race had a price that is not just a balance sheet issue. Our military stood its watch, guarded the walls, lax at times, but in a state of readiness regardless of our attitudes here at home. It kept us safe. We do not appreciate the peace time military as we should. Many of those who served may not even realize what they did. Some had good duty. Others paid a quiet price that was just as great a sacrifice as any paid on the field of battle.

Many of them never realized the toll it took on them, not comprehending why they felt as they did at times. They had the same separation from home and family. There was the identical sense of loneliness at holidays and on other special occasions. Duty stations in different parts of the world had readiness alerts that may or may not have been explained as to source or seriousness, but they extracted a price in emotional strain and tension. The military conducted tests of many kinds in the fifties and sixties as the Cold War raged and the Arms Race sped along at an alarming rate. Technology and the race into space kept an incredible pace which was more than a stride ahead of the average soldier's comprehension much of the time, yet he was the "lab rat" that made it possible. Soldiers and sailors were the test mules for America without knowing it—and for a few cents an hour.

In 1955, Harold Thomas, from Appalachia, Virginia, joined the United States Army to escape the coal mines. If a young man did not want to mine or cut lumber, there was not much but poverty or a living just above that level for him in that area. The military promised training for a skill, a life beyond the *hollers* in those hills — and perhaps a shot at a better life. He left with a plan. He became a radio technician and part of the Army Signal Corp, learning a trade he came to love. Harold soaked up all the training he could, taking every school offered, and discovered he had an interest in the new technologies that were evolving in the mid-50s. By 1956, he found himself assigned to a new duty on Eniwetok.

Eniwetok is a small atoll that is part a chain of islands known as the Marshalls which became important during World War II. The American Forces captured them in 1944 and as early as 1952, began using the remote site for nuclear bomb testing. In late 1952, the first hydrogen bomb was tested on a neighboring islet called Elugelab during an operation code-named Ivy Mike. The island was vaporized. Testing occurred on Eniwetok until 1958. Harold was part of the program during his assignment. One of his duties was checking radio equipment for post-test effects. He and I discussed the process. Compared to our knowledge of radio activity today, it was primitive. The military learned some things on the ground at Hiroshima, but atomic science and technology was still in its infancy in the fifties. The gear they wore was light weight. Soldiers were casual when they retrieved the radio equipment from the actual test sites. The assumption was, with Geiger Counters which were simplistic, that the danger centers were primarily at the blast site. Harold Thomas and others serving there did not consider the radiation threatening. The military equipment they were given did not indicate tremendous danger and the warnings provided by the Army were insufficient in hindsight. I never learned with any certainty, but felt during the discussions, that while bombs and equipment were being evaluated, so too was personal protective gear.

Harold's family shared some of his story with me, things with which I was unfamiliar. At the drop zone, the soldiers used small observation shacks not far from ground zero. They were constructed of block and had a narrow window for visual observation. GIs were given goggles for observing the blasts. They wore *suits* to protect them from radiation when they entered the blast zone to retrieve equipment and samples, but some of the work stations were also outside the observation shacks. At times, the shacks were crowded with military brass and visiting political dignitaries who wanted to observe the tests. Harold told his family that they would crowd behind the worker-bees (in effect adding their bodies to the block walls as an additional layer of protection) to view the blasts. The shanties were packed like sardine cans for some tests. Thomas laughed and told his daughters that if you looked at a blast with your arm over your eyes it was like looking at an x-ray of your arm — you could see the bone through the red glow of your own tissue. He went on to talk about swimming in the waters off the island, eating the food in the chow halls there, washing in the outdoor showers, and all the other things they did without thought of the fall-out from the blasts. Nobody understood there were consequences for the days and months that followed the tests. Nobody knew. Decades later, he endured more radiation in the form of treatments for rare cancers borne of doing the job of a peace time soldier.

The following year, 1957, Harold Thomas came home and married his sweetheart, Sue Begley. He then returned to duty and finished his stint in the Army in 1958. He had learned his trade. He worked at other things for a few years until he got his opportunity for a career in electronics. He succeeded, obtained promotions, and moved to new positions as he plied his knowledge and skills. Harold was proud of his service and what it had done for him. It had been peace time, but he had worked diligently in developing new arms to make his country stronger and more secure in a world where the threats were increasingly more dangerous. Along the way, he and his wife had two daughters, grew strong in the church, shared great times camping, and did everything that warm and loving American families do while living the dream.

In 1984, Thomas began having inexplicable problems which his doctors chased but could not corral. After many referrals, an endocrinologist discovered cancer. It was a very rare malignancy in the upper region of his mouth, or perhaps under his lower brain. It was hard to pin-point, but the doctors estimated that one in perhaps nine million cancer patients contract that variety of cancer in that particular region. He and his family learned that it was going to be difficult to treat and required some unusual techniques to combat. Harold and his family embarked on a battle that would be his Armageddon. All this was heaped atop heart problems that had arisen and continued to worsen as well.

The Thomas family was devastated. Thank God, they were people of tremendous religious faith. The treatments started with standard chemotherapy and radiation schedules. Harold endured those treatments and continued to work when he could. That ended soon, however. Heart surgery and complications forced him to take a disability retirement which intensified the financial challenges of treatment.

The weeks and months that followed were pain-filled, but they fought through the fear and kept hope. The cancer grew. The doctors looked for more aggressive and radical treatments. He agreed to be a guinea pig again, albeit an informed one at this juncture. They traveled to Charlottesville, Virginia, for treatments, living in their camper, and enjoying time together while facing hell, but clinging to hope.

Harold was married to my wife's aunt. He was family. This was a man who was a prankster, a man who accepted me at once. My father was from southwest Virginia, but I was raised in Indiana. Harold Thomas invited me to spend a weekend in his pop-up camper in the Breaks of the Mountains State Park after my wife and I married. I was fresh meat for his teasing, but that was a good thing. The tradeoff was a good deal for me. I got corn roasted in the fire in the flag-leafs. Harold shucked the corn, buttered and salted it, re-wrapped it, and roasted it. We sat around the fire and learned about each other. We broke bread and in the flickering of the fire I became another member of the family. I have to admit that I liked it much better when he traded that pop-up for a nice tag-a-long trailer a couple of years later.

Harold was a big, vibrant man. He and his family were active in many things. When we took the trip to Charlottesville to see him it was with the understanding that we would be shocked. I had been hurt during a benefit softball game, thus had the advantage of some pain meds to dull the impact. Even then, I was shocked to see the paint marking the target areas on his throat and face. The doctors made them so they could pin-point the intense radiation they were using in his treatments. By this time they had removed a lot of tissue inside his head and upper oral cavity. His spirits were good and his wife was amazingly strong. I remember Harold laughing at me because I, in my medicated stupor, stared at the "purple exes" on his cheeks. He told me that they were proof positive of his value. Harold Thomas bragged that he was a treasure and even his doctors recognized that and it was time I admitted it too.

Their faith in God was their foundation and it stayed unwavering throughout the ordeal. We were glad. We needed it too. It *was* a shock. Working was impossible. The Thomases had a Yorkie named Pebbles that was Harold's best friend and constant companion. This trip was one of many that they made to the cancer treatment facility at the University of Virginia during the next several months. I know of nothing that excluded Pebbles. The dog knew more about what was going on in Harold's head than the rest of us.

We did not stay long and left shaken. We thought we knew how desperate the situation was. After the visit, there was no question.

In 1986, doctors confirmed that Harold's cancer was due to his exposure to radiation on Eniwetok. The battle with Uncle Sam began then. His insurance was becoming burdened and his financial situation was worsening. His nose cartilage was replaced by a plastic compound. Surgical procedures reconstructed much of his facial structure. Someone first meeting him could not tell how much his features had changed. We who knew him could, but the doctors were good and his treatments were the best that could be delivered at the time.

We drove to see him several times and each trip was more shocking than the previous. First a sinus cavity was gone, then the other. When we went and the roof of his mouth had been removed I was in a state of — well I have no words to describe what I felt. Harold laughed about it. He laughed! The doctors made him an artificial apparatus which kept his tongue from touching his eyeballs! He showed me! I cringed. I was speechless. I am tearing up now as I type. He had so much heart. And no bitterness. He was doing his job. He just wanted his government to take care of his wife — that was all.

We knew things were coming to an end when, in the late eighties, we went to see him and he sat in a darkened room and cried. He could no longer stand light. He could not stand to have people see him. It was not for ego's sake. Light hurt him in a physical way. His eyes could no longer adjust. He could only wear his denture long enough to eat specially prepared foods too, so it was out most of the time. His words had become muffled and often indistinguishable. Harold would talk to us but never to strangers. His pain meds were failing. His preacher and family were the only people allowed access. Harold Thomas's body was emaciated. He did not want to be seen and he did not want to see. The dog who drank from his tea glass sat at his feet. Pebbles was his constant companion. After a while, we only spoke to him from the doorway. Harold wanted it that way. His nose had literally melted. The smiling face that had once been so handsome was gone. What was once a cheerful countenance was hollowed and cancer-eaten. The man was pain-wracked — a tortured spirit. His wife could take him food and his girls could love on him, but the rest of us had very limited access. We and our tears were best taken elsewhere. He had his Bible and his television. He had one grandson, thank God, but he never saw the next. Harold Thomas did not live until the next decade.

Before he died, he made his wife promise that she would not give up the fight for his rights to benefits for what he did on that island long ago. The week after he was buried, she got another letter of refusal for compensation. Mrs. Harold Thomas appealed. Sue and Harold's lawyers finally won. He would have been proud of her. There was too much precedent. Eniwetok.

During the summer of 2009, we sat with his widow and remembered. Harold once tried to help a lady in Charlottesville who was struggling with a grocery cart. It was dusk. She saw his face and screamed. The mall guards apprehended him. Harold and Sue had to prove he was a patient, not some kind of pervert. He was able to laugh about it at the time. The laughter was gone in the last days. He was always a kind, giving man and a man of humor. He always served his country and his fellow man.

Harold Thomas was a handsome and vigorous man, bright and capable, with a wonderful family. I loved and enjoyed him. I was jealous of him too. He had it all. Now he is dead and I write his story.

Yes, peace has its price.

A Pair of Queens

One needs to go no further than his own home town for stories if he is a writer. They exist right next to him. I lived my life among those who experienced what I now seek to tell and I was oblivious. God willing, there will be another book in my future (I am sure I have said that elsewhere in this book) which will focus more on that thought. I had no idea what a treasure I had in my grasp as I passed through adolescence, went away, and returned to nurture my family in my hometown. Through the years, I heard brief mention of Prisoners of War being encamped near my small home town, Windfall, IN, but had never asked for details. When I did at last, the search for information took me to a pair of queens, one of whom I have known for years—and the other a new acquaintance. I met two ladies who make me smile as I sit down to write the story. They are incomparable gems — forgive me, honey (my wife), but I fell for them.

    I called Jean Plummer to make an appointment to mine her memories of the Windfall POW camp on a warm June, 2010, afternoon. I was told to wait while she checked her calendar. Jean is in her nineties and had to search for an opening in her schedule for me! I knew she was active, but that was more than I anticipated. She came back to the phone and proposed a "time slot" the next afternoon with the suggestion that I better make it then before she left for a couple of weeks again. I scheduled the appointment. I have known Jean for years. I worked on her brother's farm as a teenager and played basketball with her younger son, Craig. He was one of the best pure shooters I ever saw. Growing up we shared a lot of "moments in time," but until now I never opened the door to this part of Jean's history.

    I arrived the next afternoon and as I drove onto the property, it was as I remembered. It is a pretty farmhouse where I had eaten lunch a time or two, shot basketball, and worked with hogs when they were still housed behind the family portion of the land. As I parked in the shade of the huge, old oak trees, I flashed back to the sixties. Jean's brother Bill — one of my childhood heroes — and her husband Bob have joined my father in the next life. Bill was a big, powerful man who laughed at me a lot. No matter what I did anywhere else, I was forever doing something stupid in front of him. I finished 1969 in the same way. My visit with Jean dredged up that memory as well. I graduated from high school in 1966 — from that point my life was a series of explosive events.

In October, 1967 I went to Fort Campbell, KY, for Basic Training. From there I went to Fort Polk, LA, for Advanced Infantry Training at Tiger Ridge. My next stop was Vietnam in March of 1968. I was busy for the rest of that year and into March of 1969, completing my Army commitment at Fort Riley, KS, in August of 1969. Thus much of the last part of the decade was focused on military activities. Five days after I left the Army in August, I was in Virginia registering for college, beginning a rather different part of my life. It was a dramatic change at a dramatic time. A few weeks into classes, I met the woman who was to become my wife. By winter break, I had convinced myself that I should buy her an engagement ring. I returned to Indiana in December, 1969, found work with Bill, tending his hogs during a very harsh winter on the very property where I had arrived to speak with Jean in 2010. To make the last year of the difficult sixties complete, I gifted Bill with one of the biggest laughs of his life. His laugh was much larger than my wife's ring.

My brother Jim was working for Bill as well. I cannot recall the exact job we were doing at the time, however we had been feeding and moving some stock and were in the sheds where both hogs and equipment were housed. The cold air was brittle. We had experienced several consecutive days of sub-zero weather with inches of snow and ice covering the ground. Bill had reminded me about the hog pit (a disposal pit for really disgusting things) on the other side of the fence by the sheds where we worked when we started the day. It was iced over with a thick layer of snow and looked like everything else around us. My brother was in the shed, Bill was moving a tractor, and I had completed my chore. We had finished the day's tasks and were ready to leave the cold and the stench. I was in a hurry. I grabbed the top rail and vaulted it while my brother and Bill yelled at me not to do it. Too late — it was done — and I crashed through the ice, sinking to my arms through the ice into the disgusting, undesirable yuck in the hog pit. My brother was headed for me. Bill was in a momentary panic and began to dismount the tractor. Each envisioned me drowning in hog manure. I think they had flashes of guilt because they realized that neither would resuscitate me. My reaction was so fast that it startled both. I grabbed the bottom rail and vaulted right back out of the pit and never got wet above my mid-chest area even though the pit was at least ten feet deep. Bill later described it, between howls of laughter, as a movie being played in reverse. I have no idea how many times he told that story in his life. His reaction to its telling was ever the same as well.

I was safe. Nobody knew what to do with me. The smell was incredible. I was not allowed in the Plummer house. Nor could I enter Bill's house. His beautiful wife Eileen probably did not want me in the yard. I would not get in my own car for the trip to town. Brother Jim was going to get me some clothes — when he could get the frozen tears from his eyes and face. Bill took me to the hog barn. There was *some* heat there. He took my clothes with him to his special laundry area and returned with some of his pajamas. The sight of my 200-pound frame in his clothing reignited his guffaws all over again. His robe wrapped around me about twice.

All of this came to me while I sat in my car getting the material together for my visit with Jean Plummer. I have no clue why I shared it here. In many ways, it explains how we live in the moment and forget to inquire about the history of people with whom we share those moments. We are too busy creating our own history to ask about their prior history. Now, more than 40 years later, I have been blessed with the chance to rectify that and partake of another slice of that family's history.

Jean was waiting for my knock on her door and let me into a small sitting room. Her home is inviting and well-furnished, with antiques and family pictures. It is as warm and attractive as she is — just what you would expect. She is grand. We sat down and spent at least a half an hour catching up on family things. We had seen each other, but had not talked. I teased her about her "dance card" and she showed me her calendar. Jean assured me that she was not going to sit around and get old. Her calendar had planned dates for at least a month in advance and was red with notes. She and one of her nieces (Bonita), a former high school classmate of mine, do things together often. Bonita is a Vietnam-era veteran from the Air Force and a successful banking investment counselor. Jean was preparing to spend a pair of weeks with her older son Kent as well. She was quite sincere when she told me that I was being squeezed into her schedule. She was leaving the next day. Jean then said, "Let's talk about the POW thing. I have something to do in a couple of hours. I don't really know a lot."

Jean recalls watching the POWs arriving in Windfall in the summer of 1945, although the years have rolled together. They were around from '43 to '45 in our area. During that era, the rural communities of America were important. Each small town had train stations, banks, schools, and a number of family-owned and operated businesses. They thrived and were beehives of activity. Jean was in an Eastern Star meeting in one of the town's multiple story buildings. In the forties, the town had a hotel and a movie theater among its several buildings. In the center of our town, we have an intersection we still call "the five points." There are five streets that intersect there. The angle street fronted the building where she was attending her meeting and continued to the train station, which was close to the other businesses I mentioned. The POWs arrived by train and disembarked, formed into columns and were marched northeast on the angling McClelland Street. The ladies in the Star meeting heard the clamor below and were "allowed" to gather at the large windows above the street to observe. They did not adjourn the meeting. There was far too much important business to conduct and Evelyn Bollinger led with purpose. Jean had been the leader the year prior. (I took some orders from Evelyn as a teenager. A young man in a small town can have several well-meaning mothers, with his own mother's blessing.)

People were lining the streets. It was about 7:30 PM when the parade started through the town. It was a huge event. Jean was unsure about the number of German captives marching by, but she believed that several hundred marched in formation to the camp. I do not know if they came on one train or several. She maintained that they marched by for quite some time. There were guards in many locations, all uniformed and armed. They made a left-oblique at the intersection and marched due north for two blocks. They were soon out of sight, but everyone in Windfall knew the camp was just outside of town on the eastern edge, behind the school grounds, where the fair had been hosted, as well as the circus on occasion. A virtual tent city had been erected there. Without seeing it, the ladies knew they had to make a right and march east a few blocks. The information garnered later included the fact that the local citizenry accompanied them all the way to their new housing. The Ladies of the Eastern Star were ladies of purpose. They stayed on task.

Jean and Bob lived the equivalent of four blocks from the camp. They could hear the prisoners singing at night. They saw the traffic to and from the area, heard stories, and saw the economic impact it had on the area. It was tremendous. Their first son was four years old at the time and they would not "expose" him to it by visiting the camp, as many people did. Jean was never close to it herself. She did not want to be part of it. Her father, Rome Findling, had farm ground but never used any of the labor. The POWs were there for labor in local canning operations and some of the small factories. Rome had a couple of tenant farm hands, thus he did not need field help. He owned a small farming operation and still managed Mitchell Farms at the time. It is impossible to tell the POW story without telling Jean's personal history. It explains why she remained a bit aloof from the less proper appearing aspects of the prisoner compound and its associations. It often takes years to become part of a small town social framework. Her father was growing a business in the community. She and Bob had a young family, just taking roots. Jean never said as much, but having been through it years later, acceptance is often hard to earn in a small town.

Jean's family was from the county south of Tipton County, where Windfall is located. Rome was a farmer there, but the Great Depression plowed his farm under, as it had so many others. The Findling family moved to Ohio, where Rome became a successful farm manager. His success there brought them to Windfall. The hard part for Jean was the fact that she never went to school in the small town where she landed. That makes assimilation difficult. She graduated from high school in Ohio. After they re-located to Indiana, she pursued additional education, which prevented her from being an active part of the small town social scene for a while longer.

Jean enrolled in a business college in Kokomo, IN. She had to be taken to Sharpsville, IN, to board the Inter-urban train for the ride to Kokomo. The train that came to Windfall was not for local transportation. The rail system was a major part of life then. The 16 miles separating Windfall and Kokomo were a major obstacle. During the week, Jean cleaned houses to pay for her room, board, and tuition. When she was home on weekends, she often secured work helping at the canning factory. After successful completion of her business education, she became an employee at the canning factory in the office. She was an adult before she began to develop a circle of friends. They were too precious to risk losing by getting too close to some of the frivolity associated with the camp goings-on. Girls in town were actually dating some of the guards. The military personnel had overnight passes and weekend liberty "in town" and that sort of thing. She heard that some people went to the camp and visited at the fences. She was a married lady with a child by that time and it was none of her business. She did not judge. She has never been that way. She is fun and laughs a lot, to that I can attest — but she was and is wise. It was a small town. Centralization of business and government has withered it even more. It, like me, is a shadow of its former self.

The Prisoners of War were brought into the area as a result of efforts spearheaded by Carl Scudder, a local banker, farmer, and business man. He owned the tomato and pea canning operation in town, raised those crops as well as corn and beans, and ran the bank. He had enough clout to get the camp in Windfall. It had been in Elwood for one season, 1943, and relocated to our small community. It was an important resource at a time when most men were away fighting a war. Local farmers came and picked prisoners up with their trucks (with a guard) in the morning and returned them at night. Scudder needed them for his tomato-growing operation and later in the canning facility after harvest. Sixty-five years ago, it was all labor intense. There were canning factories in Curtisville, Hobbs, and Elwood — all in the immediate vicinity. Elwood also had a factory that made cans. Labor was a scarce commodity. As I learned during this mini-project, POWs were used in several Midwestern states. They were treated well. That may be why they were never mentioned in any of the text books. There was no controversy.

Jean created a family-history book for her descendants. She shared it with me. I wish some of my family had taken the time to do at least some of what she has done. Most of my crew has a life line about two-thirds as long. Damn! I wish I had not thought of that. That does not leave many knots on the string for me either, but then again, here I am doing this and that is better than a sharp stick in the eye. We looked at pictures, some very old, shared more stories, and then she found a press clipping that raised my eyebrows. I met her brother, Garnet Findling, years ago. He owned a seed corn operation in Northern Indiana, thus I did not know him as well as I know the rest of the family. He was better known as Jack, a name given to him while attending Purdue decades ago. Jack served in World War II as a member of the Army Air Corps. The clipping Jean shared with me had appeared years ago in a Valparaiso newspaper. It was an interview done with Jack, celebrating his service. I scanned it, as my allotted time was passing all too fast.

Jean noted that she learned more from the article than she ever did from Jack. Other than perhaps his wife, she believes that is true for the rest of his family as well. He, like so many of that generation, never spoke of his wartime experiences. World War II was a void, a black hole into which he disappeared for many months. Jack re-appeared a changed man, going about the business of raising a family and walking through his life with purpose. He never spoke of it in Jean's presence that she recalls other than to say he was in Europe for the Bulge and D-Day — never with details. She did realize that he was a radio operator in the Air Corps, the only one of 600 who applied for his particular job. After joining in 1942, he became a Second Lieutenant because of his education and went overseas. The article filled in the blanks for Jean.

Lt. Jack Findling was chosen to be an early Air Controller because of his commanding voice and his calm demeanor in stressful situations. Aside from his obvious intelligence, the Army testing and observation indicated he could be instrumental in calming young, excited pilots during dangerous missions. The new radar was suspect and about to be tested under fire. The attack plans into Germany were unprecedented. The men in Jack's position were chosen to do incredible tasks. Without paper, without writing, they were expected to communicate with pilots, ships, and ground forces simultaneously. They were off-shore, yet the eyes and ears for fighters and bombers flying blind in all kinds of conditions. It had never been done before. During the course of Jack's duty, he controlled a variety of bombers, P-51s, recon planes, and the first Black Widows that flew in Europe. When the time came he floated off Utah Beach and had direct access to General Maxwell Taylor, who insisted on knowing everything at every moment. Jack considered his work during the Bulge more demanding than D-Day.

In all cases, he gave flight vectors to the pilots in horrible weather to and from targets. He gave target vectors to the Navy artillery units as well. Many of them were calculated from memory as everything was verbal. The aircraft could not return from a mission with unexpended ordinance. There was no way they could land on carriers and splash-downs were a waste of precious equipment. He and his partners often found targets of opportunity so that the bombs were dropped on prime targets and not wasted. The weather over Europe often altered missions, thus the controllers were key to effective redirection.

Jack was proudest of the fact that he was the only one in his group to get a confirmed kill. He gave a flight vector to a fighter that led to a confirmed kill of a Junker (JU-188). That was a banner moment for a remote pair of eyes. The pilot told everybody in their small world. They celebrated successful missions, but even those were stressful. They still had to get the planes and crews home in safety.

When they rotated back to England for less stressful duty for brief periods, they had other official duties that occupied them totally. During one of those stints, Jack earned a special commendation medal. The weather over the English Channel was notoriously ugly. Many times the pilots fought their way home, limping back to land-based runways. The Brass needed higher elevation positions from which to observe, both for themselves and their ever-improving equipment. For some reason all the king's men and all the military engineers could not figure out how to drain one particularly important hilltop. They needed it for observation. A good old Indiana farm boy taught them how to run a proper drainage ditch and earned a high Army Commendation Medal of some sort. Jack Findling came home from Europe a Captain. The Valparaiso newspaper told his story. He never did any other interview.

Jean Plummer is truly a queen and I had a glorious afternoon with her. She had a friend she thought could give me some more information and promised to call her. I knew the name and her son, but had never met her. Later that evening, Jean called and told me she had arranged for me to meet Mildred DeLong, the second grand lady in my pair of queens.

The next day, I called Mrs. DeLong to confirm a meeting. Each and every time I meet one of these people, known or unknown, I am a mixture of excited and intimidated. I always treated my own family of that generation with a certain quiet deference and I cannot help but approach these people in the same way. They are precious to me. If I treated them with anything less than reverent respect my parents would rise from the earth and haunt me. I may disagree, I may have something to say, but there is a way to do it and that is the way it will be done. I spoke with Mildred, set a date, time, and wrote down directions to her townhome.

Mrs. DeLong reminded me that Helen Heath had done a book about the POWs for the Tipton County Historical Society. I knew that, but Helen's is a very thorough anthology of recollections gathered over a long period of time. Helen is a local lady who retired from teaching in Windfall. I assured Mildred, as I had Jean, that I have no such aspirations as Helen had in her project. I want only to add a simple story about the POWs and the impact that aspect of WW II had on a personal level. Mildred understood that my perspective was much different than Helen's then. Helen is a grand historian and compiled an impressive local history, with many narratives.

A few days later, I knocked on Mildred DeLong's door and met another beautiful, delightful, intelligent lady who left another wonderful impression with me. She had celebrated her 92nd birthday the day before we spoke. Her mind is better than mine. She is lovely, her home is lovely, and I believe the lady should be giving life lessons alongside Jean. The two of them could embarrass a "slug-slew" of us younger complainers. We talked for some time as a way of introducing ourselves. We knew many people in common. Her comfort with me grew when she realized I was friend to some of her extended family members. Mildred shared her event calendar too. She is as almost as active as Jean. Mildred, however, does live in town and has many activities in her mini-community. She decided to leave her farmhouse at the passing of her husband, Loyd. We talked about Curtisville in earlier times. My family moved to the area in the early sixties and even then there was still a store there, a working grain elevator, and other small businesses. Many of the families in the small rural towns in our area have been there for decades. Ladies like Jean and Mildred preserve community history when they save their own.

She guided our conversation toward the POW topic with skill. It was part of her family history. Mildred had also created a history book for her descendants. She even went to the trouble of having it bound. She and Jean had both focused on identifying photographs and telling small stories in detail. Mildred had both sides of the lineage included in her children's family tree. It is an impressive, thorough work.

Her father-in-law and husband actually employed POWs on the farm when they were here, unlike Jean's family. She was not a quiet person on a distant sideline. She used her history book to show me the farm, the farmhouse where food was prepared, the 14 acres where they grew tomatoes, her father-in-law's photo, her husband's, and the truck they used to transport prisoners or produce as needed. Mildred walked me back in time. Her family moved to the Curtisville, IN, area in 1935 and she graduated from high school in Windfall two years later.

Mildred commented about the lack of interest displayed by young people about the past. I think we all feel that. Many of us realize we were guilty of it. Perhaps that is a phenomenon that was birthed with the Baby Boomer generation more than any prior. At any rate, the awareness caused her to construct her book. She knows they will ask some day. If there is nobody to answer, her book will do it. Mildred showed me her home place (once her husband's), the mechanical farm equipment, the horse (Lady) that was the most important part of the farm, and the information she wrote about farming methods. Mildred explained how they bartered, tried to plant their meager 100 acres by early summer, how they hoped to harvest by Decoration Day, and how everything was two-rows wide. She laughed when she recalled how picking was a two-person operation. If her husband threw an ear of corn at the wagon and hit her in the head, she got mad and quit, leaving Loyd to pick at half the pace. Most of the time she cooled off in a couple of hours and went back, but sometimes she did not. He needed to learn to be careful.

Mildred remembered the horse. She pulled double duty sometimes. Her husband's dad used Lady before her husband did. Lady was a "home horse." Mildred graduated in 1937, but in '36 she got a part time job working as taxi-dispatcher in Logansport, before she was married. Times were hard and everyone had to help with money for the family. She managed to get to the train station in Curtisville to catch the train to Logansport and usually returned home to find someone waiting there. Lady pulled the wagon when Loyd's father waited for her rather than someone from her family. If he had other business, he would sometimes let Lady go. She would return to the farm without guidance, every time. Mildred said Lady was a grand horse.

Mildred did not always have work in Logansport. When that was unavailable or when the busy season was raging in Curtisville, she worked at the elevator too. It is rare to hear anyone of the Greatest Generation say that idle time was a problem once the Depression was over. Even then, they searched for some kind of work. Forced idleness is a different topic.

The first POWs housed in Elwood, IN, in 1943, numbered 2000. By that time, Mildred was married with a daughter. Her husband farmed with his father. They raised 14 acres of tomatoes. When prisoner labor was made available to local farmers, it made economic sense to participate in the program. Most of the common labor was gone to war. At the time, all planting and harvesting was done with manual labor. The farmers had to sign an agreement to pay the government for using the prisoners, as did the factories which were part of the program. Mildred checked her book for the amounts. Her father-in-law paid 50 cents per day for a field hand. The factories paid 40 or 50 cents an hour. The latter information did not become public until the second or third year of the program. When it became public knowledge, it was a bone of contention among the prisoners. I suppose it was a bragging right about their value in the POW social strata, if I understand the situation.

Mildred's husband drove to town each day in the 1936 model truck to pick up their prisoner crew. A guard always accompanied the load. His mother fed them. Mildred's father-in-law permitted their daughter to stand near the gate to the tomato field — but no closer — to watch them work. The prisoners were always pleasant, treating the women well, as well as the farmers for whom they worked. She is convinced they would never have harmed the child. They were just people like anyone else, after all was said and done. They sang while they worked. Our government officials would only allow them to be utilized as labor for an eight hour day. The DeLongs found that interesting. They worked from "see to can't see" quite often, as the old saying went.

We did not discuss it, but I imagine that limitation was a combination of security requirements as well as the avoidance of any humanitarian criticism from some remote group. The local populace was aware that the prison population lived better than many of the folks in the rural communities where they toiled. Some were also upset that they did not work as hard as the locals did. It was well known that home-grown crews picked 100 hampers a day and the prison crews half that number. They were so protected that the farmers could not "lean" on them for better productivity.

Mildred pointed out one fact to me that she discovered in Helen's book. The ratio of guards to prisoners was 50 prisoners to one guard. As far as she could tell, upon arrival in the fields, it was relaxed duty. Once there, the Army men she saw often laid their weapons aside and spent the day seeking shade somewhere. The prisoners were content. They voiced the fact that they were much, much better off than at war. They were better fed, better cared for, better housed, and better treated. The POWs had no interest in escape or returning to a war-torn homeland. Most realized that at some point, they would go home under different circumstances. They were content to do what they were doing until that time came. It was a non-threatening environment.

Mildred reminded me that the prisoners had baked goods, desserts, good tents with floors, the best food, good shower facilities, clean clothes, and nightly song-fests. As far as she could recall, they had church services too. Many Americans were living on rations and envied the prisoners their standard of living. They envied the soldiers stationed there as well. The soldiers ate in the same chow halls. The local economies of Elwood, Windfall, Curtisville, and other small towns in the area gained from the program. Officers and enlisted men with families rented housing in the area. They were entertained there, became part of the social programming, and interacted in the community for three years.

For some unknown reason, the camp was pulled from Elwood after the first year. The aggregate number was reduced to 1500 and reassigned to Windfall, according to the information Helen Heath acquired and Mildred shared with me. It was rumored that the prisoners were unhappy to be moved from either location when winter approached. The Army felt that Indiana's harsh winters would be bad for the prisoners living in tents. Armchair officials forgot that the native land for these POWs was worse. They did not comprehend a soldier's living conditions in war, regardless of the season. It became quite a controversy after the first year in Windfall. The prisoners did not want to go to Camp Atterbury, where they would be housed in virtually the same kind of facility. Their guards understood. Fuel was added to that fire in 1945 as the population exploded in the Windfall camp.

The political powers decided to leave the prisoners where they were after the first winter. It worked fine. The government saved a lot of time, money, and manpower by not relocating people for no real reason. The POWs knew their jobs and those for whom they labored after the first season. Without notice, the government began shifting some prisoners to Atterbury in July of 1944, which caused problems. There was some population conflict that was covered by the local press in July, 1944. By August 24th there was a prisoner strike. They refused to work, trampled tomato plants, and had other non-violent unrest. They quit singing. The government threatened to move them all.

After the grievances were heard (most were related to the influx of trouble makers replacing the stable prisoners they had moved out — which the other POWs did not understand) things seem to have stabilized. However, during the winter the Army kept adding new POWs to the population as the war was being lost by the "Fatherland" in Germany. The population grew to 3500 by April of 1945, many of whom were hardcore trouble makers. It was an overcrowded camp. The original POWs were self-policing and wanted nothing to do with these "thorns in their sides" and reported their activities. Mildred said that she'd heard that some feared what they would say about them when they returned home. It caused me to consider the idea that the SS and other high value prisoners were arriving in the US toward the end of the War. There was fear of some kind of negative infiltration.

They managed to have some of the worst types removed to the more secure and stringent facility south of Indianapolis. I scanned the article that Helen had in her book, which Mildred shared with me. Mildred remembered bits and pieces of it, but she heard it as rumors. My second queen laughed as she recalled stories about the local girls dating soldiers. Some were reported to sneak up to the fence at night dressed like they were going dancing. She never witnessed it, but in small towns those tales become legends. Mildred heard them. She laughed, and wondered aloud how you "carry on through a fence?" Mildred assured me that those stories were just small town talk.

We talked about a discussion I had with my uncle about the POWs in Wisconsin during the same time frame. They were so integrated there that many discovered family members who had migrated to America many years prior to the War. After World War II ended and the bombs had settled, they returned to join them here and became good citizens. It was then that Mildred told me about a guard from her generation still living in Tennessee.

A few years ago, he returned to one of Windfall's Alumni Reunions to share memories about the POW camp days. He has fond memories of being an accepted part of our community. He remembers how well-treated everyone was during that troubled time. Everyone had a job to do and did what they could to survive. They did their parts. Helen included him in her book. Mildred included him in our conversation.

Jean and Mildred shared memories, history, facts, stories, and time with me. They gave me a personal touch about the time we had a Prisoner of War camp in Windfall, IN. I drew a real pair of Queens. I could not have drawn a better hand…anywhere, anyway. Thank you, ladies. I may have gotten some of it wrong, but never have I had a better time being distracted. I could see in their eyes that it was true. What greater truth is there than treating humans humanely?

POW/MIA

How can I get where his head has been?
How can I feel what he has felt in his solitary prison?
How can I see what he has seen through his bloodshot eyes?
How can I know what he knows in the marrow of his bone and flesh?

I cannot.

How can I smell the filth of his body unwashed and bloody?
How can I feel his frayed nerves and pained heart?
How can I taste through his blood and urine?
How can I sleep on his dank, cold floor?

I cannot.

How can I see through the slits in his four by four box?
How can I touch the splinters of his bamboo bars?
How can I scoop the slop from his metal china?
How can I feel creatures crawl on my skin?

I cannot.

How can I know his absolute loneliness?
How can I see the depth of the abyss into which he has fallen?
How can I know the agony caused by his keeper's boots in his ribs?
How can I feel the sting of lashes as they descend on his decaying flesh?

I cannot.

How can I know the torment of thirst with water so near I can smell it?
How can I know the throbbing in his head when he thinks of home?
How can I feel dry tears run down his face when no tears are left?
How can I feel the desolation that fills the absence of hope?

I cannot. I came home.

How can I feel his chill as he wraps himself in his tattered rags?
How can I know his forlorn spirit as he thinks of his lost loved ones?
How can I share his hopelessness as he realizes home will never be again?
How can I fight back the tears as I take myself where he must have been or is?

I cannot. I came home. I am free.

But am I?

As long as he is there am I ever free?
As long as he is imprisoned or missing, am I with him?
Does his spirit cry out to mine asking me to find him somehow?
Have we forsaken him by not demanding more be done than has been?

Perhaps.

Does remembering him in prayer and in thought free him somehow?
Does keeping his memory and absence alive pass through time and space?
Can he know it and can he feel it, and know that we care but are as helpless as he?
Is there a chance thoughts penetrate his cell so he knows he is revered in our guilt?

I pray it is so.
Am I, in my own way, a prisoner in my own land, without respect?
Am I a pawn in the hands of false prophets as they disrespect his sacrifice?
Am I weak; unable to bring him home if he lives, as long as only words are said?
If he lives, does he even want to come to a homeland that left him behind and dead?

I am impotent. All I can offer is the promise that I will never forget.
I cannot feel his pain or know his loneliness and feeling of desertion.
I can tell him I am free but part of me can never be separated from him.
Even if I ignore his plight, I cannot disclaim my country's neglect of him.

It is our guilt. Remembering is our duty; no matter the war.
But one was worse than all the rest.
It is Vietnam.
In losing him we have lost honor.
In conceding victory we gave up the strength to bring him home.

I am home.
I will always remember.
Am I free?
Part of me can never be free as long as he is there.

Michael D. Mullins, copyright 2007
Author of *Vietnam in Verse*, poetry for beer drinkers

SECTION II

Veterans' Stories — Vietnam

A Quiet Man Talks

I walk in a minefield with this story. Searching for veterans' stories takes me many places. Flying and Coast Guard eluded me. Flying no longer does. A friend flew back seat in Marine Aviation as a Radar Intercept Operator on an F-4J during the Vietnam era. Mr. A. Gale Barr shared a story which is in the "Doobie Chats" section of the book, but that one does not tell about his military service. This one does. The minefield to which I refer is one of my own making. Gale provided a lot of detail about the jet flight experience. I write about it. The mistakes I make will be forgiven, I hope, by any aviators who may read this. Up, up, and away.

I visited Gale Barr at his home. He prepared by doing some research about the F-4's participation in the Vietnam War. He loves the aircraft. Gale lived in it during his hitch in the Marine Corps. What he discovered surprised him. The F-4 flew a lot of missions, but was only one of many in service during the conflict. The pervasiveness of our air operations there elevated for Gale and became daunting when looked at statistically. The United States bombed Hanoi into near virtual submission without realizing it, yet that political reality is still unpopular to acknowledge. Their generals have, but our own social debate — well, that is another book and an argument for people other than veterans to make. I digress, even though Gale and I discussed this aspect of the 60s and 70s at length. We chatted about the civil unrest our children cannot imagine. Historians leap past much of it. Such an incredible period in American history could be a collegiate course all by itself. Back to his research:

- 649 F-4s were lost in Nam by all three branches with flying wings. The United States Air Force lost the most.
- 445 lost by the USAF, 370 in combat with 193 over North Vietnam; 33 to Migs (Chinese fighters), 30 to SAMs (surface to air missiles); and 307 to AA (anti-aircraft fire)
- 71 lost by the Navy; 5 to Migs; 13 to SAMs; 53 to AA; Navy had 40 air combat victories
- 133 lost by the Marine Corps

Gale assumed two things which appear reasonable to me. The North Vietnamese pilots were not as skilled as ours, nor were the Migs as capable as our F4s. The Navy had one Ace crew — Randy Cunningham and Willie Driscoll. The Air Force had a couple of five-kill teams. The number one Ace team belonged to the Air Force with six confirmed kills. The three branches recognized Aces in the same way — the pilot or the back seat officer could down an enemy. The Air Force called their back seat team member a Weapon System Operator (WSO). The Marines and Navy designated theirs a Radar Intercept Operator (RIO). The F-4B, first introduced to Marine Corps in 1962, began flying for it in Nam on April 10th, 1965. The Air Force used the C and D configurations, but there were others utilized as well in all the branches. The selections were appropriate to the various applications based on where the planes were stationed. They varied according to primary base locations and data storage needs such as the "black boxes" on board. Planes required to perform on aircraft carriers had much different demands than land-based craft. Gale prepared me for his story by teaching me about the F-4 he loves so much.

Gale Barr received his Draft Notification late in his senior year at Purdue University. Determined to graduate, he joined the Marines and qualified for Officers Candidate School (OCS). Given the option of going from the ceremony to Quantico or waiting for the fall class for training, he waited. It was 1971. Barr realized that four years of college life had changed his high school athletic conditioning into something less. He wanted the time to prepare for the grind he knew awaited him in Marine Corps Basic Training and OCS. Gale worked for a seed corn company that summer and ran. The choice impacted his service time in many ways, but he made the right choice. He reported to Quantico and completed OCS. Standard Marine Corps procedure demanded that he next go to Basic Training before serving as a United States Marine officer. Marine OCS, where one of his Drill Instructors had been a native of nearby Kokomo, IN, honed him physically and mentally. The Marine Corps Air Wing needed Radar Intercept Officers (RIO) in the worst way. The upper echelons circumvented their own system due to demands in Vietnam. Selected for RIO training, Barr reported to Pensacola, FL.

The training station at Pensacola, steeped in military history, welcomed both Navy airmen as well as Marines. The Navy claimed to be even tougher than the Marines. Anyone planning to land on a heaving aircraft carrier deck had to be the "real deal." The Marines sent its RIOs, the Navy prepared WSOs, navigators, and bombardiers at Pensacola. The "weeding out" process left no doubt about courage or ability.

Barr discovered that Marines trained in what seemed an antiquated basic navigation system along with their Navy brethren. Neither group ever expected to use it. In fact he never did by the book, but both branches force-fed a World War II system to the students. They learned how to navigate using the outdated three point "dead reckoning" system. Barr said it was backwards from anything he ever utilized once assigned to his F-4 squadron.

The F-4s were equipped with tactical navigation, or "tac-n" systems, which dialed in stations. The dead reckoning system permitted teams a back-up if a plane found itself over vast bodies of water where no stations maintained a radar lock. The Marine Corps demanded their Air Wings prepare for diversion to naval control in emergency situations. To Gale's surprise, an emergency situation developed later during his military service requiring the "three position" line mapping he learned at Pensacola.

Gale said, "The F-4s were quick. We were under someone's control at all times, wherever we were. Even when we had engagements, we were in someone's radar. A ground crew or a ship's radar gave us vectors for flight patterns. We got directions to bogies. We had pulse Doppler radar in the backseat where I was. It was crude by today's standards. Today's systems see bogies automatically and lock on them." Barr had to search and then determine if the target was real or ground clutter. He manipulated a "joystick" which moved an antenna up and down or "slaved" it left or right until he found a target. While at Glynco NAS (Naval Air Station), they trained three at a time aboard a Grumman business jet. The training airplane had three stations equipped with cockpit simulators where they learned to do target intercepts in the blind. After graduation, Gale received his flight assignment that remained his home — his family — for the rest of his time in the Marine Corps.

Gale Barr's assignment with VMFA 451, the War Lords, excited him. Reactivated for the Vietnam era, the group's history reached World War II, where they were the first in combat in the Pacific. Gale explained that VMFA means "Fixed wing Marine Fighter Attack" and all aircraft, whether jet or propeller driven, were classified in that broad category. Barr's graduating class joined one of two Marine Air Squadrons — his or the 333rd Shamrocks. The Shamrocks were manned by Marines whose last names were of Irish heritage. It was a Marine Corps tradition. The two units shared destinies and many assignments. When one squadron was reassigned the other found itself transferred to the same base, whether stateside or overseas. Much of Gale's duty was dictated by the timing of his OCS graduation in the fall of 1971. He did carrier support. The spring class rotated into the Vietnam combat zone. By the time the schools had been completed, troops were beginning withdrawal and air support was lessening. He flew with several pilots who did tours in Vietnam. They rotated out of combat duty after a certain number of missions or flight hours, but his flight time was confined to hundreds of hours of support and combat readiness training. Many of the pilots he flew with served in VMFA 531, the Grey Ghosts, out of Da Nang.

Barr flew the Pacific Rim area of operation for months, based at several bases from Turkey and other smaller island stations when off shore. Barr served at Cherry Point, NC; Beaufort, NC; Miramar, CA; Pensacola and Key West, FL, to name a few. Carrier cover and Cold War missions were routine but never safe. Between missions, the Marine Corps got them airborne to practice dogfights every day. Barr reflected that, "I strapped in more than 450 times." He recalls serving with a combat pilot and his RIO who survived dogfights with Mig action several times. Barry Lasseter and John Cummings experienced a lot of combat with the Chinese-built jet. They flew from the USS America on many occasions. During action on one day alone, they took out two Migs and then were hit by a SAM and forced to eject. Barr was presented a copy of a cockpit recording of that day. It is one of his treasured pieces of memorabilia. "Bear" Lasseter and "Little John" Cummings rotated into the Triple Trey, right next door to Barr's squadron. More than one of the USS America pilots landed with the Shamrocks. More than one had become a legend of that era.

Mark Keaveny, another revered Marine jet jockey, crewed with Barr on occasion. He wore a very hard-earned patch on the back of his flight jacket. The Night Centurion patch indicated that Keaveny made more than 100 successful night landings on an aircraft carrier's deck. Gale said, "Most pilots don't do that in a career and Mark did it during his tours in Nam." Keaveny flew with the 531st before he rotated to the Warlord Squadron. Keaveny also served as a Landing Signal Officer (LSO) aboard the USS America. Gale provided me with a greater understanding and respect for the pilots who are tasked with operating from the pitching decks of our carriers.

Keaveny and the flying crews aboard the aircraft which land on carriers wrapped wire around the wings of the butterflies churning in their stomachs every time they descended on the wave-riding broncos of the sea. Pilots see the target from one perspective, the LSOs from another. In Barr's words, "The LSO is the guy who stands to the side and talks the pilots in." He watches the Fresnel lens — the meatball — that replaced the deck man who waved the flags in the old days, indicating the tilt and position of the deck relative to the ocean. The carrier deck always moves in direct relationship with the heaviness of the sea swells. Gale said, "We knew that it could be a little dangerous."

The LSO and the pilot watched the glide slope when they came around "the corner" or "the 45" to line up on the deck. The "ball" lines up on the lights and the LSO tells the pilot the position of the deck for landing. Gale, as the "backseat", noted fuel level along with the pilot, and their relative position. He passed that information along with the type of aircraft approaching the deck if it was a night landing, to the LSO and added his call sign. Barr's call sign was "Swede." The LSO responded with "Hi, low, or on the line…" The pilot had chevrons and a light system just below his windscreen which gave him quick feedback for his airplane's position for approach. The system was called an "indexer." It was duplicated on the nose of the craft for the LSO's visual verification. It indicated the "angle of attack" for landing, taking off or cruising at all times for the pilot. The Navy, Marines, and Air Force each had slight differences in their systems. The pilots drilled until they had three things in focus at all times: "Meatball, line up, and angle of attack." If those were good, they were good to land. At night it was a common response among LSOs to say, "Can't see ya, but ya sound good…just keep comin'." If they were good, they "got the wire."

Barr assured me that constant carrier practice was a requirement. Aerial combat dictated emergency flight diversion. Flying air cover for a fleet sometimes resulted in emergency landings. Marine pilots trained to land aboard a floating runway as a matter of course. A mock carrier landing site existed at every air base where he was stationed. They practiced and they were graded. If they did not meet their training LSO's standards they were not approved for certain missions. He had the last word in that regard. The squadron commander was not immune from his dictates. Gale indicated that the general public has never been aware of how much air support that the Marine Corps does, from C-130s, to helicopters, Harriers, to its fleet of fighters. Preparation for carrier landings became routine during the Vietnam War. They took off and landed under the direction of the Landing Signal Officer and the results went in their records. It was serious business. He went on to explain more about the complexity and danger of carrier landings.

Barr's good fortune came from great Marine training, but more than that. He was exposed to pilots like Keaveny and others who had unusual experience beyond the textbook. The flight fraternity's normal activity is beyond my comprehension. Its members' expectations regarding daily activities include operating at the edge of danger as a matter of routine. Things that happen beyond their norm elicit conversation, becoming topics that circulate at Mach speed through their closed community. Some of the stories he shared with me were those kinds of things. Gale also tried to help me better understand the "normal" challenges in their work lives. He attempted to improve my understanding about carrier landings. The intensity, the physical demands, the danger, and the potential for calamity are much clearer to me. He talked to me as though we were in an abbreviated version of one of his flight classes.

During his "Sats Field" training, they discussed carrier take-off and landing. When they practiced they did the "touch and go" as well. It was imperative that the pilots knew how to get off the deck if they missed the bolter (the catch hook) and failed to stop. When leaving the carrier deck, the jet had two to three seconds to make flight speed. Landings occurred under full power so a miss would not result in a failed take-off attempt. The G-forces of a successful landing when the crew made the hook were incredible. The jets had arresting gears, but the deck assisted in stopping the airplane with two systems as well as the hook. There was what they called the water squeezer (a hydraulic system) or the B-52 braking system. The pilot used his arresting brakes and got an assist from the hook, resulting in a drop from full power to zero knots in a matter of yards. There was almost always another jet coming right behind. They were moved out of the way while they recovered.

Carrier take-offs were assisted by a catapult system. There were waist and bow catapults — depending on the runway you were assigned. It is difficult to call them runways. It is more akin to being shot from a crossbow. The catapult system was ordinarily a steam-assist system that generated cannon-like power that assisted the aircraft engine power. The pilots put the planes at full throttle, awaited the take-off command, and everything blasted at once. Coming or going, his hands were engaged fully. Gale explained the emergency procedures and his responsibilities when there were unexpected problems.

The catapults could fail to operate. They called the most common failure the cold cat, or the partial explosion. The decision to eject was at the pilot's sole discretion. If he made the call however, it was the RIO's job to make it happen. The F-4 pilot had his hands full with throttles for both engines. The rudder control and brake operation kept him otherwise engaged as well. The ejection valve remained in the RIO's hands. The seats were ignited by an actual explosive device in the cockpit that threw their seats 550 feet in the air, or high enough that the chutes opened with minimal risk to them. The canopies exploded off the aircraft and the seats removed them in a near brutal manner, but time was life. In fact, Gale said the Marine Air Wing's credo was, "Speed is life."

Gale told a story about a Grey Ghost who became one of those unusual topics of discussion. Even though he was an experienced combat pilot, he had to train even though assigned to a combat zone and flying from the USS America. During dogfight training, his F-4 got damaged. The jets have a number of fuel configurations for different missions. The jet he flew for his particular training session came equipped with collapsible fuel tanks in the fuselage behind the RIO's position. During the dogfight, his jet lost a wingtip. The piece flew back and ripped a hole in the fuselage, causing fuel loss. Gale heard that the jet left a 100-foot fireball behind it, adding to the drama. The commanding officer told the crew to eject, but the pilot and the RIO ignored the order. They wanted to save the jet. Like most crews and pilots, they had experimented with how slow they could fly and still maintain control of the jet. Barr explained that the F-4 was a Mach-2 capable jet, fast and well-built, but heavy with little glide capacity. Everyone who flew it tested its limits and became intimate with it. The Grey Ghost pilot was no different. Beginning his descent from 10,000 feet, he kept the jet under control down to 250 feet.

The problem was his air speed when he hit the deck. He landed at 200 knots. Most landings occurred between 140 and 160, depending on fuel load. He made it, although he did rip the arresting gear off the jet. They saved the F-4, but the story excluded the commanding officer's response.

Barr "crewed up" with a pilot he held in high regard, one who had tremendous experience in combat. Mike Ragin is a man whom Gale credits with saving his life during a 1975 deployment from their base in Turkey. The War in Nam was winding down. They had been flying missions related to the Cold War. Every flight had been done on alert status for months. Saber rattling in the Middle East and around the Mediterranean was a way of life. Their mission completed, they started back with a stop at Rota, Spain. Their squadron left to fly toward the Azores to a small Air Force base located in the Atlantic Ocean. One jet was lost in a thunderstorm near Naples, Italy, during the mission—thus they were flying with two dead companions on their minds. The members of the War Lords were upset and ready to be on the ground.

They were scheduled to meet a C-130 about 500 miles out for refueling. They arrived at the rendezvous point and found four other aircraft there with no C-130 in position. Gale received instructions to do a radar search — and then try radio contact. He could not find it on his equipment. Their ground contact found the refueling plane 100 miles ahead of them and west. When they made radio contact its pilot, whose call sign was Otis, said, "I've been in and out of the goo. Trying to find clean air space. You guys need some gas." He was right. They had been in thick cloud cover the entire flight. The problem was that Otis did not consider one thing when he made the decision to go search — the birds he left had reached their "bingo point." Gale explained that the "bingo point" is the point at which it is safe to turn around and return to the point of origination, but you do not have enough fuel to reach your destination. If you go further, you can't get back. Mike Ragin took three seconds to respond, "Negative. We're bingo." He responded before their Squadron Commander could, but everyone agreed. They turned around.

The next challenge facing Barr was finding a strange island a mere ten miles wide. They knew they were going to be close on fuel. Gale said, "At that distance, over the Atlantic Ocean, if you are off one degree you can miss your target by 100 miles by the time you get there. I started logging information on my chart. This was the only time I came close to using the old dead-reckoning system, but I had a lot of flight time by then too." He went through Cherry Point with Ragin and had absolute faith in him as a pilot. Captain Mike Ragin flew more than jets. In Nam, he flew the CH-46 helicopter between jet assignments. He had been shot down twice and survived. Before returning to Gale's group, he served as a Flight Instructor at Pensacola — but he wanted back in the fray. Captain Mike volunteered to assist with training at their sessions at the home base, even to the point of being critical of portions of the textbook training. Few pilots there matched his stick time. He and Gale began sharing information.

The Marine Corps maintained strict guidelines regarding radio discipline. Radio communications were limited to one word when possible and always to as few as necessary. There was no waste. It got to be a habit. The Flight Leader called for a fuel check: "Lead-4.5 (4500 pounds); 2-4.6; 3-4.8; 4-4.8" were the responses. They were about 100 miles out from their bogey and only two of the radars were working well enough to "paint" — or see the target. If they looked down, they could see some islands, but they were fuzzy. Gale's plotting and Mike's information from the on-board gauges indicated they should make the small Air Force base with some fuel remaining. The F-4s they flew carried fuel in the wings and fuselage. The wing tanks burned-off first and the difference then showing on the gauge was left in the fuselage. If a valve stuck in one of the wing tanks, it caused a serious problem for the pilot. He could not judge fuel remaining in the jet's tanks, but worse than that the fuel would not feed as it should. To add a little spice to their situation, it happened to the crew in the plane flying ahead of them.

Woody Ayers piloted the F-4 that incurred the gauge problem. Woody recognized his fuel level remaining the same when his RIO updated him. He was an experienced combat pilot too, having bailed out over Thailand during a tour in Vietnam and survived. Ragin got on the radio and asked if they had checked their flip chart to be sure. Gale explained that they all had a "flip chart," which was a book that showed procedures for most emergency situations. The book had tabbed pages for each topic with successful responses based on successful survival techniques from past experiences. The information gathered in debriefing sessions over the course of years created the flip chart and they were part of the gear on every flight. Their Squadron Executive Officer flew with them on the mission and was their Flight Leader at the time. He heard the radio traffic and got involved at the first exchange. He asked Woody if he had done all the things required in that section of the flip chart. Woody's RIO replied, "Yes, Sir!" Barr explained that the F-4 had three external wing tanks — one centerline and two outboard tanks. The RIO reminded the pilot to toggle the manual valve switches and noted the activity. The XO then told Woody to blow the wing tanks off to get rid of the fuel. Ragin did not like the decision, not at their distance from the base. His instincts were kicking in hard. His rank equaled that of the XO, but he was not the Flight Leader. He had more flying time too. It did not feel right to him.

Things were flashing through Ragin's mind. Too many things could happen. They'd been equipped with extra tanks for the original mission because they were crossing the Atlantic, thus they carried a load of fuel for Trans-Atlantic flight when they left. The tanks could hang, sparks could ignite the fuel remaining in the cells if they didn't drain, the plane's attitude would change with the weight differential, the drag would alter, the air speed would be different in seconds— and they could be hit by released parts the way the flight formation was organized. They were tight because of the weather and dense clouds. Dodging debris would be no picnic. Ragin told Gale that the flip chart gave him the right to make evasive maneuvers given the situation and he was backing off and going higher. He did.

Mike Ragin's experience and instincts, his quick decision, led to a lifesaving move. Two of Woody's tanks ejected and the third did not. It released on one end but not the other, causing a condition Gale described as "asymmetrical drag." The F-4 was heavier on one side than the other and they were still 40 miles from touching down. The XO's RIO contacted the base regarding emergency procedures in case they had to ditch or have the crew eject. They discovered from the tower there that the base was not equipped with any rescue aircraft at all. Only one small boat was available, and "Oh, by the way, seas are at ten feet." Gale confirmed from their position that his "tac-n" equipment showed a target lock at 40 miles. Woody's RIO confirmed Gale's data and relayed the information that his calculations indicated that they were at zero fuel. The XO told them to "trim the jet and eject." They did as ordered. Barr noted the location on his chart. Mike climbed high enough to avoid their F-4 and they lost sight of them. The XO confirmed "Two good chutes." They continued to the Air Force base. When they got within range, Gale called for permission to land. He got the okay and they landed on the lone, narrow runway. The small base also had one thread-like taxi lane. Woody's jet made it to the island, too. The gauges were wrong. There was enough fuel that it did not run out until then. It hit a farmer's field where it crashed and slid through three stone fences. Good fortune rode in the F-4; it did not hit anyone, although the farmer saw it coming.

Gale said when they came to a stop that their own plane displayed a red fuel light. They were on fumes. He and Ragin climbed out and went straight to the O Club (Officers Club) and calmed their nerves. Gale asked Mike what he planned to do if the XO had ordered Woody to bring his plane in and it had crashed on the runway. Mike told him he had already scoped out the taxiway and he was good enough to land that F-4 on it even as short as it was. Gale said, "It was great to realize that his pilot was always two steps ahead of everybody else."

They lost two jets on the mission and at that point were short four friends, two forever and two missing. They waited there for information on their team mates. A couple of hours later, the word came to them that the duck boat found them. They were safe. Several hours later, the doctors cleared them and they shared a toast together. The remainder of the squadron left soon after to return home. The two without a plane had to wait until transportation arrived. The War Lords squadron consisted of 12 jets when the mission started. It ended with ten.

I, like so many, see the glamour of flying. Danger is routine and an integral part that is shrugged off with a nonchalance that the public never comprehends. Gale said it best, "I buckled up a lot. I flew as a Marine for four years. I got out and missed it so I joined the Air Force Reserve and flew another two and half years. I had over 1000 hours in the air. Every time I buckled in I took a deep breath, but I loved it." Then he told me more.

Gale Barr never experienced combat. The Marine Corps issued orders and he followed them. He had simulated combat at every duty station after graduation from his flight schools. It was 1973 by then and troops were being withdrawn from Nam. The May, 1971, class rotated at least once. A few months had a tremendous impact, but that could not have been predicted. Gale went where pointed, as a good Marine or any soldier did. His Platoon Commander in OCS had been a Recon Officer in Vietnam as a First Lieutenant. Stationed on the Cambodian border, he once told Gale's group about receiving a call that "'friendlies' were in his area and would be in his firebase in 30 minutes." Thirty minutes later on the dot, six men dressed in blue jeans, black tee shirts, tennis shoes, and carrying AK-47s walked into the camp. They sat down, ate cold C-rations, got up and left without saying one word. Special Operations were shrouded in mystery, even to Marine Recon forces. Gale met a Drill Instructor from Kokomo, IN, only a few miles from his home town. "No slack" was fact.

Barr stood the "hot pad" against the Cubans during the Russian missile crisis. They were stationed near Key West, FL, on alert 24 hours a day, seven days a week. They practiced response times with the knowledge that a real threat existed mere minutes away — 80 to 90 miles from them. Their jets were armed with live missiles — Sparrows and Sidewinders. If any Migs left Cuban air space, they would never have made US air space, much less Miami's. When they were on the "hot pad," they were "geared up" 24 hours, then "stood down" for 48. If the alert buzzer sounded, they were airborne "in less than a handful of minutes."

The F-4 crews were taught to fight at Mach I or 750 miles per hour in ground-speed terms. The F-4 jet was rated a Mach 2 airplane, but it was hard to get it to that speed. Their saying was "Speed is Life." They did not like to go slow. They could not turn with the Migs. The Migs had lower "wing loading" as they were a lighter aircraft with different "drag dynamics." The Marine Air

Wing teams were taught not to fight them in horizontal circles, but in the vertical position. In a dogfight, after passing one, they went straight up in a hard climb. A visual rule developed in Nam that spread throughout the Air Corps. Whichever team member "eyeballed the bogey" called out "Mig!" so there it left no doubt about what aircraft was being engaged. Then the tactic choice became automatic. If the RIO made good radar lock, he could shoot them from seven or eight miles away. At one time that was classified information. It is old technology now. The range for new technology is often four to six times that distance. The Marine training preference for enemy engagement however, was a "bore sight confrontation" for psychological purposes. A healthy game of chicken at 1500 knots and closing often meant victory even if the first shot was a miss. They referred to a crosshair confrontation as putting the enemy in the "pipper." The Top Gun school discovered when that occurred, the enemy "broke mentally" if passed "fast and close, head-on." It gave your team the advantage. In a dogfight, the edge was always the goal. If the leader made that move, the wing man could break and turn, taking the enemy from another direction. The turn was called "The Hook." It did not matter who got the kill as long as the team succeeded.

I asked Gale about blacking-out after he mentioned the vertical fighting position. He talked at different times about the extreme G-forces exerted on their bodies when landing, taking-off, and in dogfights. The demands on fighter pilots fascinated me. I trained for combat, carried loads, walked miles in mud with heavy weights, but the constant pressure of gravity on the body is difficult to comprehend. How do organs withstand it? Gale admitted to blacking-out for brief periods during training dogfights when they made hard pull-ups. It occurred when doing a "six" or looking behind to locate the enemy. Even pilots experienced it. An experienced pilot named Cunningham related a real combat experience with a Mig-21 he encountered while in Vietnam. Cunningham told Barr that he went vertical and looked over his shoulder and went black momentarily. When he opened his eyes, the Mig was there, canopy to canopy with him. He was taken by complete surprise. It was a hell of fight. Cunningham told the story so Gale knew how it ended. The experience gives a flyer tunnel vision for an instant, or a flash of blurred vision. Their conditioning to the stress alleviates it in an instant. If not, the pilot slows for a moment to recover. It is just another flight hazard—and common.

I reminded Gale about a tale he shared once about an F-4 landing with fuel flooding the "backseater's" floor. Gale's buddy Domina had flown a mission in Vietnam and gotten hit by anti-aircraft fire. Their F-4 took flak in the fuselage tank. They returned to Da Nang with several gallons of fuel leaking into the floor under the RIO's seat. The gauge showed zero. Domina told Gale that the liquid covered the lower portion of his boots, maybe as deep as two or three inches. The F-4's glide ability resembled that of a rock when it had no power. Ejection was no longer an option—the seat ejector was now a miniature igniter. He and the pilot knew they were dead if he ejected. The possibility of death was high if they tried to take the plane all the way to the base, but at least that way they had a slim chance. Maybe live, or for sure not — hmmmm — they went for it. Once again, the results were obvious. Domina told the story to Barr. The pilot fought to keep the nose up and managed the last few miles on fumes, except for fuel sloshing around Domino's feet. The runway was cleared except for fire equipment. God rode with them. The fire trucks remained idle.

Gale Barr explained that there is never such a thing as a routine flight. People who fly call them routine, but are they? He recalled an incident late in his Marine Corps career as an example. It occurred in 1975 during a "routine flight" to Andrews Air Force Base in Washington, DC. He and Mike Keaveny were given the task of flying a Top Secret pouch to the Marine Corps Head Quarters from Beaufort. It was a short hop during the fuel crisis. The irony of the situation struck him at the time. They could see cars lined up waiting for gas as they circled awaiting permission to land. They were required to dump thousands of pounds of fuel before landing. Gale said, "The people below would have given their eye teeth for that fuel."

Gale took me through a landing in this story. The landing process is managed by Tower Control. After the plane is on the runway, the aircraft becomes the responsibility of Ground Control. Gale did the radio work while using his flip chart, open and attached to his leg. He referred to the airport tab — it showed all the information for airports, runways, taxiways, radio frequencies, and all other pertinent information for landing, including runway lengths. They were down and the drag chute deployed. Their ground speed reduced to about sixty-miles per hour, everything seemed normal. Keaveny listened as the Ground Control began giving instructions. The F-4 turned hard right off the taxi lane into the mud. Keaveny said, "I didn't do that."

Gale explained that the Phantom F-4s has a button designed for the pilot to engage when the jet is moving below 80 knots which enables the rudders to turn the nose wheel. Above that speed, there are aileron interconnects used that keep the rudder in a balanced condition. At higher speed, the plane is still steered with the rudders. When Keaveny pushed the button, the control box went "crazy." The plane veered off the taxiway on its own no matter where he steered it. He got hard on the brakes but it was too late. Sirens and horns blasted all around them. They turned to see what Barr described as the "biggest honkin' fire truck he had ever seen haulin' freight their way. We were at the base where Air Force One lived."

Mike Keaveny was popping his canopy and getting out of his seat. Gale did not wait for him to release him from his. The plane captains usually remove most of the ejection seat pins on the RIO's seat, except the final safety pin called the "face curtain pin." There are 13 pins in total. The last one is done by the person in the seat for safety purposes to avoid accidental ejection. He has to confirm whether it is in or out. Gale stated that, "You are sitting on a bomb. You don't leave it to anyone else. The seats come out at 22 Gs on your spine. It is called a zero-zero seat and will get you high enough, fast enough to save your life, even if it knocks you out doing it." By the time they climbed down, a Full Bird Colonel from the US Air Force was waiting on them. He was the Commander of the base fire team, which handles the president's emergencies if there are any. He has a little more juice than most base fire chiefs. He stood them at attention there in the mud and proceeded to say, "What are you blankety-blank Marines doing driving off my runway?" He warmed up from there. Even Keaveny kept his mouth shut.

The left tire was flat. The Air Force almost failed to tow it away. The Bird Colonel may have reached new heights had that been the case. They remained in DC for a week waiting on parts. At least, it proved no pilot error occurred.

Gale indicated there are amazing stories around. They are Air Wing talk. He heard two Marines ejected at Da Nang and landed in the fuel pit. The pit had been mortared by the Viet Cong. It was a mess, with fuel all over the bottom, yet somehow they survived. He heard stories that amazed him, and he witnessed unbelievable things himself. Gale knew the impossible was possible. He shared another example of the danger faced by pilots in the Vietnam combat zone. The Marine fighters armed with Zombie rockets, which carried 2.75-mm rounds in canisters for close air support, as well as 500-pound bombs. They loaded cluster bombs in alternating patterns, which opened to release bomblets on impact. Depending on the mission, the 500-pounders were altered by adding a six-foot extended fuse called a "Daisy Cutter." All these variations were designed to inflict maximum damage on enemy targets. There was intrinsic danger to the pilots in their use as well. The bomb racks mounted on the jets had two load points where the weapons attached. They were operated with electronic devices. If one end or the other failed to release, it left the weapon attached on the other end. The added danger to crews was incalculable. If the rear failed to release, the nose dropped and the bomb or rocket dangled there armed. The pilot could blow the rack off — in theory — but what if that act set off the weapon? Gale wonders to this day how many pilots and crews are included in the statistics that remain unexplained in the numbers of planes lost without a category. Or how many were there in head-on collisions or tanker refueling explosions — or any of a countless number of other ways.

Barr loves and respects the USAF. He flew with them while in the Marines and served in the Air Force Reserves after his discharge from the Corps. But… but, the Marine Corps flew F-4s the Air Force would never let off the ground. They were far more safety conscious. The Marines suffered from being at the bottom of the parts food chain. The Navy came first and next came the Air Force. The Marine Corps has always been embroiled in political battles, always fighting Washington, DC. The Corps' tradition precludes being buried in political correctness. It includes going to battle and doing the job, whatever it is. That attitude carries a price. Marines accept it and work with the tools at hand. Gale Barr is very proud of his service. Gale once met a Warrant Officer who wore wings. Not all Marine pilots were officers. The WO to whom he referred was World War II survivor whose picture is on the Hero's Wall at Cherry Point. He was a C-130 pilot with 20 log books full of missions. The old man knew Pappy Boynton and vouched for his legendary reputation. Their tradition is more important than getting along with the politicians in DC. And so they flew.

Gale recalled learning more from Ragin in dogfight training than any other pilot with whom he flew. Ragin taught all the time they were in the air. Alerting Captain Mike that their airspeed was below 400 knots became one of his responsibilities. Ragin was about speed and he flew closer to the enemy than about anyone Gale rode backseat to in most of his assignments. Barr interjected that after a head-on pass, flying through another jet's air was like going through a boat's wake. The plane bumped like a boat in rough water for a bit in the disturbance. Ragin was distracted after that and often failed to check his air speed indicator, as he struggled to maintain control. If you get slow, you die. After the pass, Mike's first goal was to keep his air speed high, then go high. Gale taught me that was when they were vulnerable. Going vertical scrubs speed and is high risk. For him to shoot, they had to climb sharply and slow, allowing the enemy to get ahead of them. Gale could make the kill then. If the enemy went with them, his pilot initiated what Barr referred to as the "scissors." This is a series of maneuvers with the enemy airplane whereby they weave around and up at the same time, gaining altitude while slowing to make a shot. The enemy pilot tries to avoid being a target. If the enemy is skilled, the danger is extreme. The explanation reminded Barr of a story about their training experience with an Air Force pilot they nicknamed "Crew Rest."

Crew Rest came to Gale's training group as an exchange pilot. He was one of the best Gale observed in action. He earned his nickname because he said he could not fly as many times a day as the Marines preferred as a rule. That jet jockey needed his crew rest. The name stuck. Barr cannot even remember his given name now. Ragin and Barr shared a memorable experience with

Crew Rest and his WSO during dogfight training 100 miles off the coast of South Carolina.

Ragin and Crew Rest engaged in the head-on and neither backed-off an inch. They both went vertical, engaging in the scissors, trying to force the other into submission. They climbed and climbed. Barr watched in awe as the altimeter neared and passed 40,000 feet. Watching the Air Force plane, Gale's mouth opened in shock. Then concern hit him like a fist. Crew Rest was dead stopped, both afterburners cold. He and Ragin were still climbing too. Their air speed had slowed too much as well. He checked air speed and they were below eighty knots. They had *all* focused so much on the maneuvers that they lost sight of the peril that they faced. Ragin fought the controls on their F-4 to avoid a flat spin. Falling back as Crew Rest's had was unheard of as far as Gale knew, but the flat spin was not an unknown in the flying world. He alerted his pilot about their air speed but it was a formality. They were still drifting upward. A thousand things went through Barr's mind as they floated there almost motionless. The classroom discussions about flat spins rushed through. He said, "You are a big, giant brick at the mercy of gravity. You are just laying there with no air going over your wings, no control without air. The plane will begin to fall and turn slowly like leaf and the nose won't come down." At the apex of the turn, they experienced zero gravity. Dirt floated up from the floor, his pencil drifted from his pocket. It was surreal to him. Mike Ragin fought the plane. They did not want to get to 50,000 feet where pressurization became necessary, where they had no chance. Somehow Ragin wrestled the jet into submission, managing to point the nose toward the earth. They had a chance.

Gale did his six before they drifted away from Crew Rest. He saw Crew Rest hanging there, beginning to slip straight back. Had there ever been anything like that before? In his mind, he told himself he was about to witness a horrible disaster. Ragin's skill gave them a chance to avoid being more than witness to it. Mike held Gale's life in his hands. As they neared the Air Force jet, they saw it slipping backwards, straight into its own contrail. Gale saw its contrail coming out its intakes. It was incredible! He could not have imagined that being possible. There was no air going in and both engines were silent — stalled without a chance of re-starting. Both engines dead meant the F-4J had no generators running. Without electricity, with no air coming into the engines there was no chance of starting them again. Mike and Gale flipped over, but their engines were running. They watched, unable to help. Crew Rest had no radio. They could not communicate with each other or with others. They were gaining speed in an uncontrolled dive. A question came into Gale's mind then.

The RAT generator — why was Crew Rest not firing the RAT generator?

He asked Mike. Ragin tried to stay with the other plane while Gale gestured and pointed at the area behind the WSO's seat. The fuselage area there housed a miniature generator. It was made for situations such as these. Gale saw his counterpart looking in his three mirror system to see if it was engaged. Barr explained the RAT generator to me at that point. The RAT is a small generator mounted on an arm and attached to a bottle of compressed air, all of which are housed in an area in the fuselage just behind the WSO/RIO area of the F-4s. An emergency button is located near the pilot. When depressed the motor assembly pops up, engages briefly, and generates enough electricity to fire one or both engines. Crew Rest must have forgotten about it in all the confusion and shock of the moment. His WSO removed his mask and began screaming. Gale saw it all. They were falling fast. The turbines had to be fired soon or there would be no chance of regaining control before it was too late. The ocean's surface was rushing toward them. At last he got the message to Crew Rest. Up popped the RAT and it served its purpose. By the time he got spark, fuel, engines engaged, and control he gathered the jet in at 4,000 feet above sea level. Ragin kept circling back to him so that they rode with him almost all the way through the ordeal.

They requested permission to approach and land without any more hitches. Once they dismounted, they walked into debriefing. The only thing the Flight Commander said to them was, "Got a little slow up there didn't you boys?"

Gale added that Crew Rest did tell them later that the Air Force had people practice flat spins before until they lost some airplanes, but he never heard of them practicing that one before. He did not think he would suggest it.

Gale recalled his OCS for a moment. The DI from Kokomo cut him no slack and in fact pushed him a little harder. He said it made him a better Marine. The recruiters never told him how it was really going to be. He does remember the DIs telling them that if they failed anywhere along the line they would start at point one again, but point one moved to Paris Island. That reminded him of his first letter home. Gale was married when he joined the Marines. Joan Barr was there for college and became a Marine Airman's wife. She has been part of the life. He remembers writing her to say, "I am in survival mode here." There were many bases where they were not together, but she knows Cherry Point.

Mike Ragin has to be one of Gale's favorites. There is a tone in his voice, a special respect for a guy he lived with and who he could have died with too. Gale told me Mike became one of the first Harrier pilots when that plane was added to the Marine Corps fleet. He was a natural, having flown choppers and fighters. Gale and Mike were at most of the Marine air wing bases.

Gale served at Quantico, Pensacola, Brunswick, Ga. for interceptor training, Cherry Point, Beaufort, Yuma, all over the US, Roosevelt Roads, Puerto Rico, Izmir, Turkey, Bermuda, and Key West.

When Gale served in other parts of the world, it left a lasting impression — not the least of which was that imprinted by his time in Turkey. Izmir was a beautiful area. The base location on the Mediterranean offered an amazing view, but Marines lived in tents right on the runway at the shared Air Force base. The space was shared with the International Air Point during the Cold War. Tensions were high and enemies difficult to identify. The local population included radical Muslims and hostile Bulgarians, both of which held ill feelings toward Americans. Bulgaria made constant attempts to drag our country into aggressive action. They were subtle at times, but did not hesitate to push us into violations of air space or borders. Theft became an easy tool or lure for them. If the flight groups did not guard their equipment, any of a number of the enemies in the area would sabotage their navigational gear to bring down a plane. The War Lords and their sister squadrons flew daily missions protecting allied ships and flight lanes.

Barr said that the Turkish military was tough. The enlisted personnel lived a Spartan existence. He likened it to the manner in which a fighting dog is maintained — keep it hungry and it is prepared to fight at all times. He was informed that Turkish officers were permitted total control over the soldiers in their command. If a soldier acted as though he questioned an order or spoke with any disrespect, the officer retained the absolute right to shoot him on the spot. While Gale served there, an incident occurred during which a Muslim insulted a Marine with a Turkish officer as a witness. He was arrested on the spot. The next day the Marine underwent questioning about the event. The Marine involved had no clue about the result of his responses. He told the truth. The Muslim was never seen in the area again. He had been a regular in the area prior to the incident. Serving in Turkey proved to be interesting, but Barr celebrated his return home.

Reminiscing about military service is a process of evolution. Stories feed on stories. We paused for coffee late in our talk and grew pensive. Gale recalled that one of the most consistent things he discovered no matter where he served was the idea that you fight like you practice. It is the same theory that good athletic coaches share with their teams as well. You fight like you practice. The premise reminded him of the time his unit sent a contingent to train at the Air Force's version of the Top Gun School. The Air Force wanted a school like that for years and got one at last. When it did, the Air Force brass wanted the Marine Corps and the Navy to come play. The USAF acquired some F-5s and painted them "No see me blue" for use as enemy aircraft. Gale explained that color blue blended with the sky very well, making the jets hard to see against the skyline. The F-5s were lighter aircraft with a definite turning advantage over the heavier, more powerful F-4s. The deck was stacked in favor of the opposing forces.

When the Marine flyers arrived at the special school, they were invited to attend a special orientation session where the engagement rules where explained. They were essential safety rules. The school leadership announced that there were 1000-foot limits on flying by the on-coming aircraft in head-on attacks. The deck was established at 10,000 feet. If anyone flew below that they were declared the loser in the dogfight. The Marine crews laughed as one. For three years, they had been trying to run into each other. They flew as low as they could, even raising dirt when over the ground or a rooster tail when over the water. At all times they went vertical as hard as they could. They did not respect the rules. It showed in the very first simulated series of dogfights. As a squadron, they came in at the F-5s from 5,000 feet. They were lost in the ground clutter and every one of them took out their bogey. It made the judges mad. They halted the engagement and called everyone to the debriefing room. The result—the Marines were sent home for not playing fair.

When the naughty boys arrived at their home base the Commanding Officer convened a major meeting. The Squadron Commander spoke for his group. He explained the rules of engagement as well as the opposing forces situation they encountered. To the man the squadron believed it was a huge waste. Gale said it boiled down to, "You think war simulation is going to boil down to training and abiding with crap like that?" In the meeting, they reached the conclusion that the Air Force school was operated by a non-combatant cadre of officers. Too many Marines flew with Air Force pilots and knew they were good. The story was the Commanding Officer spoke to his counterpart at the Air Force school soon after. He was rumored to have said something like this: "You can't let all these political and other side issues get in the way of the real purpose of what a battle unit is supposed to do. You learn to fly and fight — nothing more, nothing less. And you do it to win."

Gale spoke about pitting their F-4s against F-15s in a simulation in 1975, not long before he left the Marines. The new technology amazed him. They were radar-locked at 52 miles in the exhibition. It was an incredible feeling of helplessness and power at the same time. The awareness about what our planes could do was more than reassuring. Mig-21a had advanced. They were tough. The Chinese put screens over the engines and mud flaps, they were tough, and had guns mounted on them. Our brass would not put mount machine guns or cannons on the F-4s even though they had proved it could work in trials. Gale never understood that, nor did any pilots he knew. They were all happy to see the improvements in the other aircraft. The jets now though — that is a different story. They can do more than the men who fly them. That is saying something.

Gale met a pilot named Vernon Maddox during his rotation away from combat in Vietnam. Maddox was a Marine backseat like Gale, but he made it through Top Gun. He told Gale a story about a tragedy he witnessed involving a C-130 refueling tanker. His squadron of four F-4s had rendezvoused with the tanker and it took a while, because the tanker had to readjust its equipment. The tanker had just finished refueling some Air Force jets. The systems were different, thus the tanker had to be equipped to handle both receptacle systems. The Air Force uses a wing mount while the Marines used the pressurized hoses with basket attachments at the rear. Two of his squadron moved into position and hooked up. They were refueling while Maddox and his pilot along with their wing men waited at a safe distance. A plane came from somewhere and hit the tanker head on, resulting in an incredible exploding ball of flame in the sky. Everyone was killed on impact. The two waiting F-4s saw it all, yet could not even tell what hit the tanker. The airplane came from nowhere. There was no identification, nothing. Gale never researched it, but Maddox swore to the incident and it haunted him. As I wrote before, more than once in this story, there are no safe flights, no routine missions.

When Gale did not fly, which was not often, he had collateral duty assignments. The Marine Corps does not allow idle time. He worked in administration, the hydraulic shop, the seat ejection repair shop, and even did flight schedules. It was those times when he most often thought about the Marines in Vietnam. Barr wondered about his OCS classmates. He and two others were chosen for flight school from his entire class. All the others became grunts. Vietnam was not good to Marine Corps officers, in particular, lieutenants in a line unit. Their life expectancy in Vietnam in 1968-71 was next to zero.

Barr was Officer in Charge of the Hydraulic Shop at one of his duty stations. A Gunny Sergeant worked for him there who had recently returned from a tour in Nam. He did a couple of tours of grunt duty before his assignment in an air wing. Gale asked him one day how many lieutenants he lost in the Nam. The Gunny did not even blink when he said, "All of 'em."

Gale Barr is proud of being a Marine. He loved flying. He still does. His old unit — the War Lords — was deactivated sometime after he received his discharge. It is active again now, assigned to the hot new F-35s. Barr's pride is clouded with questions at times. While he gathered statistics for me, he asked questions for which there are no answers. What about all the losses which did not fit in the categories noted in his research? How did they die for their country? Knowing Gale Barr, I would bet he will investigate. He also wanted me to think about the fact that he focused on F-4s. Gale pointed out how many total aircraft were involved in the war. He said, "There were helicopters of all kinds, small prop-driven fighter planes as well as observation planes, B-52s, C-130s, other cargo planes, F-100s, F-105s, A-6es, the tankers…" Barr insisted I think about the sorties, the bombs dropped, the humanitarian missions, the troop movements, the rescue missions, and the man hours involved in general. Gale got very quiet. He said, "What we did in the air during Vietnam is impossible to comprehend in many ways. When I think about it, it makes World War II even more remarkable to me too."

Gale thinks of the Wall, of his OCS classmates who may be there.

Gale Barr reminded me that we lived in a time of turmoil. The 60s through the mid-70s are not discussed in the history books as they should be. Our kids will never read about them like we lived them. They will never know about Phillie, Watts, Chicago, the riots, the peace marches that were not peaceful at all, the War in Vietnam… "But", he said, "We are trying to tell them a little about it."

Gale Barr said it well. He said, "I don't look down for any man. I didn't run away. I didn't go to Canada. I served. I told my kids that being a Marine, serving my country was the most defining thing in my life. What compares to the experience, the intensity, the time taken away from home and family as a whole? Nothing in life is so large on a personal level for an individual as being separated from all other things. It was a defining time in my life and it shaped me forever."

A quiet man talks.

Blue Tag Unit

The Marines trained men as one, kept units tight.
They had to move as one when engaged in a fight.
They were quarantined for the last training journey.
They were "blue tagged"; gathered for war's unity.

One night "Gunny" offered them a chance for a movie.
It was new, about the Sundance Kid and Butch Cassidy.
They enjoyed a night of buttered popcorn and soda pop.
They ate until full with no money left; they had to stop.

They saw it five times before leaving, and guess what?
It was the feature in the air too, but they knew the plot.
The civilians on that silver bird sat there in amazed awe.
The Marines knew lines before the others were aware.

It was funny; each Jarhead took part of the cowboy script.
They made quick work of what was to be a very long trip.
It was a time to release, come down from training tension.
Laughter was their weapon with pleasure as the mission.

The "Blue Tag Unit" had a stop and a Marine was rewarded.
"Gunny" asked for volunteers but nobody stepped forward.
One was chosen, for what he knew not, but it was not optional.
He was told to get civvies and report at dawn for special patrol.

They were on a Pacific Island, a place for tourists but soldiers too.
Early in the morn he was given a job and told what he would do.
He had border duty for a pro golf tournament he heard in surprise.
He could not believe his ears and when it came true, not his eyes.

He spent several wake-ups watching the back of an old Marine.
That "volunteer" discovered the thrill of being around Lee Trevino.
They laughed, drank a little beer when the sun fell at the day's end.
Two men, with a bond of service, created some memories then.

His Lucky Day

I sat with a good friend on May 24th, 2011, eating chili dogs and fries in a fast food joint to get his story. My recorder contained the crunches and kids' laughter when I listened later. I never heard the background noise while we talked. I was surprised at the level of sound that failed to distract me. The crunch of the fries did make me hungry again. I was struck by the irony of the happy sounds juxtaposed to the topic. Dave Voris, my friend and son of Merle — "The Edge of Horror," a story elsewhere in this book — is a Vietnam veteran. Dave's theory is it is healthier to focus on the good memories than the bad. I think doing that may take more effort, but over time the results are worthwhile. The stories he chose to share with me are proof. The background noise was the perfect sound track.

Dave is one of the few men who managed to get drafted by the Marine Corps for service in Vietnam. He graduated from Purdue in 1968, received his Draft Notice in November, and left for Boot Camp in December. After completing ten weeks of boot in San Diego, he was whisked away for ITR (Infantry Training Regiment) at Camp Pendleton for combat training. All Marines share that experience. Dave was also treated to a dose of training for his final military occupational specialty. He spent several weeks learning the Marine supply and warehouse system. His total Marine school time was five months, but he does not remember ever stocking anything while in Southeast Asia.

People hear Dave's story and say, dripping with sarcasm, "Oh, you lucky guy!" when they learn he was drafted into the Marine Corps. As Dave discovered with the passage of time, he was quite fortunate. He served 19 months active duty and was paid for 24. When he came back to the States from Nam, they separated him and sent him home.

Dave Voris is involved in many activities in Tipton County, IN. The Corps drafted men in certain situations. Manpower shortages forced them away from their all-volunteer procedure during Korea and again during Vietnam. He has met several men who were drafted into the Marine Corps during the Korean Conflict, but he is the only one he knows who was drafted for Vietnam. Although he never verified it, Dave heard that 6,000 were drafted nationwide in 1968. The Corps required a lot of replacements that year. I suggested that it made sense. The losses that year, the year I went, were heavy. I Corps, where the Marines were fighting, was an intense battleground.

The Marines incurred serious casualties. It is a logical number given what I discovered when I referred to my favorite Vietnam fact site on the web. I use www.vvof.org for statistics regarding Vietnam veterans serving in Nam. It is a great reference site for "fact versus fiction" when seeking general information. The site indicates that 42,633 men were drafted into the Marines between 1965 and '73.

Dave did not know he was going to the Marines until it happened. He went to Indianapolis with a busload of people after reporting to the Draft Board as required. They did the group testing and after that the surprise happened. A spit-shined old Gunnery Sergeant stepped out of nowhere with a list of seven names and said, "Gentlemen, you are going with me or going to jail." Dave went. He has often wondered if Gunny lied about the jail part since then, but he was not about to argue at the time. In Dave's words, "I was almost 23-years old, married, but green as grass. I wasn't about to challenge that old lifer." The old sergeant gave one of the guys — a man named Camby as he recalls — a folder full of papers. It was their orders and flight tickets. They boarded a bus to the airport. A few hours later they were in San Diego where he found himself standing on the yellow footprints.

Dave and I talked about the draft process. It was a high impact part of life in the sixties. The experiences were similar for us. We registered and were called for a physical during the month we became 19. At least, that was my story. I was 1-A, or very available. There were deferments given for different reasons. Dave attended college thus was not available until he graduated. Other than that, the process was identical. A young man reported when called, suffered through a physical examination and a battery of tests, went home and waited. I did not. I went upstairs when the bus returned to Tipton, IN, to move my name to the top of the list. I was drafted the next month. Dave waited until his turn came. It did not take long after he went through the testing. The most memorable part of my physical was a young man who could not urinate. A busload of young men was held while the authorities inundated him with liquids and still his system rebelled. We were hostage to a locked bladder. It took hours. At long last we voted to make a mass contribution to his test and were freed. The bus did not travel three blocks before it had to stop for a bathroom for him.

Dave heard that the Marines relied on the written tests in their selection process during the draft. Aptitude was the key to them as the draft was an exception to their rule. Their standard was a strange mixture he never quite understood, but he thinks he was 1-A in their system. He laughed and said that he "was either at the top of the stack or the bottom. Either way it made him a prime candidate for the Marine Corps." The bottom line was he served 19 months as a Marine, came home as an E-5 sergeant making $358 per month in 1969. He made that rank two months prior to his discharge. Dave made rank at a rapid pace. When he arrived in the States his discharge permitted him to serve five months at full pay — in advance — dressed as a civilian, with more money in his boots than he ever had — before or since. Dave noted that most of his rank time in the Marine Corp came as a Corporal. He made Lance Corporal for three days. The slot became available and he was next in line. The next slot opened three days later. I will say this however — I have known Dave Voris for almost 40 years. Whatever job he had, he did well, but when he was drafted by the Marines it *was* his lucky day.

Dave Voris reported to Vietnam in May, 1969. His DD-214 indicates he was a supply man, but he never stocked anything while he was there. He was not a stock clerk in any sense of the word. He was assigned to H&S Company, with the 1st Military Police Battalion, Force Logistics Command, 1st Marine Division. They were stationed in I-Corps at the Air Force's airfield in Da Nang, located in the northern part of South Vietnam on the coast. H&S was a support company on the north side of the base. The Marines were tasked with mission security for the airfield. The airfield had two runways, but they secured the entire base. Dave's unit had a defensive combat mission. Even though the base was operated by the Air Force it was utilized by all branches.

The Navy and Marines flew there with regularity. The Army made its contribution to the controlled chaos as well. In 1969, it rivaled Tan Son Nhut as the busiest airport in the world, with a flight a minute around the clock. Dave said it was noisy beyond belief. He heard some reports that it *was* the busiest airport in the world. The area where Dave served was a hotbed for battle. The base his unit protected was central to America's war plan in South Vietnam. Dave said, "I stood a decade of bunker lines in that 13-month tour and did a bunch of six click (kilometer) patrols." We talked about how much damage was done to the base in attacks during 1968. The enemy came close to eliminating it. Our forces held, but the damage was incredible. The bomb dump exploded in one attack. The North Vietnamese Army never succeeded, but our efforts to protect the airfield defenses were elevated thereafter. Da Nang was a critical area and the Marines were crucial to its safety. Dave did more than bunker duty while stationed there.

Dave Voris arrival in Vietnam was confused by the fact that his orders were lost. After he completed in-country processing, nobody was sure what to do with him. For three days, H&S Company placed him on "Casual Orders" which required him to remain available for miscellaneous assignments. He stayed in the barracks waiting for an assignment. On the third day, he had an unexpected visitor. The battalion commander, a Full Bird Colonel, walked into his area and asked if he was Voris. Dave thought he was in trouble, but could not imagine why. The Battalion Commander said, "In all my years in the Marines, I don't know if I have ever commanded an enlisted man with a college degree. I wanted to see what one looks like." The Colonel joined the Marines during the Korean War as an enlisted man. At some point, he received a field commission and became an officer. Voris learned that the Colonel was a man of Polish descent, rumored to have been a mercenary before the Korean War began. He joined the Marines as a foreign national in order to become an American citizen. Years ago that was not unusual. In fact it was still practiced when I served during the Vietnam War. I served with several good soldiers who emigrated from Mexico the same way. They learned our language, the Constitution, and served our country well. Private Dave Voris and the Colonel became good friends, an unexpected and unconventional relationship for the military. The unusual situation evolved into a very interesting position in addition to his normal duty assignments.

Dave did not have much of a combat role. That was not his primary MOS (military occupational specialty). He learned the supply system. Voris could order material for his unit. He never stocked the warehouse, but he was assigned a work station there, complete with a desk. As mentioned earlier he spent time on guard duty and short patrols. The infantry units were responsible for the long term operations and extended combat engagements in remote areas. Dave rotated with other personnel for the daily search missions near the base. His first direct combat came on one of those patrols. The enemy ambushed them by popping out of the short palm-like growths so common to the terrain in that territory. The Viet Cong or NVA would spring an ambush, fire a few rounds and disappear within minutes. Dave never engaged in a lengthy firefight from what I learned during our discussion. His experience as a supply expert differed from those I knew. It was not long before he was asked to add another job to his assignment as well.

The Battalion Commander had a friend who was an officer in the local ARVN unit (Army of the Republic of Vietnam). That friend had an enterprise established in Da Nang that required some assistance from the Colonel, who came to Dave with a question. He asked Dave Voris if he would teach English to his Vietnamese friend's associates. Dave responded by asking how he could do that when he knew "less than nothing" about the Vietnamese language. The Colonel answered with, "Do it Peace Corps style — with objects. They only need the basics, so they can function at a very simple level." He went on to explain to Dave that there were no expectations beyond that. His ARVN friend knew pro-American people who wanted to be able to survive in an English speaking environment if they had to do so. Dave agreed.

A few days later the Colonel arrived in his Jeep with a driver and guard. They picked Dave up and drove to a building in downtown Da Nang. Dave taught his first class. Dave's high-ranking friend told him to teach them like he would a kid. He started by holding a rifle in the air and having them repeat the word "rifle." They went on to "boots", then "belt" and other simple objects. When his other duties allowed, Dave Voris taught his class in the evenings two or three times a week. It went on for several weeks. He never knew who they were or why he was doing it, but he developed a theory. Dave assumed that the class was not gratis. The people attending were not the poor people he saw on patrol. They did not wear the farmer's silk pajamas or the typical straw cone hats. He could not imagine them "chasing those pigs around with heads as big as a truck." They were people who came to the sessions in casual clothes, who appeared prosperous, and part of the business class in Da Nang. Dave theorized that they wanted to be prepared for the time when they may have to leave Vietnam. His class did not make them fluent, but they could communicate. He has wondered many times since if they are here. Teaching was an unusual job for an enlisted man, but it was not his only exceptional calling.

Dave's Supply Officer, a first lieutenant, came to Dave one morning and ordered him to meet him at a designated spot in ten minutes. He specified that he was to bring his M-16 and flak jacket. Dave had no idea what was ahead, but he followed orders. When he arrived he found the officer waiting with a Jeep. They jumped in and their next stop was Da Nang Harbor. His Colonel was waiting there aboard a friend's beautiful old three-mast sailing vessel. Dave said it was the loveliest old ship he ever saw. He and his lieutenant were waved on where he was directed to a spot on one side of the ship. Dave's job for half a day of sailing was ballast! He said it was a fantastic day, but it was the last thing he expected to be doing. He was a marine ballast Marine of all things.

As I mentioned before, Dave Voris prefers to remember those moments. They are better for his emotional well-being. He thinks all vets should focus on their moments of good fortune, the camaraderie, the unity, the esprit de corps, and those we soldiered with for such an intense part of our lives. He and I agree that a wise man struggles to find balance. It is an on-going battle. Not everyone wins. That is a sad truth. We talked about the ancient Chinese tome, *The Art of War* and its applicability still today. The North Vietnamese Army genius General Giap (who also studied it in depth) admitted we had them defeated in 1968 and 69, but biased reporting, misguided leadership in our President and then our military worked to his advantage. Giap wrote of it in his biography and the tide of the war turned. Granted, this is our considered opinion, but we were on the ground during that time. We knew the enemy would not and could not stand and fight. The South Vietnamese people had no sympathy for the North while they savaged them during that time. There had been some compassion for their brethren in the North for a while, but it was lost. We mismanaged a great opportunity to gain public support in many quarters. Not the soldiers in the mud, the leadership behind the desks. They failed us. I believe that is part of the beast that the vet has to battle — leadership failure. Dave may have discovered the best solution. We should focus more on the moments away from battle.

Four years ago, Dave heard from an old friend he had not spoken with since Vietnam. Larry Ramsey, his Battalion Armorer called "out of the blue." Ramsey lives in East Texas, near Timpson. Dave, his wife Sharon, and his father (Merle) drove to San Antonio during the summer of 2010 to see his younger son. Returning home, Dave decided to make a side trip to visit Ramsey. Merle listened as Dave and Larry reminisced about their time together in Nam. Ramsey reminded Dave of a story he had long since forgotten. They had once pulled bunker duty together on an old, well-travelled bridge south of Da Nang. It was an important position, often a target of the enemy. There were bunkers on both sides of each end. Security was high priority on the old structure. It was the link between a peninsula-like stronghold and the mainland. There was a big black man in their platoon who was a great guy, but renowned for his fear of snakes (I join him in that). His name was Mott. Voris and Ramsey were in a bunker on one side, Mott and his partner were on the other side. In the deepest, darkest part of the night, all hell broke loose. Dave said, "An M-16 started firing and it was an all-out firefight. It was just smokin'. Ramsey jumped up and we ran over there to support those guys as fast as we could. We got there and there was Mott. He was standing there with a hot M-16 and a dead python at his feet. He had a firefight with a snake. He shot it to pieces. Mott was so petrified that he could not even talk. The snake lost that one." Merle enjoyed that visit. Dave did too. He and Ramsey stay in contact now. Sometimes it takes an old war buddy to pry the lid off the memory vault. There was still the stress. They remembered that too.

Dave respects our old enemy. He mentioned how clever they were. We talked about the fact that the wounded are more of burden than the dead. They found ways to interrupt normal operations as often as they could. The enemy was expert at disruption even if they inflicted no casualties. Dave is right. They were clever. We were as good at guerilla warfare after time passed, in particular our smaller teams. We were not as ruthless in the big picture. We could not be. In the scheme of things — again my opinion, from life experience — we are not as a people. Americans are not attuned to life at war. Some cultures are.

Dave cited several examples of interdiction into the daily operations at a very secure base. Da Nang's air field was well protected, yet the Viet Cong and NVA found ways to disrupt daily operations in many ways. He saw an AWAC

(Airborne Early Warning Control) plane get shot down. The only survivors were the crew members in the rear sections of the older Tri Star Constellation, triple rudder plane (this was an old carry-over version of the AWAC and replaced for duty in most cases). The enemy brought it down with a rocket of some sort. The enemy used the Russian-supplied rockets in many ways. They also used a Chinese RPG on ground troops. The Russian version, he remembers, could be shoulder-fired or used like a mortar. It was used against the base in many ways. The attack on the plane affected him forever. When he flies, his seat is always in the rear of the plane. First class does not interest him. The VC also took down helicopters and even jets on take-off or landing with shoulder-fired weapons. Choppers were the easiest prey throughout the country. They found many subtle ways to infect a day's work.

There was a case where several hundred Marines were distracted for several hours each day with scratching. They scratched their arms, their stomachs, their legs. Their bodies were irritated day and night. They were distracted from their duty with a simple ruse as it was discovered after a very difficult investigation. Many civilian employees worked at the base and had access to the post after a lengthy clearance process. The enemy coerced a long time laundry lady into adding a very effective irritant to the rinse water. A family member, or her entire family, was threatened with something heinous if she did not cooperate with the Viet Cong. She complied. It was a little thing, but it made the war more difficult to conduct. It disheartened the soldiers. It attacked morale. It was effective. There were other methods.

There was a period when Zippo lighters were found on the ground around the base. Most Marines smoked. If they stumbled across a shiny new Zippo, they were going to pick it up and try it. When they did the lighters exploded in their hands. It happened all over the base for days. There were dozens of incidents. They were packed with a type of plastic explosive which blasted when the lighter was used. It maimed the user. A finger here, a hand there — a face — it was about inflicting harm, distraction of some sort on a daily basis.

Bob Hope came to do a show on Freedom Hill, a super secure area five or six clicks north of Da Nang. There were several thousand seats there. Tickets were allocated through a random lottery process in each unit stationed at the base. The VC got hold of one somehow and issued as many more counterfeits as originals. The night of the show twice as many or more people arrived as could be seated. The biggest brawl in history erupted in the middle of the War. It was one of Guinness Book proportions. It was another successful, major distraction. Dave was there.

At one point, the base was being hit by rocket fire which resembled mortar attacks. It was sporadic throughout the day and night, with no particular target. The rounds seemed to land with nothing in mind. They landed near bunkers, near the runways, near living quarters, or in the streets of the base. Some inflicted minor wounds but most made noise and holes in something. They caused damage that had to be repaired. They drove men into bunkers and defensive postures. They stopped all work. By the time the Marines mounted a patrol to pursue the in-coming trajectory path to its origination point, the enemy had vanished. They began patrols in earnest to catch the perpetrators in the act. Earlier patrols found launch sites. There were simple mounds of dirt with evidence of use. One patrol got lucky. It found one that had not been fired, destroyed or moved. A rocket was left on a ramp of dirt elevated and aimed at the base. Two wires ran from the round to a bucket of water through two holes that were drilled in it. The impromptu electronic device was rigged so the wires would connect when the water drained from the bucket, thus firing the rocket. Nobody needed to be present. It was a simplistic remote fire apparatus, effective and random, just like the target. It went where it went, when it went, hitting whatever was on the other end of the flight path. It raised heck with whatever was going on in the compound at the time of its arrival.

My friend was ready to get back to his other stories. Dave had access to supplies. That was his stated job. He had a desk in the battalion supply office, he had requisitions, signed papers all the time, got signatures when necessary, and really did that sort of thing while he was there. I had to remember he became an NCO. A corporal is an NCO. In the Army it is too, but not in the Infantry, except in unusual situations or for specific occupation specialties. It is an E-4 pay grade like Specialist 4th Class, which I was, but I was not an NCO. I did not command soldiers. Therein lays the difference. Dave said he could order anything from C rations to tanks and get it. The Marines got what they needed. He remembered that they ate very well at his base. Mentioning tanks reminded Dave that Marine Tankers were wild men. He said they had to be nuts to climb in those things. That comment piqued my curiosity. His point was about the bugs. They were bugged by them — everybody was. He ordered extra bug repellant. I interjected my agreement at that. I recalled a huge winged thing that had hide like an elephant. That critter was impervious to blows from a machete. I once struck one three times and it looked at me and flew away as though nothing had happened. At any rate, Dave ordered 50 cases of bug juice. The military bug spray is equivalent to "Deep Woods Off." I told him I remember it well. I often added it to my peanut butter, lit it and used it for "Sterno." When the order came in, someone had erred. He received 500 cases. Mistakes like that did not happen often, but Dave did not mind having an extra quantity of that illustrious material. It was trade capital. Barter was a good supply man's way of building morale in his unit.

Dave admitted that he never had a bad meal while he was with the 1st MP Battalion. They had an exceptional menu too. He once traded a supply of meats, a nice variety, to the Air Force for building materials which included a substantial number of marine plywood sheets. He and seven of his buddies built an elevated hooch to escape the bug population crawling on the on the ground. It stood on four-feet-tall supports and housed all of them. They were proud of their work. Dave decided that the bug repellant he had in abundance could be put to good use there too. He spent an afternoon on his hands and knees working copious amounts of the liquid into the floor of their building. When he finished saturating the floor, he returned to the warehouse to finalize his day's work. There were papers awaiting his signature. Until that moment, he felt fine. He walked, talked, and moved with his usual alacrity. When Dave began his signature on the first document his arm went stiff and began jerking out of control. He had lost his fine motor skills. The arm stood straight out in front of him. It was as though it had taken on a life of its own. He was taken to the base hospital where he was admitted and retained for three days. Dave Voris was juiced on bug repellant in his zeal to seal.

Voris fell in love with handball while attending Purdue University. One day, he had an idea about using the remaining building supplies from his deal with the Air Force. He was aware that the Battalion Commander was also a fan of recreational handball. He bounced the idea about building a handball court off the Colonel and it was approved at once. Dave got some help from like-minded Marines and constructed a building housing one court on the Parade Ground near the flag. It got tremendous reviews from the troops stationed there. The facility was utilized 24 hours a day, seven days a week. Dave laughed as he told me the story. He said, "Folks are gonna think I never did anything when they read this story." I assured him that if they ever served they will understand that something like this was a major benefit to soldiers far from home. Anyone coming in from field duty that got to use it loved it too. A thing like a handball court or a basketball court was a huge stress reliever. It became something that made them think of something other than the war for a few minutes. They were a positive morale factor. We had something else in common. While on medical profile (restriction), I operated what was known as Moon's Soda Pagoda. It was like an end of the tracks bar in the old west. The little things make a big difference. I felt guilt about my limited day duty for years until my Nam buddies validated me a few years ago (a story told in *Vietnam in Verse, poetry for beer drinkers*). He admitted that many of the things he did in his supply role had important results — often more important than he realized when he did them.

Dave and I discussed good field officers, good non-coms, and the administrative types who came for rank, but never wanted to be part of the effort or team. Men will follow a good leader without question. They will accomplish things that are often inexplicable to the non-military population. He said his good fortune extended to the officers for whom he served. One and all, they were good. An old NCO came to mind. The old sergeant was busted (reduced in rank) more than once while Dave knew him, but every time he got his stripes back. He was too proficient at his job and men would do anything the old man asked them to do. He was a golden asset to the Corps.

Thinking about the tough old sergeant reminded Dave of the E-Club (enlisted man's club). It was a ramshackle affair that served no real food, but offered ham hocks as appetizers. The only available beer was Weideman's or Falstaff. The beer cans were so old and rusty that a can opener was unnecessary. A man could use his thumb to push a hole in the top to drink. The entertainment was provided by a crew of haggard Vietnamese strippers. The club was more appealing once than twice for many.

Dave and I were chatting about how we learned we were going to Vietnam when I mentioned something I marvel at about him and his father. Dave's father served in Japan during the Post-War Occupation in late 1945 and 46. Dave was born in January, 1946 while Merle was away. Merle saw him for the first time when he was discharged. Dave's older son Clay was born in August, 1969 while he was in Vietnam. Dave was still serving when he saw him the first time while on R and R in Hawaii in January, 1970. The parallels did not end there.

When the Marines flew home from Da Nang, their flights stopped in Okinawa. There they waited for a connection to the States on a first come, first served basis. Dave was a dozen deep in the line for the last available flight on Memorial Day weekend, 1970. There were no flights for several days due to the holiday schedule. He was at a loss about what he was going to do when he remembered one of his Nam friends was stationed there. Junior Herridge was close to him and his friend Ramsey. He did a phone search and located Junior. Securing a cab ride, he arrived at the area where his former friend was supposed to be assigned. Once located and together, Junior announced he had a lot of accrued leave. He approached his commanding officer, explained the situation and was granted permission to use it showing Dave the island for a few days. Junior acquired two bikes, secured housing, and they toured the island. Dave said it is a beautiful place. His father pulled the last of his Army duty there 24 years earlier. Merle completed his Army commitment on Okinawa working with the local farmers after his assignment in Japan was completed. Dave saw the island where his father served before he ever saw him more than two decades earlier. He did not realize it at the time, but it was the end of his military service as well.

After Dave returned home, he was hired by a seed corn company and moved to Eldora, IA. Almost a year later, he got a phone call at work from his wife Sharon. She told him that a man knocked on their door and asked for him. He claimed he was a buddy from Vietnam. He called himself Junior Herridge. Dave received permission to go home, where he found a disheveled ex-Marine waiting for him. His friend was a wild-looking, long-haired, weed-smoking former Marine who hit the road to find him. They had a two or three day visit and talked about their time together in Nam. Junior left never to be heard from again. Ramsey has searched for him as has Dave. They have yet to locate him.

Some veterans do not want to come home. They cannot beat the beast.

Dave Voris and his wife Sharon are good friends. She is a Marine's wife. She survived leukemia. I never heard her complain. She is one of my heroes. In 1999, my younger son married. A week before the ceremony, Dave had a cancerous kidney removed. He sent us word that he would dance with the bride. He came to the wedding, limped into the reception, and danced with her. Once a Marine, always a Marine.

When Dave Voris was drafted by the Marines, it was his lucky day.

WompWompWompWomp

WompWompWompWompWomp…the sound!
It could be heard faintly in the distance.
It was the same but louder on nearby ground.
The dust filled my eyes, ever unmasked.
I ran to it, I ran from it, maybe I fell down.
When I needed it most my soul danced.

A Silver Bird deserted us in South Vietnam.
It took us home if we made our time.
But that big, ugly Huey was the battle ram.
It rescued us if we bled in the slime.
It pitched and yawed, I swear it even swam.
If there were trees it could even climb.

Old UH-1, in all forms, was OD green, yes.
The men inside had brass 'nads' too.
It was required, and they all were the best.
I never saw a crew that would not do.
Crazy men matched the ships, nothing less.
We Grunts on the ground…we knew!

We saw the Cobras, we prayed for fast fliers.
The B-52s made the earth shake below.
Puff made the sky red and our spirits higher.
The Bumble Bees were spotting a show.
"Chinooks" handled big stuff, major suppliers.
Hueys touched us every day down below.

Those old work horses were tough as hell.
Like a Timex they kept on ticking.
They carried ammo, supplies, men and mail.
We went to hot LZs pulses racing.
At times they carried food we even smelled.
In a firefight they heard our crying.

We watched the horizon for their smoking fallen.
If close to them, we would protect them.
Their sixties were voices to us, angels had spoken.
Those with red crosses were from heaven.

Dead or alive, they were there for us, loving iron.
They are the best horse the Army has seen.

It is hard to believe the best are to be retired.
They are like us, I suppose, and history now.
They are tough and can serve, but not desired.
A reliable, tough old Huey is not enough.
I can pull a trigger but I just can't get there.
Let's go to the bone yard and sit down.

Mike Mullins, 2/6/11

This was written at the request of J.C. Fischer for the retirement of the
Phenomenal UH-1 Huey helicopter that served us so well in Vietnam
And other soldiers for 30 or more years. We salute it and all it has done.
I could write forever. Images keep flashing. It is now the next afternoon and
The old baby is still in my mind. How do I stop it? I cannot. It was too big, too
Much a part of what we did, too huge part of our life on the ground. I was in an
Air mobile brigade and we lived with the machine…and our dead left with it.
Thank God I did not see more of that than I did. I witnessed a lot of wounded
Carried away in its not so gentle hands, but they were relatively safe there,
Soon to be in gentler hands. One vision stays with me. As we ran to her,
We were bent at the waist like subjects approaching their queen.
That was as it should have been and as it should be now as the queen
Retires to her final resting chamber. It should be something grand.

Flint

My wife's cousin, John W. Graham, is a former Marine who spent most of his service time in the jungles of South America in the eighties. He and I have become friends over the years, sharing the military tie and a love of motorcycles. John is an old school biker who knows the lifestyle in a way that a "wanna-be" like me never will. He is also a man who takes care of his body, has gotten into martial arts because of his experience in the Marines, and followed up with that in competitive fighting as an amateur. We talked about an opportunity for me to meet his teacher and friend for a year. The chance came at last. I was excited about it on many levels, but one stood out above all the others — he is a Nam vet.

John Graham served in "peace time" in a chronological sense, but as I meet those who serve I discover that in many ways "peace" is a term that is often a convenient public perception foisted upon us for reasons to sooth the mind. If one looks at history there is always discontent somewhere in the world, boiling at one level or another, just below the surface, or on the surface. The difference is whether the dictator — pot stirrer if you will — is big enough to draw the glare of international cameras. John did embassy duty in several South American countries. The big picture says that these little tin dictators are unworthy of world-wide fear, but try telling that to the local population which lives in abject fear and poverty. They maintain an "army" of vicious killers who rape and steal at will, protecting the local boss who anoints himself with a title of some sort, or jerks the chain of those who wear one at his whim.

John's job consisted of protecting the "white shirts" that worked at the embassy or frequented that locale on our dime. Many times, to paraphrase him, he and his fellow Marines had to rescue American idealists who chose to work in those countries. John finds it ironic how many American college graduates went to work for the Peace Corps in those days and looked on him and other military types with total disdain, often telling them that they could convert the local people with love and pacify them better than any military force ever could. In their liberal arrogance, they derided the service of our troops, as they did in the 70s, and in truth still do, at every opportunity.

Every country to which John Graham was assigned was filled with unrest, riots, looting, and general chaos. If there was not an outright war, there was murder and mayhem, yet the ideologues continued to pour into the countries in an endless stream, filled with the idea that they could make a difference. John is not talking about the missionaries who went into the villages, but those who thought the entire process was a giant lark, a party they could attend and play at and with for a while, then flit away. Many of them had cash to spend and did so. They became immediate targets. Sooner or later John and his friends were called upon to rescue them. Time after time their buses were attacked, they were drug off and abused. The men were stripped, beaten, and robbed; the women were stripped, raped, and robbed. They sought the local military people, if and when they were able, and begged for help to get mommy and daddy, to get money, to get home — they lost their disdain for the military. They were yanked into the real world. It saddened John and his comrades, but their cynicism increased. The embassies would not let them respond for political reasons. The reports were watered down. The press did not tell the American public what transpired and it did not stem the tide of young Americans reporting for the same kind of duty. It convinced John that there is a part of our society that refuses to learn from history. It only wants to rewrite it to fit its own needs.

John spent his non-duty hours working out and training in a variety of martial arts. The discipline benefitted him in many ways. He adapted to the environment by emotional and physical training. The practice set a life pattern for him. The physical condition hardened his body. Years ago, I saw him after a serious motorcycle accident in which a lady had crashed into him, breaking his back. His remarkable condition kept his spine from collapsing. He works and rides today, and trains. His love of the arts led him to Flint, a teacher and coach of a variety of martial arts and a Vietnam veteran. I was fortunate that John took me to meet him.

We drove to Flint's private teaching/counseling facility on a hot, sunny afternoon. We found it locked and dark. John is Flint's friend, so it was a quick decision to travel to his home and knock on the door. John was welcomed as a brother, not a student. Flint told us to meet him back at the gym and soon followed. I was a bit apprehensive. First time meetings are not always smooth. Trust is not automatic — it has to be earned. I had heard some of the sensei's exploits, as a teacher, a warrior, and a man of God. He is a dichotomy, but many of us are. He is a great man in John's eyes and my expectations were tremendous. I had been waiting for this opportunity for months. Intimidation was in my thoughts. My limited knowledge of his combat experience compared to my own made me feel inadequate about considering myself a vet in the same war.

Flint gave John the keys to his building, so we waited for him inside. Soon he joined us and I turned to meet a man with hair and in great physical shape. Damn! I should have expected that from a man who teaches self-defense, who is a certified scuba instructor, and a repelling teacher among other assorted military style activities. As I was to learn, he is a few months older than I, about six feet, one inch tall, and a solid buck ninety in weight. He wears great silver hair and has beautiful, sparkling blue eyes. Here was a man who has his demons "whupped." Flint has met them in the night, one on one or in groups, and handled them. I liked him at first sight. He was not a machine or a ghost. He was a man I could like, know, talk to, and want to know as more than a story. I wanted to be his friend too.

He looked at me, shook my hand, looked at John and said, "I trust him." In the first minutes, volumes were spoken and everything I had been concerned about disappeared. I felt a kinship had blossomed. He went on to say, "John has talked a lot about you and now I know why." I was surprised at that. I am just another guy with questions and no answers, but I care. Flint told me that he had a class soon and our chatting would be sporadic. He laughed and said his whole life is, but he would have it no other way. I told him that my mind operates that way and I would do my best to keep up with his galloping. He laughed and told me that if I couldn't, "Sen loi" and laws-a-mercy, it had been a long time since I heard that. It is how the Vietnamese said "sorry about that." I am not sure of the spelling but I remember the meaning. I laughed and he said, "Yep, you've been there."

Flint was part of the Greek Letter Projects in Southeast Asia, as he puts it, before Delta Force was created. He was a Green Beret involved in the Omega Project from 1967 through 1971 and has since given much of his life in the service to his country. He served another 21 years as a military advisor. In the Nam, his Army connection was with the Fifth Special Forces. His time in our conflict is a book. His career is a movie. I managed to chip off a few little pieces and was blessed to get those. He is still asked to train government employees in various skills on special occasions. Behind his facility he maintains a small jump tower with a miniature climbing wall. Once your name is in the Black Book it is never erased I suppose. There are things you will never pry from him, not even from his cold, dead lips. Flint is a name — steel is a smiling face surrounding sparkling blue eyes. Purpose is a way of life.

Flint was interrupted by a visitor reviewing his facility and two students who came to get their warm-up program. While he was taking care of that business, John took me through a portion of his photo gallery. We talked about a couple of his pictures — Cobras and distant lands, which included shots of Flint in his camouflage gear. There were certificates for successful martial arts competitions and training endeavors. I also saw a certification about Flint's ministerial ordination. Above his desk at the entrance was a certification of thanks for acting as the technical advisor for a film documentary. The terrain for some of the photos was much different than the countryside with which

I was familiar. I found that very interesting, yet I worked much farther south and my job was a little more mundane by comparison. I saw stories without words in some of the photography. When Flint returned, he pointed at the photo where I stood contemplating and said, "That is a special training area" and walked over to his bottle of water. I smiled to myself and followed, hoping for a little story while his students generated some perspiration in the gymnasium.

Flint worked in Laos with Air America during his first tour. He spent time there as an advisor. He was also familiar with our allied efforts in Cambodia and Thailand. Flint was well traveled in the four years he worked in the tropical paradise I came to cherish. His uniform requirements were often flexible, as was his appearance at times. His operations were covert. He was Special Forces, very elite, and worked in a six man team much of the time. His military operational specialty was intelligence and his job was always with a Study and Observation Group. His team was inserted for a close study of the indigenous population at one point for a short period of time and encountered extreme and unexpected difficulty. There was a small village of about 300 people with issues that his team had to help them eliminate. They were successful in that endeavor in its entirety and made it to their extraction point on time. Those situations were prearranged for each op and this event was no exception to that rule.

They were operating in triple canopy jungle, or worse in areas. The extraction point was an opening near a mountainside that was a mere sixty meters wide. It was a very hostile environment. Flint and his team waited on the ground for the extraction ropes to be dropped by the hovering Air America aircraft. It kept circling for some reason, calling huge amounts of undue attention to their location. It was an unacceptable situation. They could have been pulled safely out, but the Air America crew did not do it for some reason. The craft lingered so long without letting the lines down that it began taking fire. The team was trained in shinnying up the ropes and leaving, even if dangling, and that had been their anticipated getaway plan. They were pinpointed by a very angry enemy because of their activities in the region. The Air America crew abandoned them. They knew without doubt they had been deemed expendable. In the fighting that ensued, four were killed. Flint and one other team member were left alive. He grabbed the other SF operative and silenced him and his weapon. Stealth was the only choice they had deep within the enemy's grasp. Flint pointed to the top of the trees and they climbed.

Flint had watched his partners die. He was mad as hell and determined to survive. Survival is an instinct and his training gave him the right tools for it, but he had questions. When I heard the story, I felt that. It was never spoken or implied. I could envision the rage he must have felt, knowing that even if he escaped he was leaving his dead partners behind, people that did not have to die. Flint and his sole surviving team member stayed in the top of the trees while the enemy below searched like bloodhounds for them. The searched lasted for hours while they waited like Apaches in the upper foliage. At last, the enemy was convinced that they had escaped and the main force moved away to other duty. The remaining detachment stopped and after a while began to focus on stripping the bodies. While they argued over the spoils of war, Flint and his comrade descended to the forest floor and waited for the right opportunity. At long last, a soldier leaned his AK-47 against a nearby tree. Flint grabbed it and opened fire. He killed every human being in sight. Nobody escaped. Any enemy in earshot would recognize the sounds of their own weaponry. They would assume that their people had sighted the pursued invaders and write the firing off as that of their own people. Flint and his chum ended the fight with some hand-to-hand. He had in fact gotten slashed with a machete across his inner left thigh. Having been trained to fix his own wounds Rambo-style, he stemmed the flow of blood long enough to escape the region. When they were far enough away, he effected better self-repair. He carries the scars today. He half-carried his remaining teammate to safety after the battle to escape.

It took two and half weeks to return to friendly territory. Even then they were not safe. They had no idea what the passwords were, nor had they any sort of identification. Had they been seen by sentries, they would have been shot as enemy combatants. They were dressed for the occasion. Flint and friend had to break into their own compound just as they had to break out of enemy territory. He still remembers the napalm strikes from B-52s which could drop their payloads from 50,000 feet on a target the size of a queen-sized bed and never been seen by the enemy. They flew so high that he had to climb into a tree top and call in coordinates to other radio relay units because the old PRC-25s did not have the FM capacity to reach out to that altitude. The mission they had just completed had been such a mission. And Air America had left them behind. I don't know what he learned about that — or did.

After the story, we walked back to the gallery wall and Flint pointed to a photo of the Cobra that showed him with a pilot. He told me that it was a man everyone called "Bloody Bill," who remains a great friend of his. The man completed his career as a colonel. He was a chopper pilot in Nam who had many exploits. His kill ratio earned him the nickname "Bloody Bill." He was loved and respected by troops on the ground. One manic operation earned him a spot in *Stars and Stripes*. The Army was looking for a pilot crazy enough to try taking a bridge out that linked supplies from Cambodia into

Nam. It was a large, important pipeline that fed enemy forces in a major way. Starnes got involved and his ship was rigged with LAW pods on both sides and he made the attempt on the chosen day. Major No Name made the run and moved around at a bad angle trying for the shot, with the enemy taking shots when it could. The angle was much worse than believed, as the bridge was over a deep gorge and presented an impossible target for the gunship. He could not settle in long enough to let loose with his improvised weaponry. He elevated and evaluated while his backseat talked to him through the headset about aborting. Bill is another good old Tennessee boy and he settled on his own plan at the last. He told his co-pilot that he was going to show him some old fashioned Tennessee "windage" shooting. With the predictable questions, No Name lined up his mini-guns on a gigantic tree near the gorge and gave it hell. The gun sawed the tree like a buzz saw, felling it right where Bill wanted it. The tree came crashing down across the bridge, destroying it totally. The supply line was and destroyed, leaving a useful woodpile. The pair confirmed the kill — with the usual photos I assume — and returned to base. The entire incident became front page news and No Name was no longer a local treasure, so to speak.

Flint was smiling as he told the story. There was more than one reason for that. He had gotten a call a few days prior to our meeting. No Name called him and requested his assistance in a very personal matter. I mentioned that Flint is an ordained minister. No Name called and asked Flint to marry him and his fiancé a few days after our meeting. They were to be wed during a private ceremony on a nearby lake and he wanted Flint, a life-long friend, to perform the nuptials. They share invisible bonds that are unbreakable and stretch around the world and tie hearts together in this case — brothers in war, friends in life.

When Flint left the war zone in 1971, he was deemed a political risk were he to return to the World. He was given a TSSI security clearance (the highest intelligence security clearance and classification) and assignment and sent to Europe for a year. Even then, he was mistreated by his government. When he reported to the appropriate military unit, Flint was separated from other returning operatives. He was taken to a separate part of the building — upstairs and alone. The corporal who took him there locked him in, after telling him that it was done so nobody could intrude before the "higher-ups" could speak with him. Flint was left alone for three days, without food and water, without a word. The corporal made a major mistake. The lowest form of non-commissioned officer could not find the colonel he was to have informed, neglected to tell those coming on duty, and went about his weekend off-duty hours with uncommon negligence. The following Monday, a sergeant with some sense discovered the locked door, opened it and found an irate Special

Forces man inside. He was taken at once, and with deference, to the colonel and treated as he should have been. The colonel repaired some serious damage — and prevented some.

Flint lived off base, had a car and apartment, and was forced into a major cool down period for his and the government's own good. He had access to all the bases in the European theater, working on several important projects there which required special skills and travel arrangements. It was quite a period in his life. He experienced much and enjoyed a special beauty in his life. That cooled his raging emotions and brought him back into a gentler world in a warm, warm way.

Flint teaches self-defense. He teaches people of all ages how to save their own lives. In the evenings, he mixes discipline with the Bible for the youth in his community. He has done it for several years now. He says being saved, saved him. His demons are at rest. Flint has been married to a wonderful woman for 24 years and has three wonderful children. He could not marry until he was right with God and had divorced his old life. He is proud of what he did for America and regrets nothing, although he had to come to peace with much of it. Like other veterans, he too says the hardest thing is forgiving oneself. Our God is a forgiving God. He loves a warrior and understands. He is proudest of the 3000 youths and soldiers who he has saved since he became a man of God. When you meet him now you can see joy and peace in his face.

I think I made a new friend. He is starting a Christian-based Combat Veterans Organization. It is in its infancy. There has to be a place for vets who seek a different outlet than some groups offer. Flint says the time has come for that. He invited me to be part of that. I will, although it is far from the territory I range. I know one thing. I met a hell of a man.

Moody Ripsaw

Dateline, April 28, 2010…North Central Indiana

I struggled to drag my creaking body off my bike in my friend's driveway. He heard "The Duck" rumble to a halt and was outside before I got the kickstand down.

Jerry Lee Cloyd has been my friend for a while now and I've heard his story before, but this was the first time I came prepared to take notes. It was two friends having a bull session rather than a writer interviewing someone. I knew his wife Jackie had the coffee on so we could sit at the kitchen table and talk. My recorder has almost four hours of yakking saved for posterity.

There is a story to be told before I can tell the story I went to get. Jerry was awarded the Soldiers Medal when he was in Vietnam. That is a big, big deal. That is why I wanted him in my book, first and foremost. I want people outside his circle of friends to know. Before I begin that journey, I must share how privileged he made me feel before we began the journey into that war. After peeling the leather from my body (Indiana still has chilly winds in April), Jerry pushed me toward the door. I walked point for my search and learn patrol. From this point on, everything must be seen from the perspective of realizing that Jerry Lee Cloyd is a proud alumnus of the 11th Cavalry — Blackhorse!

I sat down at the table and got my notebook ready, prepped my recorder, and placed my ink pen nearby. Jerry retrieved the coffee cups and put an 11th Cav mug in front of me. He said, "Before you drink coffee I have to tell you about that cup. Jackie! I'm gonna let Mike drink outta Skip's cup!"

I realized something special was happening, but I had no idea what. Jerry began a story at a point even further back down a road we had traveled before. He and his wife took a road trip to California and the Lake Tahoe-Yosemite area on their bike a few years ago. We had talked about the California part of the trip before, but this time we began with the trip in Colorado. I was pleased. I had intended to ask some questions about the trip again anyway. It was like a magical mystery tour in my mind. I had no idea how accurate that thought was, but I was about to learn.

Jerry and Jackie were in Colorado when a storm began to bear down on them. They had been traveling US 50 — Jerry says it is called the loneliest stretch of highway in the United States — on their way to see Buffalo Bill's grave site. Storm clouds looked wicked on the horizon and they were getting communication that they contained copious amounts of hail. The couple stopped and got something to eat. It was not long before they needed a rest stop and found a sign for a rest park at Eagle River which leads to Rifle, CO. Off they went. Before they left the park, they took some great shots of the river valley and its panoramic views while sitting on the idling bike. While Jackie snapped photos, Jerry looked at the mountains nearby. He was amazed to see what looked like the 11th Armored Cavalry Regiment's emblem painted on a barn roof in the distance, atop a mountain. Pointing Jackie in that direction, they confirmed what he had seen by getting her long-range lens out of the pizza box on the back of the bike. He had to know before he could leave. Somebody on top of that mountain was proud of being a Blackhorse! He told Jackie they were going that way. She told him there was no way they could get the bike and trailer headed that way. It was the wrong direction for the exit. Jerry drove over the curbing, through the median and managed to get it done. Soon, they were parked at the fence adjacent to the property where the barn was located.

Jerry was trying to convince Jackie that it was okay to intrude on a fellow Blackhorse veteran when a man came walking toward them. The property owner had gotten close enough to see the same emblem on Jerry's bike and the welcome mat was out for them. The man was Skip Hutton, retired Command Sergeant Major, veteran of Vietnam and the first Gulf War, Desert Storm. Sutton had been in the Nam after Cloyd, but they had that war in common. He gave them directions to get into the property along with an invitation join his family for food. There were other vets (at least one was his son) there for a family cookout — a Seal — his son — and a Green Beret. They shared an incredible two hours of storytelling and warrior bonding. Sutton had been Command Sergeant Major to General Frederick M. Franks, Jr. in the Gulf War for Operation Left Hook. Jerry knew about Franks, who was also a Blackhorse legend in Nam. Sutton put flesh and blood on the personality about whom Jerry was well aware.

Franks had been a young officer in Nam, but he was a field soldier's officer, originally a tank commander. He was not a parade ground soldier. He went where his troops went, did what he asked of them. Franks was a warrior. He earned the Silver Star, the Distinguished Flying Cross, and a Bronze Star with V for Valor, the Air Medal and two Purple Hearts. During his first tour, one of his legs was so damaged that he became angry with the pace of rehabilitation. Franks demanded that it be amputated so he could be fitted with a prosthesis and return to active duty. It was and he did, where he was successful, and later commanded the 11th Cavalry. The rest became a legend for the Blackhorse and he became what was known as "visionary", according to *Wikipedia,* in the Army. Much has been written about his career. His artificial leg is in the Patton Museum.

I add that to this story only because it became important down the road after Jerry and Jackie left Sutton's home. The Blackhorse insignia on the barn roof is symbolic and has been the centerpiece in an article in Vietnam magazine. It is an open invitation to any member of the 11th Cav to stop and visit if they are in the area. The couple rolled toward their destination, but they found a room soon, as the sun set in the western sky. Jackie gave something to Jerry that she was supposed to hold until they reached California. She couldn't contain herself that long. When he came back from getting their sandwiches, she'd retrieved an 11th Cav coffee mug from a saddle bag. Jerry quizzed her about it. She told him that it was a gift from Sutton to him. Sutton knew that he would not have accepted it had he not slipped it to her for a surprise further down the road. They had shared such a special time that he wanted Jerry to have it. It was a cup given to him by General Franks, a cup that the General had personally used. I include this sidebar because Jerry allowed me the huge honor of drinking from it the day I visited him for this formal interview. I am still overwhelmed. It is a story I had to tell within this story.

Jerry and Jackie's trip was memorable for incredible coincidences. They rolled into California days later, where they spent time with Jackie's son, Tony. That young man loaned his bike to them while they had theirs in the shop for repairs. Tony's bike had belonged to Jerry and was covered with Jerry's military stickers. Jerry and Jackie took that bike to Yosemite National Park. They parked the bike at a scenic overlook and walked to an area where they could get more photos. They were walking back to the bike when they saw a well-dressed man approaching them wearing a hat with a familiar patch on it. Jerry knew the man had been an officer. There is something recognizable in the bearing. There are two kinds — field officers and desk officers. Jerry saw the Purple Fox and recognized the insignia for the Marine Corps helicopter unit in which a good friend of his had served. He said, "Bob Mayberry!"

The man reached his hand toward him and said, "Oh, my God! He was my door gunner in Nam. I was walking over to see who you were. I saw the 'Fox' on your bike." They shook hands and talked about Bob for a few minutes, exchanged information. Jerry gave Bob's address and phone number to the former pilot before getting back on the road. Mayberry had been shot down three times in combat in Vietnam. Cloyd could not believe he had encountered someone else on the trip connected somehow to his war experience, even through another veteran friend.

I had difficulty doing a "formal" interview with Jerry. When we talk, it is "Tangent City." It was time to get back on point. I went to get more of his Soldiers Medal story, but I enjoy him too much to stay on task. He was in Vietnam before I was and when he first arrived, he was in a signal unit replacement group. He did not get attached to the 11th for a few weeks. Not many soldiers start a tour of duty the way Jerry did.

After being trained in communications, Cloyd volunteered for jungle warfare training, where he earned his Jungle Expert's badge. He went in the Army in 1966 and landed in Nam in 1967. Jerry is one of those guys who does not do well with idle time, thus he took all the training he could get, including encryption and encoding techniques that got him special clearances. He hated barracks details and the training schools excused him from those. He was immersed in learning what he could and enjoyed the challenges of the work. There was value in it.

The time came for his unit to go to Vietnam. He and a few of his buddies took a last chance pass before leaving and went to a place that had long been on his wish list — Disneyland. He, like most of our generation, had been in love with Annette Funicello. On a whim, he called home to tell them he had made it to Disneyland and that was good fortune. Unfortunately, his father had fallen ill and the Red Cross had been trying to find him. Jerry returned to Fort Irwin and made immediate arrangements to fly out on emergency leave. His unit left before he returned. After his father's condition improved, he returned to his post. For this reason, Jerry Cloyd received a special dispensation and was airmailed to Vietnam while his buddies went by sea. He arrived a full week before they did and got acclimated before they did. Cloyd was temporarily assigned to the 40th Reception Unit at Bien Hoa until his unit, the 44th Signal Corp arrived. They were reunited at that point.

Cloyd's unit established a major base camp across the road from Bien Hoa and began building additions to the post there. His group established a "pool" of radio operators which back-filled needs with various operational units when not building double-decker bunkers in base camp. The radio operators also became skilled in many other jobs due to their status. The units borrowing them gave them all kinds of jobs once they reported for duty. Jerry established a very high standard of duty for himself on the first day of June in 1967. He was working as a "day laborer" traveling with a convoy getting supplies, laying sod, building bunkers, and performing manual tasks while awaiting the call to work within his MOS.

The convoy was moving down the road at a slow pace when a damaged helicopter flew over them, wobbling out of control, on the way to crashing. Cloyd observed it crash on its side in a rice paddy about 600 meters beyond the road. The convoy stopped and soldiers jumped out along the road and watched in amazement, but stood doing nothing. That was not in Jerry's nature. He could no more do that than he could stand idly by and watch people in a car wreck. With no thought about anything but helping them, he ran into the field toward the burning chopper. The Huey was shattered and lying on its side, flames beginning to engulf it, smoke billowing up as the fuel ignited. Jerry could not understand why he was the only one running to help but, in his words, he thought, "The hell with it," and he went. The fire extinguisher did not work when he grabbed it from the wreckage so he just ripped the broken metal off one of the trapped pilots, freed him, and carried him about 20 meters away. He turned and went back for the second man. It was then he noted that the other man was trapped under the nose of the chopper. Jerry Cloyd was not a big man — he weighed about 145 pounds then. Somehow he lifted the nose of that helicopter off the man and dragged him out of the mangled metal. He got him in a fireman's carry and they made it about 20 feet before the bird blew, knocking them to the ground. Jerry struggled to his feet with the rescued pilot in tow, made it to the place where he had deposited the other man. He stayed with them until a rescue helicopter arrived on the scene. He remained there and even helped with the saline drip the medics had to start in the injured pilots. By that time, three others had joined him, following his path to the site with great care. After the rescue was complete, the other soldiers told him to follow them out just the way he had entered the field. He asked them why and it was then he learned that the field was a known booby-trap area. That explained why everyone stood and watched — to everyone but Cloyd.

When he made it back to the convoy, the Convoy Commander asked his name and unit. He shook his head and asked if he was alright. Jerry turned and it was not until then that anyone realized how close it had been. Jerry had some minor burns on his hands. The officer told him to get treated as soon as they returned, but what he saw when Cloyd turned around shocked him. Jerry's hair was burned in a v-shaped wedge and the back of his state-side fatigue jacket was gone. The fire had burned hair and material away. Jerry's adrenalin rush had propelled him to lifting a helicopter off a man and kept him from feeling the flicker of flame melting the hair and cloth off his back and head. How could Private First Class Jerry Lee Cloyd be anything but a kick-ass soldier from that day forward? When the convoy returned to the 44th's base camp, he reported to sick bay, got his hands cleaned up, got some fatigues, and prepared to go to work the next day. As far as he was concerned, he had done nothing that anyone should not do.

All Army barracks are rife with complaining soldiers. It is the nature of the beast. Jerry's unit was full of specially-trained radio operators. They were dissatisfied with all the jobs they were being given. Many were saying they had filled out transfer forms for different units. Jerry had another emergency leave of absence in this period. His grandfather passed away. They had been close. He'd spent much of his youth with grandpa while his father worked away from home. When granddad died, the neighborhood went en masse to the political powers-to-be and brought Jerry home. After he returned to Nam, it didn't take long for him to join in the cry for action. He went to headquarters and filled out the form (either a DD- 1048 or 1049 — we could not remember) and with his crypto-clearance he got new orders within 24 hours. His buddies almost flipped. Where they'd been "blowing off" and bluffing, content to complain but spend their hours in relative safety, he'd really done it. He was called the next morning and told to report to the helipad with nothing but his personal gear. Jerry Cloyd was going to the 409th Army Security Agency at Bearcat, assigned to the 11th Armored Cavalry Regiment.

His new unit sent a "limo" for him. A Chinook helicopter arrived and he was the only one on board for the flight to Bearcat. Cloyd arrived and was greeted by a Lt. Col. with a Jeep at the helipad there. He was in shock. The "Old Man" had picked him up himself because everyone was working. They were waiting on him. Jerry saluted and was told to never do that again. He was taken to supply, where the supply sergeant was prepared for him. After he was outfitted, his real work in Vietnam began. In those days, his duty was split between the Bearcat and work at Suon Loc, where MACV was headquartered (Blackhorse moved there before Jerry's tour was over) — and the Special Forces group was still training ARVN forces. As a crypto-operator, Cloyd had work to do at both locations. He soon became well-known to the warriors in the entire area. He was in the war.

Jerry Cloyd remembers the practical jokes he and others played on the "newbies" who were assigned to his unit. All of us were crude. We lived hard. We played hard when we played. Some of us died hard. It was funny when we threw a dead rat in a shower at someone. It was deadly serious when we told them to shut the hell up on patrol, or to stay awake on a listening post. He took pride in sending perfect messages when he worked his radio. Jerry volunteered to man the radio banks where soldiers "called" home when they had the chance. Some soldiers hit the enlisted club when off duty. Cloyd cleansed himself of combat and work stress by assisting his fellow soldiers. One of his greatest pleasures was connecting a grunt with his girlfriend when the young man made his marriage proposal. Not long ago Jerry was sitting at his camp site at our Howard County Vietnam Veterans Reunion and a couple saw his insignia and stopped to tell their story. The man told a romantic tale about him and his wife connecting while he was in Nam. It was the very couple Jerry had helped. They met there at the reunion more than 35 years later in person! The Reunion is huge. It draws national attention from Nam veterans.

Jerry had another experience during one of the reunions which challenged credulity. He radioed coordinates for flight missions at night in Nam. His call sign was "Moody Ripsaw" and the old call sign is emblazoned on a sign near his camp site. A passer-by at the reunion noticed that and asked to whom it belonged. Jerry claimed it and the man was a pilot whom Jerry had once helped on a mission. They shared an emotional memory of a wild night in Vietnam. The warrior world can sometimes be very small. Whether at the Reunion or a scenic overlook, the bond is incredible.

Jerry Cloyd was not always on a radio in headquarters at Bearcat or Suan Loc. He toted a PRC-25 in the field on patrol. He did grunt patrols when his rotation for mud duty came up as well. Cloyd was no cherry. He has his combat time in the jungle. Cavalry is not always mounted — just as airborne is not always airborne. His most vivid combat memory is burned into his mind from the Tet Offensive of 1968, as that time is for many Nam vets.

The Army was aware that an attack was coming when the Tet Offensive started in 1968, although the size and intensity was at question in some quarters. Cloyd's outfit had been on patrol and had just returned. He was part of a strong unit and their position was pretty secure. They were told to mount up and head for Long Binh at daylight after the Viet Cong had been repelled during the first wave of the attack. The NVA were hitting in the second wave. He was in the third Huey of the first slick in, behind two Cobras and a couple of chopper gunships. The mini-guns had raised hell with the waves of attacking enemy forces. They were being mowed down and piled up like so much chaff. He could see dead bodies everywhere. Fire and smoke billowed up from two blown fuel depots on the largest American military installation in Vietnam.

The North Vietnamese Army had managed to blow two fuel dumps and the fires were raging out of control. The enemy had created a weak point and was threatening to penetrate that part of the perimeter. The 11th Cav was hitting them hard, and another Cav unit was hitting another flank from the other direction. The slicks with Cloyd and his buddies climbed over the vortex of flames and circled in search of an LZ (landing zone) where our ground troops could engage the enemy head-on and give chase. The NVA forces withdrew toward the rubber plantation north of Long Binh. Cloyd and his buddies hit the deck running, M-16s and M-60s chattering, giving chase to the enemy, which was falling away in rapid retreat. They had arrived in time and Long Binh was saved. The mini-guns from the ships had done incredible damage. They were mopping up as the stragglers from the North Vietnamese Army ran in complete disarray into the forest. They gave chase. What had been intended as a telling blow against American forces turned into a rout.

Cloyd remembers the adrenalin rush, the trembles, and the difficulty in breathing that comes with intense combat. The memory of huge piles of bodies which defy description as they were bulldozed into two enormous graves is something that lingers as well. The members of the 11th Cavalry returned to Long Binh to help secure the almost-broken perimeter and effect repairs to the damaged concertina barriers and other protective devices that had been breached by the enemy. The clerks and the non-combatants who had been called to defend the post were overwhelmed by the event. To say they were relieved by the rescue effort is an understatement of vast proportions. They had seen the end. Death was in the flames and smoke billowing into the sky. Life, for our people, was in the whirring of those helicopter blades and the tracers spewing from the mini-guns firing at tree top level into the bodies of the North Vietnamese about to overrun Long Binh. Cloyd says the view from the sky was like watching fire rain down on ants streaming from a hole in the earth as they circled waiting for their moment. It was the most electrifying moment of the war for him. It was much different than saving two men.

Jerry Cloyd laughs as he recalls when he was notified that he was getting a medal for his actions on June 1, 1967, when he saved the helicopter pilots. He had not given it a second thought. The men in his unit gave him absolute hell when they found out about it. The entire outfit was forced to fall in for a full parade ground operation, with all kinds of brass in attendance. Field soldiers are not into that. The Regiment Commander called Cloyd. By the time he was done Jerry was ready for sick call. Westmoreland was coming. The Secretary of Defense was coming. Every piece of shining brass in Southeast Asia was flying into their area for the ceremony. The place had to be spotless, including the soldiers. All because of Jerry Cloyd. He caught absolute and complete hell. He was given the Soldiers Medal. It is the highest non-combat medal awarded by the United States military. His orders read:

"For heroism not involving actual conflict with an armed enemy in the Republic of Vietnam; Private First Class Cloyd distinguished himself by valorous actions on 1 June 1967 while returning from a resupply mission near Duc Hoa. He saw a helicopter crash into a rice field near the highway as he was returning to his base and immediately dashed to attempt rescue of the crew. Heedless of the possibility of booby-traps being hidden in the tall grass. He ran across the rice paddy to the flaming wreckage. He secured a fire extinguisher from the debris and attempted to put out the blaze, but the extinguisher failed to function. Completely ignoring his own safety, he tore the twisted metal and lifted the front of the ship to free the trapped pilots. He quickly carried the injured pilot to safety and returned to assist in moving the co-pilot from the area. The ship exploded moments after he removed the second injured man, and the blast knocked him to the ground. After recovering from the shock wave, he set up a defensive perimeter and helped treat the casualties until rescue helicopters arrived. His unselfish efforts at great risk to his life greatly assisted in saving the victims and comforted them until they were moved to safety. Private First Class Cloyd's heroic actions were in keeping with the highest traditions of the military service and reflect great credit upon himself, his unit, and the United States Army. "

The orders are dated 24, November, 1967

I have a copy of his orders. Jerry has tried to find those two men. He wants only to know if they survived the war and are alive today. I have contacted a couple of people as well, to search for them. So far we have had no luck. He keeps hoping.

Like most of us, Jerry Cloyd was a different person when he came home. He was raised in the church. He left home with a briefcase. He came home with a four-piece-luggage set. His church had changed while he was away, including its leader. After he arrived home, his priest made a house call. Question after question fell on Jerry's ears. Jerry asked one of his own at last. He asked the priest when he was going to ask how *he* was. The priest had repeatedly mentioned what the church needed, what Jerry could do for it, and things like that, but he never got around to asking what *Jerry's* needs were. The priest got the message too late. He lost Jerry. Jerry, like veterans from many wars, had another battle to fight. Some wars never end and people fight them in different ways.

Jerry and I talked about winners and losers in war. Each side of a war is both at ground level. The politicians see it different than the worker bees. In the final analysis, that is an accurate summation. Jerry's trophies were in an old tin coffee can. He had them in it for years. It came to represent the hate and anger of war. Many years passed before he could share, before he could talk to anyone about Vietnam. His wife Jackie was instrumental in his opening up a bit. In 1988, he made a decision. It was time to bury the past. He buried that coffee can in his father's back yard and with it he buried his anger and hate. He forgave himself. He had his talk with God and killed the monster inside. He moved on at last.

Perhaps that is the most difficult thing of all — forgiving yourself.

Sportster-Slim

When I started riding motorcycles, I rode borrowed bikes, rode alone and did short runs only. A guy cannot ride with a group when he is on borrowed iron and he better not be gone long. I left the Army in 1969 and moved to Virginia to attend college, where I resumed riding, but this time my experience was dirt-biking in the mountains. Today some of it would be called extreme riding as we took our motorcycles into the woods high in the Appalachian mountains of Southwest Virginia.

I rode on an abandoned, reclaimed strip mine close to my house almost every day with a group of buddies who I trusted. They were people upon whom I depended in a pinch, to be there when I needed them. It was a good thing, because I was not as good as a couple of them and I broke my bike frequently. My shrapnel scars were soon hidden among the scars created by sailing headlong through the thorns of a locus tree. One afternoon, I sailed over a carrot-top in the middle of our remote 400-acre playground. The tree was benign enough to catch me in its branches and break my 40-foot fall to the ground. My God! That landing broke an unbreakable fender and I had blood all over my forearms, but I digress. That is a story I have told but have never written and do not intend to here. I did trade the bike for kitchen ware a short while later. There were many reasons, the first of which was keeping my neck whole. The point is I rode with people who I trusted just as I served in Nam with people I trusted.

Years later I got back on a bike again, but this time I was on paved roads. I was still an independent, riding alone most of the time. When my sons came along, I dismounted. I grew weary of juggling which one had more saddle time behind me and the arguments about who was next! That break lasted 25 years. The time came when I could not ignore the urge any longer. I got back in the seat, but this time it was on my dream bike. I got my first Harley. The thing that was the same was riding alone. I still had that independent thing going... until I began riding in charity events to Support our Troops.

I rode with a young friend on occasion and soon thereafter with her boyfriend (who became her husband). He is a Gulf War Era ex-Marine. I trust them. They pushed me into assaulting my "bucket list." Her family, with whom I was familiar, joined him in talking me into tackling Daytona's Bike Week in 2006 and it was one hell of an experience for me. Again, they are people I can count on—people I know will be there if I need them, whenever or wherever that might be. Life has taken us different directions but it is still true. There is a similarity between my riding friends and my Nam buds. Then I met Sportster-Slim.

Sportster-Slim is a biker and a Nam vet. He represents two lifestyles for me. One I know well, but he is teaching me a lot about the real biker's life.

Slim and I crossed paths later in life. We discovered the things we had in common and a bond grew that required no water. We ride. We fought in Nam, although I went a year earlier even though I am a younger man. Things were such that we could not be as close as we wanted until 2007 and then he pushed me into attacking another item on my "bucket list." We were joined by another young friend (one more ex-Marine who is married to a young lady I have known for years) who loves Harleys. We rode together to The Wall in DC with Rolling Thunder for Memorial Day. It was an incredible weekend and something intangible happened that weekend. All of us will carry it the rest of our lives. We traveled together and covered each other's backs on the trip. We knew if we needed anything, someone was going to be there when we looked over our shoulder. There was a thread binding us. The common bond was the purpose of the weekend and having served our country.

Since that trip we have ridden with others, but more often it is Slim and me. Slim is a Nam vet. His story is one that exemplifies the clash of two worlds and the rise of the phoenix from the ashes.

Sportster Slim arrived in Vietnam in March of 1969 and was assigned to the First Air Cavalry. He was with them until April 18, 1969. He had a really short stay in the field. Slim was a radio operator, but he was soon relieved of that duty. He was hit by an anti-personnel mine in the lower leg, shattering bone and shredding muscle, as his team disembarked their chopper that day. They were hit hard. His officer was shot as Slim watched from the deck. While Sportster-Slim lay on the ground, he tried to use the radio to call the choppers back for an emergency evacuation. Another round hit the arm he used to hold the handset. That round traveled up the inside of the arm and lodged beneath his shoulder, doing major damage to his nerves and muscles along the way. It ended his call for help. He was on his left side. Slim's right leg and arm were a matched set at that point — useless. The next thing he knew he was in a field hospital preparing for transport to another hospital in Nam where he could get better care. Slim spent the next three weeks shuffling between three hospitals in Vietnam before the Army moved him to Japan.

While in Japan, a team of surgeons tried to patch the nerves in his arm so he could regain some use of that appendage. It was pot luck. The doctors did not know what to expect, but they did all they could. They told Slim that the goal was to get him well enough to send him home where there was more expertise. While he was there, his leg developed a major infection.

Slim got embroiled in a huge dispute with the three doctors taking care of him regarding the amputation of the leg. He convinced one of them to leave it where it was — attached to him. He spent several weeks with an open wound while there, with exposed drainage tubes, trying to heal as his body rid itself of whatever poison raged in him. After an interminable amount of time, Sportster-Slim was shipped to Walter Reed Hospital back in the World (States). He endured several surgeries and several convalescent leaves home and back to the hospital, until he received a medical discharge in November of 1969. In Slim's words, "My trigger finger wouldn't work so Sam had no use for me anymore." He said it was a real joy trying to use a crutch on an arm that would not work well. It was a Godsend in a way. The pain forced him to use the leg sooner than he might have otherwise — and he used a cane ahead of medical predictions. When he left there "he almost walked the way he should."

◆ ◆ ◆

Sportster-Slim began learning the dark side of being a Nam vet during his leaves home. Although he was on a cane, he went back to his former employer, where he had been a successful car salesman, and sought part-time work. He had worked since he was a teen. Idle time was unnatural. Slim's employer saw his cane and discovered he had several limitations at the time. When he learned Slim wanted very few hours and was available for just a couple of weeks, he responded that part-time was not a good schedule, but indicated that there would be a job for him when he returned home after his discharge. His first marriage had failed. His Nam experience was beginning to ride him harder than he rode his old Harley. It seemed to him that work could be another kind of therapy. The first of many barriers began to appear. It was not a tremendous disappointment then, however, as he was still drawing his full military pay. His leave time was limited to 30 days, but the Army granted that often, not just once a year as is normal. Sportster-Slim made frequent trips between Kokomo, IN, and Washington, D C. They prevented dwelling on what would become a major issue far too soon.

Slim and I began sharing war stories, as vets do when the right opportunities presented themselves. As our friendship grew, I learned more about his "welcome home." The time he spent at Walter Reed was a great diversion for a while. He was fortunate enough to engage in a great therapy program. Suffice it to say that he found a local care-giver who gave him special attention. She was related to a legend in the male entertainment industry in those days. Sportster-Slim became a frequent visitor at a high profile home, getting some high profile therapy. He and a couple of his recovery buddies drove the convalescent center guards nuts with the creative ways they found of escaping at night to obtain their special care. In hindsight, Slim often wonders why he was in such a hurry to get home. But there was that trigger-finger thing, and when the Army gave him his medical discharge, it also gave him travel money and a final paycheck. He returned home to go to work. He thought.

Sportster-Slim arrived in Kokomo, IN, as a civilian in November, 1969—but this time he was a disabled veteran. He was tough. He walked on a leg, albeit with altered gait, that doctors wanted to amputate. His hand worked even though it did not have full strength or motion. The doctors had done tremendous work, yet Slim's pure cussedness had as much to do with his recovery as anything. He still had some healing to do before he could crawl on his old, blue Harley. The fact that it was November would not have mattered much had he been healthy. He had been a rider since he was 15. After a few days and a few drinks, Slim visited the car dealership. The old boss had sold out to his partner and the promise of a job left when he did. Slim had no wife, no job, no income, and was building a "mad."

Sportster-Slim still had some separation money in his pocket and there were several bars in his hometown. The job search could wait a couple of days. So it did. He was supposed to get disability pay, although it would not be a lot, and it would be better than a sharp stick in the eye—or a bullet in the leg or arm. The beer would be cold and would chill the heat building in his blood.

The job search was futile. Kokomo is an industrial town. In the sixties there were two steel-related facilities and two automotive. He was given a cold shoulder at each, as his limp was an obvious sign of limitations. When the hiring agents learned of his disability, they became noncommittal. At Delco Radio the personnel director was blatant in his refusal. He told Sportster-Slim, "You Vietnam guys are all a bunch of burn-outs and dopers. Everybody coming back from Nam is a junky and troublemaker. Besides, you are disabled and can't do anything. Your work would not be up to standard." Slim left before he hit the man. He was afraid if he started he would not stop until the paddy wagon came to get him. The barriers he began to sense back in the summer were built before the Christmas trees were decorated that year.

Sportster-Slim made a decision before the rising of many more suns. If the World was going to call him a "no-good piece of shit, then by god, he was gonna live up to it and be the baddest-ass, no-good piece of shit he could be." He woke up after the New Year's bells quit pealing, rolled a bed roll, packed some gear, put a gun behind his belt and jumped on his old bike. By the time Slim hit the Indianapolis city limits, the snowflakes were hitting him. He headed west. There was very little folding money in his pockets, but he would find a way. Some folks might not like the way he was going to pay for the trip, but so be it. He was going hardcore. Slim, the Harley, and the road—the devil was damned sure going to take the hindmost. He headed for Arizona.

The trip was circuitous. Slim wound his way through a number of states. It was an orgy of armed robberies. The trip paid for itself. That old bike made history as he rode into and out of town after town, unidentified, but leaving stories in his exhaust that may be told yet today. He had no plan and the rambling nature of the trip could be why he succeeded. Slim went well north and way south. At one point, he visited a family member who loaded Slim's bike up in his old truck and told Slim that he was coming too. Somewhere along the way, they stopped to eat and ordered pie. The waitress told them that it was not available and pissed Slim off again. He rode a "mad" like he rode his bike by that time. It was about a millimeter under the surface all the time. He fought at the drop of a hat and dropped the hat himself, as the old saying goes. The owner came out and told them the pie was seasonal, to which Sportster-Slim said, "Then take the damned pie off the menu. Since you don't have the #@%^&*' pie, give me all your cash" and put his pistol under the owner's chin. In Slim's words, "it is amazing how a piece in somebody's face changes their attitude." I imagine he smiled when he told the story 35 years ago. He does not now — there is sadness in his voice.

Slim and his relative hit old Route 66 and pointed west. They had enough cash to make the trip without further distractions of any major proportions. It was "Arizona or Bust" and they were worried about the latter. For some unknown reason, there was no pursuit and they traveled unmolested. The trip was tough, but they made it. Slim had a place in mind—and after a few days, he found hardcore bikers and disillusioned Nam vets who made him feel as though he had come home. They stayed a while, partied, worked odd jobs, and lived a communal lifestyle. Slim earned his sobriquet at the time. From then on he carried the nickname Sportster-Slim. I have done the Sporty thing. I hated doing 50 miles on mine. My butt flat hurt! Of course I was older when I got mine, but still — riding cross country on one? Slim had to have cast iron "nads."

Slim's relative decided that the life was too wild for him at his age and fired his old truck up and headed back home. A few weeks later Sportster-Slim decided he needed to clear out for a few weeks too. It was getting a little hot where they were and it had nothing to do with the sun. He had enjoyed a brief stay in Texas before and decided a tour of that state would be in order. The loaded six-shot ATM card was still behind his belt. He had checked things back in the Hoosier state and he had some legitimate money as well. His disability money had begun arriving sometime in July of 1970.

Slim hit the road again. It wound across the plains of Texas for a little longer time than he planned. He met some folks who insisted he stay and he did. Slim always had a weakness for the ladies and this time he could not leave for a while. There was an offer which could not be refused.

Many months later, he returned to his beloved Verde Valley area of Arizona. Slim moved around in that state for years, but he liked that area best. He was an independent. I ride alone but I learned that in the biker world that is not the same as an independent. An "indy" is a biker not affiliated with a gang. He wears no colors. They often ride in groups and are affiliated with each other, but not to a group which carries a banner and has a familial or gang affiliation of its own definition. They are as dedicated to the lifestyle as any hardcore rider, but they stay out of the warfare often associated with the competitive world of biker gangs. Sportster-Slim was submerged in the lifestyle. He was a disgruntled Nam vet who had a home and a group of people he trusted. They were his family.

To say I enjoy Slim's stories is a huge understatement. I understand the pain and disappointment that started the journey. I remember the media coverage that labeled so many of my fellow veterans the way he was labeled. I too have felt the anger, the desire to strike out, to make someone pay, felt the stress of the disdain, seen the leers on the faces of some people when arriving home, and heard the derision in certain voices during national news programs. Slim had Post Traumatic Stress Disorder (PTSD) and did not know it. None of us did. He had an incredible adventure too, when he had good times. While in Texas, he fell in love with woodworking, a passion that he has today. He is pursuing that now with a recent purchase of some equipment that will allow his creativity to reveal itself in the next few months.

Sportster-Slim rode all the mountain ranges out west at one time or another. He associated with a group of like-minded riders who were also independent of any gang affiliation. They partied. They saved people from burning homes when the firemen gave up on them. They had bar fights. The bar where Slim was a bouncer was the subject of a newspaper article in the 80s that I was privileged to read. Sportster-Slim was mentioned and appears in one of the photos. The bar was renowned for its gang neutrality. A large sign was displayed at the entrance. It said clearly: CHECK YOUR GUNS AND YOUR COLORS AT THE BAR. It was a warning and it was enforced by all who entered if someone did not take it as a serious warning. Very few mistakes were tolerated. Even bikers need a safe haven. Perhaps that is another reason why a biker has so much in common with a combat vet.

◆ ◆ ◆

Slim worked as a bouncer, a motorcycle mechanic, an escort for hookers so they could work tricks in safety, and a whole host of underground jobs that have job descriptions which polite society does not have computer codes for in any of its systems. He spent years in Arizona and loves it still. It was a more stable relationship than any of his marriages. Those are the most obvious sign of his struggle with PTSD, those and his struggle with anger and authority. The last two are the cross I bear. We vets each find a way to carry our own. Slim's way has not been mine. It took me much longer to find my way and in some ways perhaps I am still searching.

Sportster-Slim came home to Kokomo and became Slim again. He found traditional work and began to shed the old ways. He kept riding. He was on much nicer iron — and has continued to improve his rides as his economic situation has improved. Slim has found some peace with himself — some reconciliation. He is a Disabled Vet and learned that giving to our soldiers is the greatest healing mechanism there is for him. Several years ago, he got involved with his union's veterans committee, but he cannot stand the politics of groups like that and the kind of waste it often engenders. Along with a group of like-minded people, he helped form an organization that does a tremendous amount of volunteer work for our soldiers, but without all the bureaucracy. They have collected thousands of items in donations, boxed them, and mailed them to soldiers and sailors in Iraq and Afghanistan. The organization has welcomed young veterans home, sent them off in style, and loved them while they are gone. It is a small group in numbers, but a group with a collective heart the size of the Arizona that Sportster-Slim loves so well.

Sportster-Slim received very special recognition from the Commanding General of the Indiana National Guard for his volunteer efforts. The certificate says things about his dedication to serving his country, those who serve this country, and his unwavering love of the Flag under which he fought. He earned two Purple Hearts. Slim has the scars, the remnants of anger, the disability from his wounds, and the purpose that has at last allowed him to heal. Yes, I have seen the phoenix rise from the ashes. I trust him and I ride with him.

The 10th of May

This year of our Lord, 2007,
Was different for one Marine.
Today is the first time since 1976
That he has not sought a peaceful scene.
He usually takes this day alone
To reflect on when he came home.
Solitude keeps his mind filled
With peaceful images rather than
Those of a bloody war zone.
He seeks no other man at this time.
He wants to be alone with his memories.
There is no today, only his history.

He remembers the fear of coming
Back to the World, the States.
It was a land screaming with
The noise from protesting ingrates.
He thought the carnage to which
He had grown accustomed
Was preferable to a land where
He was now a returning refugee.
The noise, the fear of battle were
The sounds that he preferred.
He thought leaving that experience
Should perhaps be deferred.

He is a Marine and it is a legacy.
Many do not understand
The link of those who serve in any way.
He cannot talk about his pain today
When the words are foreign to many ears.
He cannot talk about homecoming fear.
Who could feel that when they
Had never left home, never been estranged?
They would think him odd,
May even deranged.
It was he who had left, gone to war,
But his home almost seemed home no more.

He gave up the solitude needed today
For a greater need in his life.
The lure of remembering his lost comrades
Would wait until dusk this time.
His explanation for being alone would
Confuse even his wife.
It is not rejuvenation he seeks but quiet.
If he does not, it will ruin this night.
Those minutes are demanded by
His heart and spirit, and I know why.
He has to balance what happened then
With what has happened in his life since.

He is a vet, a Marine, an American.
He knows the wrongs of doing right.
More than once in his life he made a stand.
He is a father, a husband, a grandfather, a man.
He survived for what he would give the world.
Someone has to teach the next generation,
Or try.
This is a day when he usually cries.
He still will.
Only it will not be today.
It will be tonight.

Never on Sunday — Until Now

One Saturday night, I received a phone call from my wife's good friend Connie Nance. She and her husband Larry wanted me to be sure I attended church the following morning so I could meet Larry's son-in-law, Phil Wood. Larry's daughter Christine and husband Phil were home from Arizona for a few days. He is a former Navy Seal (Naval Special Warfare Group) with combat experience during the Gulf War, unofficial combat time during the US involvement in Somalia and at other times in the Middle East, too. I went to sleep late, thinking about the stories in his life. I woke before my alarm could fire its intrusive volley of beeps into the morning's calm.

I walked into our sanctuary entrance and was introduced to Phil, a tall, handsome Native American who wore the symbols of his tribal affiliation and service to his country with equal pride. Our Native Americans have fought with valor for generations! Phil Wood placed another exclamation point on that sentence. He is slow to speak about much of it, but later — much later — I discovered he is the first Native American to complete BUDs training successfully. Services were about to begin so we made arrangements to chat later in the day. Larry and Connie were hosting an open house that afternoon for the couple. They offered me a meal — the wife is away — and I was going to jump on that opportunity like a duck on a June bug. Besides, they had chocolate cake. Connie can cook a bit, so I had visions of thick, moist, dark cake with a heavy layer of luscious icing calling my name…

First I had to visit my Uncle Bob, suffering with terminal cancer. It was a tough visit. I love that ornery old man. He is the last male in my father's clan and only one aunt remains too. I am happy to be here to turn gray but Lord, how it hurts too. I visited for a few hours with Uncle Bob, but more with Aunt Sue while Uncle drifted in and out, succumbing to the effects of his pain medicine, something he has steadfastly avoided for several months — until now. Bob Mullins is tough as nails. I could tell some stories. I have. He had a good August, better than *anyone* expected, but September has been tough. I think August must have been the eye of the hurricane. The back side of the storm is here. When he wore down, I readied myself for the trip home and the continuation of my visit with my new Warrior Brother. I kissed Aunt Sue, kissed Uncle Bob's head, rubbing it with a gentle touch, telling him I love him and left without a tear. He would not have it otherwise.

I drove home thinking about many things and my mood brightened as I neared my turf. After I checked on my spoiled dogs, I hurried to the Nance homestead, fearing most of the good chow was gone. I was later than anticipated, but my time with family was important — I felt it in every fiber. When I arrived, my sense that I was too late proved accurate. The guests were gone, but the people I went to see were still there. That too was about to change. Phil and Christi were preparing to leave as well. They had an evening commitment elsewhere. We planned to meet the next day for a visit to the Howard County Vietnam Veterans Organization's Healing Field. They left me with the rest of the Nance family and the leftover Manwich. And, there was the chocolate cake too. It was all I anticipated.

Larry and Connie have a great home amid Indiana's fertile farm fields. There is quiet there — trees and a pretty pond nearby. We gathered inside around the table, safe from the abundant corn pollens, and chatted between big bites of cake followed by well-deserved swallows of sun tea. I never hear war stories on Sunday, until now. I thought I was going to hear some of Phil's, but as things evolved I was fortunate enough to hear a pair of quick tales from Larry.

Larry's father Fred fought in World War II. He served in the Navy on a Pacific Fleet aircraft carrier. Mr. Nance was a Chief Mechanic, but Larry could not remember his exact title. He was a main player below decks keeping the muscle of the ship operational. He was the expert when it came to running the two huge and powerful diesel generators that provided the electrical power for the entire vessel. Larry's eyes sparkle when he recalls his father's favorite story. . .

The crew had prepped the ship for a major inspection for Navy brass and high ranking civilians. Fred was below decks monitoring his "babies" awaiting his turn in the spotlight. When the ship's representative (Larry was not sure if it was the Captain or his designee) came below decks with the entourage, he decided to demonstrate Fred's prowess with the huge generators. He ordered the Chief to put them in parallel phase so the civilians could see how well trained his personnel were and how much power the Navy had at its disposal. It is a delicate operation, requiring skill and timing when done right. It must be done with patience and attention to detail to avoid damage as well as surprise. Fred was bringing the two engines together, balancing the controls with care and precision. He was the maestro at the podium bringing the orchestra to a crescendo for that perfect moment. The Officer in Charge was impatient and demanded he complete the process without delay. Nance tried to tell him it would take a few more minutes, but was interrupted before he could finish his sentence. He looked his superior in the eye and said, "Aye, aye, sir!" and leveled the controls as instructed. The reaction was instantaneous.

The immense generators slammed into synchronicity with a crash, throwing all their power into the "union" with such noise and force that the entire ship was pitched on its side. The move was so violent that the flight deck listed deep enough that its edge hit the sea. Waves washed over it. The conning tower and flight control tower were even sprayed. Men and supplies above and below decks were tossed like chaff into bulkheads. Others were thrown from their stations and bunks. Politicians were slammed into iron walls below decks. They were very, very impressed with the Officer-In-Charge—and the power of diesel parallelism. It was fortunate that planes and payloads were locked in place above and below decks so the damage was not as severe as it might have been. Injuries to sailors were minor and nobody was lost overboard. But something was lost. The senior politician observing below decks made a lasting impression on all present. When everyone got their feet under them again, he reached over to the O-I-C's epaulettes and jerked his rank and the attached material off his uniform. As Fred told it, he said, "In the future, you may become a good officer when you have enough sense to listen to your men."

Connie had prodded Larry into sharing the story. I sat amazed at the images in my mind. I had visions of an aircraft carrier tossed on its side and an entire crew wondering if it had been attacked or something. The memory of Pearl had to be fresh, but there were no bombers or fighters. The ship was swarming with civilians. I was asking myself what might have happened in the shadow of that event. It was one hell of a story. Connie went on to tell me that Larry's son Duane had joined the Navy after high school in honor of his grandfather. Connie chimed in again, demanding Larry share another story. This one was funny and not as traumatic as Grandpa's, but one that fit the family tradition for leaving a ripple in the waves. Larry shared the cow story with me.

Duane became an electrical maintenance expert while he was in the Navy. After promotions and a few cruises, his job evolved. Near the end of his enlistment, he was in charge of coordinating supplies, both ordering and planning for short and long term needs aboard his ship. He got along well with his superiors, in particular the ship's Captain and Executive Officer. For some reason, his immediate superior did not like him. At every opportunity, his boss gave him crap. It was not enough to cause him to report it, but it was enough to cause some anger and distress at times. There are times in life that you just have to tread water until the rough time passes and the military is no different. Duane was angry after one incident and got a hair-brained idea. He saw an ad in a magazine that caught his attention and did something for the pure hell of it.

Duane's routine required that he write requisitions. Each day, he took a stack of *reqs* to his superior for approval. Some were for immediate release and others for release at a later date. None of them had dates or his name on them. After being signed, they were released as needed. Duane wrote a requisition for 50 cows and it was signed without the boss even glancing at it. He took his stack of papers back to his desk and put the special one in his drawer with a large measure of satisfaction, but no intention of ever using it. It was one of those private jokes that he could pull out of the file when needed. Duane could look at it and laugh when he needed to after one of the sneaky "jerk attacks." He knew that he had pulled a "no harm, no foul" trick on The Man. That harmless prank helped Duane cope with several weeks of hazing as his time in service wound toward its end.

The weeks rolled by and Duane reached his last night aboard ship. He was leaving the vessel and processing out of the Navy. He was done. He was headed home. The knucklehead knew it and could not resist one last cheap shot. Duane's officer assigned him Watch Duty on his last night aboard. He could not believe it and he was angry. As the night passed, he grew angrier. At last he said, "The hell with it" and went to his old file one last time. The requisition for 50 cows was placed in the out box. His name was not on it, it had no date, and the request was for delivery at some point many weeks in the future. Duane would be well away from all things Navy. The s-o-b deserved the gift. It was a great parting shot across his bow. The next day Duane said his farewells and the ship's Captain bade him well.

Two or three months after Duane got home Larry answered the phone one afternoon. The call was for Duane and it was the Navy. The voice on the other end was very official. Larry had no idea at that point what was going on, but he hoped nothing bad was on the horizon. Duane answered with reluctance. Duane's old Captain was on the line and told him the darnedest story. They had been on a 30-day shakedown cruise. When they returned, a truck with 50 cows was waiting to drop its load. It had been there for two days waiting for instructions. They had been trucked to a nearby pasture twice or three times for water and food. It had to be done in order to avoid problems. Duane's old boss had signed the requisition. The Captain thought Duane might know something about it or perhaps would like to know about it at the very least. The Navy had to authorize shipping them back to their point of origin. His former boss had to write that one himself and do a lot of explaining. The Captain laughed and told Duane, "Good job." He wished him well and concluded the call. It appeared he knew what had gone on between the two all along. Duane knew there was no hard evidence, but he forgot that the paperwork was from the electrical section of the ship. Who else would have had a motive? It was a good thing the Old Man approved.

I was a happy man. It was an unusual Sunday. I met another good veteran, ate some great cake, saw my uncle one more time, heard two great stories, and made plans to take a new friend to the Healing Field the next day. Pieces of stories were bouncing around with Phil's name attached. I hoped to fill in some blanks on Monday.

I met the crowd for lunch as planned that Monday. I cut Phil out of the herd and we galloped away to the Grounds for a brief introductory visit there. I wanted to show him what it has to offer. He has some open emotional wounds from his service time, as do most combat veterans. We had spoken enough for me to learn that. He and I had two or three broken, brief talks since we met the previous day. He served from 1980 to 1986 and it is my hope to learn much more about him in the future. I only turned the first few pages. My mission was to take him to our clinic and introduce him to the Healing Field.

We passed through the gate at the Howard County Vietnam Veterans Organization's Grounds with the usual teasing of one old vet of another. I was asked about my Reunion entry wristband and I blew them a kiss. I know a few of those folks there — I am a life member. The Reunion does not begin for a few days yet, but campers have been drifting in for several days, even weeks. There were probably 100 set up at least already. Flags and banners from different military units were blowing in the breeze—American Flags, POW banners, and Purple Heart Pennants fluttered alongside. We drove around the property so Phil could get a small taste of the atmosphere before we parked. People yelled and waved. Calls of "Welcome Home" and "Brother" drifted in the wind to us as we passed by the camp sites. His smile grew as we saw the aging warriors who gather each year to share memories.

I eased my car to a stop at the main building after he sighted a Navy Seal flag flying over a nearby motor home. Phil wanted to speak to the owner. We went into the shadowy interior first so he could see what the place looked like, but we did not stay long. I introduced him to a few folks inside and then we made our way to the flag he'd spied. He had found warm welcomes and knew he found a place that was special. The most important question had already been answered. He was a veteran and was at home with other vets. It did not matter what conflict. It did not matter that he was Native American. It did not matter where home was. His story did matter. The people cared.

We went to the motor home and he found the owner, all reluctance gone. The Marine was also wearing a shirt that said Navy Special Warfare Group. He had been in Nam, but had been trained by the Seals at a special school with which Phil was familiar and at which he had been an instructor when he served. They talked the kind of talk that left me on the periphery, but that is okay. It was their language. Phil was at home. He got a special invitation for next year. He had announced he will be here next year and he is bringing his best friend, a vet from my era and a 10th Armored Cavalry member. I hope he comes.

George Wilson was the name of the man and he bonded with Phil. Brothers are brothers in that arena. They looked into one another's eyes and saw truth. George told Phil that other Seals attend and one younger vet comes who was also on Grenada. That added fuel to Phil's resolve about next year. What if they know each other? The excitement is mounting. George then introduced Phil to Bruce Wilson, one of our Security Vets who attends every year. George found us about ten years ago and will not miss now. Bruce is another Marine, my contemporary. He got out of his golf cart and welcomed Phil home. We hug, we shake hands, we laugh and we cry. It is part of healing. And healing has to be renewed a lot sometimes. Like every year.

I stopped other passers-by. Phil met George and Margaret, Roy, Tommy, Terry, and later Tony, Harry, and a few others whose names fail me at the moment. I pointed out Dollar Bill, our President. Then Jimmy Smith drove by and "Ski" and I took him in to meet Short Round, a "brown water raft rider" who became a Fed after the war, working with the DEA, busting drug rings in America which had links elsewhere. Phil asked me if I knew I had a veritable cornucopia of stories to write in this place. I told him that I know, but it is impossible to do. When we are in this setting I have six or seven people talking at once and there is no way on earth to keep track of them all. If I recorded them, I could not go over them later and retrace them to the right person to separate them, so when I am there I simply enjoy. On occasion, I isolate one and share it. I feel inundated by a veritable Niagara Falls of information. My hope at this moment is to live long enough to finish this book and, God willing, live long enough to do another. If that happens perhaps I will get a good story in it about Phil.

Phil is a full-blooded Chippewa, or that is what we whites know them as. His actual tribe is Ojibwe. He has been adopted by the Hopi as well. Prior to coming here, he completed his last trial for joining the Elder's Council. He has done the Sun Dance. I have tasted a bit of his lore the last two days and I thirst now for more of his firsthand knowledge. A writer friend — jim greenwald — I know now from my writing society, shares his tribal association. I read some of his poetry a year ago. He does a wonderful job of putting their sense of oneness in nature into verse. I will learn from them if I am able. Phil and Christine have vowed to live the life of his ancestors. They live in a teepee and did survive a vicious winter last year in the way of the plains tribes. Phil and Christi will build an outdoor kitchen when they get home, then an adobe/straw-brick two room winter house attachment for the teepee for more extreme weather as well.

Phil Wood led the way ashore on Grenada, fought in Somalia, was in Afghanistan training fighters for their resistance of the Russians, and in two other major deployments. He has been shot and caught shrapnel. Like many of us, he fights PTSD and the VA. His story is like my own and hundreds of others, regardless of the conflict. I want it. He has to have the health care. His family was split on the reservation when he was a child. He ended up with a white family in CA as a child and not treated well. He loves his country and he clings to the dream. Phil is returning to his roots. That is a dream he knows he can have. Christine is going to share it with him.

He is battling the VA for care and the war is on-going. He has earned that help. Damn it, it is due him. His tribe has granted him special ink. Phil wears two Eagle Feathers — and another symbol I did not understand. They show his people recognize him as a proven warrior and it is emblazoned in his skin. He nearly died after being mistreated for a disease that he will battle for the rest of his life. Phil Wood has scleroderma. The VA has him listed as terminal and it still took him ten weeks to see his primary care doctor. Does anyone see a problem here?

Phil Wood was welcomed home. He will be welcomed every time he comes back. He is a Warrior Brother in his Tribal Council and a warrior brother at the Healing Field.

My Pet

There is no wet nose in my plate and I can't eat.
She can't sleep without her warm pet on her feet.
The loss of a pet leaves a hole in many families.
The loss is more sorrow filled than many believe.
November has been a hard month over the years.
Many loved ones, and pets, left only some tears.
No more of my big girl, wagging her tail joyfully,
Or pawing at my legs and then leaning against me.
When I look out the window and see an empty pen,
Or any of us see where a pet may have once been,
There is a longing for a pet that only wanted love.
We fool ourselves by believing in pet heaven above.
   Never underestimate what a pet means in life.
   At times it is the only thing there during strife.
   A companion, a savior, or a safe place perhaps,
   Pets have more value than just sitting in laps.
   People are slow to admit just how big a place
   That our pets often play in our personal space.
Another story revealed the truth of a pet's worth.
A Nam vet named Boston had one friend on earth.
It was a German Shepard called Chopper, his bro,
That held a glorious place in his life I now know.
He was a hunting pal, hearing all Boston's stories.
He was close to every campfire, sharing his glory.
   The day came that Chopper was unable to fly.
   Boston knew his friend was soon going to die.
   He searched for a pup, for another Shepherd.
An ad appeared, was written in the right words.
Boston made the call but the price was too high.

The numbers, the reality, made him and others cry.
A vet called the sellers; "This guy is disabled.
He has four Purple Hearts and still must grapple
With stress and memories, pain and loneliness.
He has a dog that is aging and may soon be gone.
We fear when it happens Boston won't live long."
Those people lowered the price, more than half.
The vet said, "Sold! We'll handle that." in relief.
Boston got the dog and Chopper began its education.
It was as though the two connected in communication.
They were inseparable, sleeping and waking, for days.
A day came, Boston between the two, Chopper in close.
Chopper stretched across and licked the pup on its nose.
Boston's friend quietly passed, there on Boston's thigh.
Somehow, he passed the torch to another before he died.
Who knows what spirits protect us and in what ways?
What is a source of strength to get us through a day?
A pet can be a true friend, and dogs can go to heaven.
God chooses many things in life, our loads to lighten.
They are rewarded with love, a status without equal.
Boston's load was lifted by Chopper in this parallel.
Whether little, big, docile or running all around,
The silence is deafening if they are in the ground.
This may be trite but to me truth not to be refused.
My pet is not here and she was hard for me to lose.
Laugh if you want, I really do not mind old "hoss."
I hope all who read this understand it is real loss.

An American Hero

A true American hero never stops giving.
He is more a hero now than ever.
Our lives today are what he is saving.
He has earned his spot in heaven.
The Medal of Honor on his neck brings cheers
And was earned long ago
Despite his own pain and suppressed tears.
How does that story go?
He saved others at a price; his story is told.
He has given to us *all* since.
I look in awe and think about his real load.
Is he a real man or a prince?
The Medal may lie on his heart like an anchor.
Some days it may fill him with dread.
I see now that courage is more than mere valor.
It takes over a hero's life I am afraid.
People stand in line to hug him, shake his hand.
They should look into his eyes.
Every moment given takes another piece of him.
Would he like to be just one of the guys?
They want to touch an American Hero in tribute
A greater gift may be given I am certain.
In my heart, I too offer him a pride-filled salute.
In truth our thanks is often a burden.
The line is never ending and vets just love him.
It falls away but then gains new strength.
His hero's message costs him now as it did then.
He sees lines like rope with unending length.
I felt something near this special man.

> He does not know that or me.
>
> He will live his life doing something grand.
>
> I am not a hero; it is too harsh a destiny.
>
> Mike Mullins, 9/14/07

I first wrote this on scrap paper sitting in the bright sunshine at a small table shoved against a chain link fence. It was scribbled during our annual Veterans Reunion at the Howard County Vietnam Veterans Organization Reunion on the aforementioned date. I date my poems because there is a reason I wrote them. A spur of some kind slammed into my psyche somewhere and forced them out of my soul. This day I had been angry. The stage manager at our annual event asked me to prepare a lot of material to fill in during the dead time between band set-ups. I had my book sales table about 20 feet from the stage, right below a six-foot-tall bass speaker. Having done a few poems early in the show, I was awaiting the next call to perform. The placement took me out of the traffic area and I realized that my sales were going to suffer, but it was for my group. He promised to plug my work, so perhaps it would pay off for me in the long run. No matter, it was my contribution to the weekend.

The blast of music had enraged my tinnitus, Mr. Stage Manager had not mentioned me, and one break had passed and I was ignored. He and I seem at odds sometimes. He wants nothing but party time at the reunion and I believe we have an obligation to remember why we are there — a serious note needs to be interjected at times. He thinks I am a "downer" and I suppose that is true, but I want the "reason for the season" to be interjected, and the tributes to be made. I don't sell many books there anyway. Most of my brothers bring enough money to drink beer and eat burgers. I do want to contribute and I do want to say something about those who have made sacrifices for our great country.

My blood pressure was beginning to elevate. The next thing I knew two of the stage hands were setting a table and three chairs in front of me! Now I was getting even more pissed! Five minutes later one of my personal heroes was fighting through the mob, along with his wife and another lady. Sammy L. Davis, Indiana's only Congressional Medal of Honor recipient from the Vietnam Conflict was walking toward the vacant table to my front. Sammy has been attending our reunion almost every year since its inception. The year 2010 will be our 28th I believe and it is the largest of its kind in the country — independent of national affiliation. Sammy's story is worth repeating.

This is the short version: On November 18, 1967, Pfc. Sammy L. Davis was an artilleryman in Battery C, 2nd Bn, 4th Arty Reg, 9th Inf at Cai Lay, Vn. Their position was attacked by a reinforced Battalion of Viet Cong and taking heavy mortar fire at approximate 0200 in the morning. His battery took a direct hit and his team was blown away from its gun, Sammy included. He was badly injured. Davis returned fire multiple times by himself in spite of being knocked down repeatedly by the recoil. He repelled the enemy as it attempted to cross the river. He saw three of his teams' soldiers stranded across the river, wounded and unable to swim the river. He grabbed a machine gun and swept the surrounding area, keeping the enemy at bay. Davis was a non-swimmer, but got an air mattress and crossed the river, although badly wounded, twice, retrieving his wounded comrades and returned them to safety. He then refused medical attention and joined another artillery battery and silenced the enemy mortar attack. Davis was eventually given medical treatment for his multiple, serious wounds and promoted to Sergeant. He was awarded his CMOH a year later. It was that ceremony that appears in the movie, *Forrest Gump*.

This is the man with whom I was about to spend the balance of my day. My anger with the Mr. Stage Manager was not abating, but it was being sent to the back room. I was beginning to be overwhelmed and words were jamming in my throat. Sammy Davis meets literally thousands of veterans. We had met, but I knew I was faceless. We met again then, and I met his wife and her friend. The honor of being near him was crowding out every other feeling in me. I sat down and stared. The vets queued in line before he could even take a seat. I looked around him and there stood 100 vets in the first two minutes, holding books, napkins, pictures, cameras, albums, kids, wives, tee-shirts, and anything else you can imagine. Everyone wanted a small piece of him somehow. One would move away and two got in line at the end. Sammy had a fund raiser going on for his children's foundation. He did well. He works with many, many programs and each touches a veterans' support effort in one way or another. He has given his life to it.

I spent the rest of the afternoon talking with his wife and her best friend. Mrs. Davis hovered without being obvious. Sammy was struggling. I could sense his weariness. He was not well, yet he stood and recognized everyone who approached him. Hours later, hundreds of men later, Mrs. Davis demanded he rest and I stuck my nose in as well. I was thankful when they left. Sammy was exhausted. I went home and put my poem on paper.

We returned the next day and I debated with myself about giving it to him. Mr. Stage Manager asked Sammy if he wanted to jam a little on stage with one of our bands. Davis does that too. As I recall he plays some harmonica and gets a lot of joy from that. Music does rejuvenate. While he was away I showed it to Mrs. Davis. Her eyes moistened and she said please give it to him. She said that I saw what nobody ever took the time to see. They were leaving after the music session he was doing. Sammy was going to sign a few more things and they were headed for their next event. When I had the chance, I gave Sammy the poem. He read it, looked at me with tears in eyes. I asked Sammy L. Davis, "Why do you do it?"

He said, "I owe it to them all. I love them. As long as I can walk I will do it. They are the heroes. Nobody knows them or what they did and neither do I, but most of them did what they were asked and it is up to me to thank them."

In 2008 Sammy could not come to our reunion. He was recovering from a serious heart attack. The next year he was at a major event for Medal of Honor winners in DC. I hope he is with us this year. He won't remember me, but it does not matter. I remember him. He has touched me in a way he will never know. He is a hero in a way that is quite different than that displayed on the field of battle. It is still heroism but touching another life, I think, in an even deeper way somehow. Yes, he is a real American hero to me. He touches living beings from the heart and soul in a personal way. He touched me.

WILBUR AND CAROL, A LOVE STORY

I was leaning on the bar at the Grounds laughing at one of the guys on a Saturday morning when another of our members joined us. He is a regular and well known to the guys who drift back north with the winter thaw. We have members from all over the nation who stop by whenever they are close. Those of us who live in the area visit on a daily basis. I am horrible at names, but I knew his face and he recognized mine. It usually does not matter — if we are there, we share. He reintroduced himself as Wilbur. The three of us talked about the next day's race, the pool tournament going on a few feet away, the board meeting that was on-going in the meeting room, and the upcoming mini-reunion. We almost always talk war experiences. Inevitably one of us has had a recent visit to a Veterans Hospital somewhere. Misery loves company, thus I began sharing my story about being denied benefits for my PTSD (Post Traumatic Stress Disorder) claim.

All vets have been through denial for something at least once. Most have been rejected three times (at least those whom I have met). I related how the counselor told me that I had been married to the same woman too many years and completed a couple of higher education degrees, therefore display too much stability to have a problem. Wilbur laughed and explained that he had three wives for a total of eight years of marriage after returning from the Nam — and then he met his current wife. He found his saving angel when he married Carol. Even then, he put her through hell for years and was an alcoholic, among other things. Somehow she remained by his side. He wonders why when he looks back. There are things we should not question. We should just be thankful and accept them. Wilbur had given her every reason under the sun to follow the trail made by the other three, but she walked a different road. She chose to walk with him, even when he stumbled and crawled.

The VA denied his PTSD claim for years. Frustration drove him to the point that he showed them a letter she had written him about 15 years before. He threw it on the counselor's desk in pure anger during his third appeal. Wilbur keeps the letter in a special folder at the Grounds. He has a camper there. The Healing Fields (aptly named by we who meet there — see the poem in my first book, *Vietnam in Verse, poetry for beer drinkers*) is a refuge for Wilbur, as it is for many of the thousand veterans who belong to the Howard County Vietnam Veterans Organization. He insisted on getting the letter and sharing it with me. I could tell by his voice that it was something special beyond words. After a short golf cart ride, he returned with it and handed it to me with a tear in his eye. It seems we grizzled old guys do that a lot. We allow ourselves that luxury in certain circumstances. Crying is an intrinsic part of the healing process it seems. I read the letter and I understood. It was my intent to include it in this book. Wilbur honored me by giving me a copy. I wanted it in this book in Carol's handwriting, but it was too faint to duplicate. Her heart is in the letter, just as his is in his eyes when he speaks of it. Her letter follows in its entirety:

To my Vietnam Vet Wilbur
I've waited so long for you to come to me, for me to comfort you. I listen to your complaining about this & that how your body feels. You've had a headache all day. I try to say things to you and you bite my head off.
Then some buddies call and you're off and running. Suddenly you feel good. Suddenly you don't hurt any more. Suddenly you've got more energy. You're not tired, you can drive 10-12 hours to see your friends. It hurts like a slap in the face. All you can think about is getting there to drink & party. What about me? I love you. I can't wait to get home from work to see you. I just can't stand the feelings you send me. You make me feel like I am not important to you at all.
You, know I wasn't there but you make me feel like the war vet, for me will never be over. How I long for you to hold me, make love to me like you used to. Please come home to me. I am waiting for you.
Love Always,
Carol

They have been married 25 years now. Wilbur drew stability from her, had a good career and lived well. He has his memories, good and bad. Carol is truly his angel.

Wilbur and I continued to talk after several minutes of silence. He went to Nam in 1965 as a member of the 6566th Air Force and was attached the 173rd Airborne at Bien Hoa. His unit was involved in troop processing during the build-up of forces during our increased involvement in the "conflict." They had no housing at first, thus the constant bombardment they endured on a daily basis was rain from the sky on unprotected heads unless one considers "cammies" and flak jackets sufficient protection from shrapnel and rockets. Wilbur and the men in his outfit were sent with what seemed to them, no plan. Uncle Sam seemed to say "Just unload those planes and get material to the troops some way. Wave your magic wands." They were attached to the Army as the Air Force presence was minimal at that early point in the war. Every day, they went to work with hell pouring down on them, unprotected and under fire. But work they did. The strain went deep into their souls. How could they ever explain it, much less ever be rid of it?

As materials became more available, they were able to confiscate some empty shipping containers and convert them to make-shift housing units. Those were not too well ventilated but they did provide better protection than poncho liners and ammo boxes. At some point, his unit accumulated some unshipped sandbags as well. A few months into his tour, his unit became part of a more formal Air Force unit at Tan Son Nhut in Saigon. Living conditions improved at that point, as did some of the recreational opportunities. Ugly memories had already made their indelible impression by this time. Their chain of command was confusing. They had few weapons, lived like an afterthought—and "made do" with leftovers and whatever they could pillage on their own. Wilbur got quite good at it.

Wilbur became a well-connected supply professional by 1966. He was a cook and a party organizer—a jack of all trades. He handled supplies and the wounded with equal alacrity. Wilbur knew people in the Army from having spent his early days with the 173rd and having been one of the early people at Tan Son Nhut, he was on the ground floor there as well. His connections enabled him to get his brother assigned to his area when he joined him Vietnam. They served together for 37 of Wilbur's last 40 days in-country. That is unusual. It gave the two of them a distinct connection which few brothers experience. They have some stories that cannot be shared with spouses! Wilbur's brother is deceased now, however he carries much of that brother's pain. The brother served two tours in Nam, the second as a medic. Wilbur told me a short and painful memory about his brother's experience with the VA and his battle for PTSD benefits, too.

When Wilbur's brother returned to Nam, he was in Saigon for the Tet Offensive in 1968. His duty placed him in the processing facility for the dead. The Army ran out of body bags and the dead were stacked like cords of wood according to his account to Wilbur. His letters home scared Wilbur and his brother's words, added to his memories of his own early days in Vietnam, drove him deeper into the bottle. Later his brother was assigned to field duty. He was in a heavy combat zone somewhere up north and he snapped. He was traveling in a Jeep to a combat area when a round from somewhere almost took him out. The man went into shock and drove into the middle of a fight, blindly, almost as though searching for death. He spent several months in a facility in Japan. While at home on convalescent leave, his brother realized he could never adapt to civilian life again. He returned to the military and made a career of the service. When he did retire, he went to the VA and applied for PTSD benefits. He was denied as a non-combatant. He gave up trying. Many do. The ghosts of his war never gave him any peace and he never found his angel in life. Wilbur never said it, but I know he hopes that his brother found her in the afterlife.

I was honored to hear Wilbur's story. It is a love story. It is a sad story. It is a story that is universal in many ways. Wilbur's successes and failures apply to many Vietnam veterans. Wilbur and Carol are still together. Thank God.

Topp Gunn

Did you ever wonder who was driving the cab?
Or who was next to you when standing in line?
Do you wonder about a neighborhood man?
Could he have been a hero in another time?

The man walking downtown in tattered rags
Could have saved lives as a soldier long ago.
A hero may have filled your shopping bags.
There may be a story in him he never told.

The tip you left may have made a difference.
Some have done well, others just making do.
If he spoke of old deeds, shed his diffidence,
It may have struck a chord and shocked you.

I know one Marine who survived those battles.
He did a job, took care of his brothers at arms.
The echo of rounds and those in-coming rockets
Are in his memory, even if his life was charmed.

He drove a truck and now takes care of fares.
He listens to those who may never understand
What he and others did, nor do they even care,
In some war, any war, in some far away land.

They stood tall under our flag, offering lives
And made sacrifices so others can live freely,
Pursuing pleasure and dreams of some kind.
Most are quiet people who served and believed.

He may have been a top gun or just a grunt.
He could have been in any war, at any time.
He could wonder how his youth was spent.
He may be a teacher, a welder, but he is fine.

History is them, though they are not named.
Their stories are as many as they, mostly untold.
Taken for granted, they work on, often defamed.
They complain but do not rue the youth they sold.

They gather, meet, share with others of their like.
The guy behind a wheel of a cab, showing his years,
Is a composite of so many that waded rice paddies,
Trod the sand-hills, snow, or mud, and still care.

Someone has heard them and is trying to share
What they did and tell them they are respected.
The cabbie, the bank teller, the garbage man too,
Are sources of his work; they are not undetected.

They know, as he does, what our soldiers do now.
They extend hands with wonder at all they give.
They offer arms in support; respect is bestowed
On them as they return; their lives will be lived.

The man in the crowd, with no face, no name
Will listen…when they are ready to speak out.
He's been there too, has done the very same.
They will fight another war, but are not alone.

They will disappear into those same crowds;
Will see all they did recorded in a few pages.
They will be the next worker bees no doubt.
They are what make this country so very great.

SECTION III

Mike's Stories
(Mike Mullins shares some memories)

The Moon in 'Nam

Memories crash in without sequence. A soldier's days tumble together like a ball of yarn. The days of search and destroy missions are so much the same they become as faceless as the enemy. The terrain changes but the task is the same. Heat, rain, jungle, rice paddies, dust, creatures, bugs, cramps, water, no water, filth, tired to the point of staggering, no sleep — what changes? The firefights make a day different. An event sticks in your mind. The soldier may not remember the month, the day, how long it lasted, or who was next to him — but he remembers the event. People see each incident from different perspectives, from different life experiences. They see it from a different angle when it happens if they are near each other at the moment it happened. But they both remember it and what they remember is their personal history.

I do not remember firebases. I did not care much of the time. I knew I got up at sunrise and walked until dark. I knew I lived through another night when I left at that sunrise. I knew I lived another day when I stopped at dark. Those became the only important things to me. Putting another day behind me was no different than putting one foot in front of the other. In *Vietnam in Verse*, I shared a few stories. Now it is time to tell a few more. They are in no particular order, but they happened. They exploded in my life. They still do and sometimes they explode when I do not expect it. They burst from their shell in the night or they emerge as I speak with other veterans. I tell them the way they erupted in my consciousness. When I first wrote them, they were poems. I share them here as stories, in no particular order.

The Combat Infantryman's Badge did not take long to earn. We took fire from snipers in a quick ambush by my third week in-country. I did not experience the kind of fighting many combat vets did. The guys near the Demilitarized Zone and the Highlands saw heavy combat. The enemy seldom stood and fought the 199th Light Infantry. We chased, but they retreated to the north. More often they ran to Cambodia. My fourth week in-country, I drank deep from the well of combat hell. A day late in April of 1968 crashes into my slumber too often.

A Day in April

It is a day in April 1968. No! Wait! It is now and it is quite late! I am there, but it is November 2007. NO! I was there! I was there, just now by heaven. The visions and the words are right here. They are at my fingertips. They tremble there in fear. They are just behind my lips. How do I do this? I am going back.

In-country just a few weeks, I am walking and watching in jungle, dank, through clearings littered with trees. My God! It is chaos suddenly. Hell is walking the face of the earth! Hell is here — it has broken loose. I hear "Ack, ack, ack, BOOM!" Next there's a sixty raising Cain, yet it doesn't sound quite right. Then there's a "Ssssshhhhh...Booooom!" I ask myself, "What's that hissing — that loud sound?" I realize we are being hit and guess it has to be a rocket. I have never heard one before. We are in a damned big fight!

Now the 60 *is* chattering and our M-16s. Man, listen to that crap hitting the trees. That was close! I am looking for a target. This is a day I hope to forget. My finger is pulling the trigger. My heart is frozen. It is like some kind of living rigor. My eyes try to pierce the daylight's gloom.

Where are Ronnie, Smitty, Brown and the Mad Duck, Rolhoff? There are screams for the medic. This is real. My heart is sick. Where is Sarge? How many are down? What do I do next, what now? My God, I am empty. Have I fired that many rounds? I can't see anything but flashes in the jungle. Change clips!

Time is standing still. A year has passed. I am older than I was a few minutes ago. Shoot at something. Voices are screaming. Someone needs help. Oh my God! He is pinned down! What are those buzzing noises in my ears? Are Steve and Tom here with me today? Is Clyde or Ray? There are no faces flickering in the mist. They are black powder bullets hissing, but so far they are missing. Are the guys with me now on *this* trip here?

A voice at my rear is asking for volunteers. What does he need? I answer, out of control. I will help. I will do as I am told. "What do you want? What can I do?"

That faceless voice said, "Come with me! With you, I'll need another three. Get your machete. Go cut down that tree!" He was quiet but shouting at me.

Voices disappeared in the battle's din. Soldiers lined up the bodies and the wounded at the edge of the clearing just about then. Medics were doing what they could, running from man to man.

"Get those trees down. We have to make room for choppers to land! Do whatever it takes, whatever you can." The voice of authority spoke again, but I could not see him.

There is Brownie, and so is Jim. I don't know the fourth. I hack, I sweat, I can't even laugh — or frown. I find myself shinnied up a tree. How did I get here? I don't even have a weapon with me. How am I supposed to cut limbs off with a machete? I will. I will. A chopper has to get in here. Those guys' lives depend on it.

There are those buzzes again. Something is hitting the leaves. I'm cutting limbs back as fast as I can with a machete. The choppers must have room — It takes room to land a medevac. They have to get in and out before night falls. We can't get these trees down fast enough!

There are men piling up. Body bags. I haven't seen that before. Dead. They are dead. A bunch of guys are losing a lot of blood. The medics are here, back and forth. They are damned sure earning their money.

Somebody shouted, "Get some C-4 and some detonator cord!"

The trees are coming down now. The clearing is growing, becoming a Landing Zone. We wrap the detonator cord around small trunks. We can take a bunch of trees out now, in larger chunks. I'm glad somebody came over to help who did this before. All of us are cherries.

The fight is growing — an alarming crescendo. The det cord hisses and sizzles. It works! Tree bark becomes wooden missiles. Muffled booms around the ring make this LZ useful.

Now we have to pop smoke and move hurting men. God help me, I hope I never have to do this again! I'm standing with a small, confused group. I don't know them. They are different troops. That one popped smoke as he was told but — Oh no! That is a red one hitting the ground! A gunship will hit us in all this confusion!

I drop my pot on it in the confusion. "Get some green smoke, or purple. Yellow will do, anything but more red," I scream at anyone who will listen as I try to cover the blood red target drifting through the trees. Someone who doesn't know any better will cause more to die. He's probably another of those clerks who had his MOS changed when he got here!

Where are my guys? Man, I want to be with them. These are good guys, but they're not my buddies.

I hear voices shouting more clearly. Someone says, "Look at this one I shot out of that tree. He's 190 pounds and at least six foot three. He has to be one of those northern Chinese."

"Hey, did you hear? I heard Tex-Mex bought it. There are more, too I guess."

I know how bad Tex-Mex is hurt. I cannot remember whether I learned about it after or during the fight. It's a blur. He's in a different platoon — 60 machine gun guy and walking point for his platoon. He got cut off from them. Hit but still fighting, laying down cover fire, he got hit by a rocket. It took his arm off. He fought until he ran out of ammo. He screamed for help, trapped behind a downed tree. He got hit in the body somewhere, probably in the guts because he cried for his mother. He couldn't reload due to being one armed. He rose up to roll over the log. Nobody could get to him. The intense enemy fire pinned down everyone in the area. He took a round through the top of his head. Dead, the screaming ended. His agony was over. I don't know how I know all of this.

Before the fight, our company had more than 130 men. After, I think we had 98 or something like that. We only had four killed (KIA) and the rest were wounded (WIA). It was pretty tough. We operated at this level for a long time — no replacements.

I stepped over men littering the ground. A medic asked my help to keep a man around. He handed me a plasma bag, quickly using his morphine.

"Hold this, I'll try to save him, but his wounds are unseen. The bullet hit him in the collarbone and ricocheted down," the doc explained.

"My God, his guts are torn apart and his balls are gone!" I yelled in horror.

"Do the best you can," the medic whispered.

"I have to go where I can help. Pray we can't be heard."

I hold that bag and a small voice spoke, quite lucid. "I know I've had it. Get my wedding band off my hand. Get it and my Testament to my wife."

He died, but he was not alone. I sat there holding his hand. I hear nothing but his voice. There's no war going on around me. He doesn't want his wife to know he died without his manhood. It's the only thing that matters. I promise that the people on the chopper will keep his secret too. I hear nothing else — not even bullets, if there were any. I'm holding his hand in one of mine — and the I-V in the other. I *feel* his life and soul leave his body.

Doc and I carry him to the evac chopper and place him on the floor of a gunship. We have to help the medivacs. There were too many wounded. The other companies are bringing their dead and wounded to our LZ too. I hand his Bible and wedding band to the door gunner with explicit instructions about what the message to my brother's wife is to be. I get a quiet nod in return. There's no time for tears. There have been since then — many times.

Now I am hearing numbers. Brownie's here — always full of news. "All the Companies in this operation have taken a hit. The dead and wounded are stacking up." No shit. "Moon", says Brown, "we're looking for Sergeant Smith. Have you seen him?"

"I haven't seen him in hours. Who was he with?" I answered. Sarge is no hero and is due to go home in a few weeks, but would he leave us to fight without him?

Later, some guys found him in a streambed, under some big rocks.

The firing stopped. The quiet is as scary as the fighting. Soldiers are mounting up, moving out, to see what they can see. The wounded are being evacuated. The silence is deadening. The groans are fading as some die and are set free. We have four or five companies here, it seems to me. What did we walk into that could raise this kind of hell?

Brown soon heard. It was an elite Sapper battalion. That is a North Vietnamese elite fighting unit. They ran, stuffing bodies in an old well, aware we will stop for the body count. The press will want to know, to balance our own loss.

I wish we could do that later and keep up the chase. If we finish them, they cannot come across the border again and hit somebody else. Somebody thinks this is a board game or some kind of race.

Remember that line in John Wayne's Iwo Jima movie? Forrest Tucker returns for ammo and stops for hot coffee. He tells those men that a mortar platoon lives the *Life of Riley*. Tonight, as I remember that day in April 1968, I missed Riley's hammock — his life was not my fate. Much of the time, I was just another grunt. Our tubes were not on the scene at that point.

The dream woke me tonight for some reason. As I remember it now, my heart is still frozen.

All of this is always in the dream, but the dream does not come as often as it did. Thank God.

In May came the spring attempt at a Tet offensive.

Southwest of Saigon

It was May of 1968, spring, but not one for young lovers like the old song. Still it's not one that any of us will forget. The entire brigade made enemy contact on a daily basis. We were lucky, us young-old Cottonbalers. After days of sweeps and search and destroy missions, we had the enemy pinned—and we waited to help him fulfill his destiny. "Enriched" rice would do him no good this day. Our weapons were booming and we had our way with him. There was no place for him to hide. The warning to the villagers suggested they vacate. They were not available to shield the Viet Cong or the North Vietnamese Regulars who hid among them. The only people in the small village were enemy combatants.

This battlefield was almost my own downfall. It was too close to the temptations offered by the storied Star Hotel. The enemy, encircled by several units, became an easy target for our bombers as they scored hit after hit. The ground rumbled and shook as though a continuous roll of earthquakes were slamming the region. Artillery rounds poured in, our mortars sang along too. The enemy hid, but the bunkers hidden below the huts became his tomb. Puff the Magic Dragon joined the field of play. A thousand yards of field lay peppered in every square inch, resembling Swiss cheese more than a place for water buffalo to graze. At night, the sky was red with tracers illuminating the battlefield. It was a turkey shoot. Weary grunts relaxed. It was not too easy, but by comparison to prior missions, it was lax. We had patrols out, company sized recons in force.

Everywhere we heard sounds of fighting, of course. One night, a VC doped up and charged our concertina. He got tangled quickly and a 50-caliber sang its cantata. The opium-encouraged hero and his unfired satchel-charge dangled with smoke swirling from his bullet holes. At close range, 50-cal tracers will ignite clothing when they hit. The range was less than 75 meters. One of the guys from the cavalry unit attached to us borrowed the 50. They were asleep. Our guy on watch, a crazy kid from Minnesota, heard the enemy hit the wire and jumped on the Jeep where the 50 was mounted as a sighting weapon for the 106-mm recoilless rifle. Pat used it to ensure that the perimeter was secure and any others coming behind would have a change of heart. It worked. It was not something from which the VC "hero" ever again arose.

Many things made our borrowed base camp an easy place easy to remember. There were soldiers, but there no plumber. The huge earthen jugs which became our latrines, with the addition of very uncomfortable wooden planks, teemed with maggots. Located well back of the enemy side of the perimeter, we were safe there at least. They reeked, but it was the best we could do. Oh, but I hated those maggots. There were no showers, sinks, and no working spigots. GIs planted cheeks above the mess on two-by-fours. We did not have the dignity of curtains or even doors. But where does dignity live in war?

The victory was ours and the Viet Cong were toast. In the firefights, the 199th killed many North Vietnamese soldiers. We called it making good soldiers out of bad ones. They had been filtering into the area for weeks. There were even days when we had almost warm food. We remained in the area more than a week. F-4s made daily runs. B-52s made strikes from where we could not see. There was fighting all around Saigon City, but the enemy never penetrated the town as they had during the Tet Offensive. It was an expensive and fruitless attempt by the NVA and the local VC. Our sharpshooters manned bunkers in daylight and waited for a head to pop out of the ground. It reminded one of whack-a-mole, only if they went down they did not pop up elsewhere. Gunships hovered over the area when the bomb runs ended.

One morning, I sat on the perimeter reading Stars and Stripes. An unexpected bee flew by and the paper fell in tattered strips. The buzzing in my ear was a shot that came damned close. I love reading my paper in peace now, at home.

At the end of our time there, rifle teams made sweeps of the area. The 199th assigned three battalions to the operation. The sweep rotations confirmed the same things. The stench lingering in the area from the napalm drops and firefights, along with the constant bombardment, equaled compete success. Nothing lived and body counts for the brass and politicians required a puzzle master.

Good fortune walked with me southwest of Saigon in two ways.

That was Close

I am not talking about a bomb or a sniper attack. Although those were real, this ain't about that. It's about a boy wanting to become a stud and the battle with temptation. It's about him being afraid to say no in an effort to fit in. That desire, his lack of discipline, almost caused trouble. It was something that could have burst his bubble. Right in the middle of the spring edition of Tet, a grunt had the grandest idea yet.

"Why don't we slip into town, see the Star Hotel, men? We've done nothing but fight. Nobody will miss us because we won't be gone long," he whispered, looking around to see if anyone heard.

I was from Delta, the other three from Bravo Company. They'd walked down to borrow a brick or two of our C-4 to blow a bunker in their area. I let them pass into our perimeter just as my watch ended and got replaced at the road bunker. I knew one of them.

"We can steal a couple of hours to go check things out. We heard about a place where a man can get his battery re-charged. You could get the royal treatment. The girls are number one — Asian with some French blood. Way beyond just good," one of the other guys added.

I told a buddy I was slipping away to get a bath and a beer and asked him to cover me for a while. He warned me that if caught I would not like what I might hear. Of course, I assured him, we'd be quick. It was possible we'd not even be missed. I figured he acted so pissed because he wasn't going with us.

All young men are indestructible. We're never going to get caught. Like criminals, we're smarter than everyone else. I didn't think about the kind of trouble we might find.

We slipped into the village searching for a ride of some kind. An old man's little taxi was the only vehicle we could find. He didn't want to make the trip through the fighting. It was dangerous every inch of the way. We told him that we'd pay him. He refused, but one of the guys "borrowed" the car, the first of that wild day's serious crimes.

With directions from a smiling ARVN, we found the hotel. It was a pretty old building, something special in better days. We read a menu about what things cost if we desired "love" in the spring. The choices were darned hot. We slipped into a sauna, then into a bath to be scrubbed with gentle hands. The jungles and the mud, forgotten for a few hours, were washed from our bodies and minds. After a Ba Muoi Ba (33 beer—a potent Vietnamese beer) or two, we prepared to return contented to the combat zone in the southwest.

We jumped in our little cab, fear hitting us with a sudden rush. "What have we done?" we asked ourselves in fear as we flew back. Reality was intruding on fantasy, revealing a bleak future. It was late. Where had the day had gone while we played? We meant to return earlier but the smiles caused a major delay.

We found that small village and our angry old man shaking his fist. He got satisfaction for the whole debacle when he said, "You numba 10 GIs but you in very big trouble now, stuck for sure. The fight move while you gone. You pay for what you do."

We thought fast. There was one way we had a chance. We paid him big money to take us to our outfit, no matter the distance. We realized he knew. All the villagers were aware of everything. He smiled, knowing he got his revenge. He would win. We'd lose. He drove, lights out, winding his way through the dusk into the hot zone. He stopped a mile away and told us we were on our own — a wise decision.

The B Company dudes went their way, following the sounds of a camp setting up close by. I went mine, wishing that I'd used my head and refused to go on that joy ride.

I tried to sneak to my position, but my platoon sergeant caught me.

"Your gear is rolled up over there and the Old Man wants you in his hut." I was scared more of him than the other day's sniper attack when a round had pierced my *Stars and Stripes*. That was not so bad all of a sudden. I walked to his bunker, the facts settling in like cement on feet. I was AWOL (absent without leave) during combat.

Captain Zimmerman was an NCO with a field commission. He had been around every block there was. Hell, he'd made a few in his career. He drank his Schlitz warm. He was pacing, cussing and waiting.

Irate, he asked what I did.

I told him the truth.

"Did you enjoy your stay?"

I said I did, and stood head down, waiting for the axe to fall.

He told me that the next day he needed to get supplies—and I'd accompany him. I saw torture in my future. As I walked away head down, Zimmerman's voice lashed out once again. "You are taking me where you went me young grunt, and buying. See you in the morning."

Young, my blood running hot, I proved how dumb I was and did it.

Yes, May of 1968 was quite a month. My education continued. The operation concluded there and I was still standing. And I was still free.

Intelligence knew the routes used by the NVA for slipping small groups of soldiers to town. Our next mission destined us to walk those trails in search of any supply spots or reinforcements waiting to follow. That gave us a little something to do into June. But then again, one month was the same as another.

Scared Awake

"Who the hell is kicking me in the middle of the night? I just got off watch. This ain't right man," I grumbled in the dark hooch we found in the deserted village.

The foot hit my side again and then hands shook me. A raspy whisper penetrated the darkness. "Get your ass up Moon and bring your damned Thumper. We need some HE (high explosives) to bring some thunder." I recognized my platoon sergeant's voice as the fog of sleep cleared.

I searched in the dark for my helmet and my glasses. "If I can't see, I can't kick anybody's ass."

Sarge was in a panic, but that was nothing new. I wasn't in shock. One time, Sarge was found hiding in rocks. When a grunt realizes he is getting short, life becomes more precious than before.

I stumbled out the door, rounds and Thumper in my hands. In day light, I had to squint to see a fuzzy form without my specs.

"I can't see. Can anyone else shoot this hunk of iron?" I asked.

Sarge grabbed me and made me turn. He pointed where he wanted me to fire. I wasn't at all sure I wanted to play that game. Nobody had ever seen him pull a trigger.

He yelled, "Moon, shoot at 300 meters now."

I set the movable sight at the rear of the barrel and got the right elevation. When I pulled the trigger, Thumper slammed against my shoulder. Sarge should have been behind a boulder. The round left my barrel with a flash and gave us a hell of a fright. Sarge had aimed me directly at the eaves of the hooch. Pieces of roof rained down on my head. I was happy I'd found my helmet at least.

"Jesus Christ, Sarge, who the hell do you want to kill? Us?" I yelled. "You made us the target. Didn't you check our clearance?"

One of my squad grabbed me and took the weapon. "Moon, get your glasses."

Scared awake after almost killing myself, I couldn't see squat. Stumbling back in the house, I got my glasses. When I could see and the other guys were awake, we discovered that there was at least a full platoon of enemy soldiers moving across the clearing from us. They were unaware of us for some reason. I recall putting 20 of those rounds in the night air, or more. I hope that I gave Charlie a scare. My ammo was wet and the paddies absorbed the impact.

It may have been bad ammo. We received some bad stuff on occasion. Few exploded. I remember that. It was like being charged for attacking a strange woman and being freed for assault with a dead weapon.

We didn't sleep the rest of the night. One thing is sure — Sarge never needed another reminder about aiming another man like a weapon. There are times when slow and sure are much better than panicked and stupid. The rest of his time in-country was quieter than before. He let us grunts fire our own weapons.

In spite of everything, you never know when you will take the last step — or see your last twinkling star.

Just One More Step

There are reports of enemy movement. We move through the muggy jungle in silence. The point rotates on each operation to share the risk. I set a slow pace. Our orders were no quick moves. Slow and steady. Our eyes drilled into the foliage and burned through triple canopy. Every nerve was stinging so the insects were nothing to guys like me. The sweat ran down my body in rivers, but my mouth stayed dry as baked grass.

We signaled to each other, knowing that a wrong move could be our last. Every noise, every shaking leaf held a threat of what might be a sniper. Our feet were targets for venomous jungle vipers. Our weapons pointed a different way every other man to keep the flanks covered. The man in the middle of the column was our old lifer platoon sergeant. He and his RTO (radio/telegraph operator) tried to keep contact with both ends of the line. The radio operator was the link to support from the rear. We could need support in an instant.

We cut a swath through the jungle if necessary, but walked around what looked impenetrable. The chance of contact was high, but we were seasoned and ready. Who knows why things happen, but they do, so you play the cards dealt. My pace slowed even more when it seemed open and unsafe. In one opening, I took a step and felt a small tug across the top of my worn jungle boot. I stopped almost in stride, wondering if I should crap, or give a warning hoot.

The guy close to me knew he shared my fate if I made a wrong step. It was like we were connected. He moved to our right, then left. He said, "Hold it there Moon, I'll see what I can see but, God, stay still, okay?"

I looked down. A thin wire shimmered into the jungle, visible only in places. If I had taken one more step it could have meant death, or a blown-off leg.

There had to be something at the end of the wire. It was no telegraph wire. Gently, softly, slowly — I put my foot down and inched it back, eyes to front. If my guy was tracing that wire, I would give my life to save that gutsy grunt. Nothing was very close to where we walked. It made no sense to us at all. Their traps were meant to maim, as a rule, and shallow, even very small. This one was meant to make an impression, turning jungle into a green tomb.

My partner followed it into the jungle. Scrunching into as small a target as possible, he crept along the shiny trail to its source. Those following us knew something big was happening. Hand signals sent shadowy echoes to the back of the line.

The tripwire led to a huge surprise. It was one of our own 500-pound bombs. It failed to detonate when it hit, but all of its safeties had to be gone. It became quite useful when it landed.

My buddy called for help. I stood watch over them while they worked. Each held the wire, keeping the tension so it would not trip by accident. The pressure must remain even. I asked them if they saw where the line was tied off, if there was some device. One of the guys hand-walked the line away from the bomb. He checked for a splice as he inched along. It was unusual to find a bomb like that in the jungle where we did our "search and destroy" mission. Getting that thing through dense growth was no job for a local village boy. It was a live bomb. The wire I hit only told them we were there. It did not detonate the device.

Then my guys found a trigger device that had to be manned in order for the bomb to detonate. Our enemy that day made a call to let us live — if he was even there. Each of us said to ourselves, "I'll be damned." He would have gone with us, so it wasn't our day to die. If I had taken just one more step, the choice would have been his. We were on a company-sized sweep. There was no place he could have run had he survived the blast. If he elected to hit the trigger, it would not have mattered to me.

If we had been less alert and able than we were that day, it may have been the day I was done.

You know somethin'? When I ain't hot and scared, I am wet and cold.

Bone Chilling Times

Who would believe this back home if I told them? They would be asking, "What is wrong with him?" That place is hot and humid. Vietnam has a tropical climate.

"Why am I sitting here shivering, frozen to the bone? The temperature is changing and making a big drop. Going from one ten to eighty is serious." I think to myself as I walk head down in the downpour.

Rain is pouring in stinging sheets. It will not stop. Water runs down my back, wracking me with chills. I sure as hell didn't expect this in the deal. We slog in the mud, our socks rotting off our feet. They wrinkle up and eventually start to bleed. The boots are good — at least they drain pretty well. Bless this rotten jungle. At least my feet don't smell — by comparison. I can't see three feet ahead so stumbling is common. The rain roars so loud I can't hear the booming cannons. At least it is as hard on Charlie as it is on us. He has to find a hole. He can't pull any of his stunts. If we get lucky maybe he'll drown in those tunnels. The rain is coming in buckets. Maybe the holes will fill like funnels.

I've never been so wet and damned sure not so cold. My Indiana winters are no worse. The thermometer in my brain says it may snow. Whether it does or not, the wind will howl and blow. My feet suck out of the muck. It's like walking in quicksand. It makes moving hard. I can't see the sun, so hell, it may already be dark. Dripping wet, my gear weighs much more than advertised.

We move slower and slower. I can't stop thinking of how miserable I am—and I must. At this moment, I would give a finger for a bowl of dust. If anybody steps on a Bouncing Betty, it'll just sink. I try to focus on positive things. It's difficult when you can't even keep your toilet paper dry.

This is a bone chilling time — not one of fear or fighting. The wind is much worse when it rains in the rice paddies. We go from jungle to rice paddy and back to jungle. The jungle is our shield right now, to our great surprise. The triple canopy slows the rain a bit. It is louder when hitting the leaves overhead, but it slows the downpour a little bit.

There goes the head thing again and I need to get on track. The word just came back. The old man is look for a place to bivouac. Who wants to lie down in this crap? I would rather keep on walking.

One foot in front of the other — we must keep on pushing. When we set up for the night, it will not be any better I know. I will hunker under a poncho shivering. That old poncho is six feet long. Either my head or my feet are hanging out. I always choose my feet.

We walk in rivers of mud. We swim them. We wade across them. We fish leaches out of them with our bodies. Perhaps one day we will actually ride a boat on one of them.

On the River Bank

We got to ride the river. They put us in the old WW 2 boats. We found out how the Brown Water Navy boys felt. The VC could wait along the river banks and drop nasty things in them and watch them do harmful things to our guys. We were lucky it didn't happen the few times we were along. It was cool watching a mongoose clear a bank for snakes. It was an amazing thing to see.

During river patrol, days were full, sunrise to sunset. The river ran swift. It was often a silent killer too. We had a company-sized base camp I can't forget. With night patrols and fire missions, our time flew. My education went on every day I was in the Nam. At night, three platoons set up patrols and outposts between canals or in the woods nearby. The open spaces were dotted with rice paddies and farmers working them. Were they look-outs for the enemy? Some were, I am certain. Camp followers came up river and set up not too far way. The boss lady had a few girls there. They were sampan mama-sans.

We mortar crews had missions every night. One star-lit night we had more activity than most. Our patrols needed lots of Willie-Pete (white phosphorous) in the air. We ran out of bore grease. My tube was toasted. It warped and I had a hang-fire. It was a huge scare. The night teemed with movement and sightings. Listening posts and patrols stayed on the radios. We had to fire for effect during the long evening. We fired and fired some more — the barrels glowed, going from cherry red to white hot. One by one, the mortars became ineffective. I dropped a round and only its nose poked out. The bore riding safety popped, making me shout. "Sarge" told me to clear it. I did not know how I could make it through this one. The other gun crews had their own problems. I'm not sure they even knew about my situation. Sarge sent me away with my tube. The grunts staying behind to take care of the rest of the perimeter and the HQ area saw me carrying it.

In the dark night, soldiers moved away from me. I disassembled my gun without assistance, not sure what was next. The round could detonate any second. How could I handle this? What way was best? The barrel was too hot to touch, so I improvised. Cooling made the warp worse, but I had no choice. I took it from the base. Removal by the book was ill advised. I moved it with care, nerves afire. I said nothing. I could not with my choking voice.

Grunts were to stay clear of my area, to stay away. Old Sarge walked ahead of me, by some distance, and cleared the way. It made sense not to lose more than just one — me. The game was for keeps. My God, my nerves were frayed. I went to the river bank and dropped to one knee. I lowered the barrel as I knelt on that river bank. I saw no other way except to tap it on the edge and pray. I closed my eyes and mind. My spirit shrank. I knew I was dead, but I had to make a final play.

Tap — tap, tap — tap. The round began to slide. It emerged from the end enough to pop the barrel riding safety. The round moved! The damned thing was live. I was steady (why?) but was sweating freely. Hell, I was scared stiff as the metal screeched. The round was moving. I kept on tapping. It was half out. I cringed in total disbelief.

Why did it not blow? My fears were abating. I decided this might work, if God was willing. The round inched out. Was I that lucky? Would the thing keep moving? Was this not going to be the night that I died? The mortar round broke loose and dropped. It plummeted toward the water ten-feet below. I fell prone, rolled away from the rim and flopped. I stared up at the sky. I think I cried a little. It hit the water, exploded, and my breath rushed out. I couldn't even talk about it.

I was alive. I could not understand why. I heard of hang-fires but had never been near one. My training worked. It was not courage. It was a matter of no choice.

I did what I had to do. We all did.

I walked away and hoped for better things on the river when the sun came up again. At least it looked as though I would be around for another sunrise.

What other angels waited to land near me?

The Descent

We worked the river for a while. It was a good change from the jungle. One day we got a scare we didn't anticipate. A gunship circled overhead. Alert in an instant, our eyes sought our enemies. Were they creeping in the brush across the river? Our base camp had been quiet, the rest was needed, but now that was gone. We watched that chopper, that beloved killing machine in olive-drab green.

Me posing with Cobra Gunship.

It descended, landing just outside our small base camp. The pilot needed a latrine. He jumped down and ran as though he was under fire. We grunts in camp kept our heads down. At first we did not want him to know how he had scared the crap out of us, but when we saw where he ran like a madman, we looked the other way to keep from laughing. The co-pilot climbed down then too, laughing and pointing at the fleeing derriere. He gave us the all clear. We could resume what we had been doing.

The pilot was in horrible shape, his bowels were already moving. There is just no room in a flight suit for what he was doing. We knew that the pilot would hear about this for many days to come. His maniac buddies would enjoy telling the story of a clinched bum.

Chopper pilots are a breed apart, always living on the edge of danger. They push their luck, risking life each day, but this story was stranger than most they had to share. The kills tallied on the ship would change colors from red to brown. A rocket did no damage, nor did small arms fire bring this bird down. The river winding by us, a dangerous brown ribbon of waves was a daily threat to us, but this brought a grin to our grim work.

We grunts were used to bowels demanding an explosive release. We never thought about flight crews catching the same kind of disease. Dysentery was a daily plague for people drinking from bomb craters. We acted different than we did at home our eating meat and taters. Seeing the quick descent was incredible. It was a picture I had to take.

It is a good the pilot had a helmet. It guaranteed his anonymity. I did not let him know we understood about burning, screaming tail. I took my little Instamatic out and got a shot of that war machine before it lifted into the sky. I laughed that day, but it was not too long until I became much more empathic with the pilot.

That is another story which many of us know by heart it is sad to say. Someday it will be told, but not before I figure out a good way. It cost me 35 pounds and what little dignity remained in my teenaged body. Before that however, the river gave us many more experiences.

Another company worked upstream from us. I knew some of the grunts there. Three of us shared some misadventures the first time we were close to Saigon. They showed up in a swamp boat looking for some supplies one afternoon. One of them, Kaufman was his name I think, had been a water skier in his real life back in the world. I joked with him about bringing his ski boat to our camp.

Kaufman said he would bet 20 bucks he could ski behind it. He could ski behind anything on water. I never had any money, but a couple of the other guys nearby jumped on the bet. That wild man made skis from the slats of an ammo box and a ski rope from material on their boat. He talked his boat operator into dragging him into the middle of the river and giving it a shot. He succeeded in getting out of the water and upright. The man could ski! He and his driver circled the swamp boat to create more wake — and rolled the swamp boat. We all believed that to be impossible. It was our Titanic. Our supply man had to take the john boat out and pull them out of the water. Before I drag too many skeletons out of the closet, I will end this little section by saying there was some talking done that day to keep some folks out of the stockade. Young soldiers live on the edge too, not just pilots. We had a wild morning a few days later. Oh, Kaufman won the money.

We were setting the mortars for day duty on a damp, nasty morning when a voice hailed our perimeter. The patrols were gone, having left at dawn. After getting permission to clear the woods, five LRRPs (long range reconnaissance patrol) came into camp. One of them, a short, muscular, blonde man wearing a huge knife on a buckskin thong hanging down his back, dragged a monstrous set of horns along with him. We stared at the sight. A Cobra sitting down out of the blue, a swamp boat used for a ski boat, and now this. Was everybody around this river freaking nuts? We needed to get back to the jungle before it got us too.

Our Buck Sergeant was NCOIC (non-commissioned officer in charge) of the base camp that day. He asked what the hell was going on and got as strange an answer as one could expect under the circumstances.

The blonde LRRP answered, "Sarge, we had an ambush set up for the night and this crazy assed water buffalo charged us. We knocked the big sucker down with the 60 but it didn't kill him. His head was too thick. He was waking up and we had to finish him off. Before he got up we stuffed his ass full of grenades and pulled the pin on the last one. That did the trick. The locals got a lot of meat. I decided to make some horns to put on my helmet. It took me all night to get these damned things cut off and this is the best Damascus steel knife money can buy." He pointed to the huge blade swinging on his back. "I want to borrow some C-4 (plastic explosives) to knock these horns off the skull plate. The skull is so thick I can't cut them off."

It was the wildest thing we'd heard in a long, long time. Two of the guys told Sarge to give it to him. They wanted to see it. "The Army isn't gonna miss a quarter stick of C-4 Sarge. We use more than that heating C-rats." Sarge got it for him.

I wondered how a guy five feet eight at most was going to wear a helmet with a pair of horns that spanned seven or eight feet, even if he got them off the skull. It defied my mind, but the show was going to be worth it. I hoped we did not get hit, because nobody was watching anything else.

The LRRP took the C-4 and some detonator cord and a blasting cap, walked outside the perimeter (almost where the Cobra landed) and set the charge inside the buffalo skull. He walked the cord back about 30 feet, attached it to the firing device, yelled "Fire in the hole!" and hit the trigger.

Kaaaboooom!!! The skull flew 30 feet in the air — in a thousand pieces. The LRRPs left camp with him holding two pieces, one about eight inches long and the other about six.

River patrol was different.

We passed a summer of torment. We walked hundreds of miles, filled thousands of sandbags. We flew into hot LZs and out. I fell out of a chopper on my back in a rice paddy trying to leave a hot LZ. We covered Phuc Vinh for the 101st and killed some monkeys. There are a lot of stories. Maybe I will write a book when I remember them. But I remember the pineapple groves a little.

The Groves

The Pineapple Groves were an experience for me. It was a time of hot, prickly walking in dry season. Canals were hidden in the groves. We heard about an underground tunnel complex in the area, but it was like the lost city Atlantis.

Dog teams were working with us on this mission. It was the only time I ever saw the tough Korean White Horse Division. The Koreans lived for a hand-to-hand combat. They sought it in the inky dark every night. The dogs were there to help us hunt for things unseen. They sniffed things out when not in plain sight. The dog handlers and the dogs stayed apart from the rest of us. They were a unique group.

One day an ARVN officer made a serious mistake. He took exception to one of the dogs on break. That Shepherd did not like Asians, sounding his warning. We heard the snarling and growling that morning. We looked to see what the disturbance could be. The ARVN's pistol was pointed at the canine in response. The officer looked down his barrel at Dog's head. Bolts on M-16s rammed home all around him. If he fired, he too would be dead.

He put the automatic away and shot us a glance. It was wordless, venomous, but his only chance. Most of us had little time with ARVN soldiers. They were more like civilians playing warfare as far as we knew. That day did not raise our confidence in them. It proved to us theirs was reluctant involvement. We did not know much about them, but he did not call for help as he should have. It would have been the better choice.

All operations left life-long impressions for sure. Success in that war would have been the best cure.

So much happens in war. There are scars left inside, scars left on the outside. Nobody who goes to war comes home the same even if he comes home unharmed, if in fact such a thing exists — and that possibility is remote. Most of us are unremarkable. Medals and accolades are not ours to remember. They are not ours to point to and say, "See what I did." Some people can see it in the eyes. Some can see it in the heart.

My Purple Heart

For years, I was ashamed to claim my Purple Heart. I reached a point where I had to make a decision about getting what I earned in war but felt I did not deserve. I discovered it mattered for my family. After encouraging others to claim their benefits for years, those who I had pushed, pushed back. My sons would benefit as would I. Some veteran along the way had the nerve to tell me I suffered from survivor's guilt.

Sometime in the summer of '68, during a skirmish I was bitten by a slice of concertina wire, a small gash. The snaky stuff wrapped around the calf of my leg. It hurt more coming out than going in — then bled. Our medic treated me in the field and cleaned it. Worse than a scratch were the infections we got. I was sliced pretty deep, but it was a silly thing. If kept clean my leg would not fall off, or even stink.

In September that year, we got hit late at night. Three lady mortar crews hit us before daylight. The rounds came fast and furious and on the mark. I caught hot shrapnel in the backs of my hands. We loaded our tubes, not waiting on artillery rounds. Our best gunner had the muzzle flashes in sight. We returned fire, on target, with our 81 mike-mikes.

The new guy next to me got dusted off at dawn. He was wounded and in bad shape. I looked at my tiny scratches — they were nothing. I knew what he was going to be awarded soon, or was pretty sure of it right then. I did not think about my little cuts by comparison. I believed my nameless neighbor on that dyke was KIA, a body-bag grunt that bloody night. I never saw him again — and I was ashamed that those little wounds could earn the same medal.

Purple Heart orders came many months later. By then I was in college, an English major. The official paperwork arrived 12 months late. I looked at it with flashes of still fresh shame. All I had was the certificate, a piece of paper. For all I knew, the man by me got the Grim Reaper. My minor wounds didn't deserve the same medal. Twenty years later I discovered I should rethink my shamed outlook in favor of my children. The State of Indiana had programs to consider. Someone was doing something for the soldiers. I swallowed my pride.

A war with red tape put my patience to a test. My rights unfolded over time after two years of getting records corrected in spite of deaf ears. Almost 20 years after being wounded, I received my Purple Heart. I guess getting shrapnel twice gave me a right to an award that could help my kids get a start.

After all, I *was* really in that fight. My heart is in my chest, and survivor's guilt still inflames doubt. I seldom look at my Purple Heart. I leave it in my memory chest. I can get license plates. It did help at the VA. I even got a disability for ringing ears approved.

My father earned his Heart in WWII, I in Nam. My older son is proud to be the third generation CIB (Combat Infantry Badge) recipient in the family. I pray to God he does not get a Purple Heart.

We do not want that number three.

Enough is enough for now. Really.

I stumbled across the following poem in a packet of things I had not been through in some time. It is a crude poem I wrote while in the boonies in Nam lo these many years ago. I chose to do it as it stood originally. What you see here is just as it was on July 19, 1968, when I wrote it and sent it home to my parents.

Just a Thought

Hey Mom. Ya know something?
First I became a soldier,
And Pop, then I became a man!
Nothin' wrong with havin' fear.
Just take it if you can!

I remember when I was a kid
And everything childish is what I did!
Thought it was cool to talk back
And every sentence was a wise crack!
And each taunt was a wound in my folks' back.

When I was fourteen I claimed "adult!"
But still did things required the belt.
Now I can look back-say I deserved it
And should have gotten a whole bit more
And have been sorry for hurting the ones I adore.

Then I was sixteen and screamed for a car
And Pop struggled to at least put wheels
Under me that I could run near and afar.
I begged for gas, burned his oil and ruined
His tires and caused him another financial scar.

I turned eighteen, big man, a grad
But I didn't want to work but
Still wanted support from my dad!
Got fired or quit job after job
Under the pretense of dissatisfaction or an s-o-b!

So I fooled around for a year
Did nothing but play and sneer
At those who couldn't sham their
Way through life and took their share
Of responsibilities of adulthood.

Next stop was nineteen and I
Volunteered for the draft; why?
I had to find out if I had guts
Backbone or was just going to
Be a parasite to anyone who'd listen.

Well now I'm nearing twenty
Will come home a war vet and
A live infantryman and I've decided
I want to go to college and make something of myself.

Now I know what my mom and dad
Did for me when I was so bad;
They loved, cared and tried — had faith
In God without pushing me.
Now it all falls in place, in a structure of love.

Every once in a while I may revert
But no fear, it's not really me.
It is an old shadow which I hope to shed.
I need ambition to fight
To a goal but I am yet unsure.

I realize I want something
To hold on to and cherish — and live for.
I've had most of life's experiences;
The next I want to behold is success.
Knowing I did something real,

Good, and helpful…I want to grow old
As a man who lived and profited
By his experiences; I appeal to God
To help me so my mom and dad have
A real reason to be proud!

Copied by Michael D. Mullins, 11/24/08

My father, Bernard W. Mullins, with my mother, Donna, during WWII

The Rest of the Way Home

I told part of a story but some endings are better.
Somehow, deep inside, one must find a way
To come to terms with the face of pain.
Veterans of that dirty little war
Were
Alone in a country full of confusion.

They were confused in their own minds, at a loss.
Their reputations were left to some who cared.
They could move on in one of two ways.
They turn on their hearts to believers
Or
Turn within, letting anger dictate everything.

It has been said by some wiser than ever I could be
That one's morale is really a matter of choice.
Mine, when I came home was up in the air.
My flight on the last leg of that journey
Home
Tipped up on one wheel in a cross-wind.

The fear of not making it home would not subside.
Just thirty miles from home, I still wondered.
My mind was full of that first moment
When
My feet touched our American soil.

That should have been my worst wake-up call,
But it was just the first harsh slap in the face.
I got a ride on an airport van for five miles
Yet
The driver asked me for three dollars.

In shock the money was handed over in silence.
The other voices in the van were angrier
Than I and they shamed him loudly
And
In that support I learned some gave a damn.

He tried to give it back but my back was to him
As a mixture of pride and sadness welled up.
In that moment I remembered what home
Means.

I crossed the next road and turned east.
In minutes something happened that gave me hope.
An old farmer stopped and offered me a ride.
I threw my one bag in back and got inside.
Unsure
What to say when he said, "I am taking home boy."

He drove twenty miles out of his way and it saved my soul.
He told me he knew where I had been, he read it in my eyes.
After some voices raised for me, not against me,
Someone
Actually cared, and though he did not know me, he knew me.

I was on the way where someone respected where I had been
And what I had been doing in the name of love for my Country.
An old man of seventy helped an old man of twenty
Smile.
He would have walked me to my door; I wanted to do it alone.

I strode down the street toward home but did not make it very far.
A friend's mom saw me, ran outside, hugged me and began to cry.
She hugged me and said save the kisses for you mother.
"God
Brought you home to us and we are very proud."

I stopped a moment, cried a bit, then knocked on the door.
My mother and father had no idea I was in-country yet.
Mom answered and I asked if Mike was home
And
She cried and said that he never left her heart.

Dad's voice was raised there in the background
Asking who was there knocking at the front door.
"It is our son, he is home and he is a man."
Tears
Fell and the drops hit the floor, shed in joy.

Dad quietly shook my hand then, tears in his eyes.
I knew no words were needed when I held them both.
My baby sister looked at me hiding behind my
Parents.
She had not seen me since she was a toddler.

I was reminded then that I had all the support
I needed in this world, for they all knew the price paid.
Our family had served with a heritage of duty untold.
Morale
Was a question that evening that I did not even debate.

It was years before there was a parade or people even tried
To welcome us home, but in my home I was always welcome.
In the end love from family and the circle that protected me,
Defended me
When others would not, so I could go on, climb the next hill.

Some Nam Vets did not have that luxury.
Others less grounded faded, tried to hide from themselves.
Those soldiers did not think of that option at all.
They tried to fight the battle inside alone.
At last we reached out to each other and said,
"Overcome!"

We still struggle with the trip home but many have learned
To cope, to step up, or stop burying the pain.
We gather together, sharing stories, welcoming one another.
Some do still struggle but
They find us and we tell them what we did
Was right, at our level.

We will always be "coming the rest of the way home."

I Hadn't Looked at Him in a While

I had not really looked at him in a while.
He has aged lately.
I should not have looked this time.
Those liver spots are shining like the headlamp on a locomotive.
His hair is thinning.
You can see right through it.
The hair on his left ear is two inches long.
Why the hell doesn't he trim it?
His ears are bigger.
His nose is bigger.
I read somewhere that those things are the only things that continue to grow as we age.
Emmett Kelly and Red Skelton probably didn't have to use costumes for them late in life.
At least the wrinkles around his eyes are laugh lines.
Those on his forehead could be from pain.
The scars in the corners of his mouth make me wonder.
How could he have gotten those?
What went in that pie hole that could stretch it that much?
I don't remember his wife's jugs being that big!
His nose is crooked as hell.
I think he lied about how he got that.
He never would admit getting hit without hitting back.
That chicken pox scar never faded like his mom told him it would; makes you look right at the end of that honker of a nose too.
The man is getting old.
His whiskers are white. They used to be black with a hint of red in the sunlight.
I have not stopped to look closely at him in a long time.
It is funny how we take people for granted, even when we see them every day.
My God!
It is not him anymore.
It is me.

Vietnam Vets — The Embers of Anger

People ask why Vietnam veterans are angry. It is almost 40 years since the war ended and the embers of anger still burn in the hearts of many. I can only speak with absolute confidence about my reasons, yet I have heard the explanations offered by others. An entire book could be dedicated to the topic. It is a struggle to avoid launching into a litany of reasons. I am limiting this essay to one — the lies solicited by the anti-war elements in Congress and offered by a few soldiers for inexplicable reasons.

I received a phone call on January 5, 2010, from a buddy from Nam. He is one of the men with whom I am still in contact, one of the group which gathers every other year. Clyde said, "Moon, you are not going to believe what I am doing. I am reading some Congressional testimony about war crimes from the Vietnam War."

"What?" I asked. "Why are you doing that?'

"I have been reading some history and ran across an article that mentioned some of the stuff that was said about it, so I looked it up. You are not gonna believe what I found. I found a guy who said we raped and murdered while we were there. The son-of-a-bitch said we are killers."

Clyde continued to explain what was said and where it was found. I went to my computer to look at the same material as we talked. I could not believe what I was reading. It was complete fabrication. We brainstormed until we remembered who the man was. The jerk was our company clerk. He testified that he was a boonie rat like us. The scumbag never spent a night in the bush. We couldn't even remember him coming out with our supply sergeant. Those in Congress who begged for bad information about those of us in combat obviously never confirmed what they heard. They never checked sources. They wanted only to discredit anyone who fought and did their duty. They found rats like this man and elevated them, gave them a moment in the sun. They read their lies into the Congressional Record as though their words were gospel. Clyde informed me he was going to do a little more investigation and call me later.

When Clyde and I next spoke, he told me our turncoat was dead. Clyde had tracked him and discovered his obituary. He was also guilty of *Stolen Valor* to the best of our knowledge. He had planned to visit him personally after confirming what we thought with others in our group. Clyde could do that. He is an independent businessman with the wherewithal to do so. He also has the personal character to make a direct confrontation. As he read the obituary, he learned that the false proclaimer had been buried with full military rites, claiming the honor of a Silver Star for Valor, a Bronze, a Purple Heart, and assorted other combat related awards. He would have earned unit citations, but no more than that. He was not in combat and as far as any of the dozen of us could remember, did not hold a combat MOS. Everything about his military service in Vietnam was fabricated. He lied before Congress and lived a life telling lies. Some people feel compelled to do that. The man had no reason. He had a job to do and did it. That was enough... or should have been.

Clyde and I were angry. Every time we ever heard one of these stories we doubted it. We knew that when Calley went down that the situation exacerbated it for everyone. He deserved what he got by all accounts, but it was a completely isolated, freak event. Yet stuff rolls downhill. It always does. The anti-war crowd was not about to let a good crisis go to waste. We did not trust the information that came out about My Lai after we came home. We despised the event and the cover up as well. Adrenalin and combat anger do not explain or excuse that level of savagery. Looking for another event of that nature should not have been a goal of our government, nor should it have been believed to be the norm.

We talked and decided that his family did not deserve to have his memory destroyed. It was not their fault and they should be allowed the dignity of living with the memory he created. I told Clyde I intended to write about the incident. It was proof absolute about the sort of thing that we know happened because a small group of elected officials and Americans made it possible. The press cultivated it as well. We agreed that when I told it, he would remain nameless. Not only am I telling it now, I will tell a few of the things which were entered in the record.

I will refer to our "soldier at arms" as D, which stands for denigrator. He must have been substantially older than most of us. He claimed to be from the upper eastern part of the US, but had a Master's Degree from a southwestern university. He joined the Army in 1967, completed Basic Training, Advanced Infantry Training, and planned on attending Officers Candidate School. He was rejected for views he espoused during Basic and was assigned to a duty station in Germany where he volunteered for duty in Vietnam. He believed in what we were doing there....but he was rejected for OCS for certain views? That in itself is an odd dichotomy.

I will mention here that I am paraphrasing. His testimony is far too lengthy to quote in its entirety. He began his testimony by explaining his early experience in the Army in 1967 with broad, negative criticism. D explained to the committee, in the presence of the press, that at McNamara's direction, the Army had lowered entry requirements on a wholesale scale. He called it McNamara's Brigade with lower mentality standards. In 1967, the Army required increased numbers of personnel. McNamara demanded that the ghettos, the Appalachian Mountains, and anywhere that the poor live be scoured for the disadvantaged so that they could be used for cannon fodder according to D. He seemed sure of his information. He deemed it a sort of genocide. His first example was an acting platoon sergeant who he helped in Basic Training. He was an 18-year-old "black boy with four children" who could neither read nor write. People like that young man went on to serve in the field in 1967 and even into 1968. They killed and were killed because they were told to do so. The Army had to raise the standards again because they could not use them for anything else. They — he referred to them as the "67s" — were all sent to the front. You could read about it in the Morning Reports as D had (field soldiers had no access to these documents). D claimed the Army altered the reporting system. Clyde and I found this interesting. Company clerks typed the reports as we understood it. Until sometime in 1968, the killed and wounded were reported by their service numbers. Volunteers' numbers began with the letter designations "RA" and draftees with "US." D said it became too evident that a disproportionate number of illiterate poor blacks and others were being sacrificed so the Army began reporting by Social Security Number to obscure the ratio. He was quizzed about these opinions by a hungry press. The "unbiased" moderator allowed open questioning.

D went on to reiterate that the Army did not want to keep the "67s" in the service because they were too dumb and too easily killed. They were too slow to react. Their mentality limitations caused their reactions to be slower than people of normal intelligence. They could be taught to "holler kill, kill, kill, but not to duct." I am unsure about his Masters Degree's reality. Perhaps the committee's clerk could not spell.

D spoke of a different sort of training than I received even though I was a contemporary there too. He indicated the Army managed to manipulate the draft system. D addressed the training program as well. D told the committee about learning to fire with the M-14 and screaming "kill" with every round. That came as a shock to me. My range coaches taught me breath control for accuracy. We inhaled, slowly exhaled and fired. There was no screaming. Sudden movements pulled the shot. What he claimed was a complete antithesis to accuracy in my experience. I read his expose about bayonet training and disputed it in silence. Screaming was part of that. Hand-to-hand combat is not for the faint of heart. Silent combat has a place and we learned it in basic with some refinement in AIT (advanced). D said he did his bayonet work in AIT, which was much different than my experience.

I began training for that in Basic with pugil stick warfare. We competed company-wide on a daily basis in the later weeks of Basic. When we went live, it was with range dummies. D introduced his racism theory at this point. We never yelled "gook." D explained that the Army brand of racism was not leveled at blacks or Puerto Ricans (an odd selection given that we had Cubans and Mexicans among our Latino population too). He expressed the idea that the Army began a hate-training program against "gooks" to indoctrinate its trainees for Vietnam. We had Asians in the Armed Forces as well. When I went to Tiger Ridge at Fort Polk, LA, we learned about the Viet Cong and the North Vietnamese Regulars, but "gook" did not become part of my vocabulary until I was in-country where they tried to kill me on a regular basis. In AIT, I learned about setting booby-traps and battle tactics. I learned to operate heavier weaponry. I learned my mortar. I spent more time in the field in simulated battle situations and even learned about living off the land. Basic was behind me. D must have repeated his because he did not get it the first time.

After D laid the foundation for his absolute loathing and lack of understanding for an infantryman's military occupation, he launched into the greatest lies of all. He was not infantry. In Basic he did fire an M-14, but I would wager his advanced training was typing 32 words a minute with three or fewer errors. I have no problem with that. I respect the job those people had to do. I respect the work all support people did. They served. They did what was asked of them. They were away from home, in harm's way, deprived of family and friends. I offer them my thanks and a welcome home. Ours separated himself from them by his deeds in the halls of Congress — under oath.

D arrived in Nam in March, 1968 — the same month as I. He testified that a woman was raped in the midst of a major firefight in early April and killed while escaping. He and another soldier witnessed and reported it. I tell about that firefight in this book. There were no women in any of the firefights in which we engaged in April. It is an outright fabrication. Even if there had been females around, there had been nobody in Delta 3/7 who would have done such a thing. And had there been, they certainly would not have done it and gotten away with it. We were in no villages. We were in heavy jungle. We engaged a battalion of NVA sappers. D further asserted that our Company Commander told them "that it happens all the time. You will get used to it. Just look the other way"....and that it was in the Day Report as another enemy kill. Our CO (commanding officer) at the time was a Captain who had been a senior NCO who had taken a field commission. He was tough as nails and would never have allowed anything like a rape and murder. He would have shot the perpetrator himself. The Old Man drank his Schlitz warm, would strip his blouse off and kick your ass out behind his hooch if he had to do it. He was old school.

D reported another incident later. He said he did not witness it but heard the admission about its commission. Three prisoners were taken when a village was destroyed. One of our soldiers was placed on guard duty, got drunk and killed them without anyone noticing during the night. I assume his relief never noticed when he was replaced at the given time. The next day, they were reported as having been killed in an escape attempt. That is also what the Day Report claimed. D heard the alleged guard admit that he killed them. It was unknown how and D did not offer a description of the event. He said the admission came while that individual was again under the influence. The moderator asked him how he learned about it so easily. D said it came out of the man "through his spirits." When asked if he was harassed for reporting this incident, D replied that he was told that it would be in the Day Report as enemy killed and to forget it as well.

D referred to the Day Reports often. He claimed to have read them, gleaned information from them, and had knowledge of Army information that none of us shared who served in the field. Most young soldiers "hated" the Army at times. Most young people "hate" their jobs at times. Grousing is a part of life. Why he hated us and painted us as such evil doers is a mystery. I do have a theory. That is all it is, but it is viable.

We grunts returned to the rear area on occasion. We had an R and R. We got wounded. We had a unit stand down (ordered out of the field for a temporary rest, re-outfitting, and resupply). When we came, we could be a bit rowdy. If we returned alone or in small groups, we were often not welcomed by our rear echelon brethren. We did not smell good. We did not accept red tape very well. We wanted clean socks, a pair of pants, a shirt, a bath, some warm food, and no damned hassle. We were usually met with a superior attitude. We did not like it when a spit shined Spec-4 behind a desk ordered us out of his office because we smelled bad. We did not respond well when told they would get around to it when they were ready. We might even say something a little disrespectful to him. He could carry a grudge. He might leap at a chance to get even with those nasty boys in the boonies.

Or it could be a chance for a lizard to lay on a nice warm rock in the sun.

Why are Nam vets angry? This is one reason. Lies about them and what they did. A bunch of folks in the government that sent them to do what they did which then found a way to denigrate them for doing it. Some of those same types are doing it again now to this generation of soldiers. They attacked good soldiers who served at the very best of their ability, laying everything they had on the line day and night. Isolated incidents were turned into an alleged standard operating procedure. Politicians and press were searching out liars and little jealous people to affirm their ill wishes for those who were doing what they were asked to do. The two joined hands to assail those of larger heart and courage.

While in Vietnam we read reports — when papers were available — about what was being said about Soldiers. When I attended college in the fall of 1969, I was questioned about this very thing frequently. It was a common topic of discussion among my peers in my experience.

The politicians could have verified their stories. They could have looked at something to see if there was even an iota of truth in what they were told. They wanted it to be true so they let it stand as though it were credible. They could have asked how a grunt had access to a Day Report. John Kerry was there. He knew that a field soldier had no access to a Day Report. He let it stand because that was what he wanted. The moderator was an ex-officer with a field unit. He knew it too. They were the biggest liars of all. They wanted the ill will of the American public to crash down on the average American Vietnam veteran. The committee solicited participants for months. Some of its members still serve in Congress today. I read the testimony. There were more than a dozen "witnesses" involved. Much of what appears there defies credulity. They helped create what many of us came home to.

That could be one of the reasons we have been angry for 40 years or more. Even the youngest of the Vietnam veterans is nearing the four decade mark since its conclusion.

SERVING AMERICA —
IT HAS BEEN A FAMILY AFFAIR

Desperate. No other word describes my attitude as I struggled with a way to record my father-in-law's experience in World War II. I have no information. He and I spoke of his service in the United States Navy one time while we rocked on his front porch. Harold P. Davis laughed and told me that he and his buddies got blitzed on "torpedo juice" as they sailed home after the War ended. He was passed out below decks when the ship sailed under the Golden Gate Bridge. I remember laughing at the story. Americans were drunk in one fashion or another around the world when World War II ended. Every Main Street in America hosted a parade, I imagined. Soldiers and Sailors celebrated wherever they were. I knew there was more to say than that.

Harold Phillip Davis was born in Olinger, VA, in 1925 to a farming family. He went to war like most red-blooded boys. He was young, but he was older than the girl he married after the war. She never knew much about what he did, or if she did she never spoke of it. My wife grew up with no knowledge about his experience in the war either. It is not unusual. Time after time, World War II veterans trapped the demons of war deep within only to release them late in life. Harold never had that opportunity. He died exactly four weeks after my father in 1980 at the age of 55. I have been more curious than most about what he did. Those who knew his history are gone too.

Phyllis has one treasure from his Navy years. It is a small tin filled with foreign coins. I resolved to write a story about Harold in this book, even if it is "faction." I read that term in a writer's manual a few years ago. It is a fiction story with a loose foundation in fact. The only available facts I could claim are the coins and the knowledge that Harold was in the Navy. It was enough.

I sat at my desk with the tin open, wondering if I could read a man's war story in their worn faces like a fortune teller reads the future in tea leaves. Would something drift from those 60-year-old coins into my mind and speak to me? Would Harold whisper to me and reveal where he had been and what he had done? Would they tell me about enemy planes flying at his ship, or the sound of waves beating at the sides of his vessel as he sailed to some unknown destination and fate? Did he load cannons or bombs or swab the deck and paint the rails? He survived, but there had to be story along the way.

The coins…the coins…many are faint. Many are worn. All are from the Mediterranean region. That is odd. How did he get there? Why? There are coins from India, the Philippines, Mozambique, Iran, something Asian exotic. There are several with a lion and a rising sun background…ah, they are Iranian too. There are some that say "Bank Deutscher Lander, and D G Hispon Etind Rex Philip V." There are a few that say "King George VI and Republica Portuguesa." There are rupees, centavos, centavios, MF8s, and peenies. There are a couple that Wikipedia (what a wonderful free resource) says are World War II counterfeits produced by the Chinese. The coins in the tin point to a Navy man who spent his sailing time bouncing from one place to another in the Mediterranean. The mystery deepens. I did not realize that we sailed that much in the region. The Phoenicians, Greeks, and the Egyptians, yes — but us?

I could not find a way to get Harold Davis from Olinger, VA, to the coastal regions where he accumulated those coins. I read more history about the Pacific Fleet in Wikipedia. I discovered a possible key to the mystery. The Navy needed support for the Sixth Army Group and its attack across Africa into Europe for Operation Dragoon. The Fifth Fleet was carved from the Central Pacific Fleet for that purpose. An old French port at Oran was occupied. It took months of construction and untold tons of supplies to build. The headquarters for the supply line to the Sixth Army was established at Manama, Bahrain. I had my answer for the Navy presence — therefore I knew why Harold was there and why the coins were in Phyllis' tin. I could write my faction.

Navy ships, Merchant Marine ships, personnel of every military branch worked to grow the region in support of the war in Europe. It was a huge undertaking. The French deserted the port before the war and we built it from nothing into a major supply hub. The Sea-Bees were there, the Army Corps of Engineers, and soon support facilities of every kind erupted from the coast. We built a massive Army Hospital there. The Africa Campaign was successful because of the work done there, thus the charge into Europe from the south was successful. After V-E Day, the United States government began decommissioning it. We built such a huge complex that it took until October of 1945 to move most of the material away from Oran. We turned over a huge facility to the French when we withdrew the last of our personnel. Harold Davis sailed in and out of the War with a handful of coins from a place I never knew existed for the story I had to create about him. But it has a wonderful feel of truth about it. As long as I write and say all those things about it, it will be ethical to do it that way.

Life is life. The bumps in the road took us to a safety deposit box in March of 2011. My wife came home with her father's discharge papers. She had never seen them before. Her father was discharged on March 4th, 1946 — and returned home from World War II as a Seaman First Class. His medals read, "American Area: Victory World War II: Asiatic-Pacific Area."

Phyllis was thrilled. I was thrilled. We had something solid. I had no complete story, but we knew where he was and the document showed his ships. I began to do some research in the Navy records on line. He trained at NTS Bainbridge, MD: AGS Little Creek, VA AGC Brooklyn, NY. He sailed on the SS Kettle Creek, SS John Morton, and SS John Gallup. There was a starting place at last.

The Navy web site shows every ship that floated in World War II. I was crestfallen to see that none had the "SS" designation. As I read the tiny print at the bottom of each of the pages I continued to peel another layer of the onion. Several hours later, I read deep enough to find the "SS" boats and discovered the long, long list of Merchant Marine vessels that sailed the seas for America in the War. "Merchant" implies civilian and so they were, but they were part of the Navy history web site. The ships to which Harold Davis was assigned were certainly there and a major part of the war, credited with many voyages.

I knew nothing about the training bases noted on his paperwork. The big ones are common news, but his were lesser known. World War II had a myriad of training posts for all the branches. I was not surprised at that. I was surprised to learn that he trained for a rather obscure and rather specialized group at Little Creek, VA. Harold was part of the Naval Armed Guard. He was trained in small arms warfare and in the use of anti-aircraft battle (at Brooklyn, NY, for the final live-fire phase). It was rare. During World War I and again in II, it became necessary for the Navy to protect the civil shipping contractors at sea. They were prime targets for the enemy. Our war effort would have sunk with their ships had we not intervened. In World War II, we had 144,970 sailors on civilian vessels at sea and in port. They were in teams of 28, including officers and communications personnel. It was high risk. Some records indicate as many as 2100 were killed or missing during the War.

The American public knew little or nothing about their service. Today's Navy seldom speaks about them, but the Navy Armed Guard should be held in high esteem. As part of this story, I want to thank the website dedicated to Navy Armed Guard Tom Bowman, where I discovered some facts to supplement the information I learned on line. His family helped me learn about my own.

Harold Davis did something unique and special in World War II. It is ironic that the tin of coins spoke to me. It appears that he did in fact sail the shipping lanes from the Philippines to the Mediterranean on Merchant Marine ships in World War II, but not as a swabbie. He was a Navy Armed Guard. My faction was more fact than fiction. He sailed dangerous waters in support of a major offensive into Europe.

We are fortunate his story was in a little tin box and a lock box.

◆ ◆ ◆

Uncle Harry F. Mullins (deceased), US Army Retired, left us information regarding who was the first Mullins to serve our country. He was James Carson Mullins, the oldest Mullins boy, who joined the Army Air Corps in 1938. We always referred to him as Uncle Carson. That is too old a habit to break now. He trained in Armament and Bombardier School at Lowery Air Force base before the onset of World War II. Uncle Carson was a Technical Sergeant at Jackson Air Force Base in Mississippi by 1941, where he assisted in training General Doolittle's Bomb Group in the use of the Nordic Bomb Sight. The device was complicated and could not be used in the raid. It was replaced by a unit called the "Mark Twain" so the training effort led to nothing.

Uncle Carson fought in World War II as a member of the 449th Bomber Squadron in the 332nd Bomb Group. He flew many missions as a bombardier, a gunner, and a crew chief aboard the B-26 Marauder. They saw action in Holland, France, Germany, and Central Europe — and were instrumental during the drive toward Berlin after the Bulge.

James Carson Mullins returned to the US in 1945. He served at various bases as Air Inspector, Crew Chief, and Flight Line Chief until 1952, when he left for South Korea. He was stationed at Kun San Air Force Base — and was the Air Inspector for the B-26 Night Bomber Squadron until August 1953.

T/Sgt. Mullins returned to the States once again, where he served at various bases, including a stint at West Point Prep School in Newburg, NY. He retired a Master Sergeant in 1960 at Lowering Air Force Base in Maine.

I recall visiting Uncle Carson when he was stationed near Washington, DC. Uncle Hansford (Harry F.) was stationed there too. We made family vacations out of visits to see them on more than one occasion during my childhood. Dad took my brother and me to see Uncle Carson at work. Somewhere in the treasure trove of family photos, there is a shot of us being lifted through the pilot's hatch into the dream world of a jet aircraft. The airmen at the time treated us to a high-tech cockpit that was the Jetsons and Buck Rogers all rolled into one small space. We had the run of the place. It was the late fifties and life was good.

◆ ◆ ◆

Dad's sister Margaret married one of my personal military heroes. James D. Shortt was the first in my family, extended and immediate, to serve this country. When he joined the Army on January 19, 1937, he began a chain of service in our family that has continued through today. Both branches of my family contribute to that tradition. Uncle James wrote his own synopsis. I am including an excerpt from the material he left his children.

"In July 1936, I tried the Army and I got to Bristol, Va. But because I looked younger than my age, the Sergeant told me to come back in September. But I didn't go back until Jan. 19, 1937 and went to Washington, DC, on a cold rainy day. F. D. Roosevelt was being inaugurated. I went to Headquarters Troop 3rd Horse Cavalry in Fort Myers, Va.

I soldiered under Post Commander Col. Wainwright until mid-summer 1938 and this year I was in the lead scout car on Pennsylvania Avenue from the Capital to the White House guarding King George VI and Queen Elizabeth.

We had Gen. Batista of Cuba for our horse show. I was always riding in the horse show with non-commissioned officers such as Sergeants and Corporals. In the summer we fought in lots of the old Civil War projects around Manassas, VA.

I had First Sergeant Poston and he left. I had Sergeant Jaffee, Capt. Regibald, Capt. Dewey from NY, Capt. Trapnel, Lt. Baugh, and Lt. Richardson. They were my officers from 1937 to Jan. 19, 1940 with Col. George S. Patton from mid-summer 1938 until discharged on January 19, 1940.

> # Honorable Discharge
> ## from
> ## The Army of the United States
>
> TO ALL WHOM IT MAY CONCERN:
>
> **This is to Certify, That*** _____James D. Shortt_____
> Pvt. 1cl.,
> † 6897230, Specl. 5th Cl., Headquarters and Headquarters and Service Troop, 3d Cavalry
> THE ARMY OF THE UNITED STATES, as a TESTIMONIAL OF HONEST AND FAITHFUL SERVICE, is hereby HONORABLY DISCHARGED from the military service of the UNITED STATES by reason of ‡ __Expiration of Service__.
>
> Said __James D. Shortt__ was born in __Wise County__, in the State of __Virginia__.
> When enlisted he was __18__ years of age and by occupation a __Farmer__.
> He had __Brown__ eyes, __Black__ hair, __Ruddy__ complexion, and was __5__ feet __5½__ inches in height.
>
> Given under my hand at __Fort Myer, Virginia__ this __19th__ day of __January__, one thousand nine hundred and __forty__.
>
> G. S. Patton, Jr.
> G. S. PATTON, JR.,
> Colonel, Third Cavalry
> Commanding.

I was honorably discharged, came home and went to work Feb. 19, 1940.

I have a copy of Uncle James' discharge. It is signed by Patton. Only one of his spurs still exists. He was real Cavalry. He rode behind Patton.

When he came home to work, he went underground in the coal mines of Southwest Virginia for more than 20 years. He fed the War effort. There he stayed until rheumatoid arthritis crippled him until he could no longer work. He paid the price. I can attest that he drove his wheelchair like a command car.

I went to live with Uncle James and Aunt Meg after my discharge from the Army. I went to college in a small town not far from them. I could not afford housing. In 1970, James D. Shortt performed my wedding ceremony.

♦ ♦ ♦

The next lifer in my family was my mother's brother Jack. Charles J. Washam was an enigma. He was Army. He was a dapper man in a suit. He joined the Army in early 1945, first serving in the Corps of Engineers in Europe during the reconstruction after World War II. Uncle Jack told me that he reported to Patton's outfit a few weeks after the General was killed. It was not long before he was assigned to Armed Forces Radio.

Uncle Jack worked in Europe for much of his Army career. He was with the Armed Forces Network 14 years. He had more connections with important people than any man I ever knew. Charles J. Washam began as a sound effects man, but soon found himself behind the microphone. He was an Army disc jockey for years. Every time he came stateside, it was in a suit, carrying a briefcase. We never saw him in uniform. When it came time to reenlist, somehow his assignments always took him abroad. We never really knew what he did, but until the late fifties it was with the radio network system. When he left that military occupation, it was to work with military recreational operations. There he met his wife, Faye, who until then was a professional ice skater with an Ice Capades troupe. We did see a photo of them together once when he was wearing khakis.

One assignment brought him stateside for an unhappy period. Uncle Jack's work involved travel and interesting situations about which he never spoke. Mom's younger brother, Paul, recalls when the FBI came to my grandparents' home and questioned them about Uncle Jack. He received a very high clearance level soon thereafter. That was in the early fifties. Nobody ever knew why.

When the conflict escalated in Vietnam, Sergeant First Class Charles J. Washam went. He served several tours there. He was there when Tan Son Nhut was penetrated the first time. He was still there for 1968 Tet Offensive. He was there for another tour after that. As I recall, his official records say three tours. He told me that including all his trips, he served five tours if you added all of his in-country time. He arranged a lot of travel for some very high level personnel while working at the air field. His reach spanned the world and all levels of the Army.

Uncle Paul remembers a night out with Uncle Jack when the latter admitted that during his radio career his song selection and timing had meaning. Uncle Jack just smiled and said no more. I remember wondering if dad knew more than he admitted. They often talked alone. Charles J. Washam followed the news and politics with passion. He was more aware than anyone I ever met. When I was around him, he explained what he watched — if I sat and listened. There were story lines he seemed to grasp which were not part of the broadcasts. If he was visiting us, we did not interrupt the news.

In March of 1968, it was time for me to join Uncle Jack in Vietnam. He was in the States at the time. Uncle Paul and his wife Judy met me at O'Hare Airport in Chicago. Uncle Jack came to see me off too. He shared some parting words of wisdom. I did not hear them in my mental state at the time. I was too busy being impervious. He was in a suit. We'd talked about Vietnam before — in small doses. Paul Washam is the best support one could ever have while serving in the military. (He is a superior historian still today. My son has the benefit of his support today.) They remained at my side until I boarded the plane and their misty eyes followed me into the cloudy sky until the plane was well out of their sight.

I am the only person who ever saw Charles J. Washam in military dress. I took a three day in-country R&R (rest and recreation) leave in late January, 1969. (We were entitled to a three day in-country and a week out-of-country R&R.) I wanted to visit my uncles.

By mid-summer 1968, there were five from my family in Nam. Uncle Jack was in Saigon. My cousin, 1st Lieutenant Hoyt Shortt (son of James), a graduate of Virginia Military Institute, was around Long Binh some place. My cousin Judy Kiser's husband Bud, a Warrant Officer and career man, was up north. Uncle Hansford, career man and Infantry veteran of Korea, was at Cu Chi. I thought a nice little tour would make a great travelogue at a Kiwanis Club event in the future.

Reporting at Tan Son Nhut's main gate I asked for SFC Charles J. Washam. I explained I wanted to visit my uncle and provided identification. They logged my name and unit. The guard called for an MP (military police) escort to drive me to the right hooch. After being pointed in the right direction, I walked to the door and knocked. The muscular black man who opened the door looked at me and laughed. He shook his head and said, "Boy, I think you want your other uncle." He pulled his fatigue jacket over his od (olive drab) t-shirt as he walked out the door and walked me all the way around to the other side of the compound. It was a hike. He knocked on Uncle Jack's hooch door. He said, "Sarge, I have your nephew here. He is a little too white for my family. You guys enjoy yourselves" and walked away laughing.

Uncle Jack's hooch was a palace. He had a great cot, all kinds of spit-shined boots, and pressed jungle fatigues hanging in a neat row in a real live closet. There was a stereo and a small fridge along one wall. Man! It was like an oasis. We sat and talked about my war awhile. He took me to mess. I could not believe you could get food that late or that good. I met some of his buddies and we talked some more war. I don't remember the details. When we got back to the room, he asked me what I wanted. I told him I would like to go to Vung Tau for a couple of hours. That would be a dream. Then I would like to go see Uncle Hansford. That is in a perfect world. I would settle for Hansford.

SFC Washam rolled me out for mess at his usual time. We ate off a menu! I learned why — it was a Senior NCO/Officers Mess Hall. That world was much different than mine. After a real breakfast, Uncle Jack made a call, loaded me, my camera, and my M-16 into a Jeep and took me to a heli-pad. I asked him what was going on and he informed me I had a ride to Vung Tau. I jumped into the waiting Huey and we lifted off for the in-country paradise.

I was not sure how my uncle pulled that one off, but he did. We flew to the coast without conversation. The crew I offered no information about how I got my ride or how I would be returning to Saigon. I remember that I planned to ask before I got off that bird. I think it was about an hour ride, but memories fade. When we got there, the pilot circled at our cruising elevation. He was talking in low tones to someone on the ground. Vung Tau was pretty secure, but there was something going on. He turned to me and said our plans were changed. We were going back to Tan Son Nhut. Uncle Jack was waiting when we got there.

It was mid-morning. Uncle Jack suggested we get a snack at his mess hall, or at least some coffee. He knew what happened in Vung Tau. Uncle Jack explained that it was unusual, but it had not been safe for a landing. He suggested I make arrangements for my trip to Cu Chi — and asked how I planned to get there. I had no idea. He went on to tell me he could not help until the next day and getting me back the same day would be very difficult. I could be in trouble. He offered to let me stay with him over night again. I told him I knew there was traffic that way all the time and I might just hitchhike. Uncle Jack told me I was nuts. He asked me if I had a death wish or something.

I asked my Sergeant First Class Uncle if I was right about the traffic between Saigon and Cu Chi. He confirmed it was heavy. He also said that if I got there, I could have Uncle Hansford get him word and he could get me a ride back. He knew there was a chopper going the next day and returning after noon chow. It was decided. If he could get me a ride to Highway One, I was thumbing my way to Cu Chi.

I stood near a check point at the south edge of Saigon and waited. The soldiers there thought it was funny as hell, but I had a legitimate pass and they let me go. I got a ride on an ice truck — a deuce and a half (a two and a half ton Army truck) rigged with a container that held several blocks of ice — headed south. I had my camera and weapon. They were pleased to have an armed passenger and I was happy to have a quick ride. I made it to Cu Chi to visit with my other uncle.

The return to Saigon went as planned as did my trip to Camp Frenzell-Jones (home of the 199th Light Infantry Brigade) and back to my unit in the boondocks.

I saw Uncle Jack one more time before I left Nam.

Three weeks passed after my in-country travel adventures and I was classified as a real-live short timer. Specialist Fourth Class Michael D. "Moon" Mullins was under 30 days to DEROS (Date of Expected Return from Overseas). A grunt's duty did not change, but he walked with more care. He ducked quicker. He cringed at times when he may have not before. He thought more about living than he did. He began to believe he was going to make it after all. The days, nights and hours began to drag by with lead weights attached on the second hand. Calendar pages were glued in place. Rather than hoping for contact, he began to pray for boredom. Sleep became difficult for a different reason.

I got ordered to the Old Man's Hooch one evening before dark. It was about ten days before I was due to board a silver bird for home, or about five days before I should be leaving the field to begin processing out of country. The Company Commander told me the XO (Executive Officer) was coming for me. We had been patrolling near some roads and were accessible for a change. I did not have to wait long, but it was not easy. The Captain did not tell me why and I wondered how I could be in trouble. I was clean and green.

The XO arrived in a very short time — but it seemed an eternity to me — and told me to get my gear, I was going home. I was speechless. When I could talk, I asked how that could be. He told me to get my ass moving. If he pushed the system all night, I would fly out the next day. He had gotten a call telling him to get things moving. I got everything I had and loaded in the Jeep. I had little time to talk to anyone but the people in my gun crew. I was leaving the Nam — and doing it in one piece.

We hauled freight back to Frenzell-Jones with me asking questions. He told me that my Uncle Jack called, sent some orders from somewhere pretty impressive — and I was headed home. The XO was not pleased and it showed in his voice and demeanor. My God, he was working at night! I asked my favorite First Lieutenant what I was supposed to do with my gear in the locker in the rear and he promised to ship it to me. When we got to our company area, the first thing I did was complete that paperwork. I never saw the gear I had stored in the rear area again. The pictures bother me still today. I did not expect much. That REMF confiscated my burp gun too. He took me by the hand—under orders—and walked me through the entire paperwork process all night long. I was through by dawn. My XO kept clerks working all night to get me processed out of the 199th and on my way to Tan Son Nhut one more time. He chauffeured me to Uncle Jack's gate.

Sergeant First Class Washam was waiting. After a very perfunctory salute, Uncle Jack loaded me and my single duffle bag in his Jeep and rolled toward the airport at Tan Son Nhut. I asked him how this all happened. He responded by assuring me that a seat had become available at the last minute. He held it for me. It was time. Jack told a Private to load my gear and directed me to hit the latrine and board. He shook my hand and walked over to the boarding people with my paperwork. I had a set of my orders in hand. I waved as I walked up the ramp. I was headed back to the world.

Years later, I sat in a bar on Diversy Street in Chicago with Uncle Jack after he retired. I asked him how that little deal transpired. I am not sure I ever told anyone this. Uncle Jack said there was a young officer on the plane who was not supposed to be. He put him off and put me on. I deserved to be there. When we arrived in San Francisco, I learned I was the only man on board who held a rank below E-8, or who was not an officer. How does an SFC pull that off? When I went on R&R, he knew it too. A First Sergeant sat down by me on the jet and told me Uncle Jack asked him to take care of me until I got settled in Tai Pei. He did it too. How did the man know that? He was more than he ever told any of us. A lot of things add up to one plus one is three, in hind sight.

SFC Charles J. Washam retired in 1973 and obtained a job managing a large hotel in Chicago. He maintained all of his contacts. He knew what was transpiring in Vietnam. There was a family there whose members were important to him. He reached out to them somehow, helping each in different ways. Uncle Jack was way ahead of the curve as far as the fall of Saigon went. There were two sisters in the family who he helped escape the country in 1974. He flew to Wake Island and met them, escorted them to Fort Sill for a few weeks, then brought them to Windfall, IN, in late 1974. They remained here with my parents for several weeks. Twi and Rose helped my mother, learned more English and proved to be as sweet as they were beautiful. They were refugees and safe in the heartland of America where nobody thought to seek them. Saigon fell in 1975. When things calmed and more Vietnamese were being welcomed to the States, Uncle Jack moved them to Chicago. They found jobs and acclimated to our way of life, even starting businesses of their own, with his support.

When Uncle Jack died, we took him to Arlington. He was a simple Sergeant First Class, retired.

♦ ♦ ♦

I have cousins about whom I will not write. I salute them for their service. One of them I will seek later and hope he is ready. He was shot out of Hummers on three occasions in the War on Terror. He suffers from Traumatic Brain Injury. He prefers to remain in the background at this time, but I must mention him here. He served with pride and will pay for that service the rest of his life with his disabilities. May our country never fail to care for him.

♦ ♦ ♦

I mentioned hitchhiking to Cu Chi while in Vietnam. I went to see my uncle, First Sergeant Harry F. Mullins. He enlisted in the Army on August 14, 1951, and retired July 1, 1975. His career was the exact opposite of Uncle Jack's. Uncle Hansford, our family name, was Infantry and recruiter. He fought and talked. He was a marvelous talker. He earned several awards as an Army snake-oil salesman. Uncle Jack was a talker on the radio, but his persona was much different. Uncle Hansford was a salesman. He never convinced me to join. I was a draftee. Well, there is a story about that.

I wanted to serve, but I was more interested in college. I researched the various branches of military service. The lengths of commitment bothered me. The Army offered a three-year enlistment, the shortest of the four major options. The day I went for my draft physical, I decided what I was going to do. I returned that evening, got off the bus, went to the draft office and volunteered for the draft. I moved my name to the top of the list. I joined without joining and did two years rather than three.

Now, back to Uncle Hansford — the man with all the ribbons on his chest. Private Harry (Hansford) French Mullins trained with the 10th Mountain Division at Fort Riley, KS, first and later at Camp Hale, CO. His first duty assignment came in Korea in 1952 with the 32nd Infantry Regiment of the 7th Infantry Division, where he remained until the conclusion of hostilities. Uncle Hansford saw action on Jane Russell Hill, Old Baldy, in the Kumwah Valley, the Triangle, and in 1953 on Pork Chop Hill. The 7th was the only Division to be engaged in a major battle until it was relieved by the 17th Infantry Regiment. He began accumulating his vast array of military awards while serving in heavy combat.

Harry F. Mullins earned his Combat Infantryman's Badge, the first of his many campaign badges—and the first of his awards for valor. He was wounded in combat on Pork Chop Hill and again in Vietnam, where he added to his combat medals. During the fifties, he served three tours of duty in Korea, two of which were near the Demilitarized Zone. He was committed to combat arms when assigned to overseas duty.

When Uncle Hansford returned to the States after his Korean Conflict tour, he became involved with Honor Guard service. It set a pattern when he was serving stateside. He joined the Old Guard, the 3rd Infantry Regiment, and became part of the personal detachment chosen to protect General Omar Bradley. He was selected to be part of the President's Honor Guard at Fort Myer, VA. Harry F. Mullins became involved in recruiting in the mid-fifties due to his colorful military experience. He was very successful, but he missed his combat arms assignments. He transferred to the 12th Armored Cavalry Regiment for another Korean tour in 1961 before returning to duty with the Honor Guard in Washington, DC, in 1962.

Sergeant Harry F. Mullins was again selected as a member of the President's Honor Guard in '62 and became the NCOIC (non-commissioned officer in charge) of Red Carpet Detail at the White House. He served in that capacity under President John F. Kennedy and was with one of the Honor Guard Units for his funeral. I remember watching Uncle Hansford at the Tomb of the Unknown Soldier when I was a youngster. It was the same trip when I visited Uncle Carson at the airfield. When I was even younger, we visited Uncle Hansford in Colorado. His notes indicate he was a Drill Instructor there for a short while before returning to an infantry assignment. After JFK's death, Uncle Hansford was reassigned to recruiting. We were at war in Vietnam. Soldiers were needed and he was good at finding them. He has a number of commendations for surpassing his recruitment goals.

Senior Infantry leadership was at a premium during Vietnam. Sergeant First Class Mullins was assigned to the 1st Battalion, 27th Infantry Regiment Wolfhounds of the 25th Infantry Division. He reported to Cu Chi, Vietnam in 1968, where our paths crossed. He served as a Platoon Sergeant and saw heavy combat, again earning meritorious awards and another Purple Heart. When I visited him, he had been promoted to First Sergeant for his company. He and I fought in the same areas of operation in Vietnam.

I arrived at Cu Chi, found Uncle Hansford, and was invited to share the shade of his NCO club. I could never have gotten in the places where he and Uncle Jack took me. It was good to have some connections. Those visits were the only times I saw how the "other half" lived. We shared a few beers while he ate several hard boiled eggs. Popcorn appealed to me more. We talked about Tah Ninh Province, the Pineapple Groves, the French Fort, the Rubber Plantation, and other places we knew. While we chatted an alert sounded. The firebase was under attack. In-coming mortar rounds were landing near us and he led me to a bunker not far from his command area.

It was pretty interesting for a while. My luck seemed to be running true to form. Where I went, Charlie was sure to follow. There were half a dozen of us in the bunker — those from his command post and us. Uncle Hansford's eggs were making things inside the hot, humid bunker very unpleasant. I was a grunt. Those rounds weren't that bad. I looked at him in the dim light and said, "Uncle Hansford. I am going outside and lay behind the wall. Those rounds might kill me. If I stay in here with you I am gonna die for damned sure." I went outside. It was safer.

The attack was more harassing than damaging. It did not last long. We shared mess, visited some more and when the supply chopper arrived I arranged for a ride back to Tan Son Nhut. The pilot expected me. Uncle Jack had alerted them. I made it there and Jack got me back to Camp Frenzell-Jones.

It was cool seeing family in the Nam, even if it wasn't cool having so many of us there.

Uncle Hansford had a storied military career. I could do a chapter about him. He had a son in Nam, a Marine. They were under fire together. It is a heck of a story too. I went to my first "Welcome Home Parade" with him in the late seventies. He was the Grand Marshall and a driving force behind it. I walked beside his vehicle. He retired in 1975 to Indiana, where his brothers lived. Uncle Hansford began his only other career near us. He developed serious diabetes and died in 1994. His wounds and illness took him an inch at a time. When he passed, he died as one of the most decorated soldiers ever from the State of Virginia, with more than 40 medals and commendations.

He loved serving America. It was his life.

1st Sgt. Michael S. Mullins

2001, Operation Enduring Freedom I: Task Force Mountain — 1st?87th, 10th Mtn. Div.
2004, Operation Enduring Freedom IV: Task Force Phoenix—HHC 76th BCT
2008, Iraq: Task Force Nightfighter — D co., 1st/293d Inf.

SFC Tina M. Mullins
2004, Operation Enduring Freedom IV: Task Force Phoenix — HHC 76th BCT

SECTION IV

Veterans' Stories — War on Terror

Leaving the Wire

A professional soldier doing what he is called to do
Is hard to comprehend unless you are one of the few.
Some draftees felt the momentary flash of that desire
To save the world, help people, set an enemy on fire.

There is a young soldier, an old timer in that world,
Who is in the middle of a rush, fighting, all a-whirl,
Doing things he trained for, despite danger and all.
He lives a motto, to be all that he can, to stand tall.

Weeks without much word, left my heart disturbed.
It is hard to describe being the parent of a believer.
He has seen the results of our soldiers' work, knows
They can succeed, making a difference if left alone.

The electronic age is enlightening but ignorance is ok.
There was an e-mail that turned on a bright light today.
He shared his ambition, his goal and a step in his plan.
I cannot ask him to back off; I must be more than dad.

When the warrior leaves the wire he enters his realm.
He is the captain and the battleship; he has the helm.
They who trained him well created someone to defend
The defenseless of the world, badly in need of a friend.

There is feeling ignited in him when leaving the wire.
Every nerve, every sense, every fiber is transformed.
He leans forward with eagerness, ready, embracing
Any action that unfolds when protecting this nation.

He is very ready, with his skin tingling; his eyes seek
Any sign of opposition and danger within his reach.
Excited, he would quiver but that is misunderstood.
Adrenalin and pride demand he prove he is that good.

Leaving the wire a soldier grows sharp, invigorated.
Outside the wire a soldier is challenged, motivated.
Inside the wire a soldier is just another garrison grunt.
Outside he is the king of the jungle, alert, on the hunt.

Leaving the safety a life changes, expands, demands
That he be prepared for anything in the air or on land.
It is hard to tell how a fear of death makes him alive.
His task is to break things, win, protect, and survive.

He stands beneath a flag flown over other heroes too.
Soldiers do not want to kill but do what they must do.
Inside that wire is his country, outside are invaders.
Home must be held, his heart and soul do not waiver.

I do not want him to prove that he is alive by dying.
I pray he works with care, not hotly caution-defying.
He has a wife and son he loves, but he has a mission.
We all pray for his success and want him here, living.

I can see a white-knuckled grip on his ready weapon.
His mind does an inventory as he searches the horizon.
I read his mind as he hopes his men are as ready as he.
There is no question; the task is to keep all people free.

Has he taught them enough?
Are they tough enough?
Can he handle losing one of his own?
Are they with him, in that warrior's zone?

Leaving the wire is for him, going home.
It is his world, a place he understands, he alone.
Others like him know what he knows, are linked
To him with a bond others do not understand.

They are not savages, war-mongers, haters of men.
No, they are the opposite; they love humanity.
They want people everywhere to have freedom,
Choice, joy, a chance; those things are the things
They defend
When they leave the wire.

Blinded

My son and I sat sharing small talk.
I found myself talking to myself.
He was blinded, had a faraway look.
Perhaps memory was off the shelf.

It was December 11, meaningful to him.
I called to him, got a blank stare.
It was something I had to pry loose then.
I was unsure he would even share.

"Where are you son, where have you gone?
You are with me, but are you son?"
He looked at me, suddenly back in my home.
His mind had left, leaving me alone.

"On this day, in 2001, I got my first kills.
Actually there were three downed.
I used a 40 mike-mike grenade launcher.
Your version was the old Thumper."

I looked at him, holding back my concern.
I know what he feels right now.
That kind of memory lingers, even burns.
Each of us handles this somehow.

"Dad, do you ever remember your first kill?"
I sat silently for a moment then too.
"Son, I never looked them in the eyes, still
I cannot swear I got a kill like you."

"I fired like hell when I was fired on, as you,
But I may have closed my eyes.
I did not want to know, that part is very true.
Mine were not as personalized."

He makes me think even now, my son does.
He is a warrior, a professional.
His ghosts are his own until memory floods.
I was lucky…or just forgetful.

Infantry

I have dirty feet, stinking socks.
There is also that rotten crotch.
I am infantry.

Nobody loves me, I love nobody.
With my own I am never solitary.
I am infantry.

When the bullets fly I crouch low.
It is crunch time so adrenalin flows.
I am infantry.

I walk miles, sleep in mud or snow.
Tired as hell there is one thing I know.
I am infantry.

When crossing a river or climbing a hill,
If there is a way I can so I sure as hell will.
I am infantry.

I never admit the sound of gunfire sings.
Even mortar and cannon are lovely things.
I am infantry.

We hump in mud and sand, or monsoon.
We bested typhoons; that is what we do.
We are infantry.

Shouts of "Charlie" and a firefight's noise
Are just part of the day's work for us boys.
We are infantry.

Avoid us; deride us; neglect us if you must.
We still do our jobs or our hearts will bust.
We are infantry.

Here You Stand

After all these months, here you are.
Here you stand…here you stand.
You have grown much, traveled far.
You come home a different man.

For man God's will is often masked.
He is a mystery for most of us.
This time He did everything we asked.
His answer was the very best.

We join together with eyes full of you.
Smiling faces do not grow dim.
We welcome a soldier, tried and true.
Our hearts are filled with Him.

His rod and staff were strongly there.
He kept you alive by your skill.
You are home again, this time to share.
His blessings are with you still.

God held you in His hand for a year.
You survived your time in hell.
Now you are home, you are right here.
God holds His hands in welcome.

You did your duty, followed your heart.
You served America, our home.
In another land you gave hope its start
As a soldier proud, in uniform.

The work you did was ripe with danger,
Guarding convoys with supplies.
The insurgents felt your mighty anger.
You did right and knew why.

Roads were filled with enemies waiting.
All around Baghdad you rode.
Tension and apprehension straining,
Iran a source of an enemy load.

When you left, a flag was raised high,
And there it stood all the while,
Flown with mother's love, father's pride,
Until you stood again at their side.

Here you are…at home with us again.
God opens his hands in welcome.
Wherever you go now, remember Him.
Here you stand…here you stand.

Mike Mullins, August, 2008

Ben Harlow, an airborne White Devil,
The 504th Parachute Infantry Regiment,
Serving with commitment and dedication,
Fighting for us and the safety of our nation.

Pride and respect for him should abound.
He, like my own son, laid his life on the line.
They stand for us and all who are defenseless.
Shake his hand, hug him, tell him he was missed.

I was with this fine young man and his family when he left home and when he returned. I saw his face at both ends of his journey. I saw the faces of his parents. They are good people. Brian and Rachel Harlow watched a boy leave and a man come home. Brian's father, Jim was there too. He was a World War II veteran and quite a poet in his own right. Jim joined our Heavenly Father last year, but he left this world with the knowledge that his blood runs strong and true.

I thank them for allowing me to share a moment in their life.

He is Home

A crowd gathered on a Tuesday eve.
His group was due in and I was pleased.
There were family holding welcome signs.
His friends showed too, to my surprise.
There was quite a crew to see him home.
Even though the holiday found him alone.

Now, two weeks later, he is really home,
And the strain is seeping out of his bones.
The stress and strength are not demanded.
The lines in his face are etched, indented
In his furrowed brow, without his knowing.
The frown shrinks while his smile is growing.
His face is relaxing from the war's demands.

His adrenalin is not being used just now.
He does not have a load dragging him down;
Lives in the balance, and equipment too.
He does not face the political strife in lieu
Of a grateful nation that will never know
All he and others do in war's blood-red glow.
The lines are softening, his child inspires love
And his wife feels his pain, seeks his truth.
He is home in body, but there are things,
Like a mind, which comes home more slowly.
I take myself back forty years and wonder.
"Can people see the lightning in my brain;
The questions that roll like summer thunder?
Some missed me with all their hearts yet
Others would not have minded had I stayed.
Some I love only want to continue old fights.

Will some folks grant me a little space
So I can choose my own homeward pace?
Will they crowd in and steal my air, smother me
With love, not letting me open my eyes to see?
Most mean well, others think I was on a lark.
The things I saw came with me, remaining stark.
I cannot tell them; I do not want to hurt them.
I will try to smile, yet deep in me I am still grim."

Does he feel what I felt and questioned?
I dare not ask, dare not make the suggestion.
He is home…with different things waiting.
I had nobody I hoped more than any other
Would understand, wanting only to be a lover.
But they sometimes put their own demands
Ahead of a soldier's needs and their words
And deeds can wound deeper than bombs.

What is asked could wait but often will not.
He does not need pushed ahead of thought.
His mind is still reeling, sweltering in desert heat.
He needs time to crawl, get the dust off his feet.
I walked down that street toward home, quickly,
Yet faltering, anticipating yet dreading my own tears.
He may have that same fear coursing in his veins.
It takes time, and compassion, to let war drain.

The welcome home was wonderful, special.
There was pride, the shoulders square, elation.
The love in the room was there in equal portion.
The joy and tears flowed without any shame.
Our progeny, our spouses, our heroes, our hopes
Were home, safely stepping back into today, here!
After the hoopla was pushed out, their minds quiet,
The fear, the doubt, the trepidation, again crept out.

He is home but does home want him on his terms
Or only by its own… right back into the demands
Without space, without compassion for his passion?
He does not get some of the sneers that I got.
He does hear the criticism, from some people
And the major media that see him as a threat.
In jaundiced eyes he is not more than criminal.
Or some higher form of warmongering animal.

I will wait for his stories, for his words, for his tears.
Perhaps I am the only one who deters the demands.
I fight myself; I want to rush in and ask that he unload.
I will let him walk before I push him into a broken run.
If we who are closest push the hardest it hurts most.

We must quietly understand his battle with wars' ghosts.
The old way at the end of World War II may be best.
Two weeks at sea with warriors was a detoxifying rest.

He is home.
Now I must, and so must others, make him happy about that.
I have known soldiers who wanted only to go back.
I felt that. Others have too.
Let all who love him give him the space and time
He needs… to really come home.

Down in His Cups

Bad things happen in war.
That is just a fact of death.
We wish there were no more.
Soldiers still living could rest.

Haunting memories live long.
It would be good to bury them.
They make our nights go wrong.
Memory dies with us, is the thing.

Every war is the same, it is true.
Every combatant will agree here.
Iraq and Afghanistan, too, for sure.
Images burn in the dark, in real fear.

Another story about a re-con medic
Passed through my life a while back.
I know he is in pain, feels heart-sick.
He must let go, cut himself some slack.

A young man was on a roving patrol.
Duty called during soccer's Asian Cup.
It is a huge deal in that part of the world.
In victory the people play "shoot 'em up."

The government warned villages remote
To be calm and collected no matter what,
To hold their weapons, not lock and load.
In victory a village celebrated and forgot.

A half a mile away bullets hit his team.
They had no idea what was happening.
The re-con unit was in a combat scene.
They dismounted and commenced firing.

After those initial bursts they realized
The bullets were raining down like hail.
Thirty-five civilians had suddenly died.
Men, women and youth got a coffin's nail.

Not one soldier wanted it to be that way.
It was not their fault but the tears are real.
It is an event that will live all of their days.
A good warrior does not have a heart of steel.

He has a haunted memory as do most grunts.
He has to deal; we have to love him the same.
His soul will flood; he will be down in his cups.
Ugly things do happen, but God knows his name.

He did no wrong; it was their sad, happy fault.
That does not always soothe a Christian spirit.
They live and the others are confined in a vault.
He's a fine young man; pray; his God will hear it.

Through My Eyes

Do any of you big old walking-around peoples
Ever think about the world through my eyes?
My don't talk real well and my run everywhere.
Every day me sees new things and wonder why?

What are they? What do the things mean to them?
My have everything to learn and each day is new.
The world is wonderful and a gift without ribbon.
If me smile, me smile all over, inside and out too.

My loves wooden trains and a cartoon's music.
My dances as good as me can, but without a beat.
Puppies are stuffed animals that live and breathe.
If my head don't take me there me go on my feet.

When my hurt, little or big, my screams loudly.
There is no little joy nor is there just small pain.
Every day is a new day and me am just what me be.
Papaw knows me thinks and feels and has a brain.

Me miss Daddy; me know when he dresses funny
He is leaving me again, to somewhere; it has to be.
He was out all last summer doing who knows what.
My knows something is different deep in my heart.

My look for him every day and Mommy says wait.
"Your daddy loves you, will return to us one day."
Today my saw Daddy's truck; thought it was now.
It could not be anyone else, me could not see how.

I was in the big window, on Grandma's couch.
I stood there happy, just waiting and looking out.
It was papaw getting out of Daddy's truck not him.
I love my papaw but it is just not quite the same.

Me feel stuff and sense stuff even without a book.
Papaw saw me and knows; my can tell by his look.
He sees me ask, "Where is my Daddy?" and is sad.
My want to cry and so does he; we both feel so bad.

Papaw tells me Daddy is off doing his sworn duty.
My don't know what it means but it must be for me.
Daddy never does anything without me in his heart.
My will hug Papaw so his tears stop; we are not apart.
Mike Mullins for Rylan Mathew Mullins, age 2 yrs & 8 months

My son & daughter in law & grandsons — Michael S., Tina, Rylan, & Brennan

The Torch

The morning came and the "Sarge"
Yelled at his Squad Leaders.
"Tell the soldiers to fall in on me.
Hustle, no dragging peters."
They were in the Sandbox, the war.
"Tell 'em to close it up here.
This is a talk, not Close Order Drill.
I gotta talk, but I don't yell.
Men and women, stand real still.
I'm gonna talk about being killed.
It is my job to keep you alive.
I am good at it, so listen.
I been here, done this twice before.
We can beat this damned war."

"My job is not to make politicians the smile.
It is to get you home to families in a while.
So, heads up! Even swine will get this pearl.
The women will fight like men, not girls.
You are all gonna do what I say, no doubt.
If you don't like it we peel these blouses!
Man on man, just us, we will work it out!"
"No loose cannons; I do the pointing.
A soldier next to you knows you got his back.
The one ahead and the one behind
Know you will stand firm, stay in the fight.
They know when I talk we are one.
It is about living, about getting the job done.
We stand together; we don't run."

"Whatever happens we are on the same page.
Just break that rule one time troops
And you will find something out about my rage.
When we disagree it is family.
We take care of it and each other night and day.
That is the way it is gonna be.
We move as one, our stories are told the same.
We make the rules in this game."

"We ain't Stateside; you ain't calling the I.G.
This is real, no more practice range.

When I say something, no debate.
Look and move where I tell you, the way I tell you.
No body bags allowed in my crew.
We came together; we leave here that way too!
When we report, we report the same.
Don't be a rat, don't earn that name!"

Rumor had it three challengers stepped
Out that very day.
I heard they crawled out seeing a new way.
They wanted to deny him.
I heard that the only way to do that is kill him.
This is his third combat tour.
He lost friends on the second and said, "No More."

Chatter had it that one who dared
Was bad and he was down quickly, life spared.
"Sarge" is the Man, there is no other.
He will be your friend, you father, your brother.
You do it his way or his way.
No other. Options are for ordering cars.
Say no and start seeing stars.

He is close to tabbed out and wants that too.
He is hardcore, a gung-ho fool.
He will kick an ass, then save it, and he rules!
Rumors swirl in the dust at his feet.
The battalion is having him write ops for all.
He does know what he is about.
He ain't all talk; he ain't just a pair of balls.

I hear he has some more to say.
He will do it a bit at a time, but it will matter too.
Everybody will listen, be all ears.
I wanna figure out who took him on for sure.
There may be marks we can see.
I hear we'd best not talk, that much is still true.
That is over and we stand in unity.

The weeks rolled into months.
His team did its infantry job and made a name.
They had contact often at first.
The enemy learned fighting them was not the same.
They would extract some pain.

There was a cost for ambushing this combat team.
If it took rounds something burned.

After a while the word spread.
Taking a shot at them could get someone dead.
Their name and safety grew.
When they had a job they knew what to do.
They were avoided by the enemy.
When they protected soldiers and supplies
Company leaders knew it well.
Any kind of loss could only mean one thing.
There had been a cold day in Hell.

Today's Army fights with rules.
They were written by some political fools.
Patton would have been pissed.
When he fought, only victory was on his list.
Now soldiers face an inquisition.
Even if killed they had to defend their position.
Now we seem to fight to defend
Some politician's promise given to the wind.

That stupidity started in Vietnam.
Now it is an art form.
Soldiers' lives are given in the battle
And good things are done.
Defending home and spreading freedom
Are honorable and just.
Weak politicians sell them out in their lust
For power and re-election.

Despite internal odds and bad leaders' words
Soldiers win even if unheard.
They made a difference, freed a dusty land.
Their deeds are just as grand
As any war fought at anytime, anywhere.
They fought and they cared.
Our soldiers feed children, make them safe.
They make America proud I say.

When these soldiers returned to their home
Safe and sound in a friendly zone
They knew why, they knew who they owed.
They owed a tough-assed NCO.

He told them, he taught them, he led them.
They were home because of him.
The three who stepped out in a challenge
Were among the first to thank him.

Loneliness

Her mind is where his mind is.
The feelings mirror the others'.
Never is their understanding greater.
Never could more help less.

The roof and walls are traps.
They close in like iron clamps.
The mind fills while the heart empties.
Never could empty be heavier.

Loneliness echoes in its cave.
There is no answer that saves.
The voice she hears is only her own.
She is here, sad and all alone.

Modern technology is a bridge.
Out of sight is not out of mind.
Yet being reunited is over the next ridge.
Love is anything but kind.

She understands the calling.
She is duty-bound, all giving.
It does not lessen the ache in her heart.
It stays secluded in the dark.

She is in isolation just now.
She is not alone but very lonely.
The face of her son is that of her man.
In her joy is pain and longing.

Her arms hold a pillow close.
What she wants remains remote.
The thing she clutches in the night is soft.
A blanket replaces his strong back.

Night descends, as does anxiety.
Tears run down from closed eyes.
The strength of sunshine fades into the sunset.
She faces the day but fears the night.

His days and nights are filled.
He loves duty, is wed to thrills.
His mind is occupied in that far away land.
His refuge is battle of some kind.

She looks to the horizon.
There is nobody there…
The horizon she seeks is too far away
Not one…nobody… only mirages.

She wishes this were a movie.
A blurry figure would be seen.
It would draw large and near, arms reaching.
The arms would hold her soon.

Another night passes behind.
She awakens alone, tears dried.
She wishes she had slept more than she cried.
She has to give another day a try.

Loneliness is often a monster.
It makes a mind feel captured.
Her kind of war is bloodless but has its pain.
She is loved, yet remains alone.
There are things much worse.
Being alone can be a good course.
It has been said lonely in a crowd is a curse.
Whatever…loneliness is also a war.

One Serves, One Stays

One son serves our country.
The other is left behind.
Forever one is lauded and the other
Is left in the shadow.

It is not a shadow at all.
It is so, so important.
The one with me keeps the memory alive.
He is both in my weary mind.

He has indescribable value.
That son represents all.
He is family, my son, my love, just as strong.
He serves in steadfastness just as long.

Memories, images are fleeting.
They are a will-o'-the-wisp.
A son who stands beside you keeps your faith alive.
It is value neglected, even deemphasized.

I see now what my brother felt.
It is the only shadow I ever cast.
He feels it still today when war stories are told.
Without him, my parents' hearts would have been cold.

I know now what my heroic son
Must feel when at my side.
History has a way of repeating itself I know now.
My sons have equal courage, purpose, with my love in tow.

One serves, one stays.
The lesson is for us all you see.
One fights for all, one just for me.
His mother and I will never forget.

My son Joel and his wife Olivia, son Kellen and daughter Evanne

My son, Joel, who stays home and keeps me sane.

My sons Michael & Joel

The Third Time

I sat in the Jeep with my sleeping grandson.
Our son and his bride needed to be alone.
It was the third time he was leaving home,
Flying away to enter another combat zone.

I felt a combination of fear, pride and anger.
He reveres his duty, not deterred by danger.
I sat quietly with that knot of pain inside me.
I took seventeen seconds to let my fear free.

I cannot allow myself more time to question
What all of our heroes do without reservation.
They stand with heads up serving this nation.
They go repeatedly and with little hesitation.

I have no doubt about the purpose or results.
My protest is about those who fail in support.
Politicians fail them and heed not their voices.
Our soldiers fight and victory lessens remorse.

I sing to a choir in my song but it needs sung.
Politicians snatch their defeat from our victory.
What they did was right but now they wrong
All soldiers, not learning anything from history.

This volunteer army is our greatest example.
They do not have to do this, fight this battle.
They go because they believe and they see.
A nation is healing slowly, tasting being free.

If we would commit and do what it takes
To win and bring our soldiers home right
It would bring the pride of success straight
Back to the heritage that falls from our sight.

If more people did their duty those who do it
Would not have to do it over, and over again.
It would be cheaper, faster, safer, and unite
A nation falling on its sword, for politicians.

If we had a draft our tired soldiers could rest.
The myth that a draftee army was not the best
Was just a myth that those who crucify soldiers
Perpetuated to keep our nation in its doldrums.

I have mixed emotions about all we have done.
I do not doubt our troops for they are amazing.
We have candidates who want to cut and run.
I doubt our leaders; it is they who are now failing.

Our heroes fighting do that because it is right.
Those running for office criticize and denigrate.
Our strength is in the hands of those who mind
The principles that have always made us great.

The systems in place for returning our protectors
Must be preserved, but they will have to assist.
I want to sing their praises and voice my protest
In their behalf; in belief of them we must persist.

When all is said and done, I love this land of ours.
I would go again if needed, crawling on all fours.
My son, proud of his third generation infantry stuff
Has been and been again; he has done enough.
I have only one prayer to pray on bended knee.
God, do not let my son be third generation
Purple Heart recipient
To keep us all safe and free.

1st Sgt. Michael S. Mullins & wife Tina

SECTION V

Veterans' Stories — Doobie Chats

Doobie Chats

or maybe just beer talk.

Do not take the title in a literal way. I want your attention. It has been a struggle to find a way to share smaller stories with people. There are times when veterans share little stories in very informal ways. Combat vets talk in chow lines, at beer tents, waiting at *porta-pots*, stopping by campfires, at a vendor table, and any other spot where they get caught in line together at some veterans event. Combat vets seek each other at these events for an express purpose — to talk. Many, if not most, of these stories are brief yet very dramatic. The stories should not be lost because there are not extended amounts of information or tons of data garnered from the moment. They are like the firefights we experienced. A soldier could patrol for two weeks and have nothing happen — and then in five minutes all hell breaks loose. He might lose an arm, see a friend blown to smithereens and end up shoveled into a body bag in pieces. A soldier may have an experience so intense that the next 9000 nights of his life are altered. Years later, the two-week period is hard to describe, but those five minutes flash like a nova in the sky.

It occurred to me that I should preserve those passing chats. This seems a way to record those stories too. They have been gathered over the course of two or three years, maybe longer. I keep notes, hoping that I meet their originators again. It is time to share them. Size, or lack of same, does not always lessen intensity. Ask any woman in America — or perhaps not. I may not want the answer to that one.

The "doobie chats" that I share first were given birth at the place where I meet most veterans. I belong to a local group named the Howard County Vietnam Veterans Organization. In September of 2009, we had our Twenty-seventh Annual Reunion. The Reunion began as a dream and has become a national event drawing tens of thousands of veterans and supporters. Many local veterans, and their ladies, have poured their hearts into it. Now we own 39 acres of ground where we celebrate and embrace one another in a way that has caused the Grounds to be renamed The Healing Field. Since I began writing, the opportunity to talk to more people has increased. I speak at other events and meet people whose lives have been impacted by war. When I can, I record what they share as well. As you read these tales remember — they are real.

◆ ◆ ◆

I attended the 2008 Veterans Day program at my oldest grandson's elementary school. In the hallway, a small, wizened World War II Veteran prepared to accompany the Colors into the gymnasium where the presentation was occurring. I always stand humbled in the presence of these people. I watched him for a time and then introduced myself. He wore his dress uniform from his era and I found it remarkable. I told him so. His name was Robert Parker and he wore Captain's bars.

"Sir," I said, "Thank you for what you did. It is incredible that you can still wear the uniform you wore over sixty years ago. What you did then and now is amazing."

Captain Parker replied, "I am getting old and fat. My daughter had to move this button (he pointed to the third from the bottom) over about a half an inch so I could get this coat buttoned. It pissed me off."

It was time for him to go and I had to find a seat. I asked if I could speak with him after the ceremony. His daughter said they would be there a while as he turned his attention to the procession. I hurried to the gym and seated myself where my grandson could see me. I am fortunate to be tall enough so that is not a problem.

Evan as age stooped his shoulders a bit, the old man stood proud as the Colors were presented. The National Anthem and Pledge were offered. It was a wonderful event made happy by children from first through third grades. Later in the hall, I caught up with Captain Parker again. It would be great to spend more time with him, but I thought it improbable. I was fortunate to cross his path at all. Yet I managed a few more minutes.

Captain Robert Parker served in the Army Air Corps as a security officer. His first duty station was in England, where he remained for either two or three years. After the Allies invaded Europe, he went to the mainland and accompanied our forces all the way to Berlin. Captain Parker maintained security for a number of high-level officers for the balance of the war. He was 94-years young when I met him. His daughter told me that he seldom spoke of more than he shared with me there in that hallway. What history lies in that wonderful mind?

There is a tangential story which I heard that day during my meeting with the Captain. A tall, strong, man walked up and introduced himself to the Captain. His name was Russell Eppelheimer, another World War II Veteran. Russell was a Flight Officer and glider pilot who made three landings — Bastogne, Holland, and Germany. He survived and that is miraculous. I said as much. I was — and am still — in awe. A man like this man is another national treasure. He said that one of his trips is not even recorded in most military records, but he damned sure did it. He flew both troops and equipment. Russell (forgive me, I do not want to keep misspelling his last name) said the greatest scare he had was when he was coming in for a landing on one of the runs. A Jeep rolled out the nose of his ship and got down ahead of him. I quizzed him about it having to be a "little weird flying balsa-wood airplanes." He told me they were constructed from other materials. They did not do a lot to build your confidence, but it was a hell of thrill when you cut loose from your mother ship and sailed.

These two men exchanged numbers with each other. Captain Parker's daughter wrote some things down for him. I stood by in respect, realizing this was their moment, their time, and their world. I had to step away. I could not intrude. As others have given my friends and me our space, I too had to give them theirs.

♦ ♦ ♦

I sold a few books at the Grounds in 2008, although most of the guys who come to the reunion buy food and party supplements, not books. One of my visitors was Les Miller from Louisiana, a Nam vet who served as a Naval SOG team member. He and his buddy spent some time chatting with me at my trailer. The conversation turned to the twists and turns life gives us and the control over our destiny that *we do not have.*

Les lived on the only inhabited island in the Gulf near New Orleans. He owned and operated an exclusive restaurant on shore. Les was a successful business entrepreneur. His home was large and comfortable with a phenomenal, peaceful garden out back, surrounded by a very old sea wall. It was his place of seclusion and renewal after work. Sometimes he was not alone there. His tour of duty returned while he was alone in that garden of memories. Eighteen faces visited him, floating above the lush, green vegetation as he remembered those who live now on the Wall in Washington DC, but once served with him. One night they spoke to him with one voice. The chorus said to Les, "We are in a better place. Save your prayers and energy for those who will join us in the future."

Again, on another night, as though he did not get the message the first time, they joined him in that spot once more. They advised him that he had to do something with his life that was more meaningful. They reminded him that he should quit spending so much time and energy worrying about them. He would be better prepared to join them later. His wife interrupted that interlude with a business call. They did not return again. He did not forget that night.

Katrina struck in 2005. Les and his wife were wiped out — restaurant and home. At first, he was as distraught as everyone in that disaster zone. He began to wonder if fate had followed up on the visit from his lost comrades. He and his wife began to put their life back together and made changes. Les found other work. He is a bright and resourceful man. He also thought about his biggest hero, his father-in-law. What would he do? When Les and I had our talk, it was after his father-in-law had passed away earlier in 2008, at age 78.

Les Miller chose to give me a thumbnail sketch of his father-in-law's service to illustrate what the man meant to him and why. The old man was a lifer, a Full Bird Colonel who did six tours as the head dentist in the Asian Rim countries — Nam, Laos, Cambodia, Thailand, the Philippines, and Guam. He did dental work for the "locals" wherever he happened to stay on any given Saturday. It was just what he did and what he was. He did the same thing in Nam.

One Saturday, a door gunner came to his office after a mission. The grunt had serious oral damage from a sixty (M-60 machine gun) that had broken loose, striking him in the mouth. After the repairs were complete, the soldier said he had to hurry back because he was on duty and had to be there to respond. The Colonel told him he was done for the day. He would not be flying with all the pain medications he had to take. The gunner was nervous about that. He replied that he could not stand the heat for failure to do his duty.

The dentist told him that he would see the Flight Commander himself and sent the soldier to his quarters. The Colonel went to the flight pad and told the crew chief and the junior officer that he was going to cover the gun for the hurt soldier. They were astonished, but not many junior officers or warrant grade officers refuse a Full Bird. They did get a mission and the dentist went. It was a hot one. The Colonel won a Bronze Star that day — and the crew was decorated. The "back-up" door gunner would not let them leave the scene of a pinned-down squad of soldiers until reinforcements arrived. He was a soldier. He was a hero to Les Miller and a lot more to a lot of people it seems to me. The tears in the eyes of the man telling me all of this left no doubt in my mind.

Les Miller adjusted his life. His ghosts, Katrina, and the memory of his father-in-law led him to a decision that he could make a difference in the lives of veterans in his area. Now he is doing what he can to help them. He is trying to establish a major reunion in that part of the country. It is hard work and he can't do it alone. He may be the heart and soul, but it will take a lot of arms and legs. I wish him much success, but if that does not work I know he will do well one man at a time. He will make a difference. The changes that fate made gave him the time — and the 18 faces in the garden gave him the will.

◆ ◆ ◆

Each year at the Reunion, the campground is full to the brim. Most of the visitors are from the Vietnam Era, but all are welcome. Our organization has stressed the inclusion of soldiers fighting in the Middle East. In the last three years, over the official three to four days, our attendance ranges from 26,000 to 40,000.

A large portion of our guests are not over-nighters, but daily visitors. We have two overflow lots donated by a gracious farmer in the area. The local support for the last 27 years has been incredible. One year, a vet said the further inland he drives from the East Coast the more flags he sees. I am proud of that. I see them where I travel most often — from Pennsylvania to Missouri, Wisconsin to Florida. I can't imagine our Banner not waving in front of homes and businesses celebrating the ideals for which each generation fought. I am not sure what route he takes to the Reunion, but it has to be unusual to travel that far without seeing the Flag. The resurgence of patriotism in America since 9-11 has been heart-warming. There are vets here from all over the country. They do not miss. Many plan their vacation around this huge September event and have done so for years and years. I know men and women who come to *The Healing Field* and camp for weeks at a time. We have a Firebase "mini-reunion" in June and they make it then, too — if they can. It has grown of its own volition as well. We have a select group of vendors in September each year. The food is plentiful and greasy. The participants are consistent and most are veteran-focused or owned entities. There may be a little beer and other party paraphernalia around too, while classic rock rolls across the Grounds far into the dark each night. The people have a good time while they are sharing memories, laughter, hugs, and tears. We have our own Security and a Chaplaincy group operating "24/7." It is what we do.

I stayed out of the mainstream for years. I held myself back, not wanting to share too much, not wanting to tell my own story, keeping the lid on memories except in rare cases. I opened up to a very select few and only at very vulnerable moments. I did not want to compare what I did to what others did. I have always had this nagging doubt about what I did in the war in Vietnam. It could not have been enough. There were men there who went through constant and complete hell. My own service was so inconsequential as to have no reason for mention in the company of real warriors. So what if I was a grunt with a Purple Heart? So what if I slogged paddies, got shot at a few times, got rocketed, slept in shit, had malaria, burned some villages, swam rivers, fell out of a bird trying a lift-off from a "hot" LZ? I did not do a damned thing noteworthy or of value compared to what I heard as I walked through the Grounds for so many years, all alone.

Then I went to a reunion of my own unit, with some of the guys I was in Nam with and discovered we fought in that war too, and what I did had some value too. Next I wrote a book. My stories meant something to a few guys who read them. I did salutes to some other soldiers and told their stories. I realized I was part of reaching out to other veterans and helping by listening. I *had* done what they did, more than some and less than others — but it was real and it mattered. Now at the Reunion and other places, folks want to talk to me, to share, to ask, to know somebody cares without judging. I cannot reach many. I am insignificant in the scheme of things, but I reach one vet at a time and that will have to be enough. I can tell a few stories — like this:

I was in a chow line waiting for one of those ten-inch wide, breaded tenderloins during the 2009 reunion. Initiating a conversation with another vet in the line adjacent to mine, I laughed about the lines for chow in a village outside Saigon in 1968. He and I were about 20 people back. Everyone had gotten hungry at once and we decided to wait. It was hard for me to get someone to watch my little trailer and books, so it was then or never. I was hungry. Not one to stand in silence for long, I pushed the conversation, even in the face of his obvious melancholy.

"Brother" I said, "I remember when the penicillin lines were longer than the chow lines in one little village." I could not help laughing at the memory. It was an exaggeration, but not much of one. As I recall there were a lot of guys crying at the latrine about that time. It was not often we were near a village and a few of the guys could not resist what that kind of duty offered.

"Man, I wish I could laugh right now" he said.

"What the hell is up?" I asked. The line was moving, but our conversation was moving with it. I got a misty-eyed story I did not expect.

He had done one tour as a grunt and then 18 months as a door gunner. I had no paper so I could not write down his unit. It was very dark, but I could see his eyes glistening as we stood at the edge of the lighting where the vendors were located. The man was guilt-ridden. He had somehow survived many, many missions without a scratch. The Nam vet grieved 106 names on the Wall. He was convinced he should be living there with them. He went to Khe Sanh late in his tour and 36 of that larger number died in the last three weeks of his field duty. His unit lost over 600 aircraft during the months he was with it, many of which went down during that last period. The man said that in his mind, there could not have been many worse "dogfights" in our air warfare history. His grief was living.

This was his third time to our reunion, to our *Healing Field*. The Brother needs peace in his own heart. I hope he finds it. 'Survivors Guilt' is a horrible burden. How many have I met who suffer from it? Did I reveal a bit of it as I began this narrative? I told the man that he lived for a reason. If he and others had not, who would celebrate and remember those who perished? Who would remember them with gifts at the Wall? Who would tell their stories? Who would tell the world what they did for it? If nobody survived there would be no legacy. There would have been no reason for sacrifice. Somebody has to survive or there is no meaning, no value, no going forward, no hope, no growth, no coming together, and no memories. Where there are no tears there can be no smiles. Even if trivial or somewhat trite, I reminded him that it seemed to me his buddies would be pissed if he came to a place like *The Healing Field* and spent all that time crying over them rather than hoisting one to them, listening to the music and bragging about what bad-asses they had been. He looked at me and faded to the southeast in the darkness.

I went back to my little trailer, thanked my veteran daughter-in-law for watching my stuff, and ate my cold tenderloin.

◆ ◆ ◆

The years run together. I think this story took place when my son was in Iraq in 2008. I am sure it did. My daughter-in-law and I were at the Reunion on a Saturday night without him. I was sitting in the shadows wondering why the hell people buy beer and not my books, getting pissed like I often do, reminding myself about priorities. One man I gave a book to (it is no wonder I am going broke doing this) told me about this being the thing he looks forward to most each year. He has a "Reunion" envelope and every week he puts two to five dollars in it so he can come. Three years ago when gas was four bucks, he could only eat one meal a day so he could have a beer after he got there. In 2008, gas was a little better so he could eat two meals, drink a few more beers, but he could not buy anything. He stood there and read part of my book. Okay, I gave him the damned thing — and a bag of chips. What the hell? I am a sucker. Anyway, Tina came up to me and said, "Mike, come over here. I need you. Right now! C'mon."

She dragged me to a man standing at the edge of the road where I park my little trailer each year. The sun had set anyway and nobody was buying anything. I could see it from where we were. It did not matter if anybody stole anything. I was going to give it away anyway!

Tina pulled him over to me, saying, "Talk to my father-in-law. There is nobody out here like him. Tell him your story. Tell him what is wrong. He will listen. Just stop crying and tell him." Then she turned to me. "Mike, he was walking around talking to himself about all the people he killed. I found him and had to bring him to you."

I was stunned. My eyes asked her, "WHY?" as she walked away and he grabbed me. He was drunk out of his mind and berating himself for not feeling guilty about the killing he had to do. He had been a grunt and then was sent to an in-country sniper school. Aside from the normal combat, he had more than 30 confirmed kills as I recall. His problem was he did not feel guilty for doing it. Sometimes it is odd that veterans have to find some external source of guilt in order to feel regret for what they had to do. He thought he should be sad, but he was not and he struggled with that. He was angry with himself due to the inner conflict. What bothered him was that he began to like it. I told him that it was self-defense and he only did what he had to do. He should not feel guilty because they were going to kill him or somebody else. I am not a counselor or psychologist. I have my instincts and experience, but that is all. I continued telling him that his survival and their deaths saved lives beyond his. There was purpose and something positive that meant a lot to those who lived later, without his ever having seen their faces or knowing their names.

I searched for words in the dark that night. I told him what I said to someone else at one time, but in a slightly different context. The pleasure he felt was only an emotional mechanism that enabled him to continue doing what he had to do after he thought he had reached a point that he could do no more without breaking down. If he had not taken that path he may not have survived. He would have hesitated at the wrong time and died. If he had not survived, others would have died, too.

His wife, as I learned in a moment, came through the crowd searching for him. He had disappeared from their campsite without a word. She took him by the arm and led him to a friend who was with her. She came back to me and said, "He is not crying. That is the first time since dark that he has stopped. What did you do?"

I replied, "I talked to him about reality. I hope he remembers it when he sobers up." I then repeated a short version of what I said to him. She did not need the details.

She looked at me with tears in her eyes and said, "You gave me my husband back, at least for a little while."

♦ ♦ ♦

I wish I had recorded all of the stories told me through the years. It was not until I began writing that I initiated the practice of making notes. There is a veritable montage of images mingled with words buried in my memory banks. It was not until 2007 that I became serious about the details of some chats. Even then, it is impossible to get all of them. When you are sitting with a half a dozen veterans around a table exchanging pieces of stories it is impossible to get enough information regarding individuals and events isolated into distinct experiences. If one uses technology as an assistant, recordings are often blurry. The sounds are obliterated by background noise. At times, people are talking all at once and half a dozen stories are like an explosion in a confined space. I love it, but it cannot all be captured the way I would like. I can only live in that moment. I cannot take it away with me.

One such moment was at the Grounds in 2007 during our 25th reunion. I met another grunt who shared my MOS (military occupational specialty) category. Our primary was 11-Charlie with 11-Bravo secondary. That translates into mortar man slash infantry. Unless you are assigned to a rear support group, you are, in effect, a grunt who sets up with the weapons platoon when you encamp at night. We used eighty-one-millimeter mortars in the field, and on occasion the old, old sixty mike-mike version when in dense jungle. Our outfit never humped with that big-ass piece of iron. When we had them, they were brought to us on a bird. As he and I chatted, he revealed what churned in his guts for all these years. That vet's burden was the body count system. It was our emphasis on getting data to the higher echelons, so they could relay it to the press. There had to be some quantifiable evidence of our success for the political types not in the line of fire. In a guerilla war, there is no real ground taken or definitive objectives to which anyone can point and declare as a victory in the conventional sense. The body count system became the "quality control yardstick," if you will. I was told at the time (by family members more in the know than I) that it was a *push down method* from the politicians. It became embraced by field commanders because it was the only criteria by which they could be evaluated and therefore promoted. Ambition poisons more than just politicians and upper management types.

The body count process almost got him killed. In his unit, mortar men were not issued standard M-16s. I am thankful that we were. In my unit, we almost always operated as a grunt until the sun faded, even though our assignments were often a bit different when we were in base camps or firebases. He revealed that he carried an Army issue 45-caliber semi-automatic pistol. The weapon would not eject spent shells, thus he had to eject them by hand. After one hot firefight, he was digging bodies out of a well when he uncovered two live ones hiding under the dead. They had no way of contending with the wounded or captured. They had also taken heavy casualties in the fight. The weapons platoon was given the task of guarding the captured VC. That evening, their part of the perimeter was hit in force as the enemy attempted to extract the prisoners. The American grunt was already hot as hell and had been shaken that day with the well discovery. He lost it. After firing a full clip into the jungle from the 45, it jammed, as was its wont. He was told later that he had taken out two or three of the enemy. It was the rest of his action that flipped out the enemy and friends alike. He charged into the jungle, waving the jammed pistol like a complete madman! The attack broke. The man dropped to his knees at last, cleared the pistol, reloaded and fired another clip and yes, it jammed again. He survived and the attack was over. He does not know for sure what he did that day, only what he was told. He has no clue why he survived.

I cleaned this up, but he assured me again at the end of the narrative that he hated, and still hates, the damned body-count system. I have a feeling he did not do all of this without a commendation. The vet never mentioned that part — I am just sayin'…

◆ ◆ ◆

There are several great gatherings for veterans in Indiana. Barbara Gray is one little lady I know from the southeastern part of the state who has spent her life working with and for veterans. Her husband is a Nam vet who was on a Huey crew. Barb is a wonderful little woman, full of energy and purpose. She had the original Moving Wall scheduled for the Whitewater State Park in September, 2008, and asked me to be her Keynote Speaker. I was awed at the prospect and excited. Me? I accepted and made the 120 plus mile drive to be part of something wonderful. As usual I had thoughts in mind for my talk, but I talk from the heart not notes. That Friday night, I was going to read my *POW/MIA* poem and Saturday afternoon was my speaking engagement opportunity. It was to be quite a weekend — a first for me in an event of that size. She told me I might even sell a few of my books during the event. That prospect is always alluring to a hopeful writer trying to grow and learn in the harsh world of art.

I arrived at the park and found a colorful, wooded place that I had never visited before, tucked away beside a small lake that shone in the afternoon sun. Barb introduced me to some of the folks helping with the event. They familiarized me with the layout and gave me an outline of their plans for the two days. The setting was wonderful. The Wall was situated adjacent to the lake, facing the east so the sun hit it on its back side. The beach was behind it, with a level area in front, where all the seating had been placed already. The entire area was protected in a natural amphitheater. She expected a crowd of 2500. That number was intimidating to me, but I remembered then that I had read to crowds that large at our Grounds. These were my people — I would be fine.

It was a pleasant time watching Barb and her volunteers buzz around making preparations as other participants arrived. I knew that I would have to interrupt soon so I could locate the lodging they were providing on site. It was supposed to be a cabin in the park. I had just retired, thus my income was interrupted and in transition. Her budget was limited, but she had arranged for the mosquitoes to move over and make room for me in one of the Ranger units. As I sat there watching the sun and reminiscing, a man sat down next to me. He asked if I was Barb's guest speaker and introduced himself as Glen, a Nam vet who had known Barb for years. He was a good guy and we enjoyed chatting there in the growing shadows. Glen's luck had not been good for a while and he planned to spend the weekend there in his car. Barb saw us talking, then walked over about the time I was prepared to search for her. She told Glen about my writing, which I had not mentioned. After Barb wandered away on another mission, he shared a very broken story that mirrored his broken life. He had hoarded gas and beer money to be at this event. Coming to the Moving Wall was of major importance to him. I told him to get his gear, found Barb and asked the directions to the cabin. I adopted him for the weekend. There was no way the man was sleeping in his car if I could help it. She knew it without saying a word. Rather than give me directions she found a Ranger and asked him to lead us to our lodging. It was then I learned that three others who were contributing their displays for the weekend were sharing the cabin as well. It slept eight people and we would be comfortable. All was well with Glen.

We followed the Ranger to the cabin. We followed him for six miles. That was a surprise. I was glad I was in a truck before we arrived. As the sun set over the tree line we settled in, smiling that we had electricity and a refrigerator. And yes, a shower. The evening ceremony was scheduled for an hour later and I had to read at some point during the program. I announced I was headed back to the amphitheater. It was a gentle reminder and everyone saddled up to return to the lake. By the time we got there, the skies had opened up and it was raining like it had never rained before. It descended in sheets, with wind pushing it in pages like a book written in the heavens just for us. Glen had finished a six pack by then — he had beer to replace food I think — and did not care. I had enough time to choke down a hot dog, some chips and a cream soda. The stage was small, so each of us appearing there was in for a soaking when it was our turn. It looked as though we would be speaking to empty, wet, folding chairs placed in rows in front of the Wall, but speak we would. Some die-hards would be there. There always are, bless their loyal hearts.

The ceremony was well designed and executed. Nobody spoke longer than planned. Mother Nature took care of that. I read my "POW/MIA" poem and it was well received. It always brings tears, but they were lost in the cleansing tears falling from the clouds. The 20 or 30 people in attendance showed their appreciation for our efforts. Barb made closing remarks and we adjourned to the pavilion area for hot coffee and cherry pie. It was too chilly by then to stay and talk. The part I like most was abbreviated on this soggy evening and we left for our muddy trail back to the cabin. Each of us hoped the roof was good.

Those of us in the Ranger cabin chatted until the yawns began. Glen wandered outside after an hour or so, his discomfort growing more and more noticeable. All of us had jobs and families. All of us were trying to perform some service to the veteran community. Two of the men had a display of miniatures that were an exact replica of a battlefield, complete with gunships and medevacs. A young man had joined us late who had driven a five-ton military truck over 200 miles to put on display. He and his friend had restored the machine over the course of several years, using donations when they could, but primarily their own money. He had made a deal with a sponsor to reclaim flight fuel at a small airport near his home and in turn gave them a sponsorship role in his volunteer organization. Like all our families, his supported his work and his time commitments with love and understanding.

When Glen did not return, I decided to check on him. I went out and discovered the rain had ceased. The trees dripped in the distance, as did the eaves of the cabin, but the moon was peeking through the clouds as they began to break apart. Our chatter in the cabin had diverted our attention from the weather for a few hours. I found the Nam vet drinking beer on the tailgate of my truck. I joined him and engaged him in some conversation in an attempt to let him know that there was not as much distance between us as he imagined. We all make choices, but sometimes the options we are presented differ by a wide margin. It seemed he needed an ear.

Glen struggled to pay his rent and buy gas to make his PTSD appointments at the VA. I learned that Barb and her husband had given him assistance, either outright or by pointing him toward other support mechanisms, several times throughout the years. His jobs had always melted away. His relationships had as well. With each and every talk to a veteran suffering from Post Trauma Stress Disorder (PTSD), I recall what I think it may have been called in World War II — shell shock. It is not the same, but that is as close a correlation as I can make. How did they cope? Glen had an endless supply of beer, and who knows what else was included in his "medicine pouch"? He had experienced a lot of combat and had the usual amount of survivor's guilt. He'd wounded in the war, but I think his most serious wounds occurred after his return home. Nothing was the same for him. Was it for any of us? He didn't fight back against the pain. Glen didn't struggle to make choices other than the obvious ones that the returning soldier who is disillusioned and disheartened often makes. He allowed his pain and disappointment to guide him down the path those two things prescribed. Other choices may not have freed him, but he may not have taken *every step* in *every way* that the pain and disappointment dictated. If he had fought even a little against the agony of memories, he might not have gotten as addicted to certain things that dragged him down. He may have to swallow his pride and ask for help, thereby relinquishing what he called freedom. He wouldn't have been free of responsibility for his actions. He tried to hide from himself and help. After some time I led him to his bunk and put him to bed. He couldn't have gotten there otherwise.

The next morning, we awoke to the sun shining and the birds chirping. It was a crisp, early September morning that made us glad we were there. We had to hustle through the shower process so we could get to breakfast before they quit serving. The day did not officially open until the 11 o'clock ceremony and I told Glen I would return to get him in plenty of time. I wanted to set up my table and take advantage of the people filtering in, looking at the various displays. I hoped to sell a book or two, and maybe a print of my poem. I was prepared for the usual number of people who think everything is free. My greatest delight is meeting a lot of wonderful people and talking. When I arrived at the park, I was stunned. It was even more beautiful than the previous day. It was glorious. The lake shimmered in the sunlight. Everything was fresh and clean. Barb was smiling, the weather was perfect, people were beginning to arrive, the food smells wafted up and my stomach growled in anticipation. She pointed the way to the breakfast area and told me there would be a quick information session to let us know how things would unfold as soon as I had eaten (in other words, get crackin' bub). Barb Gray may be five feet tall, but that little ball of energy got our attention. She had things planned well, including students arriving, a helicopter flyover, and dropping a wreath behind the Wall during a special moment in the service. There would be songs, prayers, salutes, speakers, including a special Native American group, and me. She had seating for 2500 people and it would fill before the main part of the program started at noon. The mayor of Connersville, IN, would be there as well as other local dignitaries. The Mayor was too old to serve in Vietnam, but he had a brother six years younger who served. He liked being part of tributes to the most unpopular war in our country's history. We were reminded that it was State property and there could be no "official" vendors, but if we happened to sell something while talking to people at our own vehicles nobody would be policing that activity. The main purpose of the day was the Moving Wall and the tribute to our fallen soldiers. The meeting was over and I made a quick trip to get Glen. I had reserved parking.

It was a beautiful day and a wonderful ceremony. Glen looked at my book before I went to sit in the row of speakers. He had no money, but it did not matter. I gave him one and my card. I told him that he could take care of it when he could. I also let him have one of my "POW" prints. I am proud of that poem. It speaks. The man was moved at being trusted. I met some wonderful people sitting there on the tailgate of my truck, watching the proceedings and listening to the singers and musicians. It was time to gather in front of the Wall. The day was fabulous, the mood somber, as the Wall tends to make it, wherever you find it. I walked down the hill and found a seat next to a man who introduced himself as Jim Disney, the County Service Officer. We had a few minutes to chat. It was a blessing.

Jim is a preacher now, a man who serves his fellow man. He has been a Veterans Service Officer for years, also working at the State level. Mr. Disney did five tours in the brown water Navy. I would love to have more detail about those years, but our location and timing did not give me a chance to dig out much else. Suffice it to say, I know he gave grunts like me rides, floated down rivers in World War II leftovers that were great targets for rockets and grenades, and cleared some rivers of mines and other such minor gigs as that. He became an ensign at some point.

One story he did share with me before the opening prayer was about his adventure on an old LST on the open sea. Jim explained that an LST is about 300-feet long and the average wave is approximately 150 feet in length. They were sailing a rough sea as they cleared one wave, they hit another, repeatedly, without cease. The old boat was taking a beating. Their destination was 600 miles away and the purpose was to dock for repairs that were long overdue. Jim said the LST began handling wrong, getting very sluggish and riding low in the water. The captain was concerned and believed they were sinking, but did not know why. He called Jim and another sailor to the wheelhouse. He asked them to dive in the ballast tanks to check for leaks. He was afraid they were damaged. The ship had three ballast tanks, the largest of which was mid-ship and held 30,000 gallons. Jim and the other sailor were the certified divers on the boat. They dove in one tank and found nothing. Jim went into the largest. He found a huge slab of steel bent back at a severe angle with water pouring in faster than it could be pumped out through the bilge pumps. He got out of the tank before he got caught in some kind of backwash. It was just what the captain feared and it could not be repaired at sea. They had to slow the engines, pump fast, and sail with a prayer for harbor. They made it somehow. It took three months in dry dock to effect repairs. Tugs were waiting on them. If they went down in the harbor's mouth, they would block the harbor for months. It was serious. Jim preferred his brown water. I almost asked him then if that is when he was called to preach.

The speakers each delivered their remarks, all running over a few minutes. We came to a section of the program devoted to a very impressive Native American Ceremony directed by Arthur Running Bear who told a story about a dream he had at one time about a little girl taking him on a train to a place where it was revealed that he would receive a special drum. A few days later a friend told him he had for some reason been compelled to make him a drum. It was a beautiful creation he was using in the ceremony that very day, one he has used many times in the years that followed the dream. His ceremony ran very long. Barb came to see me a few minutes before my introduction. The Gold Star families were tiring and threatened to leave. The shadows were growing long. She asked me to shorten my remarks. I had been reduced from key note speaker to cut note speaker. At least I did not have notes to abbreviate!

I was introduced and after asking a simple question I talked about The Wall. First I asked the crowd what you get when you add dignity to beauty. You get the day God gave us for the ceremony there by that beautiful little lake in southeastern Indiana. Then I talked about The Wall in earnest. I remembered the controversy at its inception. Vietnam vets were torn at first over the concept of black granite in a hole. Once again, we were reminded that we were a stain on the American psyche. It seemed symbolic of that. The design contest, the results, the drive for funding, all those things were a battle individually and collectively. I remembered relenting and donating. It was not easy for me. I had no money, but it was important that somehow we recognize what we did even in the face of our nation's rejection of our efforts. I closed by saying that breaking ground for that Wall led to all the other tributes that are on the site today — Korea, World War II, the Nurses — and that it awakened a nation in many respects. The Wall did that. I sat down and we had a wonderful concluding ceremony at the Moving Wall and the Gold Star Families stayed.

Glen sent me a check a few weeks later. He sent a note too. It said that it had been a long time since anyone had trusted him to pay them when he could.

◆ ◆ ◆

The local ABATE (American Bikers Aimed toward Education) chapter began a *Support the Troops Ride* soon after we engaged in the War on Terror. It is the purest ride for any cause about which I am aware. There is no entry fee and it is not commercial in any way. Riders come together for one reason: To Support the Troops. The event is held in late April each year. Weather is the greatest deterrent to attendance. We have been fortunate the last two or three years. The greatest crowd we drew was in 2008 when we had 2100 bikes. That is staggering participation for a ride of this kind. It brought tears to my eyes. A young friend of mine, a former Marine, has been trying to get his dad to participate for several years. The weather and his schedule cooperated that year. We staged early and I had the chance to chat with him for a few minutes before we hit the road. Scott's dad, another Mike, was a Marine as well. He went to Nam in 1965 with the First Marine Recon Expeditionary Force. Although he was there just a few months the first tour, he spent time at both Chu Lai and Khe Sanh. It does not take long to get filled with survivor's guilt. I sat astride my black Harley and Mike leaned against the backrest on his three-wheeler. We talked as the other bikes roared by, finding their places in the lines readying to leave the memorial park where we stage gather in Kokomo. The worst fight Mike recalls is when his unit walked into a North Vietnamese Army Regiment's ambush. Their artillery had them pinned down for four hours about 2000 meters from their pick-up zone. It was hell. The shells rained on them without s break until they could get enough separation to call for air strikes and artillery support. Mike was a Radio Operator/Communications/Encryption Specialist. A squad member on one side was killed. One of the other, a man lost an arm. Mike was unscathed. His reinforcement battalion lost one-third of its manpower in that operation, code-named "Harvest Moon."

After Mike choked out his story, he could not provide more details about the rest of his experience. I understand that. I did learn that he was back in 1968 for a while, then again in 1969 for a year with the Force Logistics Command in Da Nang. He left in 1970 for the last time. The current war has brought back memories and old pain for him, as it has for me. He is proud of his service, his son's service — and we will talk again. As for now, Mike is around, wrinkled, limping but remembering — as am I.

We rode our 100 miles, smiled at the crowds along the route, and waved at the children jumping with their small flags as we passed by. We shared the three hours of patriotism you find in Central Indiana on a day like this. Looking around, we saw other faces beaming with the same pride, and sometimes the same shadowy look in their eyes, as we were sure ours had. Our bikes roared down the roads. The local police and volunteer fire departments blocked intersections so we could pass and nobody is upset at the delay.

We are Supporting the Troops.

♦ ♦ ♦

I sat down next to a young man I knew in a local American Legion one evening and renewed a long forgotten acquaintance. He is younger than my sons and I know his older siblings better. I discovered he served in the Army during the "missing" years as a member of the Special Forces in South America. He is a veteran of the hunt for Manuel Noriega. Jerry Frazier survived the jungles of Panama.

Jerry did not relate any details about the actual search. He was reticent due to the mixed company I believe, but he laughed and shared a funny story.

Jerry said the monkeys in the jungle were as big a threat as Noriega's guerrillas. His platoon learned to secure their weapons at night. If they didn't the monkeys stole them and disappeared into the upper jungle while they slept. It was very difficult to explain to the brass that their M-16s were somewhere in dense forest in the possession of a thieving simian.

Frazier assured me that he was scared for his life on more than one occasion. The first came as he hacked his way through heavy jungle one day. He became entangled in a thick, rope-like web from which he could not seem to extricate himself. The harder he struggled the tighter he was trapped. He couldn't even turn his head. As he attempted to hack the thick strands with his machete, someone at his rear fired a two round burst. When the firing ceased, a pair of soldiers added their machetes to his and cut him loose. After dragging the heavy web from him, he discovered that he had become entangled in a huge spider web. His teammates directed his attention to a monstrous spider on the jungle floor. It was a banana spider which was at least two feet across in the body. Jerry learned they are carnivorous. He was lunch. They had to shoot it save him from a savage bite at the least.

Jerry said that was the only war story he could share then. It was a good one. Neither of us care much for jungle spiders.

♦ ♦ ♦

My wife and I had to make an emergency run to Fort Benning, GA, in May of 2009 to "rescue" our older son. He participated in the pre-Ranger qualification school and injured his left ankle. As we learned, the accident occurred during the first week, but he continued without telling anyone about it. He almost completed the entire two weeks before being discovered. He was considered successful and was invited back to finish the course after healing. In fact, SFC Mullins was accepted for the course prior to going to Iraq (having done two tours in Afghanistan prior to that). He had to get an age waiver as well. He did so, thus when he went to the school he was 35. That is a little long in the tooth, to be frank, but he was determined to finish. The instructors caught him doing push-ups with one foot elevated on the final day. He washed out and had to call us to come get him. He made it, but he did not. Fate takes a hand in all things.

While we were there, and the time was very brief indeed, I went with him to an off-post, military supply store to purchase some things and met a retired Nam vet who was working as a greeter. The big, black man was as grizzled as I. We recognized each other for what we are on the spot. We smiled and the greeting was a little different between us than it was for most of the other customers that day. That Nam vet had seen a lot more Army life than I, but we were still brothers. He was a retired "lifer" who had spent his last seven years teaching airborne techniques to those who wanted to be airborne. The man was a career-long member of the 173rd Airborne. It was his love and his pride. Wife and son were doomed to wait while we talked. That is just the way it is.

My wife and I drove from 50-miles north of Indianapolis straight through to Fort Benning. We rented a room, slept three hours, showered and began preparations for departure. The stop at the store was part of that, but leaving had to wait just a little while.

My new veteran acquaintance arrived in Nam in early April, 1968, or a couple of weeks later than I did. He was in the air when Martin Luther King, Jr. was assassinated on the fifth of that month. I was in the field. We talked about the event. Having written a poem about the event and its impact on us sharing field duty, we had things to say to one another. We agreed that people not in combat could not understand how we shared the pain of the moment with our black brothers. He saw the conflict when he landed. Black soldiers serving in the rear took their anger out on white soldiers quite often and it was a horrible, tense time of misunderstanding and conflict that none of us deserved — not in either race. He knew what I was talking about. The man also understood the bond we shared in the field, covering each other, fighting and bleeding together. It was not like earlier wars. Some race baiters tried to make it seem like it was a black man's war after the tragedy, but it was not. Historical data proves that fact. Nonetheless, he and I, and all combat soldiers, know that we were all mud gray, bleeding red, and caring for each other. We shared a different bond than blacks and whites who were non-combatants ever understood. He told me a story that underscored that better than I could ever have explained to anyone.

His squad in Vietnam happened to be composed only of black soldiers. They were proud of it, given what occurred before he joined it. They called themselves the Midnight Squad. Their Area of Operation was the Central Highlands, which was often a high enemy contact area. There were times they crossed into the Tay Ninh AO as well, so he and I shared a lot of memories about bamboo and the border which were very similar. After several hot firefights, the Army assigned a white man to the squad. It was an awkward time for them, worsened by the fact that the new soldier had been raised in a prejudiced household. The "newbie" spent a lot of time with another squad when they had down time, but Fate stepped in here too. He was saved by a black man named Henson. They became inseparable. It not only saved him, it "saved" him. The white man changed. He learned. The prejudices fell away. Henson and my new *lifer* acquaintance were in contact for years. The story is amazing. The reformed white soldier took Henson home with him. He wanted his family to meet the man who saved his life, believing that it would matter to them. When they arrived at his home and he knocked on the door his father greeted him with warmth, looked at Henson and said, "People like you do not come under my roof."

The son said, "Dad, if he is not welcome, then neither am I" and they left. My storyteller said they went to a motel and shared a room for the first part of their leave. The young soldier spent time at home, but then accompanied Henson to his home, too. It was no easier there in many ways. The pain in the black community was palpable. The one thing that runs true, however, is the bond of serving together in war is strong. It is hard to explain and it is difficult to break. The soldier I met there in that store did not tell me more than that. We were out of time, but I can assume those two had to go their separate ways, yet what they took with them is with them still — a little of each other.

We came home after that moment of sharing. Fate had taken a hand in my son's life. Oh, he was disappointed. We talked of it for hours. He could not even help drive due to the pain. There was a time limit on his return to complete the school. Two weeks after we returned home — and I discovered power-driving that far with three hours of sleep is tough on a worn-out old fart — my son received a phone call. If he had not been home it would not have happened. The National Guard made him a First Sergeant and had him take over an Infantry Company.

We made a quick trip, I met a wonderful veteran who served this country with honor, heard a great story, and my son took another step forward. It was a hell of a trip.

♦ ♦ ♦

My little home town has a surprising number of people who have served this country. I live in a farming community and the ratio of people who have military experience to total population seems quite high to me, but I have done no studies to provide data for that opinion so you will just have to take my word. I went to my high school reunion (my high school, like all my schools, has been razed) and the 1951 graduating class, which was the smallest since 1921 or something like that, had 13 male students and 11 of them were in Korea. I wish I had the time and ability to chase everyone down and do a book dedicated to my hometown. These people deserve it. The point is, I see someone every day who served and it is far too easy to take him or her for granted. I overlook them like they overlook me. We just did what we were supposed to do. We are not special. We are Americans.

I made a list off the top of my head that I wish I could talk to for this book. There are 23 people on it who live in the immediate area. There are more, but that was a quick review by memory. I live in a town of fewer than

700. The cemetery is dotted with small flags at Memorial Day. I ran into one of my town's veterans at the local convenience store and remembered to ask him to talk while my mind was working.

Gale Barr was in the Marine Corps Air Wing as an RIO (Radio Intercept Officer) during the Vietnam era. He flew backseat in an F4 Phantom. He was a year behind me in high school. Gale is a quiet, funny guy who is very, very bright and tough to the core. He is a Marine and a Purdue graduate. That is two reasons not to like him, but what the heck — I still asked him to give me some time. We blocked an aisle for a few minutes while he shared an amazing story with me. We discussed having a longer session later. Gale has told me some great stories and I want more.

Gale attended a nursing conference in Arizona with his wife in February of 2010. He was sitting in the hotel lobby people watching one day as several Marines began walking through. They were Native Americans wearing their tribal colors as well as their Corps unit insignia. Marines hail Marines. Gale initiated a conversation with one. As a result, he was invited to a Pima Indian tribal Pow-Wow. It was a much bigger deal than he imagined. He was one of a few white men permitted to attend a special memorial ceremony conducted each year by the American Legion Post 84 (Ira Hayes Memorial Post) on a local reservation. It was a huge event honoring Ira Hayes, who was the Native American involved in raising the second flag on Iwo Jima. There were 6000 Indians in attendance, with an inner circle of 200 braves (Barr's estimate) who were military veterans, playing drums and Native American instruments during the ceremony. The veterans wore vests much like bikers, proud of their individual heritage and as proud of their military unit affiliation. The ceremony is open to the public in Sacaton, AZ. Gale was given access to the inner circle, which is a rare and very special opportunity.

Barr was swept away by the power of the ceremony. The beat of the drums was an impassioned tempo that pulled him into the moment. The echoes were primal, pulsing and powerful. They spoke to him, running along his nerves like an electric pulse. He had to react. He had to move with the beat. Every man there moved with the beat. It was impossible to resist. It mesmerized him in the moment with what those men feel in their very spirits. The tribes represented have their own histories, but their stories are the same in many ways. These men fought for the country that pushed them onto reservations in a wasteland. Yet it is a wasteland that has been their home for centuries, where they too pushed others before them. Their histories are told in the beats of those drums, in the stories they still tell, not written, but in song and stories that they struggle to preserve. Ira Hayes and those who composed the circle that Gale observed with awe are the warriors—the tribal heroes of today. They are still proud warriors. He listened to stories which few outsiders hear. I get as emotional listening to the stories I hear as those who share them with me. I worry about telling them with accuracy. This is one of those moments. Gale was speaking with another invitee when a World War II hero was brought close. He was an elder, an icon in a wheeled chariot pushed within their hearing. He was a *Wind Talker* who was as revered as Ira Hayes himself. Another old hero was brought to him and introduced, who caught Gale's attention at once. The latter was a Marine pilot from World War II who had flown an F4U Corsair. The two heroes chatted within earshot and as Marines, Gale and his companion were drawn into the conversation as welcomed admirers. The pilot shared a story about dropping a bomb on an entrenched artillery position on a mountain. The 250-pound bomb went right into the cave opening, taking out the big gun. Gale's new acquaintance grew excited. He had to get involved in the conversation. He told the Marine pilot from World War II that his uncle had told him that story — he had been on the ground right there and had seen it himself. They were all stunned at the irony of the moment! Gale's companion dialed his uncle on his cell phone and handed the phone to the Marine pilot. He allowed the two of them to share a moment at long distance. The ceremony had taken on an even more ethereal and personal meaning for them.

Gale Barr left that day with another thing weighing on his heart and mind. The reservation where he visited was a place of indescribable squalor. I worried about using the word "squalor." It is a harsh word, but we take so much for granted sometimes. They are happy and proud people. Gale would not use the word perhaps for fear of offending one of them. I do not mean to be offensive. It is my intent to call attention to their living conditions as described to me. There were no doors on many of the dwellings. The houses were ramshackle at best. The kids were poorly dressed, but smiling. His life's work has taken him many places and he has seen poverty. Never has he seen anything worse than what he saw that day. It is right here in America, on our soil, in existence where it should not be. Our government has poured billions into the inner cities, where it has disappeared often into a bottomless pit. Somehow it looked as though nothing had ever been done here, at least on this particular site. It may be presumptuous to paint a landscape from one oasis of poverty, but Gale could not avoid wondering why. The thing that tore at his heart was the fact that not one word of complaint was heard. Not one word of regret for having served, having bled, having sacrificed for America, was heard. Nothing but pride in their service was displayed. The Native American veteran who invited Gale to attend wore his Silver Star with pride. To the man, it seemed that everyone he met had no regrets and would do it again. America is still their home.

They would fight for her still.

◆ ◆ ◆

I attended an informational meeting for veterans hosted by a large American Legion Post in a nearby city in 2009 with two friends. The guest speakers were all associated with veterans services in one fashion or another. The agenda indicated they would be providing information regarding burial services and housing for aging veterans. As a result, there were many older veterans in attendance. We felt a bit out of place and then realized that we too are on that precipice. The debate about leaving dissipated.

As the empty chairs filled, a World War II veteran was helped to a seat by a lady as old. I assumed they were man and wife, which I confirmed soon after. I read the old warrior's coat. I am pleased when our older vets wear their association gear so they are recognized for what they are. He was a former member of the 875th Bomber Squadron, part of the 498th Bomber Group. Other older veterans began to filter into the front rows near us. I could not see all of their hats and coats to get a read on their affiliations. Several of them acknowledged others in the area. I found myself wishing for different circumstances.

One slight man walked up to the gentleman at my front who wore the same 498th coat, but his squadron was different. I could hear them as they spoke of operating from different islands in the South Pacific. After he left, I leaned forward to introduce myself and ask my neighbor's name. And that's how I met Bill Krum, World War II veteran. We spoke very in short bursts before the meeting was called to order.

Mr. Krum flew in B-17sfirst, graduated to B- 24s and then to B- 29s. His first duty was as a gunner and then he became a flight engineer. Near the end of the war he was training gunners. He mentioned the attrition rate in some of the aircraft was quite high. Mr. Krum became quite animated when he talked about his early experiences landing on one of the islands where we first established air fields in the Pacific islands. I could not understand if he said New Guinea or Okinawa, but when he landed the first time, the Japanese were pushing the natives off the cliffs to drown, then jumping in the ocean to commit suicide. They did not want the natives to help Americans. When his crew left the ship, they ran to the cliffs where the Marines were firing on the Japanese in the water. They could not understand why they wasted the ammo on them when they were going to drown anyway. That is when he discovered they were pushing the natives under water to assure they died.

Bill Krum was among the first to land on Iwo Jima. He said it was not secure yet and it was hell. Small arms fire did more damage than flak during the bomb run. He remembered the early computers used on the B-29s. He had been training gunners for a while by then, but we were out of time. I did get his address and phone number and a promise to talk later.

I called several times over the next year and a half. His wife and I spoke. He was ill. She took him to Arizona for the winter at one point. She promised on two occasions to call me when he was able to talk. I never got a call.

If he is still with us I am happy about that. If not, God keep him and bless him.

◆ ◆ ◆

I have heard stories from veterans since I was a kid. I did not mentally catalog them like I have since I started writing them. Hence most I share have been given to me since my first book was published. It was then I began speaking at small events and having book signings when possible. We had a meeting in our town hall in 2007, where I was telling some of the stories I heard at the events where I attended. The meeting must have been after Veterans Day. I told a story which I heard before I spoke to a group of senior citizens at their center in recognition of that day. They were widows or participants of World War II or Korea. It was astonishing to speak to them. What could I say to them?

Prior to the meeting, one of the men at my table shared a story about his uncle who passed away a short time earlier. His uncle had been part of the D-Day invasion. The man who told me about his uncle was a Vietnam veteran. The other man at our table was the new Veterans Service Officer for the county. He was interested in the Nam vet's story too. When they hit the beach, his uncle's best friend was a few steps away from him. A German rocket hit a few yards in front of them, killing his friend. The blast took him and another member of his squad to the sand. Wet and blood-splattered, they struggled to their feet, looked at their dead friend and continued the assault. A few steps later, a rocket landed behind him, killing the other friend. Again he went down, this time with shrapnel wounds. He was treated by a medic there on the beachhead and rejoined the battle. The three of them had gone through all their training together since entering the Army. They met in Basic Training and went ashore together. He fought on without them. Fifty years later, he was suffering from those old wounds as the shrapnel was still working its way out of his body. A surgery a few years prior to his death revealed that the shards in his body were bone fragments from his dead friend, not metal. He had not only lived with the horrible memories of that day all that time, he had lived with parts of his friend imbedded in his body. It was a discovery that left him trembling and with horrible dreams until the day he died. I was, and am, overwhelmed by the story I heard that day.

I shared that story as I waited with friends in our town hall. Another story had also been recalled which was included in my impromptu conversation that day. I met a World War II B-17 belly-turret gunner from Kokomo by the name of Charlie Ornsby. He is an active member of a Military Rights Burial Detail yet today. Charlie shared a quick story with me after showing me his original 1941 driver's license. He and his twin brother were in the same bomber squadron in Europe. The twin was a tail gunner and flew on Charlie's wing. They were on a bomb run deep into Europe and his brother's plane was shot down by flak. Charlie watched it go down. The next day he had to make another bomb run to the same target. He said that the feeling which came over him as they flew over the area where he lost his brother was something he could not find words to describe. At the moment he could not see to take out a target, even though he would have welcomed one. His brother had lived, became a POW, survived — and was recovered. The brother passed away in 2009. Charlie is an amazing man and tells wonderful stories — of all kinds.

I began to tell a third story when an older man sitting in front of me turned around and asked me to shut up. I have known him for years. I went to school with two of his daughters. I dated one of them and he never shot me. He had tears in his eyes and his lip was trembling. He asked me again to just shut up. I asked what was wrong. The man is a good man, honest and straight-forward — and I had never known him to be vindictive in any way. He told me that he had made the invasion too on D-Day. He fought all the way to the end of the war, seeing his friends die, receive wounds, get maimed, while he never got a scratch. He cannot talk about the war, nor listen to it. The dear man left the building in silence — refusing to speak of what he saw and did in World War II. Until that moment I was unaware he had served.

Some things were confirmed for me that day. Survivor's guilt is not generation-specific. Nor is it confined to one war or one battle. Neither does it have an expiration date.

♦ ♦ ♦

My search for help with my PTSD claim led me to a man whom I had met but not engaged because he is a Service Officer in another county. People urged me to see Bob Ladd. We met at a Veterans Day event, which I believe was his introductory event in his home county. Bob is one of the most dedicated and hardworking people I have had the pleasure to meet. I met him as the State Commander of the Disabled Veterans Association, but he does double duty. I had not joined yet. I refuse to join groups when I feel that I cannot participate in a meaningful way. Bob assured me that when I carry the message for and about veterans that I am participating. That did assuage my reluctance to a degree. We met and I discussed my anger and frustration with the continued rejection of my VA claim. Once beyond that we had a wonderful discussion about our experiences with the vets we encounter at veterans events. Our roles are much different, but the stories he shared and I hope he shares in the future, were wonderful. I could do a book about Bob. He deserves it. I read that he has gotten 3.1 million dollars in benefits for veterans since he began working as Service Officer. He has earned his wings in heaven. His halo is in the mail for all the things he has accomplished outside that role.

Bob told me about two Master Sergeants at Grissom Air Force Base near Bunker Hill, IN. It was a magnificent facility a few years ago. It is a reserve base now — and has a variety of units using the facilities now. The government, in its infinite wisdom closed it for all practical purposes, and moved a very important refueling wing to a hurricane-riddled base in Florida. I am sure they have spent enough money relocating due to storms to have kept the base open for half a century. Everybody knows the government is more into spending money to look like it is "doing something" than it is into making sense. It passes idiotic laws where laws already exist in the same way. Oh My God, did I say that? Pshaw! How dare I editorialize in my own book! At any rate, these two senior non-coms decided that young soldiers need to see what older veterans have sacrificed for this country. In that spirit, they initiated a program for volunteerism to help disabled vets in some way. They have little funding, thus it is a program of direct and personal assistance. They encourage involvement by giving recognition and a ribbon for every 100 hours of service. Their group is comprised of some eight or nine air-persons at this point. I would have to call them fine young people. I read between the lines, but I believe Bob gets them some information and perhaps funding sources. I am not betting the farm, but I am just saying…

The Air Force group has built nine handicap-access ramps as of mid-May, 2010 and that is a heart-warming accomplishment. They built one for a Vietnam veteran who draws a small disability check for his service, but he does not receive all he should for political reasons. His is not the only case like this I am sure, but it is the first I have encountered. He lost a foot to a landmine, but he does not get 100 per cent disability because he was in either Laos or Cambodia when he lost it. The government does not acknowledge that we had ground forces in either country, therefore they will not pay for wounds received there. They pay for his in-country disabilities. If they paid him for his "loss" the government would be telling the world we were there. We had to go there. We were being attacked from there. Our POWs were there. The Khmer Rouge did not appear from nowhere in 1975. The man has a serious handicap and it is from his service to his country. Our Air Force people chose to help him in their quiet way.

The man lived in a very poor neighborhood and had not been out of his home in over two years. He had gotten quite heavy as he aged. His wife could no longer lift him over the five-inch drop to get him in and out of the house. He was missing his medical appointments at the VA. Some of his conditions for disability were being threatened. The man needed help. So they built him a ramp.

It was an unnerving experience at first, as the neighborhood watched with distrust. They stood out from the crowd in their crisp uniforms and for other reasons. With many pairs of questioning eyes on them, they worked on and as they progressed the crowd warmed. By the time they were done, they were cheered and a woman cried and loved them in a way not expected. They have learned about sacrifice, giving, respect, and a kind of love that crosses all kinds of lines. And all for a ribbon.

◆ ◆ ◆

There is a huge network of Nam vets on line with whom I communicate, without having seen or met any of them. Thoughts and information they share comes to me and visa-versa, via shared acquaintances. I have developed some very good internet friendships with people whose hearts and minds show in their words. Our common experiences bleed into the airwaves. Recently one of my friends sent me current photos of an old in-country R and R (rest and recreation) area which was used during my time in the Nam. The photos of Vung Tau provide proof of how the country is changing. Vietnam is evolving into a tourist lure, with its coastal beauty developing into some of the most attractive anywhere. Vung Tau shines in the photos that I then shared with the friends in my mailing list.

Many Soldiers and Marines from III and IV Corps tried to spend some time there if they were able to finagle a three day, in-country pass. Enemy activity in the area was seldom seen after it was developed heavily, although there were scattered firefights at its perimeter. There are many stories and rumors why that is so, but I cannot provide a definitive reason. I have no real experience there personally, although I tried once at the wrong time. Memories rushed out, experiences from Nam vets came back to me and I read things about that long-lost haven that I never knew. It became mandatory to share an electronic "doobie chat" even though I cannot give you names and I will not reveal e-mail identities. As I read my mail, it was as though we were sitting around a fire at a reunion somewhere sharing stories of our time in Vietnam.

"I was with the 224th Avn Bn (RR) at Bear Cat in '71 and the 146th Avn Co (RR) at Long Than North next door, both ASA units. I transferred crypto equipment all around Nam via convoy and chopper. I started up north at Nha Trang in '69. The 11th Cav was up in I Corp by that time. I was at Vung Tau once for an afternoon, but it didn't look like that. We rolled up to the beach in a convoy with 3 gun trucks, 2 with quad 50s. We unloaded, swam for a couple of hours and headed back for Bear Cat."

"Several years ago I rode the hydro boat to Vung Tau from Saigon. There are a number of Aussie vets hanging there — several ran bars on the waterfront — that was their AO in Vietnam. I remember being downtown and it was really Vietnam-hot and humid. I was drinking a lot of water and had to find a bathroom in a hurry. The statue of Ho Chi Minh on the edge of the strip, beautifully decorated with flowers, seemed like a good place to take care of business. Most Vietnamese totally ignore the communist statues in Vietnam because they represent repression-so no one was around. Take that you commie bastard. If they would have caught me I would still be in jail."

"I got sent to Vung Tau for CIA school. We were told it was in-country R&R for VA and ARVN so there were no attacks to speak of. At that time, Jan 69, it was a whole lot smaller and dirtier. There is now a Russian retirement community in VT. An OCS classmate and I were *detained* for a couple hours by the MPs for calling an LTC a "straphanger" when he tried to tell us we were in a "hot" war area and we should not be walking around late at nite. The CIA night duty officer had to come fetch us and verify we worked for them and not the Army."

"Vung Tau was the in-country RnR spot. No VC in the area and the Aussies had a base nearby or was it the Kiwis artillery unit? A huge freighter was aground in the sand right by the cape. I do not recognize a thing in the photos you provided. Actually Vung Tau was a bit boring after a day or two rest. But it was nice to sleep the night without fear of the first mortar is the one that might get you. In the Da Nang area, there was China Beach but it was crawling with Korean grunts walking the beach with swim suits and combat boots. Looking ridiculous. The best RnR as we all know was Bangkok, Hong Kong and Sydney. Married guys mostly went to Honolulu."

"Was Vung Tau the in-country RR area? If so, us Covans at least the ones I knew, never got a whiff of it. We did, however, know of a place in Nha Trang right on the South China Sea owned by a French/Lebanese guy I think he was. It was a hotel used by the Air America pilots. He had rooms, a bar, and great food. Everything you could ask for including a "full service" hooch maid. About every two or three months when we started to back talk the District Advisor, he would send us to Nha Trang for three days or so. Did wonders for your attitude. As I recall, late in my tour Nha Trang was put off limits. I went once and had to stay on whatever base it was there. No fun. Didn't go back but real soon I went home so no problem GI."

"I made it to Vung Tau after Tet 68. They had a Revolutionary Development HQs and training center there. Also made it to Con Son Island and Phu Quoc. I understand they are all tourist traps now."

"Any of you Co-Vans make it to Vung Tau? I didn't — hell I did not make any of the "pretty" places in Vietnam. I was just a dumb ass "swabbie" at My Tho."

"Somewhere along that beach in Sept of 1965, I stepped off an LST for my first tour in Vietnam. Bet good American money, it is still there today."

We have a network which acts as a vent mechanism at times. When we cannot see each other, we still feel each other. Technology scares me, but the guy in Texas, the man in Washington State, and the man in Florida are only seconds away.

We had a campfire and we raised a glass.

◆ ◆ ◆

How do I draw a line in the sand and say, "No more — I am adding nothing else to this part of my book." That is a rhetorical question. It is not even a question. I don't ask it, I don't even say it. My book is not static. I meet new veterans wherever I go; in the Wal-Mart parking lot, the river at Barbarosa campgrounds east of Newport, TN, and anywhere I happen to wander in between. This particular evening, I happened to be invited to one of the first meetings of a new organization being formed for Christian combat veterans. There are those vets who believe they should have a forum for sharing that is exclusive of groups devoted to the infusion of alcoholic truth sera.

I had the tremendous pleasure of riding with my wife's cousin John Winton Graham in the summer of 2010 when he was not driving truck. John has an old Harley Duo Glide Pan Head. He led me through some incredible scenery and introduced me to new people. The first man he introduced me to was the first step to this evening. It was also on this evening that I learned more history about my friend John.

John Winton Graham's name is to honor his uncle who died in World War II. Winton Sommers Graham is considered the *white sheep* of the family. He was a brilliant man who grew from boyhood near a small town in Southwest Virginia. He graduated from high school in Big Stone Gap, VA, where he was a star track athlete. Winton set school records, many of which stood unbroken for years. The family saga includes the story that Winton used to run to town as part of his training regimen. It was difficult. In those days, the only people who ran to town did so only in an emergency. When he ran, it often took him all day. Everyone who saw him stopped him to inquire about the problem and offer assistance. He had to stop and respond. People cared and offered help — he had to reply. What else could a kid do? It made his training much more difficult, but he persevered. He did in all things he attempted in his life.

Winton Graham succeeded in the challenges he undertook as well. He was a brilliant student in science and math.

Winton Graham went to graduate from West Point. John has his hand-tooled boots and engraved, wooden boot stretchers in his possession. I had no idea, but that was a tradition at the Point. All graduates were given a pair a custom boots upon the successful completion of school, replete with their own hand-made stretchers emblazoned with the cadet's name. He became a fighter pilot in the Army Air Corps and went to fight in World War II. Not much is known of that experience now in family lore. The family is gone, but John knows how Winton's life ended. Winton S. Graham was flying a mission somewhere in Europe and crashed into a mountain during a violent thunderstorm. John has his encased 48-star flag in his room.

We drove the rest of the way in silence to Blountville, TN, each filled with thoughts about another sacrifice made to our country. We stayed at a historic hotel owned by a Nam veteran who had managed to keep the only building in town that stayed with a family with roots over 100-years deep. The building is on the National Historic Register. Others in town have been sold and are gone — monuments in memory only. I was going to meet men who shared a common bond: service to America. We met in an historic place where the words of the Founding Fathers were not quite so distant.

John and I were welcomed as we walked down the cobblestone entrance. It was not a large building, but character oozed from its old lumber. There was a large porch and a narrow entrance. Inside, there were small rooms and the smells of old wood. It was the real deal. The furniture was period-correct. The pictures on the wall were old family photos, yellowed with age. Our host took us into his military room. Some of the founding members had donated memorabilia that made the room quite special. Immediately to my left, I saw a World War II era flag (like John's), photos, and a display of medals, including a Purple Heart. I met the young man who provided it. The items were a tribute to his uncle who died in combat. He too had been in the Army Air Corps — a pilot who was shot down in Europe. The same young man had a display of every medal offered by our military including an old style Congressional Medal of Honor. I asked how he managed to acquire that. The answer shocked me, as it did him when he found it. The family had no attachment to it. It had been earned four or five generations earlier and meant nothing to them. They sold it in a garage sale. The young man to whom these items belong is a Gulf War veteran and a combat medic. He struggles with the chemical effects of that experience. When we talked later, he spoke of raining oil and the thick smoke from the destroyed oil wells as Saddam and his forces left as they retreated before American might.

Three other men drifted in shortly thereafter. I met a Seabee who worked in Nam in 1967, for more than one tour, and who served for many years all over the world. Another man was a Marine Recon veteran who has also worked as a private contractor and consultant for years, with multiple trips to the Middle East. The fourth man was an eight-year Navy veteran who served as a medical doctor aboard ship, providing care to the wounded. He has been a VA doctor for years. Our host is an Army vet of multiple tours. I will meet them again and there will be others in attendance.

For now their names are unwritten. I will learn more about them and tell their stories. God willing I will write another book. They will be part of a larger story. I will see them again.

◆ ◆ ◆

You never know who you are walking by on any sidewalk or in the mall. You never know who you are meeting in a local business. *Vietnam in Verse* became a key that unlocked doors for me that would never have been unlocked without it having been written. In 2008, I stopped in to take care of some business in a nearby town with a man who knew me and my book. He introduced me to his boss. I wish I could reveal his name. Many Vietnam Veterans would stop just to shake his hand for the work he did. The man was a member of a Special Operations Group (SOG) team. He calls his team a Repatriation Team. It is another of those teams that did not exist. My new acquaintance served 21 months and helped recover 96 Prisoners of War. We did not discuss failures. It is best that nobody dwells on that. He was a corpsman when he became a member, but was soon cross-trained as a sniper. At first, the irony of the added MOS was an emotional challenge to him. He had mental and emotional difficulty balancing the assignment conflict. It would take an operation or two for him to understand how important it was to the team and those they were inserted to rescue. The team was composed of four members, from different combat branches of the service, but they became one team with one purpose. They were skilled at it too.

My newest source educated me about another silent operation that was unknown to me. It made my chest swell to learn that something like this occurred during our war. He and his team operated on information gleaned in a variety of ways. The CIA had sources, but the Army and Marines were always getting leads about the missing as well. Our captured soldiers were seen by villagers sympathetic to what America went to Vietnam to do, or what we thought we went to do.

Our recovery teams went on two-week recovery missions as a rule. If the leads were confirmed, they acted. The corpsman/sniper learned that his role was to lie in the bush while the other members made the actual insertion.

They killed whoever was guarding the prisoner(s) and brought them safely from their confinement. He was to stay disengaged unless one of the enemy soldiers escaped the initial attack. If they did, he took them out. His job was to live so he could administer first aid to the POWs who were recovered.

It has taken several trips to visit this unsung hero to get this smattering of information about his incredible service to our country. It would be wonderful to tell his story and pay him tribute. Each time I see him, I try to learn something else. He was in other countries seeking our stolen soldiers. His team knew names and dates. Those who were saved may or may not even know who brought them "home." One of the questions I asked was about his very odd juxtaposition of duties. Being a sniper and corpsman at one time had to play on his mind, it seemed to me. He says that it was reconciled after his first mission. When he saw the way our people were treated the lust for retribution, the desire to extract some justice for them was hoped for rather than avoided. They were in horrible condition when found. His medical skills were often taxed to the utmost in order to get them strong enough to return to the safety of an American military compound.

I heard once that VC and NVA avoid palmetto plants. I never knew why, but he confirmed that they would not go anywhere near them. They hated the palmetto bugs. I discovered that certain varieties of snakes loved the cover of that plant. Special Ops troops cleaned the area and used the plants for cover when they were operating in enemy territory. The Repatriation Team members used them as a matter of course, curling around them to sleep in enemy territory, knowing they could rest with little chance of discovery.

Unsung heroes are walking among us. I try to remember them when I bow my head on special military holidays. They deserve our thanks. When I can, I tell them face to face. I told him every time I talked to him. I will keep hoping that he tells me more of his story in the future.

◆ ◆ ◆

Sportster Slim tells me stories quite often. It would be interesting to do a novel based on him, but I have not convinced him yet. When he lived in the wild, wild west, there were Nam vets gravitating in and out of his bike crew with regularity. One evening during his shift at the bar where he worked as a bouncer, such a man arrived and sat alone at the end of the bar. Slim recognized the look in his eyes and the way he watched everyone around him. He was well aware of the signs of a man walking the raw edge of control. He was there most of the time himself. The man was new in their territory. It was not a problem. The stranger was just another loner in a group of loners who rode together.

That solitary figure at the end of the bar became a fixture each night. It took Slim a few evenings, but he did break the sound barrier with him at last. As Slim anticipated, their stories were much the same. The loner was homeless and verging on penniless. Slim invited him to a party at his place after work one evening. He was not surprised when the new guy arrived astride an old Harley just as he had when he arrived in Arizona. When the party faded into sunrise, Slim told the loner to spend the rest of the night at his place. The loner did, but not inside. He went to his bike, pulled his pack off the backrest and erected an old two-man pup tent just like they both used when they were in the Army. Slim's overnight guest had a ground sheet and light camping gear. He spent the night alone in Slim's back yard. It was the first night of many.

Slim's new friend was no longer homeless. He also managed to land some odd jobs after he hooked up with the crew which was family to Slim. He was paranoid and remained aloof, but he was part of something and grabbed hold of it like a drowning man grabs a thrown life ring. The man would not spend a night in a house, but he had people who cared about him and a bathroom within useful distance of his tent. Life was better than before he found that barstool in Slim's favorite watering-hole-place-of-employment-bar.

A few weeks later, the stranger earned the nickname that he would wear into perpetuity — or at least as long as he was part of Slim's band of brothers. That bunch danced to its own music. They set their own schedule when they could. Almost everything they did included the bikes they rode. They made a weekend run from Prescott to Flagstaff often. It was a ride of 170 miles or so, but just under half-way, they had a stopover where they loved to eat, top off with gas, and drink a beer. The guys with the smaller gas tanks liked the eighty-mile break a lot better than those with greater fuel capacity, but after they had been accommodating the smaller bikes for a while it became an important part of the trip. They all looked forward to leaving the interstate for their respite.

They partied in Flagstaff, crashed for the night and made the return trip the next day, with their rest park as a half-way point in both directions. They were known and the money they spent was loved. During one of these excursions, the loner filled up and pulled out ahead of the main body. He blasted out and flew down the road. The rest followed as soon as they fueled up and even riding hard they could not catch him. It dawned on Slim that the quiet man had screwed up. He was willing to bet that he hit the loops wrong and went the other way. He got everybody's attention and as fast as they could find an exit they reversed course. They had to scream down the interstate. It was one hell of a ride, but they did see him in the distance at last. By the time they caught him, they decided to go the rest of the way back to Flagstaff. Sure as God made little green apples, he had turned the wrong way onto the interstate and did not notice. They spent another night in Flagstaff and replayed the entire journey home again the next day. That time though, their new friend had a name. He was known as Wrong-Way from that day forward. He was reborn and whatever his given name has faded in Slim's memory. Wrong-Way is the friend he remembers, the man who slept in a tent in his back yard, but never in his house. Wrong-Way stayed with them for months. One day, he woke up and went away. He left friends behind, but the monkey on his back left with him.

◆ ◆ ◆

September, 2010, was the 28th annual Vietnam Veterans Reunion for the Howard County Vietnam Veterans Organization. It is an all-veteran event now and we encourage our current crop of warriors to join us for a genuine "Welcome Home" with respect and encouragement every year now. The crowd was huge! I arrived at my small cargo trailer to arrange my small book sales display for the day, expecting nothing. Generally I have a great time but must admit to a portion of frustration due to a failure to sell many of my books, either print or audio. Poetry is tough and the people who come are there for other reasons.

This year I made the decision to visit, enjoy the people and any sales were icing on the cake, so to speak. I have given up on my fellow members utilizing my skills for anything during the programs. Physically I have nothing to offer the group now, but talent-wise I do. I guess they are the wrong talents. So be it. Acceptance made me happier going into the event than I had been in a couple of years. I think opening that door allowed the wonderful things that happened to occur. I was blessed at our Reunion in many ways.

Campers started drifting into the Grounds as many as three weeks before the event officially began. We actually have an unofficial gathering on Thursday evening with music and fun, but the official opening is not until Friday morning. I was on site by noon Thursday — enjoying the vets, wandering and chatting with the regulars I have gotten to know over the years. A great by-product of my location is greeting the first-timers who stroll by and meeting repeat visitors who wander up to my trailer out of curiosity. One of the new men I met was Rick, a Nam vet who served from April or May of 1967 until 1968. He wore a patch that declared he was a Tet Survivor. We talked for almost three hours — mostly he did. Rick has a horrid problem with Post Traumatic Stress Disorder, although he declares he is much, much better. Keeping up with him was like trying to capture Niagara Falls with a bucket.

Rick was an artillery man. He was in the Central Highlands on Firebase

16, which was overrun during the Tet Offensive of 1968, firing 105-mm beehive rounds at close range and fighting hand-to-hand at the end. He was one of something like 70 survivors, many of whom were walking wounded, of the six or seven hours of battle. He said 11 were killed and 26 were wounded and listed as serious. The day left him forever scarred emotionally. It would. He was 18.

We discussed his hospitalization, his VA experiences, his trauma, other war experiences, and a host of other issues. He has not spoken to his three children in two decades and he is barred from contact with his grandchildren. We also discussed that he had been saved and becoming a Christian has made the biggest difference in his life of everything that he has undergone. He had to leave all the negatives behind so he left his home in the Rockies and moved to Berea, KY, where he has a quiet life now. He carried a letter from the VA to prove he is safe, but will "react violently if approached violently or threateningly." After a couple of other visitors, he was compelled to retrieve it from his campsite and bring it to me as proof of his improved nature. It was valium for the moment, but I get ahead of myself.

Several people came by and chatted, but he interceded in all those conversations. Those people did not stay in the competition very long. One who did with remarkable patience was a Marine who served with Kilo 3/5. He was an E-6 Recon Sniper with 27 confirmed kills as I learned when I could get a few words in that he could hear. It was tough getting information, but he was a good man and I would like to get more of his story. The Marine won the Silver Star and had the Purple Heart ribbon with clusters. He was wounded a total of three times. He also wore a scalp on a special ribbon on his right breast just under his jungle blouse pocket. Rick got in his face about that, challenging his right to that, asking if he was Native American and other unintelligible questions. Rick had a bad habit of frothing at the mouth when he got over-charged.

I got in Rick's face at that point and challenged him. It was my turn to ask him why he thought he had the right to question what any vet did with his person, why he thought he could demand answers of anyone else when he was so adamant that people respect his space and individuality. He backed up at last. The Marine had been shot in the upper thigh when he was wounded the third time. He was down, but he came up to his feet when the Cong came up to him for the kill shot. The Gook was taken by surprise but reacted by bayoneting him in the abdomen. That weapon went in to the left of his navel and came out over his left hip. My Marine visitor grabbed the VC by the hair, yanked his head back, pulled his 45 automatic from its holster, and shot him in the top of the head. When it was over, he was standing there with a scalp in one hand and an enemy at his feet, a bayonet in his body, with fighting to do. He removed the knife and continued to fight, helping his team repel an ambush. He kept the scalp. As far as I was concerned, he earned it. He did not go hunting a souvenir. Many months were spent in recovery and nobody took his symbol of victory and life. Rick asked to be forgiven and changed his tone. Some of his belligerence receded for a while.

Rick was really a good-hearted guy, but he had a bad habit of having to outdo every story that anyone shared with me while he was around. He was Airborne. He was Recondo. Twice. He had the *baddest* Drill Instructors. He could not hear a story without telling one that was worse. Not one person could tell me something without his having had something just a little worse happen to him. Over and over, he berated *wannabes*.

I was worn out by Rick and went home early, fearful that he would be back all day the next day.

In truth, I sympathized with him. He was sincere. He cared about other vets. He was also a ticking bomb and seemed unable to control himself under duress. He told a couple of stories about confronting people who he thought had a demeanor that indicated they believed they were better than he. Rick exemplified classic paranoia. The Marine and I both told him that it was good that he had not approached us that way. His response was that, "by God, nobody intimidates him or acts as though they are better than he." We calmed him down again, reminding him that he did not have a license to treat others that way either, in particular, other veterans. He was in the wrong place to behave that way for damned sure. It took a while, but the message penetrated at last.

I saw Rick each of the next two days. He made a quick visit and moved on, to my relief. I had other friends there who did not have my patience — or that of the Marine. He visited with a World War II acquaintance of mine and treated him with extreme respect and regard. I think he took his meds. It was a good thing.

Friday was a pleasant day that became a day of wonder for me. The Opening Ceremony was passionate and emotional as usual. I saw a friend from Ohio who I look forward to seeing each and every year since I met him. Another friend brought a first-timer who took part in the Posting of Colors (our stadium-sized flag) and stood near me to get good photos as they passed by my location. Campers drifted in all day until the Grounds were swollen to capacity. We stuff 1000 campsites into 39 acres and there are often three people per site. Walk-ins add to the number every day. In fact, a camper often sets up and others join, erecting tents in the same area. In the last ten years, we surpass 20,000 attendees in total on Saturday. It is one hell of a sight. There are over 400 golf carts rented, small vehicles and ATVs of every kind, and motorcycles roaming the Grounds. We have our own Security Staff and even have to control traffic flow during the heaviest hours. It is a small, crazy, party town larger than many "cities" in Central Indiana for three days.

A dear friend from high school sat with me for two hours and we talked old times. He served in Nam for 27 months — very dangerous duty, duty about which I can never write and reveal his identity. I did write one story about him in my first book. We are both late entries into the VA healthcare system. We are also slamming into the same walls when dealing with buried PTSD issues. I introduced him to other vets who are regular visitors to my little trailer. For some reason I received a couple of nibbles on my book variations. My friend is a loner in many ways. His work in Vietnam took place in four-man teams (at the most). We talked about residual guilt and the difficulty of ridding oneself of it no matter what is done. In the last few months of his last tour, he was given a "cool-down" job with a mechanized transportation unit. He attempted to protect one of his good guys. The man was getting "short" and inside his two-week window for DEROS (Date Eligible for Return from Overseas). My friend assigned him to a short supply run in order to protect him from more dangerous convoy duty. As Fate would have it, he dodged a civilian to protect some children, rolled the three-quarter ton truck he drove and was killed. The short-timer's wife was widowed and his child fatherless. And my friend sees him in his sleep regardless of what anyone tells him. The demons live, alternating with the other demons flashing their ugly yellow eyes in the gloom of night. It was great when my friend Ray showed up and lightened the mood. Ray is good for that. He is hilarious and he was manna from heaven at that moment.

Ray and I met a couple of years ago when he bought my old motor home. He is an absolute character. His wife is his match too. After introductions, I gave my other friend some background about Ray. My Buckeye Buddy did not want to get drafted. He moved every 30 days so his notice could not catch up to him. He realized he was a bubble boy. He evaded, he eluded, he partied, and he hid. Successfully he delayed the inevitable for a year. Memory is playing with me, but a friend or two may have joined him in his reindeer games, but one day he awoke and said "#%_* it!" and went to the local Draft Board Office and asked if they were looking for him or went to the recruiter's office and joined. Either way, he was in the Army. He still did not want to go and was determined that whatever he did he was doing it his way. Ray volunteered for every school he could get. He is a very, very bright man.

He made it through Basic Training and a litany of other schools. I think there was Jump School, Ranger School, Jungle Warfare School, and Advanced Infantry Training School (oh, that is sorta-kinda-like what I did after Basic too, so I got that one out of line). He was an E-5 when he arrived in Vietnam. Once in-country, he volunteered for that version of Recondo School as well.

At any rate, when he was finished with all of his schooling, he had rare skills as warrior and became a Ranger. He was assigned in-country to a Special Forces Group attached to the 101st Airborne.

Ray won promotions, valorous commendation awards, a Purple Heart or two, and I think spent more than one tour. Not bad for a red-assed, block-moving, draft-avoiding, wild man. After being wounded the second time, the Army tried to get him to go conventional warfare. He refused. It was not safe. We grunts moved in larger numbers, made more noise by comparison, and had less freedom to operate. Ray went back to his specialty work. My old high school chum understood how he felt about that. The two had many things in common. They drifted away and I sat down to eat a "Lunchable."

Later in the day, I had a wonderful visit with a man and woman from a nearby city. While chatting, I noticed another couple waiting patiently for us to disengage, as it were. I turned to the lady who was nearer to me than the man and asked if I could help her. She greeted me warmly, introduced herself as Donna Elliott. As it turned out, she was a member of Military Writers Society of America, the writing group with which I have proudly been involved for three or four years. Donna was named Author of the Month for her book *Keeping the Promise*, a story which evokes all kinds of emotion in the reader as it relates her dedication and courage in the search for the remains of her brother. He has been missing in Vietnam for more than 40 years. It is an incredible story and Donna is an amazing woman. She was accompanied by her friend Mick. Her smile and sense of humor were compelling and I was drawn to her on contact. We chatted for quite a while. Mick is a Nam vet — the bond was immediate there too. It was another special moment in the Reunion for me. I was emotional before they came over from their book sales table in the vendor tent.

I was sitting alone in mid-afternoon Friday, enjoying the music and thinking about one of our speakers from the day. We have an annual guest who brings me to tears of pride each time he appears. A Triple War Veteran, retired Sergeant Major Arnold Wallace, who fought in World War II, Korea, and Vietnam, spoke to us. He is amazing. I sat there in the chaos hearing nothing when I saw a golf cart go by and I jumped to my feet waving. It was Congressional Medal of Honor winner Sammy L. Davis. His wife saw me and waved. I heard her tell Sam, "Turn around. There is our poet." To my amazement they did. She recognized me and they both remembered me. I was stunned. I am still stunned and honored. In all the thousands of faces he sees, he remembered me.

We talked for ten minutes and he is well. I asked him to sign something, anything, for me. I grabbed my personal copy of our new audio book *Kings of the Green Jelly Moon*. It was already precious to me because I did it with three other wonderful Nam vets and fellow writers, Lloyd King, jim greenwald, and James Jellerson. It is even more so now. Sam signed it. He had to go, but he had time for me. They were not staying Saturday due to other commitments. I gave him a copy of my original audio book, shook his hand and hugged him. I kissed Mrs. Davis's hand and stood there like a dolt. I did not get a picture. My poem mattered to them. He spoke to us all from the stage, played Shenandoah on the harmonica, and left the Reunion to his usual standing ovation. I was misty-eyed the rest of the day and along came Donna. Damn.

Later my friends George and Montana came by. They work their butts off for veterans — all the time. I love them. They were checking on me. I was there with my oxygen hooked up by then. Music was hammering us, thus we could not hear each other, but they learned what they wanted to know. George had open heart surgery last spring. We were all reassured.

Saturday leaped off in a wonderful way too. As I unloaded my display material from the trailer that morning, I turned around to find two ladies waiting and a couple of men walking into the area. Company in my space was not unusual. There were a half a dozen port-a-pots nearby. My friend Connie Salsbery was outside the trailer with a lady. Her husband Bill was walking my way with a man. They brought her sister and brother-in-law to the reunion for the first time. They were visiting from Connie's home in Missouri. Harold was another Nam vet. I did not get a lot of information, but a decent thumbnail sketch. He was there before I was in 1968 and was the first man I ever met who was with an air-mobile artillery unit. Harold was in the 5th of the 27th and it was attached wherever needed. He was an assistant gunner on a 105-mm Howitzer. The unit fired over 10,000 rounds in one month during heavy combat. He said the worst hour he ever experienced was firing with a split barrel when they were under direct attack and slamming more than 1000 rounds in an hour. I listened slack-jawed. That is amazing. My unit had arty cover several times, but we were often on our own deep in the jungles. We relied several times on our own mortars. Our arty could not reach us. Once we set up with a 155-mm battery and another we were a few miles from a thunderous three-battery station of 175s. I never experienced that kind of bombardment. It was incredible to consider.

The five of us enjoyed a great visit. Connie bought almost one of everything I had. She turned my sales experience into a great one almost by herself. She did change my momentum entirely. I introduced them to several of my Nam buddies as they drifted in and away during our talk. Bill and Connie are ministers who have a church a few miles south of the Grounds. They are wonderful people seven days a week. Bill is a farmer by heritage, salt of the earth. My kids grew of with theirs. I have known them for years. Good folks started my day in a good way. It stayed that way.

The Reunion was exceptional that entire Saturday. I had a wonderful time with the people, the too-loud music and great weather making the day special. Then my family began drifting in too. My younger son Joel had not been there in years. He and my oldest grandson Kellen arrived and stayed with me until dusk. My veteran daughter-in-law, kids in tow, came much later. Her cousin had been visiting me (former Navy) to check on me for three days. Brian has been a regular for five years, coming from Wisconsin. My older son, serving for 18 years now, arrived very late in the evening.

It was my best Reunion ever in almost every way. What else can I say? Nothing.

PTSD

A Personal Perspective

The VA, a tough bus to catch

This section of *Out of the Mist, Memoirs of War* is different than the rest. It is information for those who still struggle to get care, to understand, who have yet to try. It is my personal story. I must say now that it turned out well in the end. Rulings changed and results changed, but not about PTSD (post-traumatic stress disorder). My wife asked me to stop fighting and I have. The battle rages on for many. As you read the pieces that follow, please understand that some are akin to a daily diary and others are an out-pouring of emotion during crucial times in a difficult process. We Nam vets joke and say that a vet is sure to be denied *any* claim three times. The VA hopes we will either die before we can prove our case or quit trying. That is the process in a nutshell. We also realize we are old news. We will keep fighting for our rights; there are a lot of us who need care. We also know that our deepest concern is for those coming home from the War on Terror. One and all, our message to you is never quit, cast off your frustration, and stay in the game. The hardest battles are often the ones at home.

This is my opportunity to tell the American public that I love it for funding the VA program. It is your money — and mine. I know that. In troubled times, in hard economic times, everyone is searching for ways control budgets. The Department of Defense, thus the VA, is always in the crosshairs first. The American public has supported the veteran when aware of threats to VA programs. The various veterans' organizations toil to keep our citizens apprised of what is happening in this arena. It is also a wonderful time to dole out kudos to the caregivers in the VA system. Each and every one I meet emphasizes the "care" portion of that word. The issue is in the administrative side of things and its threatening, cumbersome design. It is regulated to death, as are all things government. I understand the need to exercise due diligence in the protection of tax dollars in case of fraud. Combat veterans hold DD-214s that are often self-explanatory, and in my case a DD-215 was included due to the late arrival of some of my paperwork. We were a small percentage of force in Nam. Too often things were harsher for us than necessary. When I have an official document stating I have a Purple Heart why do I have to provide a daily diary showing I was in combat? If my paperwork shows I hold a Combat Infantryman's Badge why do I have to prove somehow I was in combat? The issues with the VA are systemic.

The men and women serving now, or who have served, must be prepared to stay the course when seeking help from the VA. Do not be afraid to ask for help. Do not be reluctant to hold your ground. You are a political force. Get involved with a veteran's organization. Their dues always include a portion to fund activity in DC. It is important. It is the only voice outside your district that you have. There are people in your area that will help you. I can't say that enough. The system is flooded and caregivers are already not being replaced. Where I have gone for help, the counselors are not being replaced. The psychologists are not being replaced. The public does not know this. While DC fills desks there, facilities across the country are neglected. That is why I am saying this here and now.

I am angry with the system. I am not going back to my counselor. He does not want me there. I am fortunate. Writing and meeting the wonderful people about whom I write has become therapy for me. I promised the men in my group that I would assemble some information for them and share it. The writers' organization with which I am affiliated, The Military Writers Society of America, has people involved at many levels in PTSD programs. I have successful ideas available to me. I mentioned that before I left my last session, but the leader looked as though I had stepped on his toes. One would think he would welcome anything that could help his group. But as you will see when you read the material that follows, I seemed to him a threat. I may have read him wrong, but I haven't gotten a call asking where I am either. In that regard, I broke my word to some fellow veterans, but after I left I feared I would do more harm than good.

The medical side of the VA is more productive than the psychological side in my estimation. The greatest stumbling block there has always been what the government does not want to admit what happened in the way of exposures or events outside the norm. I give you Agent Orange as one example of that. We add the exposure to black dust during the Gulf War as another. The chemical warfare weapons of mass destruction that our troops have encountered in the last decade will become more apparent in the future I fear. Emotional trauma is not as immediate sometimes, or as scientifically simple. The suicide rates in our current gallant warriors group continues to escalate.

The VA and the various branches of the Armed Forces search for reasons about the suicide problem. The reports I have seen indicate that it is worse with our National Guard forces and the reservists. Having spoken to many of those troops, most of whom have served multiple tours, the support they were promised has not been delivered. They come home to learn that the laws passed regarding the promise of safeguarded jobs are not enforced. The toll-free numbers for help with utilities or house payments are unmanned recording stations, from which there is never a response. I travel in different states and speak to young men at different places. Most have stories to tell that echo of similar experiences. If not their own, then they have happened to someone they know. They are going through emotional hell. Financial trauma leads to familial destruction, which leads to more emotional hell. The VA can't see them all. How prepared are they to seek help there or anywhere else? Can the Armed Forces even allow the chaplaincy to suggest they find refuge in religious counseling or is that precluded now? I don't pretend to know, but I want all tools in the medicine cabinet for our veterans. Meditation, medication (a last resort I pray), group support, writing, older veterans, and anything else there is available to prevent this epidemic. One young man told me about a friend's recent suicide that stemmed from a second tour, a return home to no job, and the discovery that his family's utilities had been stopped while a pay problem was resolved. The last straw was when his wife left him. He committed suicide for the insurance money after volunteering to return overseas. My informant could not guarantee that happened, but he was convinced. The point of this is all the programs that were promised do not exist. Many of the things that are expected in the way of support for returning veterans are not there.

There are contracts with Guardsmen to join that promise college will be funded. They go but must assume huge debt. They complete their service and after two or three years of separation they still have not been paid. It is happening. Some are still serve and fear complaining. There would be serious repercussions.

As I said, I understand budget cuts. I want to believe that most Americans prefer to cut funding for things other than those going to American citizens, much less American veterans. But that is just me.

The VA is a tough bus to catch. It can run you down, but it means more than words can express to thousands of veterans. There are more to come.

Today I Cried

I drove to the Veteran's Administration Campus in Marion, IN, today. It is hilarious that they refer to them as "campi." They certainly are not collegial. It was my first appointment with a counselor. Somehow I have never been steered to one during the entire claims process while being evaluated and denied for my request for compensation for Post-Traumatic Stress Disorder.

I never wanted to admit I had a disorder. I have had nightmares and anger issues for years without admitting why or even understanding why. Even though I counsel others, listen to them, tell them to seek help, claim what they've earned, and care, I have never heeded my own advice. The first step in any process is taking one. I believed I had, by being evaluated, but I had not as it evolved. The man who evaluated me did not like me. His only purpose was to reject me. He did. He pissed me off, made me fight harder and he inadvertently made me take a real step.

The little yellow car I was crammed into was my wife's cute bug of thing. She is using my vehicle for a well-deserved respite from her mother and me. I had the radio humming on some oldies while I thought about an essay I plan on writing about the man I consider the number two enemy to the Vietnam veteran, right behind Jane Fonda. It will be an opinion piece. It will be controversial. I am going to speak about a dead icon in the American news industry, but in my opinion he is not as good a man as any man whose name appears on that black granite Wall in DC. My mother used to tell me to never speak ill of the dead. The quasi-intellectual crowd does not let that little moral boundary muffle them, therefore I will not. I had not planned on writing this tonight. I was going to write some mini-stories for a section in my new book — yet here I am — "'a-settin'" and 'a-pokin'" at the "puter."

Last night I was taking a break from a short story I was writing, thinking about the same topic in my head now. I mulled over it this afternoon as well. The cruise control was set right on the money. I have grown averse to speeding tickets and the accompanying fines. My cell phone was set on vibrate, resting in a comfortable spot under my testicles so I would not miss an important call. I could focus and sort thoughts, thereby committing them to some memory card inside my withering mind. Walter Kronkite was a news giant at one time. His word was gospel. His employer made money from every word he spoke. By the sixties news was no longer a break-even proposition for the networks, with regular programming as the cash cow. It was a cash cow on its own. The role of newscasters had changed. They were rapidly becoming "opinion-spewers" and not objective news reporters.

It was subtle, but now we have seen the evolution so thorough that the main stream media relies almost 100 percent on opinion pieces. As an industry, it actually does very little news. It revels in controlling public opinion. The industry learned about that power while covering the Vietnam War. It was not the reporters as much as it was the puppet masters. The puppets had to respond to keep their jobs I believe. Salary increases and success were tied to doing it well eventually and "eventually" had begun.

Kronkite looked right into the camera while the smoke still wafted into the air from the battle and said we lost the 1968 Tet Offensive. He told the American public we lost! He stood right there, knowing that he only saw what was around him, knowing in his heart he had no facts, only an opinion, knowing he was *against* the war. He said we lost! He said we had no chance! He blatantly lied to America. And because he was who he was it was taken as irrefutable and true. It twisted the mind and heart of American supporters and her future warriors.

We did not lose that battle. I'm resorting to memory here, but I am very sure I am close to the numbers. We killed 70,000 enemy troops around the country that day and wounded approximately another 150,000 NVA and Viet Cong. We sadly lost 2,000 dead and 20,000 wounded. Their supply lines were in disarray. Their communications were almost destroyed in South Vietnam. Their bunker complexes were intact in parts of the country, but populated by few. Many of the professional troops had retreated into neighboring countries. It would take time for the VC to mount a successful recruitment campaign. Kronkite's words gave them that time as it turned out. They were so defeated that the Spring Tet was a miserable failure for them. The *facts* never supported his assertion.

Kronkite's words were so powerful that Lyndon Johnson stupidly resorted to prevarication about our successes and inflated numbers rather than doing what was making us successful with our Search and Destroy missions. Johnson crawled in a hole and gave his political enemies the country. Doing what is right works. Lies do not. I believe Westmoreland lied because he had to do so. He became a political scapegoat. Johnson was a goat. We became the sacrificial lambs. The public was in large measure poisoned. The proof is in the pudding. Many soldiers came to war then believing they were fighting a lost war, for a lost cause, and all for false reasons. They were half-hearted and there was weak commitment then at all levels. Kronkite did that from his pulpit and he was the strongest preacher in town. Young men fled to Canada. Nobody wants to play on the losing team. Kids use to leave the school yard when they were the last to be chosen for a team. Professional athletes ask for trade clauses in their contracts today to get away from losing teams. It is an undeniable mindset. I am convinced that had the assertion never been made it would have made an incredible difference.

The soldiers who came after me often believed they were joining a bunch of losers, only to be wasted themselves. Soldiers did not lose that war. Wow, I have shared the gist of what I was thinking about writing. My point in sharing it is that I had opened my mind and heart during the drive to Marion. My soul was unbuttoned before I ever got there. It is opinion too.

The session started late. I remembered the counselor. After we started he remembered me. I once donated a book to his group after the first one was released. He had read my file, but we still had to dance. The questions came then. I usually deflect. I never talk, *really,* about me. I avoid the real tough stuff although I have talked about some of it with a very select few. In short, I opened up to a complete stranger and I have no clue why. He seemed to doubt I had dreams. He wanted proof. He wanted to know how many, when they started, why they were bothersome, how they interfered with my life. He had me answer 17 questions — after I calmed down. Always questions that quantify! I told him that what is normal and common to me may be different to someone else. Those things are subjective as hell. If someone else were in my head, they may think every thought was extreme. I have come to view my thoughts as acceptable and normal. That whole routine is bogus, but they have to have a baseline of some kind I realize. Suddenly I am sitting there with my guts in my hands, like I had been shot with an AK-47 from about 100 meters. They were spilling all over the floor and I was crying like a freaking baby. God, I could not believe I let myself go like that in front of anyone, much less him! Tears were streaming down my face and I couldn't talk. My shoulders were shaking like they were when my dad died. I stood in the shower that morning all alone and screamed into the showerhead like it was a microphone linked directly to God. I did not even do any kind of sequence. It was exactly the way dreams hit me — randomly, out of order. The demons were all screaming and leaping out of their boxes, the lids were off and the flames were screaming out of my ears. I told him that the ringing was enough by itself to keep me from sleeping at night, but add the demons to it and the world explodes!

I remembered the sampan being pulled up to the river bank and us pulling body parts out and trying to match them up so we could get a body count from the morning patrol.

I remembered laying there in the dark of the night by myself, as ordered, tapping my mortar tube on the bank of the river to get a live hang-fire out without killing myself. My God, I was scared.

I remember holding the saline bag for a man I never knew while we waited for a medevac chopper. He had been hit in the collar bone and the round ricocheted down through his body. It hit his heart, his lungs, his guts, and went out between his legs, castrating him. He begged me to cover him and not tell the guys on the ship so it would not be reported. He did not want his wife to know he died less than a man. He took off his ring and had me put it in his New Testament and promise not tell anyone. He died there while I held him. My God, I am crying again! I will forever and ever. Tell that frigging psyche doctor I have no damned memories or dreams. Tell the pencil-neck geek that, will you? I did everything he asked. He died.

We could not shut the combat photographer up in my first experience of being ambushed. It took many, many shots of morphine to quiet him. The leech almost got me shot. It was my first one. I learned to smoke that night too. That is killing me now. That is funny as hell, is it not? That same operation — my first — a guy throws a grenade up hill. I am walking drag. The grenade comes back down the hill. The fuse delay gives it time to go off about 20 feet from me, but I am not dead. I should be, but God's hand turned my poncho into some kind of invisible shield and the shrapnel went all around me. Why? I earned my CIB (Combat Infantry Badge), the second week I was in the field.

He asked me if I was in combat. That is funny. I told him I was rarely out of the field. Maybe three times in the entire year. We had some duty that was around Saigon, but it was always combat type duty, not REMF (rear echelon mother-f***er).

Three days in-country and I am doing in-country orientation. We are Tet replacements. Now I have known since the fifth or sixth week of Basic where I am going and what I am going to be doing. No surprises for me, and I have been well-trained. Hell, I like throwing hand grenades and stuff. But the desk jocks who's MOSes (jobs) were changed in transit ain't so happy. We are going through an impromptu grenade training course. Some of us have jumped in twice already. The sergeants force us out of line and let them go again. There is a sandbag barrier where we toss them. All you have to do is pull the pin and throw. If you get in trouble, you simply drop the live pineapple on the other side and everything is cool. No panic, no sweat. Ain't no thang, ya know? One guy drops the pin and freaks. He drops his grenade and panics, knocks the grenade out of the guy's hand next to him. The next we know we have two or three of them exploding behind the wall. We have four dead and seven wounded. We have a head blown 20 feet in the air. We have a Sergeant First Class dead. He is due to rotate home in two weeks. We have blood and carnage and guts and screaming and gore and dead bodies all over the f-%-ing place and we ain't even in the f^&*ing field yet! It is real! Man, this is real. We could be dead right now! This ain't a game no more! Yah, I got some memories.

It is late April. Tex-mex is down in front of us. He has a sixty (machine gun). He has been hit. Damn! His arm is gone. He is screaming for help but he is still firing that gun. Oh God, a B-40 got his leg. It is gone! He is still fighting. He is yelling for his mother. Oh my God, nobody can get to him. He is trying to crawl over that log. Damn, that sniper just took his head off. Good, he wasn't gonna make it anyway. He doesn't need his momma anymore. F+*^ those Gooks. Yes, I heard all of that. I saw that. Yes, I have memories.

Today I cried. F@#* it, it don't mean nuthin'.

Addendum:

As I began final preparations for publication, I had second thoughts about this section of the book. My words regarding Walter Cronkite are opinion — my opinion. Although many veterans share it, some do not. He is an American journalistic icon. There were Huntley and Brinkley, Cronkite, and before them Edward R. Murrow. Cronkite was a powerhouse. That is my point. He was known — as far as I can recall — to be against the war. Many journalists had begun to mix opinion with their reporting at that time. It is standard procedure today. Very seldom does the viewing public see or hear a news report without it being as much opinion as news. Careers are created that way. Follow the money. That aside, I owe it to the vets who survived Tet, and those who did not, to speak my mind. Every American has a right to their opinion. I do too. Be angry with me. I accept that.

I spell Mr. Cronkite's name with a "K" because I think he was kryptonite to the American war effort in Vietnam, thus to the Americans serving there. He was a tremendous force. He was obligated to wait for battlefield reports from the entire country before he damned us and our efforts. He did not. He was my generation's Ernie Pyle. If Ernie Pyle had done that in World War II, he could well have stopped the sale of War Bonds and destroyed our war effort. That is how much power there is in the pen. I resent the lack of discipline and the lack of loyalty to our fighting men who shed their blood during the Tet Offensive in 1968. I reported to Nam in March after Tet. I learned how to fight from those who were there. They told me how it was. Many of them were disturbed by that report. They knew we repelled the enemy forces and how much damage was inflicted on them, yet America believed the opposite due to a live broadcast given from a man in one location. Damage and destruction in one location can always be shaped to present a story however the storyteller wishes to present it. It was his choice. He could have waited for the right information. He did not. He was more interested in beating somebody else on the air than he was in being accurate in my opinion. If he had been broadcasting from one of our rescue locations, he could have done the same thing. It still would not have been true. We never lost a firefight, but we lost people and people were hurt. It was war.

I have my nightmares. I have my anger at times. I have my demons. There are names that stood out from all the rest during the Vietnam War who represent the source of angst in Vietnam veterans. Cronkite is one of them for me, but most of us have no disagreement about many of the others. I cannot change that and I will not apologize for it.

Our VA

I wrote "Today I Cried" on June 14th, 2010, late at night, as I reflected on the afternoon's events. I was alone in my home, frustrated and angry. More was said than I wrote about and residual angst roils in my soul. I was told when I entered the system to be prepared for huge roadblocks at every turn. Most vets believe the system is designed to deny anything except the irrefutable. I have the stressors that the VA regulations cite as causal for compensation in PTSD cases. Period, end of story. Men who fought in my unit are being compensated. Men who fought in my Brigade at later dates are being compensated. They did not work through the Marion facility. They did not get an evaluation by the same jerk who evaluated me. I know I made mistakes in the process. I also know that my representative had a physical problem which caused me additional delays. The VA did not help when I went there and asked for assistance in rectifying the situation.

The system is designed to take advantage of those things. They can be mired in crap for years and that is okay, but you have one misstep and they slam the door with your face still in the crack. Near the end of the interview, the counselor told me essentially the same thing the psychologist told me. "You have been married almost 40 years, received two degrees, had good jobs, (even though I told him about my problems with authority and anger — and being moved due to that), have written a book, been successful in your career and life. What has PTSD cost you?" I told him that I was never able to get a really good job anywhere because of my anger and relationships with my superiors. I could not even get approved for further schooling at my last job. PTSD cost me my chance to do better, to be upwardly mobile. I survived. I should have said that is just like what I did in the war.

The dogs at the top of the VA food chain are smiling when they get their reviews because the curs at the bottom of the pile are yelping in pain. I know in my heart that the system is preparing to do its worst for the soldiers serving now. I know we Nam vets are yesterday's news. Any of us with claims in the pipeline are dead meat. They are going to rape and pillage us now and sweep us into the dust bin, there to curl inward on ourselves until death doest we depart. They will have been well-trained to make it even worse for the tens of thousands of new claimants coming home from Afghanistan and Iraq. WAKE UP AMERICA!!!!!!!!!!!!!!!!! IT IS OKAY TO GIVE BILLIONS TO ILLEGAL IMMIGRANTS, to let them steal the money out of our treasury, to send money to the Palestinians so they can rocket our only real ally in the Middle East, and *deny money to our own troops coming home with God knows what kinds of issues*! Just sit back and keep your mouths shut folks. The Sleeping Giant is in a coma.

Today, June 15th, 2010. I read where a Vietnam vet who is a high muckety-muck in the VA, a man who we believed would make things better for us, asked the Senate not to have the hearings required to approve three new diseases proven to be Agent Orange related because he did not want to pay for them. Science has showed them to be real, with a direct link to our service in Vietnam. He has become one of *them*. He does not want to pay us. I asked that my claim be reopened because of the new findings. Now I know what is going to happen to that too. The hearings have been quashed. There will be no funding. The regulations will not be forthcoming. The claims will go nowhere. The die is cast. It is just that simple. How hard is it to block all the studies relating to the new chemicals and related illnesses from the War on Terror?

I am putting this in a book. It will be old news about this particular issue. The sentiment and the process will be relevant. It is a warning to all who read it. It is something to remember. Keep a weather eye out please. It is not about me. It is about a generation of young people who deserve better. I will tell you about one now.

I sat in the waiting room with a young man who was obviously preoccupied. He too was waiting for a counselor. I could control my curiosity no longer and asked him what he needed. He replied that he had a very unique problem over the weekend, something he never expected to experience. The young veteran said he was unsure if he could even discuss it. I assured him that I understood and that we all went through that. He was silent for a few minutes and then rocked forward in his chair and spoke softly to me. The young man had contracted leukemia four years earlier while serving in Iraq. It was rare, but it happened. The doctors were not sure exactly what he was exposed to but there was no question that his duty in Iraq was the problem. There are other cases.

Many of the diseases displaying themselves now are new to the military. Nobody can blame them for not knowing at first. Some things cannot be anticipated. The issue is their reaction — denials. I understand that there are deadbeats and those who would abuse the system, but a vet's job, time served, and location reveals much.

The young man continued his story, telling me he had gotten a bone marrow transplant two years ago and the drugs he was taking had the cancer under control at this point. Then he looked at me and said, "The drugs are why I am here now. My weekend was weird. I never thought anything like this would ever happen." His explanation was halting after that, but he went on talking to me. He told me that the drug caused an odd reaction in very, very rare instances. For some unknown reason, it could generate a reaction like Viagra. I was taken aback by that and thought I had heard something wrong. He repeated it when my mouth dropped open. The young, former soldier informed me that the erection would not go away, even in his sleep Saturday night. Sunday he went to the emergency room in complete misery. The doctors told him that most men will not do that. They do not have enough sense. Their egos prevent them from making a good decision and they would have made a huge joke out of a serious problem. If he had not, his sexual apparatus would have exploded for all practical purposes, and been useless for the rest of his life. In his words then, "It would have gone down and stayed down forever." He shook his head at his close call. He is a young man. The idea had to shake him to the bottom of his tennis shoes. The description of the procedure was rather gruesome, but he did the only thing he could. He used his hands to show me a kind of corkscrew operation into the organ to drain it and release the pressure while giving me a verbal re-cap. I was cringing inside. Men are wont to joke about what they would do in similar circumstances. This kid knows it is no joke. The other side effect was a kind of hallucination. He told me that the weekend, combined with the cancer experience, had put his life in a different perspective. It is easier for him to prioritize the pettiness in his life.

The VA has no choice but recognize the hell he is going through. He was there to see the counselor about the stress of the weekend. He was being crushed and had the additional fear now of where he goes next with effective drugs to battle his cancer. From being in remission, he now was faced with the very real threat of leukemia reentering his life. He had an appointment today, the 15th, to see a doctor about that. Did I remember to put him on the prayer chain? I was so stunned by all of this I forgot to get his name. He told me before he left with the counselor that his dad was a Nam vet. They are from Wabash, IN. When he was going through his treatments, his dad took off work two or three times a week, whatever it took, and was with him every minute. His father is a busy, successful man, but he stepped up. I think that young man has as well. He had courage and common sense. He was meeting his enemy face to face. In this case, the VA has to as well. I pray to God it never backs away. Shall we also pray, they never have a hearing about funding for this?

P.S. July 11— after much daily rumination
PTSD Mea Culpa
Experts from the many fields of self-conflagration — the ways we self-

destruct emotionally, mentally, and physically — universally agree that the first step in healing is admitting there is a problem. Until three years ago, everyone I met had Post Traumatic Stress Disorder but me. I had no problem for a variety of reasons. First, I am not entitled. Second, it is a sign of weakness. Third, there is nothing wrong with me. Roll them all up and you get a whole ball of self-denial. Coming to grips with the summation has opened the proverbial can of worms. Having done that, I had to turn myself wrong side out and look at my innards in an honest way. That is tough. I do not like it. The activity is gory and unpleasant. Let me say before I paddle any further up this stream that I am not giving our glorious Veterans Administration system a pass. I am looking at my own culpability and mistakes in the process because I have not understood myself and they have done nothing to help me with that.

Before I get into "tearing down my own meat house" as many of Louis L'Amour's characters are wont to say, I want to add that my personal counselor got me involved in group therapy after our one and only meeting. Unlike the other vets in group, I have no other one-on-one counseling sessions scheduled. I assume he has washed his hands of me. For some odd reason, most of the others in group speak of on-going individual sessions. I am unsure about how to interpret that.

How do I proceed with this self-deprecating revelation? I have been peeling back the layers of this aging onion for a while now and I just keep finding layers. Denial is an interesting process. It is like a callous on a callous on a callous. You take the needle and prick a layer and think you have finally reached tender hide and you find another layer of toughened skin buried there that you forgot about from some bygone hole you dug at an earlier time. My wife has a letter started about what she has gone through during our years together that relates to this topic. It is not complete and she had not shared it with me until a few months ago. I should take it to the VA. It fits in well with item one of my tripartite explanation for not believing that PTSD is a factor in my life. I suppose going through those three items is a way to proceed. How about that? I stumbled across away to meander through the revelation.

I am not entitled: it has been 41 years since I came home from Vietnam. About 32 or 33 years ago, I went to my first parade welcoming us home, sponsored by us, for us. My uncle was heavily involved in organizing the event. I could have the date wrong, but no matter, it was not a huge gathering of eagles. I was the only person there from my brigade. Most of those there were from much more highly recognized units and I was an outsider. I listened to their war stories and kept mine to myself. I was also only a year removed from a bad experience in a small town VFW where an older vet had told me that I had not even been in a war. The national sentiment at the time was still pretty much negative toward Nam vets and the event I was attending was good, but low key and close-knit. For years, even when our local event blossomed, I retained my reluctance to join in and share much of my own experience. I heard astounding stories as I walked through our ever-growing Reunion and was convinced that my own combat experience was so insignificant that it did not bear the telling. In short, these guys had a right to have demons. I had earned none. My wife's note about an incident early in our marriage had been long forgotten. I had compartmentalized it for years, recalled it a couple of times, then neatly folded it again, and resealed it. One night, without ever waking, I put her in a stranglehold, told her that if she moved I would kill her. She spent the night on the edge of the bed, supporting herself with one arm on the floor, in abject fear. I don't believe I told anyone at the VA about this. If I told the chicken-necked sob of a psychologist about it, he did not note it at all or discarded it entirely. I never told the counselor. Perhaps I should take her letter to group, I don't know, but when she let me read it at last, the full impact of the night on her came to me in living color.

A sign of weakness: my dad fought in World War II and was part of three of four major jumps, was discharged from the Army at an Army Hospital and never spoke of it. He never drew a dime from the VA and often said, "Leave that money for those who need it worse than I do." I was emotionally tough. I had a great support unit in my family and friends. I was, and am, luckier than most in that regard. I have a family full of folks who served and are serving. All of these things are absolutely true, but wrapped in there is the fact that I never shared with them either. I shared some of the anger, some of the time, but I never fully explained it or discussed it with any of them. Usually we vets only do that with other vets, and I only did that in very recent years. When I at last told myself that number one was wrong, only then did I even allow myself the luxury of doing that. My wife's letter mentions the anger that seethed just below the surface, usually well controlled, but on occasion erupting in an amazing way. Never did I harm her or my family, but I had learned to find a way to be alone. In the process of going to the VA, I have, at long-last, admitted that I was a work-a-holic, but that was also partly because I wanted things for my family. I was heavily involved in community affairs, but the same motivations were part and parcel to that activity. I have addictive behaviors, but smoking is the major self-destructive activity — and the VA does not even consider that one — only drugs and alcohol. That is interesting. In all government literature about smoking cessation, the habit is treated as a drug addiction until it comes down to compensation! I had anger issues. I learned to walk away. My wife wrote about them. I still have them at times. I have known for years to get away from everyone. You don't always have the luxury, so you yell. A lot. I blow up and it is over. Then you hope to God you are forgiven. I have been most of the time I believe. Perhaps that is why I have done so much in my community — to pay for my transgressions. But keep in mind — I do not have any weaknesses.

There is nothing wrong with me: the most recent awakening I had and that I need to share with those at the VA counseling group, even though it will not mean a damned thing, is the realization that my brother saved my job for me. Don't misread me. I was good at my work. Everywhere I went, I was successful and it was always acknowledged, but I was known as rebellious, argumentative, more in tune with the floor rats, than upper management, and not promotable because of my temperament with my management. Every department I ran, I was a well-liked and respected floor supervisor, was successful. I was forced out due to my age and rumors led to that, but in the end, upper management came to me asked me to reconsider. Review of my work showed that I was successful and there was a place for me. I knew that my course had been run and what would happen if I stayed. I really liked and respected the man skipping a level up, but nobody in the next immediate level of management earned my respect. I was done with them. In retrospect, I know now that in all those moves, I was fortunate to have been given multiple chances. I earned them, but if I had not had a brother with tremendous influence it would not have happened. I am the caliber of leader to have been promoted. My anger issues preclude that eventuality. In 2000, a former antagonist had the opportunity to be rid of me and was successful in that. I was escorted out after utilizing my expertise in reorganizing a production line one day. I was not fired, but I was unceremoniously laid off to EVERYONE'S surprise. I was given the inside scoop about it a few years later, but regardless, it happened. My brother got me in at another location two months later. I managed to survive four moves in eight years there and retire. He and I have never spoken of it. I have asked but he ignores me. A demon in the night hit me with a club after my first group session and made me face the truth. In Nam, I was angry with leaders who made me watch Saigon get rocketed during a cease fire while we did nothing. In Nam, I was angry with a Platoon Sgt. who disappeared for 45 minutes while we got our asses embroiled in hell. In Nam, I heard about us paying five million USD for a blasted, plaster-of-Paris "religious" shrine, a shell left over from the war with France that was close to nothing, because an errant round hit it. In Nam, I read about our ignorant leaders arguing about the shape of a table at the Peace Talks. In Nam, we stopped successful search and destroy missions to do search and search and search and search and frigging search missions, while the enemy rebuilt and resupplied so more of our guys could die. But I ain't mad and there ain't anything wrong with me.

By the way, my counselor asked me if I wanted the intense program after the first and only session or the slower repair program. I told him that my family had travel plans already, thus we went with the group program. I have no clue what the intense version is, but the indication of options told me that he took me seriously. The question followed my breakdown, which is partially documented in "Today I Cried." I said more than that, but that displays enough of my weakness. A huge layer of onion fell away that day.

I owe it to a good friend's brother to tell one more VA story before I seal this story up for the day. He was not in-country. He was in this country. It is about Bud O'Neal. My dear friend was in Nam, but his older brother was here. Bud has been denied his Agent Orange Claims repeatedly because of that. He never left the United States and he is disabled, suffers a great deal, and deserves to be compensated as much as anyone who went to war.

Bud was stationed at an Agent Orange distribution point. He loaded the stuff. Everyone told him it was perfectly safe, but signs were posted all around the property that farmers should keep their livestock at least a mile away. Bud was given an asbestos suit and he and the members of his team were limited to handling the materials in 15-minute intervals. They loaded the barrels and then another team palletized them. They rotated on schedule, but it was an all day job, five days a week. Bud did it for over a year before he was assigned different duty as I recall. They did it in the wind, the rain, the hot, the dry, the whenever. Bud performed his required duty in the mid-sixties. He is still paying for it — dearly. The VA is not.

No Room in the Room, er, uh, System

I had my first one-on-one PTSD counseling session in September, 2010. It may be my last. I don't think the system wants me. It does not matter if I need it or not. I don't fit the little box they want me in or something. I am not ga-ga in the correct way. My lungs are too bad to climb a water tower and I don't own an illegal automatic weapon. I have refused psychogenic drugs. There is no trail of empty alcohol bottles behind me. I have not started my own graveyard. When I smoked regularly, the butts all said Winston or Marlboro on them. And there were no paperclips on the floor under the coffee table. What am I to do?

Group therapy has been interesting. There are some good men in the session with real problems. I talk too much and that problem has plagued me since elementary school. I sensed that our group leader wants me to "stifle" and began making that adjustment in the last session. Ironically, that was the session after which he asked me to meet him alone. It was about time. I could not ascertain why that had not happened previously. I hoped that I would at least learn why when we did have our "man-to-man" discussion. I planned to draw him out during that. Can you fathom the fly trying to elicit conversation from the spider?

We met at the appointed time and had the scripted opening statements. It was enlightening for me. I learned from some of my brothers that my first counselor did not like many of his students. He often handed them off, keeping only a select few. That explained my having been dropped-kicked into the group where I am. Additionally, he often acted as though the only people who earned the right to have PTSD were those who shared his Marine Corp affiliation, even though the attendees universally believed he was a peace-time Jarhead. I realize there can be a sort of personality clash residual bitterness in these environs. We are in these sessions because of anger and paranoia, thus statements like this, and many of my own, are not infrequent. Hmmm. I may have just damned myself in incredulity.

I will summarize his evaluation of me. He determined I had all the stressors, tested in the PTSD limits, broke down in his presence, and showed visible signs of measurable issues. He then classified me as a "sub-Post Traumatic Stress Disorder" sufferer. That is an interesting result given all the previous findings.

Counselor number one asked me if PTSD had cost me anything. The

VA wants to quantify everything. In my case, they wanted the cost to be measurable in dollars and cents. Once again, since I had kept my job the last few years, I was determined to be successful. Once again, since I was in manufacturing supervision, I was slotted in a unique place. I reminded him that I was ambitious and had failed to get promotions because of anger issues. I therefore lost much better bonuses over the years, got smaller raises, and retired on a much smaller pension due to my anger issues. None of those things made an impression on him. The result was much like the result of having finished college and being married for many years on the pencil-necked geek of a psychologist.

Counselor number two recognized what I was talking about. These factors had a huge financial impact on my life. They amounted to thousands of dollars at work and in retirement. They mean the difference between living a careful lifestyle and one much freer from stress. I took an in-depth look at myself after spending some time in group therapy. I also looked at myself with greater honesty. For the first time I admitted out loud that my brother had probably saved me at work on more than one occasion. I explained that to the second counselor. He reevaluated my situation and told me he reclassified me as a PTSD sufferer and disagreed completely with the prior assessment. Then we talked about what was bothering him. I opened that door as we chatted. The fly was getting the spider to share at last.

The next 20 minutes of talk was both enlightening and shocking for me. The guys in my group did not trust me. I am invader. I am a writer and they are fearful that I am going to write about them. I am going to violate their confidence. I am there to learn about them and turn that knowledge into a story. Well, it has become that, but not about them. It is about me and the experience. Immediately, I assured the counselor that there is no way I am capable of doing that. I am a man of integrity. Then I said that he should have defended me, knowing that were I of that caliber I would never have admitted to being an author. He in essence admitted that he had not looked at it that way. He should have — he should have come to my defense. It would be corrected. What followed these words caught me almost as by surprise.

My group counselor, and new found solo counselor, told me that in some sessions certain individuals try to take control of the group and push the leader into a follower's role. He wants to be sure that I am not doing that. Again, I assured him that is not the case — and that when I speak, it is because I have issues and I want to share them. I am there for that. I should be able to air them, get a response, and at some point, resolution. I thought that was the intent. He responded that I am extremely well-spoken and that can intimidate others, forcing them into silence. I admitted that I had sensed that he wanted me to say less at times. We discussed that further and agreed to a subtle hand signal when he wants me to back down. Then I dug for more info on the intimidation factor.

My group partners do not think I belong there. Here it was again. I do not belong there. They view me as successful. That was a shocker. I know how broke I have been — how many times I have been forced into starting over — how many times I have struggled. I am well-spoken. I am well-educated. I have had a career in management. I have a resume of accomplishments, including a book with another in progress. My vocabulary is far in excess of theirs. My ability to see things in a way that gives life to images that are fuzzy in their minds is far different to them. In my counselors words — and they were not meant in a mean way or to denigrate at all as he appears to have great affection for his people and means to protect them — many of them cannot put one word on top of another, much less write a book. They are good men, but live in a different universe than I. I do not belong. I am a success. Why am I there with them in that room?

It is as though I have no right to a problem like theirs. It does not matter what I did forty years ago. It does not matter that I had more combat time than all but three sitting in that room. It does not matter that of nine people there, only four of us even have combat experience at all.

There is no room in the room. There is no room in the system. I am a misfit for the VA and for those suffering from PTSD. I don't fit the mold for the VA because I have gone to college and been married for four decades. I don't fit the mold for my fellow vets for the same reasons.

Irony has slapped me right upside the head like a big ole ugly stick. In my survivor's guilt, I always said I had no right to have a problem. Now I am in a system that says I have no right because I have worked hard to do things in my life in spite of my problems — and have handled them in my own way, fighting through the curtains of anger, tinnitus, pain, frustration, failure, and dead ends. I have had some minor successes, although I have never looked at myself in that way. I was taught long ago that when you accomplish something you set another goal and keep moving forward. I was also taught to try to get up when I was knocked down too, as hard as it is sometimes.

Where do you go when there is no room in the room? Do you stand in the hall? I have pride. I am going to be myself. That has been good enough or bad enough at different times. It will have to do this time as well.

Mike Mullins, 9/23/10

PS — I must add that the only time I mentioned my book was during introductions into the group session at the very beginning. If it came up after that it was in terms of bringing other resources for PTSD remedies.

Awakened Again

These thoughts came to me in the night and awoke me, demanding release. I shared them with my vet buddies and have been shocked at their universal impact. I worry that our soldiers today are aimed in the same direction due to the criticism that is pouring out now — and the approach to this war.

My Disturbing Dream:

I had a hard time going to sleep. I knew I would. I stayed awake longer than I planned… by a little. I knew my night would be checkered by intrusive memories. A book I'm reading has brought back the old pain. Every day, I get a morsel of the old animosity as our government is pulled away from the ghosts of those who died to make our country great. I feel the anger I've buried inside as our troops are disrespected by not letting them do what they can do. Ambitious officers are more concerned about their own promotions and how the politicians view them. When that happens wrong decisions are made and wrong deeds are done. Morale is destroyed. "Why are we even here?" echoes as the will to serve and fight is eroded.

I was awakened early by visions that were created by resurgent ideologies. They had taken the form of people I know attacking my credibility, doubting my participation in the 10-year-long ordeal that was Vietnam. They said I was not there. That I did not act like so many vets they knew. That I did not strike out or suffer as they do. It made me killing mad. I turned over the table where we were. The vision transformed into someone I knew sitting across from me with face skewed in derision. He stomped on my self-doubt, my belief that I had not done enough, had not bled enough, had not wept enough…had not won as my heroes had. I had not suffered enough. Here I am, surrounded by people who do not know how many times those thoughts belittle and torture me. They do not know my bottled-up shame which is so unlike the proverbial genie which grants wishes for its savior. My genie sneers at me for not having been heroic enough.

Am I supposed to suffer more now to excise my evil genie? Am I to get angry and deliver a killing nose-bridge strike to my acquaintance to prove that I have been there — have done a little of what my more involved comrades have done? Must I rip off the vision's ear to show my training? Will the smell of blood convince them or me? Should I kill one of them to prove I have PTSD, that I am angry, that I feel what others feel? I offered to go get a gun and shoot at them. I have been shot at so I want *them* to feel what I felt. It will do no good. Bullets can't kill dreams. Bullets can't riddle doubt, regardless of where it resides. I am too much in control they think. I am too jovial. I am too cynical about the politicians and that *is* something shared by my brothers. I write about others because I did not do enough to write only about myself.

Am I angry at the forces that comprise my night visions? I sit here on my toilet typing with tears in my eyes begging the heroic ghosts of the past to forgive me. Am I angrier at myself for all that has been released?

I want to strike out and feel the vindication of inflicting pain on someone else other than me. I did serve. I did my job. I felt the anguish and pain of war — but I did not do enough. I lived.

I may be surrounded by those who quietly whisper that I did anything at all. I have the wrong demeanor. I can show the scar on the back of my leg, painted there by flying concertina. I can show them the fading scar on my hip, pressed there by the rubbing of a loaded, wet web belt, grinding my flesh day after day. I can show them the almost invisible tiny scars on the backs of my hands, burned into my flesh by tiny shards of shrapnel. I cannot show them the scars on my heart. They are the only ones which remain unchanged. No. They are larger. Maybe they caused my blockages. My by-pass can never avoid them. More by-passes will not.

I survived. I did not do enough. I did not pay a high enough price. I must keep paying installments. I am not a hero. Really I am not much. My guilt and self-doubt are alive and well. They have joined forces perhaps, to become paranoia.

Ask the psychologist at the VA. He will tell you I don't suffer. I've tried too hard to serve since the war and I have done it well. I am in control and well adjusted. I am until the visions that destroy my sleep escape and attack the cages where I've kept them and then I give them real faces so I can hurt them as much as they hurt me!

Control is tenuous and everyone has a button. Shall we pray, for them and me, that it never gets pushed? My demons won tonight. They attacked me at the start of sleep and scraped off the scabs. I am bleeding freely from my emotional jugular. Even though I have nearly killed myself with tobacco, my weapon of choice, I am going to go smoke a cigar and try to re-load. I have to speak about Memorial Day to some little old ladies tonight.

PTSD Compensation examination results

(VA 2011)

2. *Service connection for anxiety disorder, not otherwise specified.*
Service connection for anxiety disorder, not otherwise specified has been established as directly related to military service.

You wrote to Congressman Burton regarding your previous denial of service connection for post-traumatic stress disorder (PTSD)...Your award of the Purple Heart Medal and Combat Infantryman Badge are annotated on your DD Form 214 and 215, and are considered prima facia evidence that you suffered traumatic combat experiences.

Correspondence from your wife reports that you have a long history of anger management issues, nightmares, and a need to control. We electronically retrieved your treatment records from the Marion, IN, VA Medical Center. These records show that you are not clinically diagnosed with PTSD or any mental disorder at the time of treatment, rather a clinician is observing and noting your symptoms and behaviors. You were assigned a social worker who enrolled you in PTSD group therapy program since June 2010. You participate in group therapy, but soon began to control, lead, and dominate the sessions with your observations, opinions, and recollections of your published writings. After a number of sessions, your social worker, during single therapy, attempted to guide your behavior into more of a listen and support mode. The social worker reported improvement in this, which has helped the group sessions. Throughout therapy, you have reported symptoms of intrusive ideation, nightmares every other week, flashbacks, avoidance of conversations of combat, detachment, sleep disturbance, and foreshortened future. There is no evidence of prescribed medications for a mental condition within the treatment records.

We requested a VA examination to determine if you were diagnosed with PTSD, and if so, its severity. At the examination, you reported depression once in a while but you don't allow it to stick around long, never more than two or three days; periods where you struggle with finances; worry about your kids; poor sleep since the military due to ringing in your ears where you rarely get more than 4 to 6 hours of sleep. You hold two Bachelor's Degrees, one in English, and another in Operations Management, as well as assorted classes and certificates in human resource management. You have been married greater than 40 years with two children and four grandchildren. You report family life as caring and supporting of one another. Your wife is laid back, while you are more volatile. You enjoy drives with your wife and spending time with your grandchildren. You maintain contact with your siblings through email, and holiday gatherings. You report having military and non-military friends from high school that you get together with every two years. You reported a "wide network" of friends. You also attend church every Sunday. You report being a writer, working on your second book, and a monthly column as part of a writer's group published nationally, and you have authored an audiobook.

 The examiner observed that you have historically good psychosocial adjustment and supportive relationships with both family and friends. However, you report struggling to control the negative impact of your anger on your family. You felt your wife has stayed with you more so due to her commitment to you, rather than some aspects of strength within you. You have well-defined, active interests and a variety of accomplishments including being published several times. You describe yourself as driven and goal directed both a work and play which has been a positive coping strategy in some ways, and also a way of avoiding more negative aspects of your emotional experiences, such as dealing with anger and emotional distress related to your combat experiences. You reported always having a defiant streak and know how to push buttons to get a reaction from people, which you deliberately do to antagonize people, especially authority figures.

 The psychological portion of the examination reports that you were clean, appropriately and casually dressed with a cooperative, friendly attitude toward the examiner. You verbalized feelings reflecting bitterness and resentment that VA doesn't believe you deserve to be at the examination because you don't fit typical patterns and don't fit into the box that defines a mental disorder or illness, especially with respect to a diagnosis of PTSD. You were further described as intense at times, and you were initially upset with yourself because you left your teeth at home, as well as being somewhat distressed because you weren't sure if it meant anything. Your concentration and mental fluency were within normal limits or above. You repeated five of five digits forward and backward. You were intact to person, place and time. Your thought content was described as preoccupied with one or two topics — being told that none of your experiences matter because you don't fit into any categories because you've been married for a long time and have functioned well in life; and your anger that the past C&P examiner did not listen to you or let you present information that you had brought to the previous assessment. You were under no delusions. Your judgment was intact, and you have good insight. You did not report any hallucinations. In the examiner's opinion, you have appropriate behaviors, you interpret proverbs correctly, you have no obsessive or ritualistic behaviors, you do not have panic attacks, nor suicidal or homicidal thoughts, you have good impulse control, you can maintain your personal hygiene, and you have no difficulties with your activities of daily living. Your remote memory was unimpaired, your recent memory was mildly impaired, and your immediate memory was normal.

The examiner reported your stressors as combat experience for 12 months while in Vietnam. You reported exposure to firefights, mortars, seeing dead and injured bodies and parts, and that this resulted in fear and feelings of horror. However, you were not out of control. You were scared when hit by shrapnel, but noted that the guy next to you was hurt more. The examiner specifically related these experiences to fear of hostile military or terrorist activity.

The examiner reported PTSD symptoms of persistent re-experience the traumatic events as evidenced by the recurrent and intrusive distressing recollections of the event that include images, thoughts, perceptions, and recurrent distressing dreams; persistent avoidance of stimuli associated with the trauma and numbing of general responsiveness as evidenced by efforts to avoid thoughts, feelings or conversations associated with combat; persistent symptoms of increased arousal as evidenced by difficulty falling or staying asleep and irritability or outbursts of anger; the stressful events cause clinically significant distress or impairment in social or occupational areas of functioning; and your symptoms are delayed onset.

The examiner stated that your stressors meet the DSM-IV criterion as PTSD stressors. However, the examiner stated that you do not meet the DSM-IV criteria for a diagnosis of PTSD because while you have intermittent symptoms of re-experiencing, avoidance of talking about combat, and prominent hyper-arousal, you do not meet the full criteria for PTSD due to not meeting "criterion C" within the DSM-IV for PTSD. The examiner further stated since you do not meet the full criteria for PTSD but still have some symptoms which cause clinically significant distress (for which you are receiving treatment), you do meet the criteria for Anxiety Disorder, not otherwise specified. The examiner specifically stated that your disorder is linked to your traumatic combat stress exposure. The examiner stated that your anxiety disorder symptoms are not severe enough to interfere with occupational and social functioning.

Since the examination has resulted in a diagnosis of anxiety disorder, not otherwise specified, which is medically linked to our traumatic combat experiences, service connection has been granted. Even though the examiner has stated that your symptoms are not severe enough to interfere with occupational and social functioning, you have a long history of anger management issues. Sleep issues, sleep impairment, avoidance of combat discussions, hyper-vigilance for which we have assigned a 10 percent evaluation.

An evaluation of 10 percent is assigned from March 4, 2010, the date we received correspondence from Congressman Burton's office and the date we inferred a claim to reopen your claim for PTSD. And evaluation of 10 percent is granted whenever there is occupational and social impairment due to mild or transient symptoms which decrease work efficiency and ability to perform occupational tasks only during periods of significant stress; or symptoms controlled by continuous medication. A higher evaluation of 30 percent is not warranted unless there is occasional decrease in work efficiency and intermittent periods of inability to perform occupational (although generally functioning satisfactorily, with routine behavior, self-care, and conversation normal), due to such symptoms as: depressed mood, anxiety, suspiciousness, panic attacks (weekly or less often) chronic sleep impairment, mild memory loss (such as forgetting names, directions, recent events).

My wife, Phyllis Davis Mullins

Saving Grace

I know a man, Bill McDonald, who writes. He is also a Nam vet, a former door-gunner, who received a few medals and at least one Purple Heart. He is a reverend, has been a technical reference for some movies, traveled the world, spoken to a wide variety of audiences, and helps veterans at every opportunity. He demands that whatever is written be ended with a hopeful note whenever possible. That sounds so simple it is deceiving. Writing about war is emotional, crass — violent by its very definition, haunting, personal, and often angry when you tell the story of any veteran of the conflict in Vietnam.

I have a dear friend who works constantly. His name is Dave O'Neal. Our responsibilities have prevented us from sharing any uninterrupted time together for quite a while. We went to high school together. He went to Vietnam before I did and came home the last time after I did, for a total of 28 months in-country. I am aware of much that he did, but I told him that I would not write until we had spoken. One day I came home and found an envelope in my front door. Dave had decided what he wanted to share. He wrote his story and left it there for me. Our schedules were simply not jelling. Dave decided to write about the experience he had each time he came home. I am including his experience in his words.

"The Vietnam War was a very unpopular time in America during the 1960s; a time that split the American people in various ways. The media primarily displayed the anti-war protesters, peace-niks, and the anti-government side as being the only view. Yes, it was a very trying time for America. However, there was a large segment of the population that would do whatever they could to support the troops in that war. I would like to share a few events that were very positive for me during that time. I have tried to place all the negative events that happened to me in places that I no longer visit.

I volunteered for the US Army in 1966, and served in Vietnam for 28 months. On my first return to the United States in the spring of 1968, I was thankful to be home and was enjoying life to the fullest, visiting my extended family and seeing friends.

I recall traveling from Indiana to Michigan and US 31 was under construction, being turned into a new, modern four-lane highway from Kokomo to South Bend. I was driving my step-father's 1962 Studebaker Hawk. I was thinking just how good it was to be driving a powerful car on a smooth highway with no traffic jams or the limitations of a Jeep M-151, or a deuce-and-a-half truck. Plus no one was trying to ambush me.

It was a beautiful day, the sun was shining, and there was very little traffic on that brand new stretch of highway. So I decided to see what the old Studebaker would do. I put the pedal to metal and let it go. I was enjoying life and the old Hawk was on the other side of the 100 mph mark, and running well.

I noticed after a while that there was a vehicle approaching from the rear with blue lights flashing. Well, when I was last in the USA, blue lights were on volunteer firemen's cars. So I started looking for the fire, just in case I could help out.

After a while, the "volunteer fireman" got close enough that I could see that the car was a big Plymouth and the "fireman" was indeed a State Policeman. I knew then that I was in a heap of trouble, pulled over, and stopped. As the policeman approached my car he had his hand on his pistol and was very upset. He stated in a very loud and commanding voice that I get my registration, insurance papers and driver's license and 'get my ass into his car.' I did, in a very fast manner.

Here I was, in a car not registered to me, driving like a crazy person. I had no valid driver's license since my permit had expired while I was in Vietnam. I just knew that if he did not shoot me, I was going to jail at least. What a way to spend my leave time.

His first statement to me was, 'Boy, do you know just how fast you were going?' I did, but I also knew that this was not a good time for any admissions or confessions, or the right time to brag about how fast the Studebaker Hawk was.

The officer was still quite upset, and his hands were still shaking with rage. He demanded the vehicle registration, and wanted to know who the car belonged to and why I was driving it; also why I did not have a valid license. I then explained that I was in the Army and that my license had expired, but my commander had assured me that I could drive on my leave orders while in transit.

The officer looked my leave orders over and started to calm down. He asked me a few more questions about when my leave was over and where my next duty station was. I told him that I would be returning to Vietnam. He looked at me in disbelief, and wondered out loud why anyone would return to a place like that.

He returned my papers and told me that since I was still in the Army, he would not give me a ticket this time. He told me to slow down because we were losing more people on the highway that we were losing in Vietnam. I thanked him, because I certainly did not have the money for a fine. He then did something that I had never had done to me. He extended his hand and thanked me for serving my country. I was at a loss for words — that just did not happen in 1968.

The second time that I received gratitude for serving my country during this period of time I was on my way back to Vietnam. I was traveling stand-by, as all military personnel did. I was waiting on a flight in St. Louis, MO, and there was a 4 or 5 hour delay before my next possible flight. I met another soldier who was also waiting for his next flight. We had plenty of time so we decided to do what good soldiers do best — and that was to find a place to have a few drinks.

We grabbed a cab and told the driver to take us to a 'friendly bar' since we had both experienced some of the anti-war protesters before. The cab driver said he knew just the place and he drove to a small, neighborhood tavern. The cab driver decided he would wait in the bar for us so we would not have to wait for another cab. When we entered the bar, all the patrons of the place looked us over and then they all stood up and started clapping their hands and thanking us for our service. We did not have to buy one beer all the time we were there. The people would not let us empty one drink before they had another setting in front of us. They all treated us like heroes. They shared stories of their past, and of men they knew who were serving in the military also. They made sure we had enough to drink and left no doubt they were part of the Americans who really appreciated the people serving their country.

The cab driver loaded us into the cab and took us back to the airport. He waited until we were safely on board the plane before he would leave us and he would not accept any money for his services.

On the third occasion that I experienced the thanks of another individual, I was returning from my second tour of duty in Vietnam. I had extended my tour but had delayed my return home until I could return home for Christmas. I had not had a Christmas with my family for three years and I really wanted this one to be special. I had written a letter to my younger sister Helen and told her of my plans, but asked her not to tell anyone, just in case I was unable to be there.

I was flying stand-by and it did not look good that I would get a seat on the last flight to Indianapolis before Christmas day. The plane was loading passengers and I was the last person in the waiting area. After a long delay, the lady at the desk looked my way and checked the manifest one more time. She then came over to me and said there was one seat left, so I was in luck.

The only remaining seat was in the first class section of the flight. I sat next to a man who was returning to Indianapolis from a business trip to San Francisco. We shared conversation and drinks all the way back to Indiana. I told him of my plans to surprise my mom with a visit home for Christmas.

When we got to the airport in Indianapolis his wife was there to meet him. They decided to take me to the north side of the city. They thought it would be easier to catch a ride there for the remaining 50 miles to Windfall, IN, where my family lived. They let me out at a small restaurant, where I went in to get some coffee and warm up. It was cold and snowing, to the point of being a blizzard. There were not many people traveling north at 8 PM, so my chances of hitching a ride did not look good.

After I warmed up I picked up my duffle bag and started walking north, with the hopes of getting home for Christmas. I had not walked very long when a car pulled over to pick me up. It was the same man and his wife who had taken me to the north side of the city. The couple decided that they would make sure that I got home in time for Christmas. They said they would take me home just to see the look on my mom's face when she opened the door. They went over 100 miles out of their way just to help me surprise my mom. I tried to convince them to come in and meet my mom and family. They said that they had a long drive back and just to see the happiness of my mom was enough.

My sister had made sure that mom was the only one near the front door that night, so she would be the one to answer the door. When mom opened the door, it was one of the best moments of both of our lives. Without the help of people who did not even know me it would not have happened. The man and his wife smiled, waved goodbye, and drove back to Indianapolis.

I wish I had written down the names of the State Policeman, the cab driver, and the most generous man and his wife who went out of their way to help me and thank me for my service to our country.

Now, when I see a man or woman in uniform, I always try to extend my hand and thank them for their service to America. I am truly grateful to the people who continue to serve in the Armed Forces of America.

"D.O."

Dave and I, in fact most veterans, retain a cynical anger that boils over sometimes. It is borne of losing a war in meeting rooms, in the streets of our home towns, in our nation's newspapers. We did not lose it on our battlefields. We are not debating the right or wrong — it is too late for that. That has been debated ad nauseam and will be debated ad infinitum. More importantly, we all...all, I firmly believe — have a core of knowledge deep down inside that says we believe in the core values that made our country special. Nobody can take that away as long as there are a few people who believe and feel as we do. And we still do. We love America and would fight for her still. It is hope and that hope is raised to new heights every day as we see our glorious men and women in uniform parade, toil, live and die for us, stand at the ready in peace, and do what they must in battle. No group, no enemy, can push us beyond that which our forefathers wrote for us and we re-wrote in blood and sweat. And in that, there is HOPE.

Dave gave me much with his letter. He gave me saving grace for the end of my book. He allowed me to conclude with a strong, positive note that says thank you to all who care about us who fought and will fight. I thank all of the people who allowed me to tell their stories. They are all special and incredible. They blessed me. God blessed me by giving me the heart to try this. Dave gave me a letter in an envelope. It allows me to say thank you to all of those who are fighting. As Dave says so well, all of us extend our collective hands to you as you fight for us now.

Thank You. God bless you.

Index

A

Afghanistan 45, 184, 192, 271, 302, 335
  Operation Enduring Freedom IV 259
Air Force
  6566th 201
Aluminum Alley ---Himilayan Mtns. 54
American Legion Post 84 (Ira Hayes) 305
Anvil Operation---World War II 19
Arizona
  Verde Valley 183
Army
  3rd Infantry Regiment 258
  11th Armored Cavalry Regiment 169, 170, 175
  12th Armored Cavalry Regiment 258
  17th Infantry Regiment 257
  32nd Infantry Regiment of the 7th Infantry Division 257
  110th Infantry Regimental Combat Team 95
  173rd Airborne Division 201, 303
  199th Light Infantry Brigade 255
  409th ASA, 11th Armored Calvary Regiment 174
  442nd Combat Engineers, WW2, Europe---WW II 24
  613th Field Artillery Battalion 35
  5332nd Long Range Penetration Brigade 37, 41
  Airborne 19, 20, 155, 320, 322
  Bloody 32nd Infantry Regiment 31

Davis, Sammy L.---CMOH; Battery C, 2nd Bn., 4th Arty Reg., 9th Inf. 197, 199, 322
Elliott, Earnest, Pvt. 31, 32
First Air Cavalry 179
First Cavalry Division 71, 74, 75
Frank Merrill, General 40
Frazier, Jerry---Panama 301
Harlow, Ben---504th Parachute Infantry Regiment 267
Headquarters Co. of the 3rd Battalion, 517th Parachute Regiment 20
Hutton, Skip, CSM retired 170
John Trimble 47
Lederle, Stephen D., Sgt. 271
Mars Task Force 35, 37, 41, 46, 52, 54
Marsmen 35, 40, 46, 48, 49, 51, 53, 54, 55
Mullins, Bernard W., Pvt. 20
Pathfinder 21
The Bloody Bucket Division 91
Vinegar Joe Stillwell, General 39, 52
Williams, John C. (Old Claude), 517th PIR, Army 20, 23, 25
Army, 10th Mountain Division 257
Army Air Corps
  421st Night Fighters 11
  875th Bombardment Squadron, 498th Bombardment Group 307
  Flying Cadet Program 85
  P-61 Black Widow 11, 12, 13, 14, 15, 16
  Parker, Robert, Capt. 287

Army Air Corps
Dodge, Ralph 11, 15, 16, 17, 18

B

Barbara Gray---Vietnam veteran
 supporter 295
Battle of the Bulge---World War II 97
Boston---Vietnam veteran 41, 194, 195
Bradley, Omar General 258
British
 Lord Luis Mountbatten, Vice Admiral 52
Bronze Star 170, 289
Browning Automatic Rifle 19, 43, 44, 90, 91, 92, 93, 94, 183
Burma 16, 34, 35, 36, 37, 38, 39, 40, 41, 44, 48, 49, 51, 52, 53, 54, 56
Burma Road 34, 35, 39, 40, 41, 44, 48, 52, 54

C

Calcutta
 Bombay 38
Camp Landis 36, 37, 40
Chiang Kai-shek 39, 40
China Sea 14, 312
Cold War ix, 107, 131, 134, 144
Colorado
 Camp Hale 257
Combat Infantryman's Badge 208, 257, 326
Congressional Medal of Honor 197, 314, 322
Connie Salsbery 323

D

Dallas Hange 58
D-Day---World War II 79, 117, 308, 309
DeLong, Mildred 118, 119

E

Elugelab 108
Eniwetok 107, 110, 111

F

Florida
 Boca Rotan 11
 Key West 131, 137, 144
 Kissimmee 11
 Miami 11, 137
Fort Sill 35, 256
France
 Ardennes---World War II 19
 Le Mans---World War II 91
 Normandy---World War II 19
 Reims 104

G

Geiger Counters 108
Geneva Convention 102
Georgia
 Fort Benning 21, 59, 302
 Glynco Naval Air Station 130
Germany
 Black Forest---World War II 19
Grenada 192
Guam 28, 30, 289
Gulf War 170, 178, 187, 314, 327

H

Hawaii
 Pearl Harbor 24, 28, 56, 58, 66, 80, 81
Healing Field 188, 191, 193, 200, 286, 290, 291
Heston, Charlton President of National Rifle Association 18
Hopi---Native Americans 192
Howard County Vietnam Veterans Organization 188, 191, 197, 200, 286, 318
H & S Co., H & S Bn., 3rd Marine Division 148

358

I

Indiana
  American Legion Post #46 2
  Camp Atterbury 55, 122
  Kokomo ix, 18, 116, 129, 137, 143, 180, 181, 184, 301, 309, 351
  Tipton 2, 69, 150
  Windfall 58, 76, 112, 114, 115, 116, 118, 119, 121, 123, 256, 354
Indiana National Guard 20, 184
Iraq 184, 259, 271, 292, 302, 335, 336
Irrawaddy River---Burma 37, 42, 48
Italy
  Anzio---World War II 4
Ivy Mike 108

J

Japan
  Bofu 16
  Hiroshima---World War II 61, 108
  Honshu 16
  Nagasaki—World War II 61
  Tokyo---World War II 61, 62, 63
  Yokohama---World War II 61, 63
Japan---World War II 15, 28, 51, 61, 62, 63, 64, 65, 66, 68, 71, 81, 158, 179, 202
Junker (JU-188)---Nazi aircraft 118

K

Kachinas 37, 40, 45, 46
Kansas
  Fort Riley 113, 257
Kennedy, John F. President 258
Korea
  38th Parallel 72, 73, 81
  Demilitarized Zone 81, 208, 257
Korea War
  North Korea 17, 72, 73, 74, 81
  South Korea 81, 249
Kwajalein 31

L

Ledo Road 37, 47
Luxembourg 94, 95

M

Madame Chiang Kai-shek 39, 40
Marine
  Graham, John 162
  Gunn, Tommy---VMA Attack Squadron 252 204
  Mike Hartsock 301
Marine Air Wing
  Night Centurion 131
  Ragin, Mike, Captain 134
Marine Corps
  Ramsey, Larry 154
McKinney, Marie 78, 82
Missouri
  Fort Leonard Wood 76

N

Navy
  Captain McVey 30
  Naval Special Warfare Group 187
  Pilot Marks 29
  Smith, James Seaman First Class 28, 29, 30, 31
  USS Essex 17
  USS Indianapolis 28, 30, 31
Nazi concentration camp
  Camp Berga 98, 101, 102, 106
  Stalag 9b 97, 106
New Guinea---World War II 11, 13, 15, 31, 307

O

Ojibwe---Native Americans 192
Okinawa---World War II 12, 30, 31, 64, 158, 307
Operation Harvest Moon 301

359

P

PBY---World War II 29
Pearl Harbor 24, 28, 56, 58, 66, 80, 81
Peleliu 31
Philippines
  Leyte---World War II 12, 31, 79
  Luzon---World War II 12, 13
Philippine Sea 12, 14, 29
Plummer, Jean 112, 114, 118
Prisoner of War 2, 3, 105, 106, 112,
    114, 115, 119, 120, 123, 124,
    191, 296, 298, 309
Purple Heart 20, 44, 170, 184, 191,
    195, 231, 232, 241, 258, 284,
    290, 314, 319, 322, 326, 347,
    351

R

Richard Lugar, Senator 85, 105

S

Sailing in support of USN
  Jose Navarro 56
Shweli River---Burma 42
S. Korea
  Inchon 72
  Jane Russell Hill 257
  Kumwah Valley 257
  Old Baldy 257
  Pork Chop Hill 257
  Seoul 72, 73, 74, 75
Soldiers Medal 169, 171, 176
Somalia 187, 192
Sun Dance 192

T

Texas
  Fort Bliss 68
The Mauretania---private passenger
    ship under contract for troop
    transport 90
Thomas, Joe POW World War II 2, 3, 4

Tina M. Mullins 279, 280
Tomb of the Unknown Soldier 258
Turkey, Izmir 144

U

Utah Beach--- World War II 91, 117

V

Veterans Day 287, 308, 309
Veterans of Foreign Wars 2, 338
Vietnam i, ix, x, xi, xii, 2, 52, 78, 82,
    113, 114, 125, 126, 127, 128,
    129, 130, 132, 135, 137, 138,
    140, 146, 147, 149, 151, 152,
    153, 154, 157, 158, 159, 160,
    161, 163, 169, 170, 171, 172,
    174, 175, 176, 177, 179, 181,
    197, 200, 201, 202, 203, 208,
    222, 240, 241, 243, 245, 252,
    253, 256, 257, 258, 277, 290,
    298, 300, 303, 305, 308, 310,
    311, 312, 313, 315, 318, 321,
    322, 329, 330, 333, 334, 336,
    338, 345, 349, 351, 352, 353
  Bearcat 174, 175
  Ben Hoa 172, 201
  Chu Lai 301
  Cu Chi 253, 254, 255, 257, 258
  Duc Hoa 176
  Freedom Hill 155
  Khe San 291, 301
  Long Binh 175, 176, 253
  Saigon 202, 213, 214, 227, 253, 254,
      255, 256, 291, 312, 332, 340
  Tah Ninh Province 258
  Tan Son Nhut 151, 202, 252, 253,
      254, 256, 259
  Tet Offensive, 1968 175, 202, 252,
      319, 330, 333
  Vung Tau 254, 311, 312, 313
Vietnam in Verse, poetry for beer drinkers
    2, 126, 157, 200

Vietnam veteran
  Arthur Running Bear 299
Virginia
  Arlington 256
  Quantico 129, 144
  Virginia Military Institute 253

W

Wake Island 256
War on Terror ix, 45, 82, 257, 261,
    300, 326, 336
Wind Talker 306
Wisconsin
  Camp McCoy 65, 90
World War I ix, xi, 1, 2, 3, 11, 15, 19,
    24, 32, 34, 40, 42, 45, 49, 55,
    56, 58, 59, 61, 67, 68, 69, 70,
    71, 78, 79, 80, 81, 83, 85, 90,
    105, 107, 117, 122, 129, 130,
    141, 147, 188, 246, 247, 248,
    249, 252, 267, 270, 287, 297,
    299, 300, 306, 307, 308, 309,
    313, 314, 320, 322, 333, 339
World War II ix, xi, 1, 2, 3, 11, 15, 19,
    24, 32, 34, 40, 45, 49, 55, 56,
    58, 59, 61, 67, 68, 69, 70, 71,
    78, 79, 80, 81, 83, 85, 90, 105,
    107, 117, 122, 129, 130, 141,
    147, 188, 246, 247, 248, 249,
    252, 267, 270, 287, 297, 299,
    300, 306, 307, 308, 309, 313,
    314, 320, 322, 333, 339
  Bataan Death March 66